THE VERY RICHNESS OF THAT PAST

Canada Through the Eyes of Foreign Writers

Volume II

Edited by Greg Gatenby

Alfred A. Knopf Canada

PUBLISHED BY ALFRED A. KNOPF CANADA

Introductory essays and editorial arrangement of material
© 1995 by Greg Gatenby

Canadian Cataloguing in Publication Data

Main entry under title:
The very richness of that past   :   Canada through
the eyes of foreign writers, volume II

ISBN 0-394-28118-7

1. Canada — Literary collections.   2. Canada —
Description and travel.   I. Gatenby, Greg.

FC70.V47 1995   820.8'03271   C95-931488-1
F1012.V47 1995

First Edition
Printed and bound in the United States of America

The very richness of that past as I discover it now makes
me irritable to have been cheated of it then. I wish I could
have known it early, that it could have come to me with
the smell of life about it instead of the smell of books, for
there was the stuff of an epic there, and still is for anyone
who knows it right.... All of it was legitimately mine, I
walked that earth, but none of it was known to me.

Wallace Stegner, *Wolf Willow*

Gustave Doré's depiction of the spectacular ending at Niagara Falls for the 1863 French edition of *Atala* by Chateaubriand. Doré (1832-83) remains one of the greatest book illustrators ever. The caption for this romantic and mysterious landscape read "We soon arrived at the edge of the cataract, which announced itself by the most frightening roars."

CONTENTS

INTRODUCTION

THIS ANTHOLOGY is the second I have edited to showcase and to discuss how foreign writers of adult fiction, poetry and drama have perceived Canada or Canadians.

The first volume, *The Wild Is Always There*, published two years ago, seemed to surprise, even stun, many of my compatriots. They were astounded because they could not understand how, or why, they had been kept in the dark—for generations—about the importance of Canada to so many internationally acclaimed authors. That William Faulkner and Willa Cather actually lived in Canada, or that Charles Dickens and Arthur Conan Doyle had spent considerable time in Canada, and that these four, along with most of the three dozen other writers in the first volume, wrote positively, even glowingly about their experience of Canada, this came as news—delightful, exciting, pride-inducing news—to many readers of *The Wild Is Always There*. That they will also be astonished and uplifted by the contents of this second volume I have no doubt.

The idea for compiling such histories arose in 1978 when I decided to write a literary history of Toronto. Being young and brash, I presumed that such a book could be written in less than two years. Of course one of the reasons I made such an assumption was that, like most Canadians, I had been raised to believe that my city, indeed, my country, was of little literary consequence compared to centres such as Paris or London. So writing a literary history of

Toronto, I thought, would be largely a matter of collecting data about the few eminent souls who had passed through the town on their way to somewhere more important.

As my researches progressed, however, I came to realize how wrong my assumptions were. One of my errors was to believe that most important literary visitors to Canada would probably have stopped in Toronto at some point in their itineraries. While many certainly did stop in Toronto, I quickly discovered that many others did not. Discovering the reasons why some travelled here or there in Canada became fascinating to me, and so I chose to put (temporarily, I trust) the literary history of Toronto aside in order to write about foreign authors' perceptions of a nation, not just a city.

In deciding which authors to include in this volume, I was faced, as I was in the first volume, and as I will be in the future, with an embarrassment of riches. At last count, I had found more than fifteen hundred authors who had written about this nation. That number alone is sobering. At the beginning, and while working on this project, I had been warned repeatedly by other writers and colleagues in the Canadian book trade that there was not enough material to make one decent anthology of the sort I proposed, much less a series. Alas, they, as I had been, were ignorant of the very richness of our literary past. I confess that I started to have mischievous fun watching the jaws of these Canadian naysayers drop in astonishment as I began to cite the legendary names among the hundreds of foreign authors for whom Canada had been an irresistible subject.

In fact, I am wrong to use the past tense when speaking of such writers. As the Artistic Director of the Harbourfront Reading Series, I am responsible for bringing scores of eminent writers each year to Canada from all six continents; indeed, in the past twenty-one years the number of foreign authors who have been my guests exceeds one thousand. And I watch with wry mirth and with much pride as these authors, their voices full of awe, tell me how overwhelmed they are, after days of exploring, by what they have seen in Canada. The letters, journalism, fictions and poetry that they have written or are going to write will be added to the hundreds of enticing works by their predecessors which I have been able to uncover. Taken together, these works form a unique, endlessly seductive facet of our literary past.

A shocking amount of this historical material is writing that is superb, even brilliant. So, in the belief that a collage of entertaining selections would be of far more interest to the general reader than any encyclopedic approach, I have chosen again to present an array of approximately three dozen authors whose writing, ranging from the extravagant to pursed-at-the-lips, illuminates aspects of our country much as a starburst from fireworks brightens the land more radiantly, more magically, than any streetlamp.

In addition to seeking material that is exceptional in some way, I have chosen to mix writers who are currently famous with those who were famous in their own day, or with those who were never famous but should be. Almost as punctuation to the larger entries, I have included a few shorter entries which are, despite their possible artistic shortcomings, historically important or simply amusing.

While all of these entries are historically important to Canadian letters, there are some entries that are especially significant; for example, Margaret Blennerhassett, an intriguing, mysterious woman, gave no hint from the facts of her life that she would write such a delicate poem set in Canada. Blennerhassett, as a poet, is admittedly no Emily Dickinson. But her omission from previous accounts of our literary history is a reminder to the general reader of the lamentable poverty of research in that same literary history by our academics. While many British and American scholars revel in the study of their literary records, writing biographies and histories that celebrate figures important in those records, too many Canadian scholars in English Departments seem to sneer at literary biography even as a viable area of research. As a result, the histories of the literatures of the traditionally powerful countries continue to be well documented, while, at Canadian universities, our literary history is practically ignored. A telling measure of the undeserved obscurity of our literary development is this: when I opened the only copy of Blennerhassett's book in the entire University of Toronto library system (a book that was published more than one hundred and fifty years ago), I found the pages uncut, the book unread. In more than eighteen years of research I have seen no more poignant symbol of how much work is yet to be done in exploring our nation's past.

The entries in this volume are arranged so that the writing can be read either as one reads a novel or as one reads a guidebook. In other words, there are subtle reasons why one author follows another, but the links are not intractable and a single entry can be read on its own without reference to its predecessor or successor.

For a country that still considers itself young, Canada has been written about for a long time. This volume, for instance, contains writing that covers nearly a millennium: from the sagas of the Vikings to the ruminations of Joyce Carol Oates on Canadian identity. Obviously, within that period, some perceptions of Canada changed, but, amazingly, others have remained constant. Again and again and again, writers came to this country and marvelled at its landscapes, and expressed unashamed compliments for, and optimism in, the intelligence, energy, drive and capacity of the citizenry. Almost all writers were awed by the looming danger of the Canadian wilderness, a danger made all the more titillating because it could not be discerned, could only be sensed viscerally. Some, such as Chateaubriand, flirted with this danger until they were almost undone by it.

Canadian readers will be flattered to learn that most of the authors in this volume, as in the first of the series, relished the vistas of the country, even the seemingly (to us) mundane. The Rockies, of course, have their champions, and Niagara Falls endlessly evokes competitiveness in authors, each trying to outdo the last in describing this wonder of the world. But the hemisphere of the prairie sky, the awesomeness of the Labrador coast, the charms of the Halifax *demi-monde*, the terrible beauty of an Arctic storm, the poetry of the name Medicine Hat, these, too, are singled out by the authors in this volume, their vocabulary in describing all parts of this country a mixture of awe, reverence, acclaim, and certainly envy.

My editing of the texts has been light whenever possible: obvious

typographical errors or spelling mistakes have been quietly cor-
rected; abbreviations and most numbers have been spelled out. Male
authors greatly outnumber the female in this volume because many
more male authors wrote about Canada; until recently, of course, it
was very much easier for a man to travel here, then publish accounts
of that travel. Descriptions of the east outnumber those of the west
because literary travellers have been exploring the eastern half of the
nation for far longer than they have the west. When authors wrote
about Canada in a variety of forms (for example, in published
poems as well as in their private diaries), I have tended to choose the
format in which the writing is more evocative, regardless of its polish. All other aspects being equal, I have chosen to include excerpts
which have never been published or are relatively unknown.

Some readers may be shocked by the casualness with which many
eminent authors of the past uttered what today we regard as racial
slurs. This is not the place to debate the complex attitudes of most of
these authors to racial questions. However, rather than try to pretend that these authors were saints, and because their words are a
matter of public record, I have left their remarks unedited where the
remarks are relevant to the theme of this book.

Through the eyes of some of the most famous and respected
authors in the world, what follows in these pages is a remarkably
invigorating, and for many readers, completely new way to see our
country, an amalgam of refreshingly affirmative and always curious
images of Canada.

Fans of *film noir* and the hard-boiled school of detectives will be
amazed by Raymond Chandler's emotional homage to Canadians
and the majesty of the Canadian regiment with which he served.
They will certainly be amazed to see him proudly dressed in a kilt.
The fiasco of Theodore Dreiser's "dirty weekend" in Toronto had
repercussions felt around the planet yet it appears in none of our literary histories. I hope its telling here might make it part of our common folklore. Peter Freuchen's descriptions of the North, and his
chilling account of being trapped in an Arctic storm are told with
engaging anguish, and remind us that Canada is not just a country

from coast to coast, but a nation from coast to coast to coast. Donizetti's opera shows that others have been singing our praises for centuries. While all fishermen boast about the ones that got away, Zane Grey, using only a primitive rod and reel, came to Canada and caught a world record tuna, a fish weighing more than four times an average man. That he caught the fish at all is amazing, but a paltry accomplishment compared to his skill in making the description of the experience compelling even to people who hate fishing.

Finally, Wallace Stegner's moving account of his boyhood on the prairies is a wonderfully gentle prod, an arresting reminder to all Canadians, that our country, our people, our past is rich beyond imagining, and needs only to be better known to take one's breath away.

Greg Gatenby
Toronto,
May 1995

PETER FREUCHEN

WITH THE EXCEPTION of the Canadian author Farley Mowat, no novelist has been so associated with the Canadian Arctic as has the Danish writer Peter Freuchen (1886-1957). As with W.H. Davies, it was the loss of a limb in Canada (achingly described below) which forced him to rethink the direction of his life, and pushed him into the profession of authorship.

Freuchen was born in Denmark and had a conventional middle-class upbringing, peppered by a modest lack of respect for authority, especially teachers, and a lust for tales of adventure in Australia, North America and the North Pole. Upon obtaining his undergraduate degree, he signed on as a general hand for an Arctic expedition by a Danish explorer who was more romantic than scientist. The ensuing trip to Greenland was a fiasco from the technical point of view, but it served to pique Freuchen's love of the North.

A similarity of interests soon brought him, in 1909, into contact with the Danish explorer Knud Rasmussen. By this date, Rasmussen was moderately well-known in his native Greenland and in the mother country, Denmark. But it was not until he began exploring the breadth of the polar regions (with Peter Freuchen as his chief lieutenant) that Rasmussen achieved the international reputation and acclaim that his name maintains to this day.

Their first memorable adventure involved the establishment of a trading station (similar to a Hudson Bay outpost) on the extreme northwest coast of Greenland. Freuchen chose the name for the barren spot where in 1910 they founded the post: Thule. Several legendary Arctic expeditions of archaeology and exploration were later to be named in honour of this pioneer post (the first four Thule Expeditions were in Greenland; the fifth explored the Canadian North). The town of Thule has since become an important military base for the Americans, and a vital medical centre for Greenlanders.

With Rasmussen as his mentor, Freuchen took to Arctic living like a polar bear to water. He became fluent in several Inuit dialects, married a native woman (with whom he had children), and with Rasmussen conducted exploratory trips across the top of Greenland so gruelling that, reading descriptions of them, one cringes at the ferocity of the insults to the body that the two men endured.

Late in 1921, Freuchen's wife passed away, one of several aboriginals throughout Labrador and the Greenland coast to die from the influenza epidemic. Full of grief at her death and anxious to be distracted, Freuchen, although not a university-trained scientist, agreed to travel with Rasmussen and two other scientists to northern Hudson Bay on what history has come to call the Fifth Thule Expedition.

This journey of exploration has achieved the status of legend among northern ethnographers and other polar scientists: its principals were colourful characters and its work in cartography, ethnography and a myriad of other branches of science remains seminal in Arctic research. The Expedition was also one of the first scientific campaigns to report its findings dually: specialists received one set of data, but more tellingly, several books aimed at the general public of Europe and North America were published by the trek's protagonists; these books became bestsellers, and their authors were portrayed by the media as brave, bright, heroic adventurers (Freuchen, for example, made a winning appearance on a popular night-time TV quiz show, "The $64,000 Question").

The Fifth Thule Expedition lasted for four years. Freuchen and his colleagues fought the bellicose Arctic climate and mapped and excavated land known only to the Eskimos of Canada; even as late as the 1920s, they encountered natives who had never met Caucasians. The formal *Report of the Fifth Thule Expedition*, although it inspired ominous murmuring among some Canadian scientists as an assault on our sovereignty, helped awaken Canadians to the desirability, nay need, for Canadians to explore their own nation, rather than leave the task to others, no matter how talented.

As the following excerpt shows, the cost of the Fifth Thule Expedition was high for Freuchen in particular. Restricted mobility forced Freuchen to return to Denmark for proper medical treatment. To his pleasant surprise, his exploits and discoveries in Canada had made him a celebrity. He gave lectures about the Arctic, and the success of these talks encouraged him to tell his stories in the form of novels. These, in turn, became bestsellers, were widely translated, and led to a brief involvement with Hollywood.

Freuchen struck his contemporaries as a bruin of a man: he stood six feet, six inches and had a massive red beard. By his own admission he was ungainly and generally uncomfortable with sophisticated urban life. Yet he counted among his acquaintances and friends such luminaries as the King of Denmark, Herbert Hoover, Louis B. Mayer, Jean Harlow, Rockwell Kent, Niels Bohr and Robert Flaherty.

While he spent but four years in Canada, his experience in this country had a disproportionate effect on his fiction. Several of his novels were set in our northern latitudes, including his first. *The Great Hunter* told the story of an Eskimo who has killed a man according to the laws of his people and of his escape from the RCMP, who try to enforce our more familiar laws concerning murder. Almost all of his work was overtly autobiographical and concerned itself with the clash of cultures and the value of Inuit existence.

In our time, Freuchen continues to be a much-revered figure in the Nordic nations, and in Denmark his stature approaches the mythical. According to Arctic specialist and Freuchen authority Edmund Carpenter, Freuchen is the only author who has managed to convey in his novels the nuances, the very mode of syntactical construction of the Greenland language into a European tongue.

Perhaps the highest compliment to Freuchen in this regard was paid by Rasmussen who said that when he read Fruechen's fiction he knew he was reading in Danish but was thinking in Inuit.

In his lifetime, Freuchen published three books of memoirs, of which the last, *Vagrant Viking*, published in 1953, was the most honest, the most understated and most polished. The following extract (taken from *Vagrant Viking*), details the knee-buckling hardships and pitiless terrain encountered by Freuchen on his return to Thule. Despite the fact that the book appeared as late as the second half of the twentieth century, it remains one of the earliest descriptions of the Hudson Bay district penned by a creative writer.

The following is an excerpt from Freuchen's *Vagrant Viking* (1953) as translated from the Danish by Johan Hambro.

---

from VAGRANT VIKING

We had planned to leave Canada in 1924, each by a separate route in order to cover as much territory as possible. Dr. Birket-Smith was to go south through Canada, Dr. Mathiassen north to Pond Inlet on the east coast of Baffin Land, Knud Rasmussen was to go west through Arctic Canada to Alaska. It was my intention to go across Baffin Land, Devon Island and Ellesmere Land and across Smith Sound to Etah and Thule. But before I set out on the long trek to Thule, I planned to make an extensive mapping tour of the large area east of Igdloolik along the coast of Baffin Land. The maps of this region were very incomplete. I also hoped to make contact with some of the Hudson Strait Eskimos and to study their way of life.

In the early spring of 1923 I was ready and set out with Bangsted, our married Eskimo couple from Thule and a Canadian Eskimo,

Patloq, as a guide. We were in high spirits when we started, but the going was slow as the sleds were loaded with equipment and supplies. The dogs were in good condition and the weather was fine at first. We made progress for five days until we met our first snowstorm and had to stay on the same spot for three days. I had hoped to make up for this loss of time as soon as we got going again, but before long we were delayed once more. Halfway up the coast of Melville Peninsula we had to travel inland because the ice was no longer reliable. We had to go through deep snow and our loads were too heavy for the dogs going uphill. Finally we were forced to unload something from each sled to maintain any semblance of speed. We stored the unloaded supplies in a big pile and planned to send one or two sleds back for them the next day.

When we made camp that night I was annoyed at this extra delay, which meant we would waste another whole day. I knew that my dog team was stronger than the other teams and I was sure I could get the extra load onto my sled. So I started back for the load. The thought of going thirty-six hours without sleep did not bother me. The dogs did not like going back, but as long as we traveled with an empty sleigh I had no trouble with them.

I had gone only a short while when the wind began increasing rapidly and with it the snowdrift. At first there was only a brisk "floor sweep," as the Eskimos call it. But the wind mounted by the minute. In Greenland the temperature always rises with the wind, but in Hudson Bay the wind did not have this effect upon the temperature. It remained at fifty-four degrees below zero, and the snowdrift increased until it was like a heavy fog that cut sharply into my nose and ears. It seemed to penetrate my very brain, and it made me dangerously sleepy.

Soon I could no longer see our tracks, but I managed to stick to the right course until I found the pile we had left behind. I got the whole load onto my sled and, although it was heavy, I thought the dogs would get new strength when we turned around and they knew that food and rest were ahead of them. But the wind was straight ahead and growing stronger by the minute. Soon it was so violent my whip could not reach the dogs. I tried running ahead of the sled to stay close to the dogs where I could whip some speed into them, but it was no good.

I thought it would be easy to find my way back since I had only to follow my own tracks, but they were already obliterated by the whirling snow. I determined the direction by the wind, which is an unreliable indicator. Without knowing it, I got off course and soon the dogs knew that something was wrong. There were hills we had never climbed before and several times we got stuck in rocks. The moment we got stuck the dogs simply settled down in the snow and refused to move again. I first had to get the sled loose and then struggle with the dogs, screaming and swearing at them and using my whip brutally to get them up. When this had been repeated a few times I finally lost all sense of direction.

Suddenly we came to an enormous boulder where there was a deep depression in the snow on the wind side. It was like a small cave giving shelter against the howling wind. The dogs dived into the hole, and I decided to spend the rest of the night there.

I set about building an igloo, but for the first time in my life I found it impossible to cut through the snow. It had been packed solid by successive storms and I gave it up as a hopeless task. But I made up my mind to stay awake and wait for daylight.

At first I kept awake by walking back and forth in front of the boulder. When this got too boring I tried the old trick of walking with my eyes closed. I walked ten paces straight ahead, turned right, ten more paces and another right turn, another ten paces and the same thing a fourth time before I opened my eyes to see how far I had strayed from the starting point. But for once this game proved too cold, too windy and too uncomfortable. I felt an unbearable desire to lie down and saw no reason why I should not do so without risk, and I decided to make a small cave-like shelter where I could stretch out.

I began digging in the solid snow and soon I had a depression long enough for me to lie down in. I put my sled on top of this strange bed, then I put all the lumps on top of the sled and around the sides. I had built my bed in such a way that the end opened into the cave where the dogs were asleep, and I left this side uncovered, since it was well protected by the large boulder.

On my sled I had the skin of a bear's head I had killed some days before, and I took this along for a pillow. Finally as I crawled into my snug little shelter, I pulled my small seal-skin bag in place with my foot, so that it covered the opening like a door. It was a little like a berth on a ship—rather more cramped but I had room enough to stretch out.

I was well protected against the sub-zero temperature, dressed like an Eskimo in two layers of fur—one with the hairs inward against my skin, the other facing out. I had heavy boots and good gloves. Strangely enough I have never been bothered by cold hands, not so my feet.

Warm and comfortable at last, I soon fell asleep. I woke up once because my feet were cold and I tried to kick out the bag which served as a door. I wanted to get out and run around to increase my circulation, but I could not move the bag. It was frozen to the sides of my house, I thought. In reality there was an enormous snowdrift in front of it. I was annoyed but not enough to keep me from going back to sleep.

When I finally woke up I was very cold. I knew I had to get out and move about at once. What worried me most was the fact that my feet did not hurt any more—a sure sign of danger. To get out I had simply to crawl out through my little door, I thought, and I inched my way down to the bag. I could not move it. I used all my strength, but it was obvious that I could not get out the way I had come in. I was not worried because I expected to turn over the sled which covered me and get up that way. And I managed to turn over and lie on my stomach so that I could push up the sled with my back. There was not room enough to get up on my knees, but I pushed with my back the best I could. The sled would not budge!

At last I was really worried. My friends would soon begin to search for me, of course, but the question was whether I could survive until they found me. Perhaps I could dig my way out. But the snow surrounding me was now ice, and it was impossible to make the smallest dent in the surface with my gloved hands. I had left my snow knife outside on the sled with all my other tools. I decided to try digging with my bare hands. My hand would freeze but it would be better to lose one hand than to lose my life. I pulled off my right glove and began scratching with my nails. I got off some tiny pieces of ice, but after a few minutes my fingers lost all feeling, and it was impossible to keep them straight. My hand simply could not be used for digging so I decided to thaw it before it was too late.

I had to pull the arm out of the sleeve and put the icy hand on my chest—a complicated procedure in a space so confined I could not sit up. The ice roof was only a few inches above my face. As I put my hand on my chest I felt the two watches I always carried in a string around my neck, and I felt the time with my fingers. It was the middle of the day, but it was pitch black in my ice house. Strangely enough I never thought of using my watches for digging—they might have been useful.

By now I was really scared. I was buried alive and so far all my efforts had failed. As I moved a little I felt the pillow under my head—the skin of the bear's head. I got a new idea. By an endless moving with my head I managed to get hold of the skin. It had one sharply torn edge which I could use. I put it in my mouth and chewed on it until the edge was saturated with spit. A few minutes after I removed it from my mouth the edge was frozen stiff, and I could do a little digging with it before it got too soft. Over and over again I put it back in my mouth, let the spit freeze and dug some more, and I made some progress. As I got the ice crumbs loose, they fell into my bed and worked their way under my fur jacket and down to my bare stomach. It was most uncomfortable and cold, but I had no choice and kept on digging, spitting, freezing and digging.

My lips and tongue were soon a burning torture, but I kept on as long as I had any spit left—and I succeeded. Gradually the hole grew larger and at last I could see daylight! Disregarding the pain in my mouth and ignoring the growing piles of snow on my bare stomach, I continued frantically to enlarge the hole.

In my hurry to get out and save my frozen legs I got careless. I misjudged the size of the hole through which I could get out. My hand had, naturally, been able to move only above my chest and stomach, and to get my head in the right position seemed impossible. But I suddenly made the right movement and got my head in the right position.

I pushed with all my strength, but the hole was much too small. I got out far enough to expose my face to the drifting snow. My long beard was moist from my breathing and from the spit which had drooled from my bear skin. The moment my face got through the hole, my beard came in contact with the runners of the sled and instantly froze to them. I was trapped. The hole was too small to let me get through, my beard would not let me retire into my grave again. I could see no way out. But what a way to die—my body twisted in an unnatural position, my beard frozen to the sled above, and the storm beating my face without mercy. My eyes and nose were soon filled with snow and I had no way of getting my hands out to wipe my face. The intense cold was penetrating my head, my face was beginning to freeze and would soon lose all feeling.

Full of self-pity I thought of all the things in life I would have to miss, all my unfilled ambitions. And I thought of Magdalene, my friend, whose letters through the years had always been a little melancholy. It was the thought of Magdalene which made me want to go on living.

With all my strength I pulled my head back. At first the beard would not come free, but I went on pulling and my whiskers and some of my skin were torn off, and finally I got loose. I withdrew into my hole and stretched out once more. For a moment I was insanely grateful to be back in my grave, away from the cold and the tortuous position. But after a few seconds I was ready to laugh at my own stupidity. I was even worse off than before! While I had moved about more snow had made its way into the hole and I could hardly move, and the bear skin had settled under my back where I could not possibly get at it.

I gave up once more and let the hours pass without making

another move. But I recovered some of my strength while I rested and my morale improved. I was alive after all. I had not eaten for hours, but my digestion felt all right. I got a new idea!

I had often seen dog's dung in the sled track and had noticed that it would freeze as solid as a rock. Would not the cold have the same effect on human discharges? Repulsive as the thought was, I decided to try the experiment. I moved my bowels and from the excrement I managed to fashion a chisel-like instrument which I left to freeze. This time I was patient, I did not want to risk breaking my new tool by using it too soon. While I waited, the hole I had made filled up with fresh snow. It was soft and easy to remove, but I had to pull it down into my grave which was slowly filling up. At last I decided to try my chisel and it worked. Very gently and very slowly I worked at the hole. As I dug I could feel the blood trickling down my face from the scars where the beard had been torn away.

Finally I thought the hole was large enough. But if it was still too small that would be the end. I wiggled my way into the hole once more. I got my head out and finally squeezed out my right arm before I was stuck again. My chest was too large.

The heavy sled, weighing more than two hundred pounds, was on the snow above my chest. Normally I could have pushed it and turned it over, but now I had not strength enough. I exhaled all the air in my lungs to make my chest as small as possible, and I moved another inch ahead. If my lungs could move the sled I was safe. And I filled my lungs, I sucked up air, I expanded my chest to the limit— and it worked. The air did the trick. Miraculously the sled moved a fraction of an inch. Once it was moved from its frozen position, it would be only a question of time before I could get out. I continued using my ribs as levers until I had both arms free and could crawl out.

It was dark again outside. The whole day and most of another night had passed. The dogs were out of sight, but their snug little hole by the boulder was completely covered by snow, and I knew they must be asleep under it. As soon as I had rested enough, I got to my feet to get the dogs up. I fell at once and laughed at my weakness.

Once more I got to my feet and once more I fell flat on my face. I tried out my legs and discovered the left one was useless and without feeling. I had no control over it any more. I knew it was frozen, but at first I did not think about it. I had to concentrate on moving. I could not stay where I was.

I could only crawl, but I got my knife from the sled, pulled the dogs out of their cave and cut them loose from the harness. I planned to hold to the reins and let the dogs pull me on the snow, but they did not understand. I used the whip with what little strength I had left, and suddenly they set off so fast my weak hands could not hold the reins! The dogs did not go far, but they managed to keep out of my reach as I crawled after them. I crawled for three hours before I reached the camp.

Fortunately I then did not know the ordeal was to cost me my foot.

As soon as I had been inside our igloo for a while and began to warm up, feeling returned to my frozen foot and with it the most agonizing pains. It swelled up so quickly it was impossible to take off my kamik. Patloq, our Canadian Eskimo companion who had had a great deal of experience with such accidents, carefully cut off the kamik, and the sight he revealed was not pleasant. As the foot thawed, it had swollen to the size of a football, and my toes had disappeared completely in the balloon of blue skin. The pain was concentrated above the frozen part of my foot which was still without feeling. Patloq put a needle into the flesh as far as it would go, and I never noticed it.

The only thing to do was to keep the foot frozen, Patloq insisted. Once it really thawed, the pain would make it impossible for me to go on. It was obvious that we could not stay where we were and that we had to give up the whole expedition to Baffin Land. And with my foot bare to keep it frozen, we returned slowly to Danish Island, where Knud Rasmussen was completing all preparations for his long journey to Alaska.

He was horrified when he saw what had happened to me, and he wanted to give up his trip. But I insisted I could take care of myself with the aid of our Eskimo friends, and I persuaded my companions to carry out their plans according to schedule. And after a few days Knud set off to the north with two of the Eskimos, Mathiassen to Pond Inlet at the northeastern tip of Baffin Land, and Birket-Smith south through Canada.

I was left with Bangsted and the two Eskimo couples from Thule, who refused to leave me.

I was nursed by Patloq's wife Apa and I was in constant discomfort. It felt as if my foot had been tied off very tightly. The leg above was all right but the flesh below turned blue and then black. I had to lie quietly on my back while my nurse entertained me by recounting her experiences with frozen limbs. She knew a number of people who had lost both legs, others their arms or hands, but many had been killed because they were far too much trouble to take care of. And as the flesh began falling away from my foot, she tried out her special treatment. She captured lemmings—small mice—skinned them and put the warm skin on my rotting foot with the bloody side down. Every time she changed this peculiar kind of dressing, some of my decayed flesh peeled off with it, but she insisted on this treatment until there was no more flesh left.

Gangrene is actually less painful than it is smelly. As long as I kept my foot inside the warm house the odor was unbearable, so we arranged to keep the foot outside. We made a hole in the wall by the end of my bunk, and I put my foot out into the freezing temperature whenever the odor became too overpowering. As the flesh fell away from the bones, I could not bear having anything touch the foot, and at night when I could not sleep I stared with horrible fascination at the bare bones of my toes. The sight gave me nightmares and turned my nerves raw. I felt the old man with the scythe coming closer, and sometimes we seemed to have switched roles and my bare bones to have become part of him.

One day Apa told me that I needed a woman to take my mind off my pains. She brought along a young girl, Siksik, whose husband had kindly put her at my disposal while he went off on a trip with

Captain Berthie. I felt like King David who was given young girls to keep him warm at night, but I told Siksik that I was in no condition to take advantage of the kind offer.

In the meantime it seemed as if Apa's cure was having some effect. The gangrene did not spread beyond the toes. Once the decay had bared all five toes to the roots, it did not go farther, and the flesh stopped peeling. I could not stand the sight, however, and one day I decided to do something about it. I got hold of a pair of pincers, fitted the jaws around one of my toes, and hit the handle with a heavy hammer.

The excruciating pain cut into every nerve of my body, an agony I cannot describe. Siksik had watched me and was deeply impressed. She offered to bite off the rest of the toes, and if her teeth hurt as much as the pincers, she said that I could beat her up. Ignoring her offer, I fitted the pincers around the next toe, and this time it did not hurt so much. Perhaps one could get used to cutting off toes, but there were not enough of them to get sufficient practice.

I admit that I cried when I was through with them—partly from pain, partly from self-pity. But it was a great relief to have the toe stumps off since they had kept me from walking and putting on my kamiks. Now I could at least get on my boots and hobble around.

During the winter we moved from Danish Island to nearby Vansittart Island where we spent some peaceful and lazy weeks. My wound did not heal, however, and I realized I had to do something about it. We had heard that the Hudson Bay station in Chesterfield Inlet was visited every summer by a steamer which carried a doctor, and I decided to go down there by boat, once spring arrived. I knew I could not make the long sled trip to Thule next year if my foot did not improve. And Bangsted and I went to Repulse Bay to see Captain Cleveland about it. But just before we departed a child was born in our camp. Arnanguaq, the wife of our Thule Eskimo Akrioq, had a baby daughter, which they decided to name for my wife. By calling her Navarana they made me responsible for her future, and I was very touched by this tribute to my dead wife....

I went to see the doctor and asked him to look at my foot. His name was Hart. He told me afterward that he was only a medical student at the time, but I had complete faith in him as a doctor and a surgeon. He told me he would begin operating at noon and, as he had to anesthetize me, he asked me not to eat anything during the morning. But I had seen potatoes on board, a delicacy I had not tasted for years, and he reluctantly agreed to let me have some....

When it was my turn to be operated on, I was put on the table and given ether. When I awoke I was lying on a mattress in the corner of the mess room. The doctor said he had cleaned up the foot as best he could, but he had done only enough of a job on me to get me home safely, if I was careful. I must go to a proper hospital for further treatment, and he wanted me to go south right away on the *Nascopie*. But I had to go back to our headquarters. I was glad just to be able to walk again....

As soon as the steamer had left, I boarded a company schooner to Repulse Bay. It was to take Sergeant Douglas up to his station under a post manager called Thom, who had taken Cleveland's place. We went north together, and I said good-by to Douglas in Repulse Bay, where I got an Eskimo to take me to Hurd Channel in his whaleboat. The crossing should normally take two days, but we spent most of the time repairing the small craft which leaked like a sieve. We constantly had to pull it up on an ice floe to cover new holes, and while we repaired it the current would send us back as fast as we had moved ahead. When we finally reached the tip of Vansittart Island I went on shore to make the last leg of the trip on foot and told the Eskimo Usugtaq to take his leaking boat home.

He left his younger brother Inuyak to accompany me overland to our camp. It was only a short distance but it took us a long time to travel it—thanks to my foot. The stitches opened the very first day, and the wound began oozing, making it impossible for me to wear stockings in my kamiks. We could not stay where we were, slowly starving, because I had no equipment with me, and we continued our short and painful marches along the southern side of Vansittart Island. Fortunately the foot did not get worse, and after a number of painful days we reached our camp again.

The Thule Eskimos had taken good care of the camp and had quantities of meat in store. My dogs were in excellent condition, and we had sufficient supplies for the long trip ahead of us. Shortly after my arrival we moved back to our headquarters on Danish Island to spend the last few days before we began the return trip to Thule. We had run out of coal, but we kept warm by burning our bunks and various pieces of furniture we needed no longer.

We moved all our scientific materials, notes and diaries to Repulse Bay to have them sent home by the Hudson's Bay Company, and by Christmas we were ready. The last Christmas Eve was celebrated by baking cakes with all the flour left over. The local Eskimos were eager to see us leave as they had been promised our house when we were gone, and the longer we stayed the more wood we tore off the house for firewood.

At daybreak two days after Christmas we were ready to start. We said good-by to Bangsted, who was going to Repulse Bay, and set off with our three sleds—the Eskimo couples had one each, and I had one. The sixth member of the expedition was Navarana, the little girl who had been named for my wife. We went north by the familiar route and passed by the place where my foot had frozen. My dogs knew the way and I did not have to watch them. I sat on my sled, thinking about Magdalene and the future. I had some qualms about giving up my carefree life in the Arctic and settling down at home, but all that was still in the future.

When we got to Pingerqaling we met an Eskimo couple on their way north, and we liked them both so much we asked them to join us. The husband whose name was Aguano was going up to meet a friend of his with whom he was *Nuliaqatie*—which means with whom he was sharing a wife. Both couples were childless and were happy in this communal marriage. Every year Aguano took one of the women south with him, the next year the couples met to exchange wives, and Aguano went away with the other woman for a year. The wife we met was called Qinoruna and our two Thule women were happy to have her as a traveling companion.

When we passed Igdloolik we met my old friend, missionary

Umiling, whose son Nuralak had been sentenced to ten years in prison for the murder of a white trader, and taken down to Ottawa. Umiling was very proud of his son's achievement and insisted that this great success of his family was due to the fact that he had been converted to Christianity!

We continued across the Fury and Hecla Strait to Baffin Land which we had to cross. The local Eskimos, who often made the crossing to Pond Inlet where there was a trading station, gave us a detailed description of the route. I carefully wrote down all the names they mentioned while my Eskimos just remembered them. The good thing about Eskimo names is that they always make places easily recognizable. Thus we had to go to Pingo, which means a round mountain top; then to Kuksuaq, meaning the great river; then to Tassersuaq, meaning the large lake; and so on across Baffin Land....

After days of heavy and slow going we approached Milne Inlet at last. All the sleds sank deep down in the soft snow, except my small sled which was equipped with bone runners. I let Arnanguaq and Navarana take over this sled while I used my skis. It is now at the Ethnographic Museum in Copenhagen. At the mouth of Milne Inlet there was a large settlement where we met great hospitality. The fame of Nuralak, the murderer, had reached the place ahead of us and was still the great sensation. He had been promised room and board for ten years in a great house in Canada! The house was kept warm in winter, there would be women to sew his clothes for him, and he would never have to go hunting for his food! But his prison stay in Ottawa did not last as long as expected. After a few years he contracted tuberculosis and was returned to his tribe. I don't know if he had time to spread the infection before he died.

Three more days brought us to Pond Inlet, the Hudson's Bay Company station at the northern tip of Baffin Land. We met the hospitable post manager and his interpreter, a half blood called Edwards who had been to the World's Fair in Chicago, in 1893, one of a group of thirty-six Eskimos. And I met some of the mounted police, that splendid Canadian police corps. They gave me some genuine pemmican, made with tallow from the bison that still exists in Canada.

In Pond Inlet I saw a most regrettable sight. The wealthier Eskimos were living in filthy huts made from wood acquired at a great cost. The dirt and smell in the houses were unbelievable. For generations they had been used to living in tents during the summer and igloos in winter, so they had never developed any sense of cleanliness. They left all refuse on the floor and in piles outside the door. In the corners and under the bunks the dirt and rotten food had piled up for years. No wonder tuberculosis was thriving under those conditions. A new way of life is to no purpose without proper education.

As we left Pond Inlet our adopted Eskimo couple decided to go with us all the way to Thule. We planned to cross Lancaster Sound, in order to reach Cape Warrender on Devon Island, but our plan did not materialize. We drove across the inlet and all along the coast of Bylot Island and out the bay to the west of the island, Eclipse Sound. When we approached Lancaster Sound we went up in the mountains where we had a good view which showed us open water all the way across. We had to go still farther west.

A day or two later we met a sled coming south. It was driven by Sergeant H.A. Joy of the mounted police, one of the finest men I ever met in the Arctic. He had intended to go north the way we had planned, but he thought we would reach Devon Island if we went farther west. And he advised us to go overland through the valleys instead of following the coast. The overland route would be the quickest and there were plenty of musk oxen to feed us on the way.

We continued west along Baffin Land. Twice a day we climbed a mountain to get a view and see if it were possible to cross Lancaster Sound, always in vain. We crossed the mouth of Admiralty Bay where the open water went far into the bay. We had to go a great distance south before we could cross the ice and return to the coast of Baffin Land on the other side of the bay.

Suddenly we saw a bear, and we set off across the ice after it. By the time we had killed and skinned the animal, it had begun to snow and soon we had no idea of direction. The compass is of no use in this area, which is so close to the magnetic pole, and we had to stay overnight on the ice. The snow continued the next day and I went out to see if I could find my directions from the snowdrifts. The prevailing wind in the area was from the northwest, and if I could find the old snowdrifts piled by the wind, I could find our way back to land again. I soon discovered that the ice floes in Lancaster Sound had been drifting and turning in all directions so that the snow piles were no longer of any use to me and I returned to the Eskimos with no idea where we were.

In the evening the wind set in. It mounted during the night and soon turned into a regular gale. Suddenly Akratak screamed that there was water under us. The ice had cracked, and we did not waste a second getting into our clothes and out of the igloo. Outside we were beaten by a brutal hurricane, and we could hear the ice rumbling and breaking around us. All at once there was open ice in front of us as far as we could see. We turned about quickly and set off in the opposite direction.

In a very short time we met open water again, and as we moved away from the edge the ice suddenly cracked once more, and all the dogs in Agiok's team fell into the water. The next moment the two ice floes crashed together and killed all the dogs but one. The sled fortunately was not lost. Since Agiok had only one dog we had to divide his load among the other sleds. With frantic speed we unloaded his sled, and just as we had all his supplies ready to be divided among the rest of us, the ice opened and the water swallowed up everything.

We could only stay where we were and hope for the best. After a while little Navarana began crying. She was cold and hungry and Arnanguaq had to take care of her. The two other women stood in front of her to give shelter against the wind, while the men went with me to see the possibility of moving from the spot. After a minute or two we heard a wild scream behind us. Once again the ice had cracked, this time separating the three women from the baby.

I grabbed her up and put her inside my fur jacket with her feet inside my pants. She was delighted and screamed with laughter, but she slowed me down and kept me from jumping across the rift. Agiok and I were in a panic, rushing blindly around to find a way across, when suddenly our two separate ice floes ran into a third one which formed a bridge. Before trying to cross, I quickly tore off my fur jacket, turned it inside out and put Navarana inside. As soon as I had closed the jacket around her, I tossed her over to her mother. But the delay was enough to separate us once more.

Now Agiok and I were left alone and soon lost sight of the others. He was dripping wet, and I was shivering from cold without my jacket. The snow was still very heavy, cutting visibility to zero, but we had to move around to keep from freezing to death. After a miserable night of trudging about we suddenly saw something dark ahead of us—our companions with the two sleds! Some miracle had brought our two ice floes together again, and we walked over to them without any risk.

The next few hours were almost the worst I have ever lived through in the Arctic. The ice broke up continually all around us, and we had to be on the move all the time, running in different directions as the cracks seemed to come closer and closer. Sometimes the ice floe on which we found ourselves was so small it could hardly carry us all, at other times the ice seemed to stretch endlessly ahead. It stopped snowing at last and we could once more see a good distance, but we did not know which way to go. We were cold, exhausted and hungry. We saw seal and bear, but we had not the strength to take up the hunt. And during the night we lost several more dogs.

The terror and the agony came to an end at last. When the storm finally abated we found ourselves in the middle of Lancaster Sound. Both shores were equally far away, and though we were on reasonably solid ice open water was everywhere. We had only nine dogs left of our original team of thirty-four, only two sleds, no primus stove, no kerosene, few matches and hardly any ammunition for our guns. I had lost all my ammunition, and I threw my gun into the water as a sacrifice which Aguano assured me would placate the spirits of the sea. And we had only two sewing needles safely tucked away in Akratak's hair.

In these sadly reduced circumstances I did not think it advisable to continue north on the long and risky trip to Thule. I suggested that we give up the crossing of Devon Island and the heroic return to Thule by sled in favor of a safer way, and they all agreed. And Aguano, our adopted friend, asked us to forgive him for all the misfortunes which were his fault. He had broken his promise to meet his friend and exchange wives in order to stay with us and keep Qinoruna longer than he was entitled to. The hurricane and all our troubles were due to the revenge of the spirits, he claimed. Since the date was April 24 I thought it likely that the hurricane had been part of the equinoctial storms.

Somehow we had to get back to Baffin Land, and the simplest way out would be to wait until the sound froze again, but it was too cold for us to stay where we were. We loaded the sad remains of our once impressive equipment on the two sleds, with five dogs to pull one of them and four dogs the other. Aguano and I walked ahead to find a way to shore and the others followed. And we made our way from ice floe to ice floe. Some were small and not very solid, and they swayed dangerously under our feet and made the going very tricky. I had to admire the way the Eskimo women managed the dangerous trip. Arnanguaq, who was usually heavy and clumsy, danced across the ice like a ballerina. I could not move fast because my left foot was useless and without feeling. Whenever I had time to think of anything but keeping alive, I worried about the foot, certain now that I would lose it.

When we finally reached land the women began complaining. As long as our lives were in danger they had kept quiet, but now they were angry with me. Why had my sled been saved and not the others? Why had I kept most of my dogs while the Eskimos had lost most of theirs? And what was the use of saving my theodolite, my books and my diaries? My fancy equipment had been unable to make good weather and solid ice, so what was the point of my staring at the sun through my instruments?

The time was not right for any scientific discussion, and I only answered that we must keep going. But we were all tired, we had hardly any food left, and we had to break off parts of one sled to make a fire. Fortunately we found a cave which gave good shelter, and we left the women there while we went out to catch a seal or two. Once more we returned to the ice, taking care this time not to trespass on any ice that was not anchored to land, or so we thought.

We missed the first seal, the second one disappeared under our ice floe, and by the time we had harpooned the third and pulled it up on the ice, we were once more adrift. This time we were carried west to Prince Regent Strait before our ice sheet bore us back to shore. We had to cut up the meat and divide it between us in order to carry it back to the women, and in our exhausted state the return trip took us several hours.

The women were furious when we finally turned up, particularly Arnanguaq who screamed at us: "It appears that the men intend to go home alone and leave the women here to starve to death!"

I was rather shocked at the violent reception, but Akrioq, the experienced husband, smiled for the first time in many days. "There is bad temper here," he said calmly. "The situation must be back to normal when there is time to be angry!"

The women were mollified when they saw all the meat we had brought them and soon we had a roaring fire going and began eating, but I was only halfway through the meal when I collapsed. I had not slept for five days and nights. I have never been able to stay awake longer than five days, and I settled down in the cave to sleep. The others soon followed my example, and when we awoke we were ready to be on our way again.

We had to get to people somehow, but with two sleds and nine dogs our progress was painfully slow. We made our way along the coast until we reached Admiralty Bay where there was still no ice at the mouth, and we had to go far down the bay to cross over to the east side. We saw quite a few seals, but we had to save our ammunition and did not dare shoot any. Akrioq, who had been to the bottom of Admiralty Bay with Dr. Mathiassen two years before, assured us there was never any shortage of caribou, rabbit and seal. We decided to go all the way down to the end of the bay, but before we got that far we met a strange procession on the ice.

At first we thought it a herd of caribou, but as we came closer it looked more like a family of musk oxen. Through my binoculars we finally made out that it was a group of twelve Eskimos on the point of collapse.

They could hardly be recognized as human beings, but some of them appeared to know us. It seemed that we had met them the previous year as prosperous happy people in Igdloolik. Under the leadership of Tulimak—The Rib—they had made an excursion to Admiralty Bay, had run into one storm after another, and for a whole month they had been unable to hunt. Tulimak had worn himself out trying to get food for them, and one day was found dead close to their camp. He had kept them from eating their dogs, which they had to depend on if they were to make their way back again. Once he had died the dogs were killed and devoured, but it did not keep thirteen of them from starving to death. The twelve survivors had been on the move for days without hope until they heard the howling of our dogs.

We quickly made camp and gave the starving people food. At first they could not swallow a thing, and we had to force small morsels of meat into them. I gave them mainly soup and some seal fat, and gradually they recovered and cheered up a little. But they did not want to talk about the experiences they had gone through at the bottom of the bay. After four days they declared themselves strong enough to return to their camp for all their possessions, if we would lend them our dogs and sleds.

I offered to go with them, but as soon as I had made my offer I noticed Aguano whispering to Akrioq, who quickly called me and asked to have a word with me.

In all the fourteen years we had been traveling companions he had never refused to do my bidding. But on this occasion he insisted that I stay where I was and let the strangers do the job alone. Dead Eskimos had been left behind in the camp. Who could tell what had happened to the bodies? Perhaps the dogs had eaten them, perhaps the people had done it. Such things should not be seen or known by white men, "because you like to talk together," he said. "It might be better to be ignorant in a country where rules are made by police and ministers who do not know the way people may have to live and act." I agreed with him and our friends went off alone.

They made two trips and they brought back four loads of valuable possessions—sewing needles, lamps, knives, axes and matches, all things useful under the circumstances. We had to agree to remain where we were in order to help these poor people recover. They were terribly weak, but they did not miss their dead friends and relatives so badly as we had expected. There were enough women left for the surviving men.

The weather turned warmer, and soon we could not stay in igloos any more because the ice thawed too fast, but we had already got enough skins to make our first tent of the season. Most of our visitors had to stay under their sleeping skins for days, and those who could walk around spent most of the days sitting outside the tent in the warm sun and eating. But as they got stronger they all developed boils.

My Greenland friends came to ask for a private talk. We had to move out on the ice where nobody could hear us, and they told me that the boils, according to Qinoruna, were proof that the Eskimos had eaten human flesh. But next morning when my Eskimos from Greenland also broke out in boils, they changed their tune. Their wives claimed that their men had been unfaithful—the boils were a proof that they had slept with the cannibal women. They denied the accusation and insisted that the starved girls were too emaciated to arouse any desire.

Peace reigned the next day, however, when the wives themselves woke up with boils! The husbands had a wonderful time making fun of them.

I tried to stay outside the marital squabbles, which I could do easily since I was above suspicion—being the only one without boils, except a half-grown boy from Igdloolik. The drawback was that the sick people were unable to go hunting so that this boy, Mala, and I had to feed all the patients. We kept each other company on hunting expeditions, sometimes lasting two or three days, but Mala refused to go south toward the old camp where he had starved. He was very friendly, but he shut up like a clam whenever I mentioned the camp.

The patients did not improve much, and I realized it would be impossible for us to go on without assistance. In addition to our own group of seven, we had the twelve Eskimos from Igdloolik, and we had only our two sleds and nine dogs. As soon as my three Eskimos were well enough to walk, we decided the only way out was for me to go overland to Milne Inlet and Pond Inlet for help from the trading station. From Pond Inlet a boat could be sent up to bring the whole group back. In my absence my three Eskimos could take care of the others.

I packed a minimum of supplies and tied them up in the Danish flag, which I had taken along from Danish Island, and I took a gun with our last eight rounds of ammunition. I did not want to go all alone so I asked Mala to accompany me. He was willing, but he asked as a reward that I get him a wife.

We set off to the east, marching through the most forbidding district I had ever come across. For eleven days we made our way through an endless plateau of soft wet clay. My frozen foot was getting more and more painful, yet day after day we went on and on, without sight of any kind of game. Except for a small ptarmigan which Mala killed with a stone one day, we had nothing to eat for eleven days. We chewed rabbit excrements which we managed to get down as long as our blubber lasted, but afterward it was impossible to swallow the disgusting stuff. We ate grass and chewed the Arctic saxifrages which we ran across now and then. We were famished and I was sorry that Mala, who had just gone through a terrible ordeal, should suffer starvation again.

To make matters worse the warm weather had turned the rivers into roaring torrents which were hard to cross. Sometimes I had to carry Mala as ballast when the current was too strong for me, and the extra weight was bad for my foot.

The clay was the worst of all. It covered everything, there were no stones, no cliffs, no dry place. We had to sleep in the slippery stuff, close together to keep warm and covered with the Danish flag. The flag, our clothes and our faces were covered with clay and quite unrecognizable.

Time and again I was ready to give up, but the thought of Magdalene kept me going. I thought of her day and night, and only the knowledge that each step brought me closer to her made it possible for me to move my feet. I decided to name the place Magda's Plateau. If it bore her name something good must come out of it.

When the eleven days came to an end I had given up all hope that things would ever change. In fact, I was reconciled to the idea that we would keep stumbling through deep clay to the end of our days, when finally we caught a glimpse of the ice in Milne Inlet.

Mala had been very quiet the last part of the march; we hardly talked at all. The hunger did not bother us much any more. Hunger pains usually last only three days. Once this initial suffering is over, one feels only an increasing weakness and an unbearable desire to lie down and sleep. But reaching the ice did not mean the end of our troubles. The snow was deep and soft in spots and sometimes we fell into pools of water. When I finally removed my kamiks and socks my foot was a horrible, bloody, pussy mess. I tried walking barefoot, but the ice felt like needles shooting into my sole, and I had to give it up.

The ice meant seals, however, and soon we saw the first ones. They were shy and kept at a distance, and we dared not risk a shot we were so short of ammunition. Our hands trembled so from weakness it was hard to take good aim. And at the end of the first day we had still not killed a seal. The second day we saw a wonderful fat fellow a short distance away, and I decided to get him or stay there and die. When there is no possibility of hiding behind a camouflage, one has to go to the opposite extreme and let the seal see as much of one as possible. One has to pretend to be a seal, which is what I did.

I went wholeheartedly into the act, and the seal watched me curiously as I crawled slowly along the ice. He obviously did not think I was worth worrying about, and every time he slept for a few moments

I crept a few yards closer. My path went through pools of melted water. I was soaking wet in no time, but this was our last chance. I spent hours at the game, realizing I would have neither physical nor mental power to go through it again.

At last I tried to take aim, but my hands trembled so violently I had to drop the gun and rest. I simply closed my eyes and dropped my head on my arms. While I waited to calm down I realized that I did not care any more. If I killed the animal we would survive, if not we would die—it did not matter any more. With this conviction I became calm. I took quick aim and with a single shot I killed the seal.

Once I had fired I did not bother to look at the animal or to get up. I heard Mala splashing through the pools, and he ran as if he were in perfect condition, and I let him handle the animal. He skinned the seal and cut it up into large pieces, while I cut through the skull to the brains. I mixed it with fat from the skin until it turned into a paste which I gobbled down. It was the most delightful food I had ever tasted, and I finished by eating some raw liver, part of the tongue and fat—more and more fat. And in a few minutes we were asleep, covered for the last time by the dirty Danish flag.

When we woke up we were hungrier than ever. I gathered cassiope, enough for a fire, and we soon had a roaring blaze going on which we grilled seal steaks. We satisfied our hunger, and I washed in the icy water, cleaned the flag, and we settled down to sleep once more.

Our muscles felt more tired than ever when we got going again but we moved ahead slowly and in four more days we were at Toqujan, where a crowd of Eskimos came to meet us. Mala sat down on the ice, covered his face with his hands and began to sob. The closer the Eskimos came, the more wildly he cried until he was finally ready to tell them of the disaster that had taken the lives of thirteen of his companions. All the dead people had relatives in Toqujan, and soon the whole crowd joined Mala in his mourning. In the end I had to pull him into his sister's house where we both collapsed and slept, while the women took care of our clothes and equipment. They were fascinated by our appearance—we looked like skeletons with our sunken eyes and cheeks and our protruding bones.

After some days the good Eskimos drove us the last leg of our journey to Pond Inlet, where the post manager received me with open arms and took wonderful care of us both. And in a few days I was able to fulfill the promise I had given Mala. We met an old Eskimo by the name of Suna—meaning What is that? As soon as I heard that Suna, who came from the River Clyde district, had a daughter who was ready to be married, I gave Mala all sorts of gifts, praised him to the skies—which was no less than the strong and courageous boy deserved—and suggested a marriage arrangement which was quickly accepted.

I left him behind in Button Point on Bylot Island, as he said that "his feet were no longer hungry for walking." The next time I saw him was on the silver screen. A good friend of mine, Reginald Orcutt, went to Pond Inlet sometime later to make a film, and he assured me that the young man was happy and prosperous. If it had not been for Mala I would never have survived the march across Magda's Plateau.

W. H. DAVIES

Few men of letters are able to date their beginnings as authors with the certitude of the Welsh poet and autobiographer William Henry Davies (1871-1940). Even fewer can say that an incident in Canada caused a change in professional ambition: in Davies' case, from gold prospector to poet. Accidently slipping under the wheels of a train, he lost a limb and was forced to reconsider how to make a living.

Davies was born into souring poverty in Newport, Wales. His formal education was, not surprisingly, nearly nonexistent. As a youth, he lived like the Artful Dodger, thieving either solo or at the head of his own gang of boys, until he was caught and, by way of redemptive punishment, was forcibly apprenticed to a picture-framer. He counted the days until he was free to leave, peripatetically worked at menial jobs for half a year, then convinced the trustees of his grandmother's estate to advance his share of a meagre weekly allowance so that he could travel to North America and exploit the riches it offered.

After years tramping across the United States, and because of the accident befalling him in Canada on March 20, 1899, Davies moved to London, determined to be an author. Unable to interest any publisher in his poems, he paid for them to be privately printed in a modest edition, and had the wit to send copies to famous authors who might be potential admirers. Among those famous authors was George Bernard Shaw. The eminent playwright happily became advocate and cheerleader for Davies, and the major literary critics of the day agreed that an exciting new talent had been discovered. Shaw even wrote the preface to Davies' literary recollections of hoboing across North America, isolating Davies' account of the Canadian disaster for special commendation.

Handsomely encouraged by Shaw and other esteemed authors, Davies emitted a Niagara of words, publishing twenty books of poetry and eight of prose in the following two and a half decades. His eminence secured, he fraternized easily in London with colleagues such as Shaw, Joseph Conrad, Edmund Gosse, Edward Thomas, Osbert Sitwell (who wrote an introduction to Davies' *Collected Poems*) and Augustus John, but eventually he moved to the Gloucestershire countryside and the quiet life of a scribbler—in mute contrast to his wayfaring youth. Following a lengthy illness, he died in 1940.

The parallels between the following excerpt and Jack London's account of riding the Canadian rails (in his book *The Road*) are uncanny. Not least among the coincidences is their decision to "beat" west by the same train route, and relate incidents that took place only a few years apart on the same short stretch of track.

The following excerpt from Davies' *The Autobiography of a Super-Tramp*, although it is careless with dates, includes Davies' expressions of gratitude to the Canadians he encountered (in Renfrew and elsewhere). In *The Autobiography of a Super-Tramp*, W. H. Davies wrote as a wolf walks: supple, almost laconic, and always alert.

from THE AUTOBIOGRAPHY OF A SUPER-TRAMP

One afternoon, when passing through Trafalgar Square, I bought an early edition of an evening paper, and the first paragraph that met my eye had this very attractive heading—"A Land of Gold." It was a description of the Klondyke, and a glowing account of the many good fortunes that daily fell to the lot of hardy adventurers. It would cost me sixty pounds, or more, to travel to that remote part of the world, and forty-four pounds were all I now possessed. This thought did not for long discourage me from making the attempt. I knew that I could beat my way across the Canadian continent, without using a cent for travelling, and I could save these few pounds for food, and cases in which payment would be absolutely necessary, when forced to travel on foot, at the other end of Canada.

That night I exchanged thirty pounds for their equivalent in paper dollars, placing the latter in a belt which I wore next to my skin, determined that this money should not see the light until my journey was nearly done.

It was now the month of March, and the navigation of the St. Lawrence had not yet opened, so that I would be compelled to beat my way from Halifax, or St. John's, to Montreal, which would not be necessary later in the Spring, when the latter port would be the destination of all emigrant ships. I was very happy at this time, with these prospects in view, which were really too bright to decoy any man who had an average amount of common-sense. My conception of that wonderful land, for all my travels, was childish in the extreme. I thought the rocks were of solid gold, which so dazzled the sun that he could not concentrate his glance on any particular part, and that his eye went swimming all day in a haze. I pictured men in possession of caves sitting helpless in the midst of accumulated nuggets, puzzled as to how to convey all this wealth to the marts of civilisation. What I wanted with all these riches I cannot say, for it was never a desire of mine to possess jewellery, fine raiment, yachts, castles or horses: all I desired was a small house of my own, and leisure for study. In fact I made up my mind not to waste time in hoarding more wealth than would be necessary to these small comforts, but to return home satisfied with a sum not exceeding two thousand pounds, the interest from which would, I thought, be ample for any student who remained true to his aims, and was sincere in his love for literature.

In this month of March, the first day in the second week, I left Euston Station at midnight and arrived, cold and shaking in Liverpool, early the next morning. On making enquiries, I learnt that a ship was leaving for St. John's on the following Wednesday, from which place emigrants must needs go by train to Quebec or Montreal, owing to the ice-bound condition of the river. I decided on making St. John's my destination, from which port I would beat my way towards the west, going easy at first, and faster as the spring of the year advanced.

The accommodation for steerage passengers on this ship was abominable, and their comfort seemed to be not in the least considered. This was owing to the small number of English speaking people that were travelling as steerage passengers, and the disgusting, filthy habits of the great majority, who were a low class of Jews and peasants from the interior of Russia. None of the ship's crews could be expected to treat these people as one of themselves, seeing them sit to eat in the filth of their skin and fur clothes, without the least thought of washing; and again, hiding food in their bed clothes, making the cabin too foul to sleep in. After seeing the first meal fought for, and scrambled for on the steerage floor, where it had fallen, we Englishmen, five in number, took possession of a small table to ourselves, only allowing one other, a Frenchman, to sit with us....

So many of these aliens were landing in Canada at this time, that when I approached the Custom House officers, one of them, judging by my features and complexion, which were not much unlike those of a native of the south, addressed me in an unknown tongue. I looked at him in surprise, which made him repeat his question, probably in another tongue, equally unknown. Being rather incensed at this, and flushing indignantly at this tone to a dog, I lost no time in answering him according to Billingsgate. "Ho, ho!" he laughed, "so you are a blooming cockney, and so am I. Why didn't you say so at once!"

The blacksmith had booked through to Quebec, and would take train to that place before morning. Three other Englishmen had booked through to Winnipeg, and would travel with him by the same train. The other Englishman, a carpenter by trade, had relatives in Montreal, and, having only a couple of dollars in his possession, was willing to take instructions from me how to get there. I promised to get this man to Montreal in three or four days, providing he did not at any time question my actions. He kept his promise, and I kept mine, for on the fourth day after landing, I wished him good-bye outside his sister's house, which he had had some difficulty in finding. I was now alone, and seeking a companion for my journey west.

Now, once upon a time, there lived a man known by the name of Joe Beef, who kept a saloon in Montreal, supplying his customers with a good free lunch all day, and a hot beef stew being the mid-day dish. There was not a tramp throughout the length and breadth of the North American Continent, who had not heard of this and a goodly number had at one time or another patronised his establishment. Often had I heard of this famous hostelry for the poor and needy, and the flavour of its stew discussed by old travellers in the far States of the South. When I thought of this, I knew that a companion for any part of America could most certainly be found on this man's premises, and I would there hear much valuable information as to the road I was about to travel.... I was strolling along with these thoughts, when I met the man of my desire, leaning lazily against a post. Not wishing to accost him outright, and yet eager for his conversation, I stood beside him lighting my pipe, striking several matches for this purpose and failing owing to the wind blowing in small gusts. Seeing my dilemma, the man quickly produced matches of his own, and, striking one, held it lighted between the palms of his hands, leaving just enough space for the bowl of my pipe to enter. For this I thanked him, and secondly, invited him to a drink, asking him where we should go, being in hopes he would mention Joe Beef. "Well," he answered, pointing to the opposite corner, "the nearest place is French Marie's." We entered that place and, in the course of conversation, I told him how I had beat my way from state to state, but that this was my first experience in Canada.

"The United States," said this man sagely, "are nearly played out, and of late years there are far too many travellers there. You will find the Canadian roads better to beat, and the people's hearts easier to impress, for they are not overrun. When did you get here?" Knowing that this man was under the impression that I had just beat my way into Canada from the States, and not willing to undeceive him, I answered quickly "This morning," and for a time changed the conversation into a praise of the beer. "Where are you going to sleep?" he asked. "Meet me here in half an hour, after I have begged the price of my bed, and a drink or two—and we will both go to Joe Beef's, where I have been for this last week." Not wishing to lose sight of this man, I told him that my pocket could maintain the two of us until the next day. "All right," said he, appearing much relieved, "we will go at once and settle for our beds, and come out for an hour or so this evening." Leaving French Marie's we walked beside the river for some distance, when my companion halted before a building, which I knew must be Joe Beef's, having just seen two seedy looking travellers entering. We followed, and to my surprise, I saw it was a rather clean looking restaurant with several long tables, with seats and a long bar on which the food was served. But what surprised me most was to see a number of Salvation Army men and officers in charge of this place. Without saying a word to my companion, I took a seat at one of the tables, to order a beef stew, asking him what he would have, and, for his sake, the order was doubled. "When Joe Beef kept this place," whispered my companion, "he was a true friend to travellers, but you don't get much out of the people except you pay for it!" Although I winked at him, as though the same thoughts were mine, I noticed that the meals were well worth what was charged for them, and, in after days, I often compared this place favourably with similar institutions in London, that were under the same management, and where men did not get the worth of their money.... I remained three weeks in this inexpensive hotel, and decided to travel on the following Monday, although the snow was still deep in Montreal, and would be yet deeper in the country. I had a small room for sleeping purposes, at a cost of fifteen cents per night. There were several others of the same kind, each divided one from the other by a thin wooden partition, which was high enough for privacy, but did not prevent curious lodgers from standing tip toe on their beds, and peering into another's room. Going to bed early on Sunday night, previous to continuing my journey on the following day, I was somewhat startled on entering my room, to hear a gentle rap on the partition which divided my room from the next. "Hallo!" I cried, "what do you want?" The man's wants, it seemed, were private, for he seemed frightened into silence at this loud tone of demand, which would most certainly draw the attention of others. At last he cleared his throat by a forced fit of coughing, and then whispered, in a low. distinct voice—"I want a match, if you can oblige me with one." Of course, smoking was not allowed in the bedrooms, but in this respect we were nearly all breakers of the law. Taking a few matches from my pocket, I threw them over the partition, and heard him feeling in the semi-darkness, after hearing the sound of them falling. Then he gently struck one, and, by its light, gathered in the others. In a moment or two he addressed me in his natural voice, and, to my surprise, it sounded familiar, and filled me with curiosity to see this man's face. I encouraged him to talk—which he seemed determined to do—thinking a word might reveal him to me, and the circumstances under which we had met.

His voice in the dark puzzled me, and I could not for my life locate it. A hundred scenes passed through my memory, some of them containing a number of characters. In my fancy I made them all speak to me, before dismissing them again to the dim regions from which they had been summoned, but not one of their voices corresponded with this voice heard in the dark. Above this voice I placed thin and thick moustaches, black, grey, brown, red, and white; under this voice I put heavy and light beards of various hues, and still, out of all my material, failed to make a familiar face. Still sending Memory forth in quest of the owner of this voice, and she, poor thing! bringing forward smiling men and stern men, thin men and fat men, short men and tall men, tame men and wild men, hairy men and bald men, dark men and fair men—until she became so confused as to bring back the same people the second time; still sending her forth on this vain quest, I fell asleep.

It was a dreamless sleep; no sound broke its stillness, and no face looked into its depths; and, when I awoke the next morning, this voice seemed to be already in possession of my thoughts. I lay awake for about ten minutes, and was just on the point of rising, thinking the man had left his chamber, when I heard a stir coming from that direction. He was now dressing. Following his example, but with more haste, so as to be the first ready, I waited the unbolting of his door, so that I might meet this man face to face. I unbolted my own door, and opened it when I was but half dressed, but there was no necessity for doing this, for my arms were in the sleeves of my coat when his bolt was slipped back and we simultaneously appeared, at the same time wishing each other good morning. I recognised this man without difficulty, but apparently had the advantage of him. To make no mistake, I looked at his right hand, and saw the two fingers missing, knowing him for a certainty to be Three Fingered Jack, who had been a cattleman from Montreal, whom I had met in Glasgow when I had gone there from Baltimore, three years previous to this. On that occasion I had been in this man's company for only half an hour, and since that time had heard thousands of voices, but was still positive that I had heard this voice before.

We stood side by side washing, and preparing for breakfast, and, although I remained a stranger to him, as far as former acquaintance was concerned, I mentioned to him in confidence that I was going west that very morning, after breakfast. "So was I," he said, "as far as Winnipeg, but thought to wait until some of this snow cleared. Anyhow, as a day or two makes little difference, we will, if you are agreeable, start together this morning. I know the country well," he continued, "between Montreal and Winnipeg, having travelled it a number of times, and, I promise you, nothing shall be wanting on the way."... Three Fingered Jack was a slow traveller for, as he with some emotion said—"It broke his heart to hurry and pass through good towns whose inhabitants were all the happier for being called on by needy men." This slow travelling suited me for the time being, for we were having another fall of snow, and I half regretted having left Montreal, although, day after day I was certainly getting a little nearer to the gold of Klondyke. But I determined to shake off this slow companion on the first approach of fine weather.

We loafed all day in the different railway stations, in each of which was kept a warm comfortable room for the convenience of passengers. Although we were passengers of another sort, and stole rides on the trains without a fraction of payment to the company, we boldly made ourselves at home in these places, being mistaken for respectable travellers, who were enjoying the comforts for which we paid. Sometimes a station master would look hard on us, suspecting us for what we were, but he was very diffident about risking a question, however much he was displeased at seeing us in comfortable possession of the seats nearest to the stoves. Towards evening we made application for lodgings at the local jail, at which place we would be accommodated until the following morning. I was now without money, with the exception of that which was concealed and reserved for the most hazardous part of the journey, which would be its western end. Now, in all these jails we were searched and examined before being admitted for a night's shelter, but often in a very indifferent manner. One night we arrived at a small town where a double hanging was to take place in the yard of the jail early the next morning. A woman, it seems, had called on her lover to assist in the murder of her husband, which had been brutally done with an axe, for which crime both had been pronounced guilty and condemned to die. Thousands of people had flocked in from the neighbouring country, which in this province of Ontario was thickly settled, and a large number of plain clothes detectives had been despatched from the cities, there being supposed some attempt might be made at rescue, owing to one of the condemned being a woman. We arrived at this town early in the afternoon, and were surprised at the unusual bustle and the many groups of people assembled in the main thoroughfares. Thinking the town contained, or expected, some attraction in the way of a circus or menagerie, we expressed little curiosity, but returned at once to the railway station, intending to possess its most comfortable seats against all comers, until the approach of darkness, when we would then make application at the jail for our night's accommodation. When this time came, we marched straight to the jail, and boldly hammered its door for admittance. It was at once answered by a police officer, to whom we explained our wants, and he, without much ado, invited us indoors. Expecting the usual questions, and being prepared with the usual answers—expecting the usual indifferent search, and having pipe, tobacco and matches artfully concealed in our stockings—we were somewhat taken by surprise to find a large number of officers, who all seemed to show an uncommon interest in our appearance. The officer, who was examining us previous to making us comfortable for the night, had finished this part of the business to his own satisfaction, when one of these detectives stepped forward, and said—"We cannot admit strangers to the jail on the present occasion, so that you had better make them out an order for the hotel." This order was then given to us, and we immediately left the jail; and it was then, curious to know the reason for this action, that we soon made ourselves acquainted with the true facts of the case. When we arrived at the hotel, we were informed that every bed had been taken since morning, and that, as it was, a number of men would be compelled to sit all night dozing in their chairs, and it was with this information that we returned to the jail. For the second time we were admitted, and were advised to walk to the next town. This, Three Fingered Jack absolutely refused to do, saying that his feet were too blistered and sore to carry him another hundred yards. All these detectives then got together, and, after a rather lengthy consultation, one of them came forward and, after plying us with a number of questions, proceeded to examine our clothes, and that so thoroughly that I feared for the result. At the beginning of the search, I gave him my razor, a small penknife, my pocket handkerchief and a comb, but he was not satisfied until his hands were down in my stockings, and bringing up first my pipe, then my tobacco, and lastly the matches. What worried me most was the belt next to my body, which contained my money. I had not much fear of Three Fingered Jack, when confronting each other openly, though he was a tall active man, but had he known of these dollars, I had not dared in his presence to have closed my eyes, believing that he would have battered out my brains with a stone, wooden stake or iron bar, so that he might possess himself of this amount. This detective certainly discovered the belt, and felt it carefully, but the money being in paper, and no coin or hard substance being therein, he apparently was none the wiser for its contents. At last this severe examination was at an end, and we were both led through an iron corridor and placed in a cell, the door of which was carefully locked. I don't believe we slept one moment during that night but what we were overlooked by a pair, or several pairs, of shrewd eyes. They could not believe but that we were other to what we pretended and had come there with designs to thwart the ends of justice. Next morning our things were returned to us, and we were turned adrift at a cold hour that was far earlier than on ordinary occasions.

The snow was still deep and the mornings and evenings cold when, a week after this, we reached Ottawa. This slow travelling was not at all to my liking, and I often persuaded my companion to make more haste towards Winnipeg. This he agreed to do; so the next morning we jumped a freight train, determined to hold it for the whole day. Unfortunately it was simply a local train, and being very slow, having to stop on the way at every insignificant little station, we left it, at a town called Renfrew, intending that night to beat a fast overland passenger train, which would convey us four or five hundred miles before daybreak. With this object we sat in the station's waiting room until evening, and then, some twenty minutes before the train became due, we slipped out unobserved and took possession of an empty car, stationary some distance away, from which place we would see the train coming, and yet be unseen from the station's platform. This train would soon arrive, for passengers were already pacing the platform, the luggage was placed in readiness, and a number of curious people, having nothing else to do, had assembled here to see the coming and going of the train. At last we heard its whistle, and, looking out, we saw the headlight in the distance, drawing nearer and nearer. It steamed into the station without making much noise, for the rails were slippery, there still being much ice and snow on the track. "Come," I said to Jack, "there is no time to lose"; and we quickly jumped out of the empty car.

This fast passenger train carried a blind baggage car, which means that the end nearest to the engine was blind in having no door. Our object was to suddenly appear from a hiding place, darkness being favourable, and leap on the step of this car, and from that place to the platform; this being done when the train was in motion, knowing that the conductor, who was always on the watch for such doings, rarely stopped the train to put men off, even when sure of their presence. If he saw us before the train started, he would certainly take means to prevent us from riding. When we had once taken possession of this car, no man could approach us until we reached the next stopping place, which would probably be fifty miles, or much more. At that place we would dismount, conceal ourselves, and, when it was again in motion, make another leap for our former place. Of course, the engineer and fireman could reach us, but these men were always indifferent, and never interfered, their business being ahead instead of behind the engine.

The train whistled almost before we were ready, and pulled slowly out of the station. I allowed my companion the advantage of being the first to jump, owing to his maimed hand. The train was now going faster and faster, and we were forced to keep pace with it. Making a leap he caught the handle bar and sprang lightly on the step, after which my hand quickly took possession of this bar, and I ran with the train, prepared to follow his example. To my surprise, instead of at once taking his place on the platform, my companion stood thoughtlessly irresolute on the step, leaving me no room to make the attempt. But I still held to the bar, though the train was now going so fast that I found great difficulty in keeping step with it. I shouted to him to clear the step. This he proceeded to do, very deliberately, I thought. Taking a firmer grip on the bar, I jumped, but it was too late, for the train was now going at a rapid rate. My foot came short of the step, and I fell, and, still clinging to the handle bar, was dragged several yards before I relinquished my hold. And there I lay for several minutes, feeling a little shaken, whilst the train passed swiftly on into the darkness.

Even then I did not know what had happened, for I attempted to stand, but found that something had happened to prevent me from doing this. Sitting down in an upright position, I then began to examine myself, and now found that the right foot was severed from the ankle. This discovery did not shock me so much as the thoughts which quickly followed. For, as I could feel no pain, I did not know but what my body was in several parts, and I was not satisfied until I had examined every portion of it. Seeing a man crossing the track, I shouted to him for assistance. He looked in one direction and another, not seeing me in the darkness, and was going his way when I shouted again. This time he looked full my way, but instead of coming nearer, he made one bound in the air, nearly fell, scrambled to his feet, and was off like the shot from a gun. This man was sought after for several weeks, by people curious to know who he was, but was never found, and no man came forward to say—"I am he." Having failed to find this man, people at last began to think I was under a ghostly impression. Probably that was the other man's impression, for who ever saw Pity make the same speed as Fear?

Another man, after this, approached, who was a workman on the line, and at the sound of my voice he seemed to understand at once what had occurred. Coming forward quickly, he looked me over, went away, and in a minute or two returned with the assistance of several others to convey me to the station. A number of people were still there; so that when I was placed in the waiting room to bide the arrival of a doctor, I could see no other way of keeping a calm face before such a number of eyes than by taking out my pipe and smoking, an action which, I am told, caused much sensation in the local press.

I bore this accident with an outward fortitude that was far from the true state of my feelings. The doctor, seeing the even development of my body, asked me if I was an athlete. Although I could scarcely claim to be one, I had been able, without any training, and at any time, to jump over a height of five feet; had also been a swimmer, and, when occasion offered, had donned the gloves. Thinking of my present helplessness caused me many a bitter moment, but I managed to impress all comers with a false indifference.

What a kind-hearted race of people are these Canadians! Here was I, an entire stranger among them, and yet every hour people were making enquiries, and interesting themselves on my behalf, bringing and sending books, grapes, bananas, and other delicacies for a sick man. When a second operation was deemed necessary, the leg to be amputated at the knee, the whole town was concerned, and the doctors had to give strict injunctions not to admit such a number of kind-hearted visitors. At this time I was so weak of body, that it was thought hopeless to expect recovery from this second operation. This was soon made apparent to me by the doctor's question, as to whether I had any message to send to my people, hinting that there was a slight possibility of dying under the chloroform. A minister of the gospel was also there, and his sympathetic face certainly made the dying seem probable. Now, I have heard a great deal of dying men having a foresight of things to be, but, I confess, that I was never more calm in all my life than at this moment when death seemed so certain. I did not for one instant believe or expect that these eyes would again open to the light, after I had been in this low vital condition, deadened and darkened for over two hours, whilst my body was being cut and sawn like so much wood or stone. And yet I felt no terror of death. I had been taken in a sleigh from the station to the hospital, over a mile or more of snow; and the one thought that worried me most, when I was supposed to be face to face with death, was whether the town lay north, south, east or west from the hospital, and this, I believe, was the last question I asked. After hearing an answer, I drew in the chloroform in long breaths, thinking to assist the doctors in their work. In spite of this, I have a faint recollection of struggling with all my might against its effects, previous to losing consciousness; but I was greatly surprised on being afterwards told that I had, when in that condition, used more foul language in ten minutes' delirium than had probably been used in twenty four hours by the whole population of Canada. It was explained to me that such language was not unusual in cases of this kind, which consoled me not a little, but I could not help wondering if the matron had been present, and if she had confided in her daughter. The latter was a young girl of sixteen years, or thereabouts, and was so womanly and considerate that her mother could very well leave her in charge of the patients for the whole day, although this had not been necessary during my stay.

For three days after this operation I hovered between life and death, any breath expected to be my last. But in seven or eight days my vitality, which must be considered wonderful, returned in a small way, and I was then considered to be well out of danger. It was at this time that the kindness of these people touched me to the heart. The hospital was situated at the end of a long road, and all people, after they had passed the last house, which was some distance away, were then known to be visitors to the matron or one of her patients. On the verandah outside sat the matron's dog, and, long before people were close at hand, he barked, and so prepared us for their coming. When it was known that I was convalescent, this dog was kept so busy barking that its sharp clear voice became hoarse with the exertion. They came single, they came in twos and threes; old people, young people and children; until it became necessary to give them a more formal reception, limiting each person or couple, as it might be, to a few minutes' conversation. On hearing that I was fond of reading, books were at once brought by their owners, or sent by others; some of which I had not the courage to read nor the heart to return; judging them wrongly perhaps by their titles of this character: *Freddie's Friend, Little Billie's Button*, and *Sally's Sacrifice*. With such good attendance within, and so much kindness from without, what wonder that I was now fit to return to England, five weeks after the accident, after having undergone two serious operations! My new friends in that distant land would persuade me to remain, assuring me of a comfortable living, but I decided to return to England as soon as possible, little knowing what my experience would be in the years following.

When the morning came for my departure, the matron, in a motherly way, put her two hands on my shoulders and kissed me, her eyes being full of tears. This, coming from a person whose business was to show no emotion, doing which would make her unfit for her position, made me forget the short laugh and the cold hand shake for which my mind had prepared itself, and I felt my voice gone, and my throat in the clutches of something new to my experience. I left without having the voice to say good-bye. On my way I had to wish good-bye to everyone I met, and when, at last, this ordeal was over, and I was in the train on my way back to Montreal, I felt that I was not yet strong enough to travel; my courage forsook me, and I sat pale and despondent, for I never expected to meet these people again, and they were true friends.

Soon I reached Montreal. Only two months had elapsed, and what a difference now! Two months ago, and it was winter, snow on the earth, and the air was cold; but I was then full limbed, full of vitality and good spirits, for summer-like prospects golden and glorious possessed me night and day. It was summer now, the earth was dry and green, and the air warm, but winter was within me; for I felt crushed, and staggered on crutches to the danger of myself and the people on my way. I soon got over this unpleasant feeling, roused by the merry-makers aboard ship, the loudest and most persistent, strange to say, being a one legged man, who defied all Neptune's attempts to make him walk unsteady.

BESSIE RAYNER PARKES

A<small>N EARLY</small> and certainly important British feminist, Bessie Rayner Parkes diligently combined a modest literary career with an inveterate commitment to improving the rights of women.

In her lifetime (1829-1925), she published three volumes of verse; these were collected and published only in 1904 as *In Fifty Years*. At twenty-one, scandalously for the era, she left London and went to the Continent accompanied only by a friend of the same age. Upon return, she became active in petitioning for the legal rights of her sex, and as an *engagé* woman of letters, fraternized comfortably with authors better known in our own time, writers such as George Eliot, and Elizabeth Gaskell.

In 1858, with the assistance of Barbara Bodichon, an old friend and a seminal thinker on feminist issues (Bodichon, for example, was one of the founders of Girton College, Cambridge), Bessie Rayner Parkes established a magazine for women—but not just any magazine. It was written and run completely by women.

At the time of the periodical's creation, England was slowly discovering the facts behind the loss of Sir John Franklin and his expedition to discover the Northwest Passage. The anxiety experienced by Britons in their efforts to confirm that Franklin and his officers had died like gentlemen, that they had died with the honour demanded of their class, that as officers they had not committed cannibalism, that the cannibalism was resorted to only by the lower ranks—such anxiety over these matters but not over whether the explorers were actually alive is scarcely conceivable to us from the distance of a century and a half. Indeed, their preoccupations with table manners versus actual survival seem almost obscene. The literary response to the loss of Franklin and his men was voluminous, reaching its climax with the play by Wilkie Collins and Charles Dickens, *The Frozen Deep*.

Parkes contributed to the Franklin literature. Despite her concerted attacks on the British Establishment's refusal to let her vote, to give her even legal rights over her own body, Bessie Rayner Parkes still managed to have sufficient sympathy for one of the Establishment's heroes to write a panegyric for his death in Canada. She herself never visited Canada.

In addition to having an interesting biography, Ms. Parkes is of interest to us because she had two children: a daughter, Mrs. Marie Adelaide Lowndes, who wrote successful crime novels and plays little read today, and a son who wrote much that has proven enduring. He also wrote about Canada. His name was Hilaire Belloc.

THE FATE OF
SIR JOHN FRANKLIN

In summer, eighteen fifty-eight,
  A ship sailed out from Aberdeen;
A gilded pet for summer state
  The little Fox had been.

But ringing hammers night and day
   Her coat of iron mail did fix,
Before they sent the Fox away
   With sailors twenty-six.

I call them sailors every one,
   Since all were true in time of need;
A very little band to run
   Great risk for doubtful meed.

True English hearts sent food and drink,
   And everything the crew could store,
And every blessing heart could think
   Pursued them from the shore.

And so, across the great salt deep,
   From Aberdeen they steamed away;
And, doubling Greenland's ice-clogged steep,
   Pushed up to Baffin's Bay.

But there the cruel ice grew thick,
   And hemmed them in, and hemmed them round;
The little Fox she could not pick
   Her way into the Sound,

Which opens westwards towards the Bay,
   And leads to endless mysteries,
And kept for many a weary day
   The secret of the seas.

So, being finally beset,
   Her prow was wedged as in a vice;
And month by month was never wet
   Amidst those leagues of ice.

For eight long months seemed motionless,
    While game and tale the gloom beguiles;
Yet she, in darkness and distress,
    Drifted a thousand miles!

All down the length of Baffin's Bay,
    A southern drift the Fox did keep,
Till darkness melted quite away,
    And she into the deep.

A solemn and an awful track
    That silent passage seems to me,
From midnight and the Frozen Pack,
    To sunshine and the sea!

And then the gallant little ship
    Put joyfully into the shore,
And soon her slender paddles dip
    In Northern seas once more.

This time the summer days were long,
    The little Fox is very wise,
And soon she paddles, safe and strong,
    Beneath the western skies.

Now Heaven direct her in her track,
    And send some sure and guiding breeze,
Or she will never bring us back
    The secret of the seas.

She struggles up the Northern route,
    The Northern ice is hard and broad;
The little Fox must put about
    And seek some other road.

But, though she struggles day and night,
  She cannot reach the wished-for land;
The captain and his men alight
  Upon a frozen strand.

An awful thing it was to be
  Alone upon the icy plain,
Which broadens imperceptibly
  Into an icy main!

And then they sledged both east and north,
  And then they sledged both south and west,
Till the dread doubt which drove them forth
  At last was set at rest.

What did they find? A paper, scored
  With English writing, English names,
(How long by English hearts deplored!)
  Signed Crosier and Fitzjames!

Scant record of their hungry grief
  That blotted page supplied;
But one faint gleam of sad relief—
  The day when Franklin died.

At least he died within his cot,
  While kindly eyes were watching there;
We know no tribute was forgot,
  They buried him with prayer.

And thus the secret of the seas
  Was yielded to their quest,
The mystery of mysteries
  Was solved and set at rest.

HILAIRE BELLOC

S HORTLY AFTER becoming an English citizen (he was born in France to Bessie Rayner Parkes) Hilaire Belloc (1870-1953) was elected to the British House of Commons. But it is as a poet, historian and essayist that Belloc is remembered today. His overt anti-Semitism also increasingly makes him the subject of literary argument in our own time. He shared this unfortunate trait with many of his erudite cronies, but—by way of perspective rather than excuse—it should be noted that the anti-Semitism did not occupy his every waking hour. He found time to write well-regarded biographies of, among others, Robespierre and Cromwell; he penned several histories of European interest; he wrote poetry continuously; and he collaborated closely with G.K. Chesterton in the editing and writing of anti-Imperial, often pro-Catholic works.

He visited Canada on only one occasion, in March 1923, stopping in Toronto and then Montreal, as part of a North American speaking tour. Throughout his entire tour of the continent he was curmudgeonly; even the trees in Canada offended his sight:

Thin trees everywhere with branches running stark upwards— most hideous—and thin scarred trunks and all haphazard: never grouped in regular woods and *never*—even in the wildest parts— dense. A wooded slope some miles away in this snowy winter looks like ... a lot of toothpicks stuck more or less regularly with salt. It is—to our eyes—uglier than anything imaginable.

49

His immediate impression upon entering the country was super-ficial: "There is no appreciable difference between the two sides of the border." In recounting a discussion (transcribed below) with a Canadian about John Morley, the renowned English editor of the *Fortnightly Review* and a leading opponent of British entry into both the Boer War and World War One, Belloc has fun with what he clearly feels are the barbarities of Canadian speech. But it is a tribute to the range of his interests, and certainly his curiosity, that after a mere seven days in Canada, he was able to write to a friend with per-spicacity about the Quebecois (albeit without much sympathy) and their relationship to English-Canada.

––––––––––––––––––––

To Mrs. Raymond Asquith
Mt. Royal Hotel, Montreal
March 11th, 1923

That not inconsiderable gulf which separates Europe from America has 2543 manifestations—most of them superficial—but the most constant is in the employment of time. No one between the Arctic and Mexico does anything consecutively and no one thinks of time by spaces of one hour's leisure any more than we think of it by one year's. They cut the day into ten-minute snippets and spend them one after the other in moving from place to place (half the time) and talking very slowly with a very small vocabulary the other half. And as they don't know of any other way of dividing the day, a man trained in another world is lost. No lie—or hardly any—is of avail. If you sit down to write, a man at once sits down beside to talk—very slowly, heartily, full of good heart and with a limited vocabulary. If you are in a house, it is your host. If you are in a public place, then any stranger. As this talk (to a foreigner) is mostly of simple questions (Do you think Lloyd George will come back? Is the Duke of Connaught loved in England? Will the French stay in the Ruhr? When did you land? Was it rough? Ought the United States to do this or that?), there is no shutting one's ears.

If it is eating time they provide a meal with very very many guests and each guest makes a speech. Also they put you into vehicles and take you past miles of Residential Neighbourhood and Alpine Scenery, and if you say you must get some work done they stare kindly and send for a typewriter and two women. These do not catch the language and it is heavy going—and all the while metal clashes against metal all day and all night and a buzzing and a clanging and a ceaseless interruption of violent ringings in the background.

This morning I have wangled three quarters of an hour by leaving a message with my host that I was going for a walk through the deep deep snow. Then I did and furtively slunk to this room. I may at any moment be discovered and dragged back to the fullness of life.

Canada is more amazing than the United States because the nightmare of false similarity is more general. In the United States the half incomprehensible language is the main shock: like a machine dressed in human clothes. But here there is more: news from England solemnly printed and discussed and the Royal Arms over signs, and a half English flag, and also a deliberate imitation in incongruous and sudden corners. It is like a machine not only dressed up in human clothes but every now and then making a half-human gesture with some crack or other, grotesquely imitating an arm.

The French are everywhere—and quite unlike the French of France. A silent—in the sense of only talking mechanically (though incessantly), I ought to say, a *bouché* people—pressing on the Orange civilization which has the official machine in its power. You see a shop marked "E. Bezard. Footwear Vogue. Come Right In. Grab day," and when you go inside they are all talking a mumbling and closed French. In Ontario which is as violent Orange as Belfast (though not at all of our European savour) they pass laws compelling all children to learn in English: their English. But those laws are not obeyed and the strange denaturalized French (full of Indian blood I fancy) press in from the north. They go west and establish islands in the empty spaces. The Railways and the Press and the announcements are in their English. But the French spreads beneath like water under ice. It is very strange. The Canadian French have this power through an intense, rather sullen organization. They love to call themselves a Conquered People—and you know what that means in the way of expansion and tenacity! They treat their hierarchy as a sort of Cadre, like the officers of an Army.

The counter-proposition is to call in immigrants at any price from anywhere and drill them in Orange schools. It is a system now pitted against the grotesque fertility of the French-speakers. There were seventy thousand in 1760. They are now three million. Camouflaged down in Official Statistics but not escapable from the senses—and the geometrical progression goes steadily on. Immense families following generation upon generation. There is no French immigration. There is very little intermarriage—it is negligible. The whole thing is a battle between something deeply rooted, indigenous, and prodigiously expansive against something imported and with shallow roots, like the conflict between a luxuriant weed and a garden vegetable—without the gardener being allowed to weed but only to plant in snatches of energy.

I am caught. I shall fold this up.

It is indeed a strange life: I have been up since half past seven. It is now three: and in the interval I have not had a moment save the forty minutes in which I wrote the beginning of this: and yet nothing has been *done* either by me or any of the pesterers. It is all waste—or anyhow, not what is called work in Europe.

I have seen a bishop—rubicund and jolly and talking a French like the muffled sawing of wood. I have heard an address in the same idiom. I have been motored through deep snow up a shapeless lump of earth about five hundred feet above the river, called a Hill, and from it I have seen a vast white expanse dotted with innumerable toothpick trees and a big undefined white plain which is the frozen St. Lawrence and further off other lumps of earth—thirty, sixty miles off—called mountains, one of them called Hilary after me— or more probably that Trinitarian of Poitiers, whose Mass house still stands and is used profanely by the Poitevins as a museum.

I have also engaged in this conversation with a rich railway magnate and a Papist.

"D'jer knaw Djaun Morley?"

"I've met him half a dozen times."

"Dawse he live yet? Heh?"

"Yes, I think so."

"Say." A very long pause. "He waz against this yer war? Heh?"

"Yes, I think so."

"What call had he to act so?"

Then a long discourse from me under seventeen heads showing how, why, when etc. many Englishmen, some of high value, some of good judgement, opposed the entry into the war.

At the end of this the magnate suggested a walk through the drenching snow to a stick where there was, he said, a viewpoint. For the first time in many weeks, I showed a trace of manhood and refused: but it was very flabby manhood for I took refuge in a most elaborate lie about cold and my voice: like a prima donna: for I have to speak this afternoon—indeed in a very few minutes.

I have acquired the right to sit down at this desk for a few moments on the pretext that I am making notes for this same speech. Another lie. I don't mind lying, but I like to lie at my own time and not be driven to a cataract of lies morning, noon and night. In a moment I shall be called away. It is a solemn thought. I am beginning to speculate as to what I shall see before me. I count heads, multiply by dollars and a half, and count about a quarter for myself—less travelling costs: a mournful prospect. But I believe the Erleet will come in this town because, like Boston, it is overwhelmingly Catholic. Rich cliques in these towns are called "the Erleet," which came from and is spelt "Elite," the French word. As a Papist am I hauled from place to place and little other basis have I.

I have given my lecture. There were rather more than a thousand people and I spoke to fifteen hundred dollars, as their phrase goes. That's three hundred pounds. But I shan't get more than fifty pounds for myself, I fear.

PAUL BLOUET

Travel writing about English-Canada by writers from France—especially during the nineteenth century—is rarer than fine wines in a greasy spoon, but one of the wittier Victorian commentaries on our allegedly bicultural land came from writer Paul Blouet (1848-1903).

Not much is known of Blouet's early life. He always claimed to have been a cavalry officer wounded in battle, but regrettably for the truth, his name figures in no military lists. He did move from France to England in 1873 and became a teacher at the Ecole Française de St. Paul. A decade later, he published to colossal success his first book, hailed by one authority as a masterpiece of humour and a superb critique of British manners. The book was later translated into English by his wife (a Briton) as *John Bull and His Island*. A bestseller in both languages (more than four hundred thousand copies were sold in English alone) the following year Blouet was able to quit teaching to pursue, for the rest of his life, his two loves: travel and writing. Some sense of his affection for the job he was leaving behind can be had by citing the title of his memoirs of teaching: *Drat the Boys!*

Blouet's success may have evolved, in part, because he enjoyed, actually relished, in contrast to the finger-drumming impatience of so many of his French compatriots, the peculiarities of the Anglo-Saxon world. Indeed, such was his easy bicultural nature, he employed for most of his professional life the unlikely *nom de plume* "Max O'Rell".

Subsequent work included travel books (with such titles as *English Pharisees, French Crocodiles, and Other Typical Anglo-French Characters*) interspersed with novels of the lighter sort. Although relatively unknown today in the English-speaking world, the situation was clearly different while he was alive: he made a great deal of money from his writing, large audiences throughout North America came to hear him speak, and he mixed comfortably with the rich and famous.

In 1894, he published *John Bull & Company*, a canny title to describe Victorian Britain and her colonies. The work includes some comments on Canadian life and customs. The following excerpt, however, is a section from a later, better book, *A Frenchman in America*, published in 1891, which includes shrewd observations, made during an 1890 lecture tour, of our two founding cultures.

———————————————

from A FRENCHMAN IN AMERICA

Montreal, Quebec, February 1, 1890

I begin my Canadian tour here on Monday, and then shall go West. I was in Quebec two years ago; but the dear old place is not on my list this time. No words could express my regret. I shall never forget my feelings on landing under the great cliff on which stands the citadel, and on driving, bumped along in a sleigh over the half-thawed snow, in the street that lies under the fortress, and on through the other quaint winding steep streets, and again under the majestic archways to the upper town where I was set down at the door of the "Florence," a quiet, delightful little hotel that the visitor to Quebec should not fail to stop at, if he like home comforts and care to enjoy magnificent scenery from his window. It seemed as though I was in France, in my dear old Brittany. It looked like St. Malo strayed up here and was lost in the snow. The illusion become complete when I saw the grey houses, heard the people talk with the Breton intonation, and saw over the shops Langlois, Maillard, Clouet, and all the names familiar to my childhood. But why say "illusion"? It was a fact: I was in France. These folks have given their faith to England; but, as the Canadian poet says, they have kept their hearts for France. Not only their hearts, but their manners and their language. Oh, there was such pleasure in it all! The lovely weather, the beautiful scenery, the kind welcome given to me, the delight of seeing these children of old France, more than three thousand miles from home, happy and thriving—a feast for the eyes, a feast for the heart. And the drive to Montmorency Falls in the sleigh, gliding smoothly along on the hard snow! And the sleighs laden with wood for the Quebec folks, the carmen stimulating their horses with a *hue la* or *hue donc!* And the return to the "Florence," where a good dinner served in a private room awaited us! And that polite, quiet, attentive French girl who waited on us, the antipodes of the young Yankee lady who makes you sorry that breakfasting and dining are necessary, in some American hotels, and whose waiting is like taking sand and vinegar with your food!... Yes, it was all delightful. When I left Quebec, I felt as much regret as I do every time that I leave my little native town.

I have been told that the works of Voltaire are prohibited in Quebec, not so much because they are irreligious as because they were written by a man who, after the loss of Quebec to the French Crown, exclaimed: "Let us not be concerned about the loss of a few acres of snow." The memory of Voltaire is execrated; and for having made a flattering reference to him on the platform in Montreal two years ago, I was near being "boycotted" by the French population.

The French Canadians take very little interest in politics—I mean, in outside politics. They are steady, industrious, saving, peaceful; and so long as the English leave them alone, in the safe enjoyment of their belongings, they will not give them cause for any anxiety. Among the French Canadians, there is no desire for annexation to the United States. Indeed, during the War of Independence, Canada was saved to the English Crown by the French Canadians, not because the latter loved the English but because they hated the Yankees. When La Fayette took it for granted that the French Canadian would rally round his flag, he made a great mistake; they would have, if compelled to fight, used their bullets against the Americans. If they had their own way, the French in Canada would set up a little country of their own, under the rule of the Catholic Church, a little corner of France two hundred years old.

The education of the lower classes is at a very low stage: thirty per cent of the children of school age in Quebec do not attend school. The English dare not introduce gratuitous and compulsory eduction. They have an understanding with the Catholic Church, who insists upon exercising entire control over public education. The Quebec schools are little more than branches of the Confessional box. The English shut their eyes, for part of the understanding with the Church is that the latter will keep loyalty to the English Crown alive among her submissive flock....

The French Canadians are multiplying so rapidly that in very few years the Province of Quebec will be as French as the town of Quebec itself. Every day they push their advance from East to West. They generally marry very young. When a lad is in the company of a girl, he is asked by the priest if he is courting that girl. In which case he is bidden go straightway to the altar; and these young couples rear families of twelve and fifteen children, none of whom leave the country. The English have to make room for them....

What is the future reserved to French Canada and indeed, to the whole Dominion?

There are only two political parties, Liberals and Conservatives, but I find the population divided into four camps: Those in favour of Canada, an independent nation; those in favour of the political union of Canada and the United States; those in favour of Canada going into Imperial Federation; and those in favour of Canada remaining an English Colony or, in other words, in favour of the actual state of things.

Of course the French Canadians are dead against going into Imperial Federation, which would simply crush them, and Canadian "Society" is in favour of remaining English. The other Canadians seem pretty equally divided.

It must be said that the annexation idea has been making rapid progress of late years among prominent men as well as among the people. The Americans will never fire one shot to have the idea realised. If the union becomes an accomplished fact, it will become so with the assent of all parties. The task will be made easy through Canada and the United States having the same legislation. The local and provincial governments are the same in the Canadian towns and provinces as they are in the American towns and States: a house of representatives, a senate, and a governor. With this difference, this great difference, to the present advantage of Canada: whereas every four years the Americans elect a new master, who appoints a ministry responsible to him alone, the Canadians have a ministry responsible to their Parliament—that is, to themselves. The representation of the American people at Washington is democratic, but the Government is autocratic. In Canada, both legislature and executive are democratic, as in England, that greatest and truest of all democracies.

The change in Canada would have to be made on the American plan....

Montreal, February 2nd

Montreal is a large and well-built city, containing many buildings of importance, mostly churches of which about thirty are Roman Catholic, and over sixty are devoted to Protestant worship, in all its branches and variations, from the Anglican Church to the Salvation Army.

I arrived at a station situated on a level with the St. Lawrence river. From it, we mounted in an omnibus up, up, up, through narrow streets full of shops with Breton or Norman names over them as in Quebec; on through other broader ones, where the shops grew larger and the names became more frequently English; on, on, till I thought Montreal had no end, and at last alighted on a great square and found myself at the door of the Windsor Hotel, an enormous and fine construction, which has proved the most comfortable, and in every respect the best hotel I have yet stopped at on the great American Continent. It is about a quarter of a mile from bedroom to the dining hall, which could, I believe accommodate nearly a thousand guests.

My first visit was to an afternoon "At Home" given by the St. George's Club, who have a clubhouse high up on Mount Royal. It was a ladies' day, and there was music, dancing, &c. We went in a sleigh up the very steep hill, much to our astonishment. I should have thought the thing practically impossible. On our way we passed a toboggan slide down the side of Mount Royal. It took my breath away to think of coming down it at the rate of over a mile a minute. The view from the club house was splendid, taking in a great sweep of snow-covered country, the city and the frozen St. Lawrence. There are daily races on the river, and last year they ran tramcars on it.

It was odd to hear the phrase "After the flood." When I came to enquire into it, I learned that when the St. Lawrence ice breaks up the lower city is flooded, and this is yearly spoken of as "the flood."

I drove back from the club with my manager and two English gentlemen who are here on a visit. As we passed the toboggan slide, my manager told me of an old gentleman over sixty, who delights in these breathless passages down the side of Mount Royal. One may see him out there "at it" as early as ten in the morning. Plenty of people, however, try one ride and never ask for another. One gentleman, my manager told me of, after having tried it, expressed pretty well the feelings of many. He said: "I wouldn't do it again for two thousand dollars but I wouldn't have missed it for three." I asked one of the two Englishmen who accompanied us whether he had had a try. He was a quiet, solemn, middle-aged Englishman. "Well," he said, "yes, I have. It had to be done, and I did it."

Last night I was most interested in watching members of the Snow-shoe Club start from the Windsor on a kind of picnic over the country. Their costumes were very picturesque: a short tunique of woollen material fastened round the waist by a belt, a sort of woollen nightcap with tassel falling on the shoulders, thick woolen stockings and knickerbockers.

In Russia, in the northern parts of the United States, the people say: "It's too cold to go out." In Canada, they say: "It's very cold, let's all go out." Only rain keeps them indoors. In the coldest weather with a temperature of many degrees below zero, you have great difficulty in finding a closed carriage. All, or nearly all, are open sleighs. The driver wraps you up in furs, and as you go, gliding on the snow, your face is whipped by the cold air; you feel glowing all over with warmth, and altogether the sensation is delightful.

This morning, Joseph Howarth, the talented American actor, breakfasted with me and a few friends. Last night, I went to see him play in Steele Mackaye's *Paul Kauvar*. Canada has no actors worth mentioning, and the people here depend on American artistes for all their entertainments. It is wonderful how the feeling of independence engenders and develops the activity of the mind in a country. Art and literature want a home of their own, and do not flourish in other people's houses. Canada has produced nothing in literature: the only two poets she can boast are French, Louis Frechette and Octave Cremazie. It is not because Canada has no time for brain productions. America is just as busy as she is, felling forests and reclaiming the land; but free America, only a hundred years old as a nation, possesses already a list of historians, novelists, poets, and essayists, that would do honour to any nation in the world.

February 4th

I had capital houses in the Queen's Hall last night and to-night.

The Canadian audiences are more demonstrative than the American ones, and certainly quite as keen and appreciative. When you arrive on the platform, they are glad to see you, and they let you know it—a fact which, in America, in New England especially, you have to find out for yourself.

Montreal possesses a very wealthy and fashionable community, and what strikes me most, coming as I do from the United States, is the stylish simplicity of the women. I am told that Canadian women, in their tastes and ways, have always been far more English than American, and that the fashions have grown more and more simple since Princess Louise gave the example by always dressing quietly when occupying Rideau Hall in Ottawa.

Ottawa, February 5th

One of the finest sights I have yet seen in this country was from the bridge on my way from the station to the "Russell" this morning: on the right, the Waterfalls; on the left, on the top of a high and almost perpendicular rock, the Houses of Parliament, a grand pile of buildings in grey stone standing out clear against a cloudless, intense blue sky. The "Russell" is one of those huge Babylonian hotels so common on the American Continent, where unfortunately the cookery is not on a level with the architectural pretensions; but most of the leading Canadian politicians are boarding here while Parliament is sitting, and I am interested to see them.

After visiting the beautiful library and other parts of the Government buildings, I had the good luck to hear, in the House of Representatives, debate between M. Chapleau, a Minister and one of the leaders of the Conservatives now in office, M. Laurier, one of the chiefs of the Opposition. Both gentlemen are French. It was a fight between a tribune and a scholar; between a short, thick-set, long-maned lion, and a tall, slender, delicate fox....

Kingston, February 6th

This morning, at the "Russell," I was called to telephone. It was his Excellency who was asking me to lunch at Rideau Hall. I felt sorry to be obliged to leave Ottawa and thus forego so tempting an invitation.

Kingston is a pretty little town on the border of Lake Ontario, possessing a university, a penitentiary, a lunatic asylum, in neither of which I made my appearance to-night. But as soon as I had started speaking on the platform of the Town Hall, I began to think the doors of the Lunatic Asylum had been carelessly left open that night, for close under the window behind the platform, there began a noise which was like Bedlam let loose—Bedlam with trumpets and other instruments of torture. It was impossible to go on with the lecture, so I stopped. On inquiry, the unearthly din was found to proceed from a detachment of the Salvation Army outside the building. After some parleying, they consented to move on and storm some other citadel.... To-morrow I go to Toronto, where I am to give two lectures. I had not time to see that city properly on my last visit to Canada, and all my friends prophesy that I shall have a good time.

LLOYD C. DOUGLAS

L LOYD C. DOUGLAS (1877-1951), the American author of such
mega-bestsellers as *The Robe* and *Magnificent Obsession*, regarded
himself firstly as a church minister and only secondarily as someone
who, in his spare time, wrote religious or inspirational novels. He
was refreshingly modest about his literary talent and openly abashed
by his commercial success. As he said in a speech to the Empire Club
in Toronto in 1942, "*Magnificent Obsession* has been so pleasantly
referred to here, I think I should say when I wrote the book it was
strictly experimental. I had never written one before and I didn't know
how to do it. A good many of my critics think I don't know yet."

Douglas never allowed the vigour of his intelligence to succumb
to the dictates of faith, an approach to the theological which, early in
his priestly career, brought him into such feisty conflict with the
elders of his churches that occasionally he and his family were
politely asked to move on. Promptly.

It was after one such setback that he was invited to give, at St.
James United Church in Montreal, a series of sermons over six consecutive weeks, starting in March, 1929. It was made clear to him
that he would be offered the pulpit on a full-time basis if the sermons were a success. They were. For the next four years, he worked
and resided in Montreal before returning, in 1933, to larger possibilities, both as a novelist and a minister, in the USA.

Douglas and his family enjoyed Montreal immensely. In the

biography published in 1952 by his daughters, he is quoted as uttering only one negative comment about his adopted land:

> When we were living in Montreal [a] dilatory butcher had called forth a fine stream of Daddy's choicest sarcasm. "Just cancel our account!" was his final snort into the telephone. "Very well, Mr. Douglas," was the butcher's mild answer. Daddy came away from the phone highly pleased with the fresh twist to an old situation. "That's Canada for you," he laughed, "business when they feel like it."

Years later, back in the USA, he wrote to his daughter Virginia, who had remained in Canada, married to a member of the Dawson family, prominent for centuries in Montreal:

> Sorry to hear that you are bedevilled with colds up there. I do think that Montreal is one of the coughingest, handkerchiefingest, sniffliest cities between the North Pole and Pawtucket, Rhode Island. Sometimes I found myself in a street car in your town. On these occasions I invariably had to hold on to a strap, swaying like a decayed corpse on a gibbet in a wild November gale. The strap was always clammy with heaven knows what, and the pestilential air seemed to be a saturate solution of every known disability that could do havoc to (a) the turbinates, (b) the bronchia, (c) the incus, (d), the stapes, (e) the hammer (to say nothing of the whiffle).

As a popular novelist, Lloyd C. Douglas has been ignored by academia and scholarly biographers. The following letters to various family and friends are excerpted from *The Shape of Sunday*, the daughters' biography of their father. Apart from the Empire Club speech noted above, these letters seem to comprise all that is left of what must have been an extensive correspondence penned in Canada.

April 1, 1929

Montreal is everything we had hoped it would be. We were met at the train by cordial people, shown to an apartment owned by a lady now en tour around the world. Living room, bedroom, bathette, kitchenette, hallette. She had moved the contents of a ten-room house into this place before she left. To the clutter we added seven pieces of hand-baggage and two hefty wardrobe trunks.

Yesterday was a red-letter day at the church. Fully two thousand were there in the morning and at night hundreds stood around the walls after the place was packed. Large chorus choir of excellent voices led by superb soloists accompanied by organ, piano and orchestra. It was quite lifting.

A most intelligent audience. I couldn't flatter myself they came to hear me.

We are delighted with everything as far as we have gone. Weather yesterday delightful, today pretty terrible; sleet, etc. The city is beautiful: massive buildings, weathered gray stone. Our kind of a place. We will have to learn French if we stay. Very Frenchy.

The church is huge. When I looked out over the sea of faces in that big tank I wondered what my voice would sound like when I uttered my first yip. It's a very queer feeling when you get up to make a noise in a place that seats so many people.

I guess my sermon went all right. Everybody stayed through and I heard no complaints. I was tired when it was all over last night.

April 12, 1929

Sunday was a good day with us. We had thought that Easter would be the record breaker, but last night the big pack was there again. I am still not sure that they came to hear me. There had been announced some special numbers of a touring Welsh Choir and after the evening service was over the crowd stayed to hear them do some more. But whether I pulled the crowd or the Welsh they were there—some 2700 of them, and I, myself, had a whale of a good time.

I have learned from friends that they didn't think my Easter night sermon was as good as I thought. They said it was too heavy for the evening crowd. One man, whom I have known for a long time, called on us yesterday and said that if I should continue to preach sermons as heavy as that, I would empty the church in five nights. He is quite British and outspoken, but not offensive. He seemed much pleased with what I did last Sunday night and predicted it was the mental gait which that crowd could follow. I think they underestimate their mental value. They all looked pretty intelligent to me from where I stood. Of course, I can't see very well. And I'm a stranger here.

Anyway, it's a lot of fun and I'm glad we came. I have made no attempt to delete the occasional drollery that I like to indulge in and the British seem to like it.

The only trouble will be the Old Guard who are horrifically sober—just as old folks are in every country—just as I shall be when I am munching my gums and wearing bella-donna plasters on the small of me back. To my surprise they haven't let out any shrill yelps of distress yet, but I am all braced for a riot at any time.

Last Sunday an old friend who has more political power than any four men in the Congregational outfit in the States was in town and ran out to see us at our apartment. He wants us to come back and look over a place in the east which will be open in a few months. I shall be interested if the church here does not measure up to full expectations; or if, to put the matter more bluntly the Canadians should decide they can jolly well do without my interpretations of the Gospel.

But—let the heathen rage and the people imagine a vain thing—; the fact is I like this place. It's quite a tremendous tug that big crowd makes on me. If I learned I had to stay here for a long time I think I could bear up.

Bessie—she thinks she'd rather live in the goodole USA.

Write to us often, won't you? We're perishing of loneliness up here. I haven't much pastoral work to do and am pounding away on a few religious articles for the *Christian Century*. Doubleday reports of my novel, "It has many fine points and some publishing possibilities, but it is not for us." I am sending it out for the last time to a little religious publishing house in Chicago. If they don't want it—t'ell wid it.

Well, anyway, my Sunday night mob here, as compared intellectually with some I've seen, are a lot of Platos, Aristotles and Einsteins. The church is massive and beautiful, and it has as bad ventilation as any holy temple I ever preached in. So that's that, no matter what Bessie says.

May 12, 1929

Well, little children, your sweet mama and I have been here in this city of the frozen north for about six weeks. The powers that be are having a meeting tonight or tomorrow to decide whether to extend us an official call. We aren't worried because there are several other supply jobs we can step into until we make up our minds about a permanent place, but we rather like the people here and would like to get our plans settled.

I am anxious to get a report of this meeting for, however blessed we have been,

> What we shall be eating next May
> Depends on this meeting today.
> We are not very thrifty
> And the age of past fifty
> Does not apprehension allay.

> A fellow who works by the day
> For $three-fifty or $four let us say
> He may never be rich.

The poor son of a b—
But he knows what he gets for his pay.

This poem comes to you by the courtesy of an anxious parson, and is copyrighted in all langwidges, including Scandinavian and the dialect spoken by persons living in Ohio who have spent a few days in N'Owleans.

May 14, 1929

We feel securely anchored again. The negotiations when we finally got around to making them proved easy and brief. Not only have these people made me the most generous proposal, but they have gone out of their way to be considerate. They had previously engaged a London preacher to supply here during July and August and I am to have the two months on full pay. Isn't that quite sporting of them?

We cabled the girls (they have been horribly worried about us for fear we might not get a good job) and had a reply in a few hours. Two words only, for they have been living very frugally and cables are costly. They wired "Hot stuff." Sounds like them, doesn't it?

I haven't taken to wearing a monocle yet, but I've been looking at them. I must get a cane. If I don't stop taking on weight I'll have to get crutches.

Besse is having a good time here. She is quite content about my decision to stay. The people are rather shy and reserved on first acquaintance and that is to her advantage for she is that way herself. I can see from the fuss they are making over her she is going to be taken in as a kindred spirit. I am glad. She was wretched in Los Angeles. In the racket of all that strident ballyhoo she was as helpless as the fellow at the party who ordered ginger ale and was soon drowned out of the conversation.

February 17, 1930

It was cold enough up here yesterday to freeze the hinges of hell. Some said eighteen degrees below. Notwithstanding the weather large quantities of the saints assembled at divine service to hear the Word. Unknown to them their minister was wearing a new suit of woollen underwear into which had been knit every manner of thistles and burrs. Ordinarily I am a man of few gestures, but yesterday I flung myself about in an abandoned fashion whenever there was the least excuse for it....

October 29, 1931

I haven't done another line on my new novel since I came home from Cape Ann. *Magnificent Obsession* is steadily mounting in sales. It was in the list of the first twelve best sellers in September and October according to the Bookman's monthly score. My publishers are bringing out new editions every four weeks. They tell me they are hard pressed to keep up with the demand. This is all very amazing but gratifying to us.

Montreal looked pretty good when we came back this fall. It's really a very lovable old city. It would not surprise me much if we were to be here for some time. Ginger will return to England to marry her doctor but they will eventually settle here and this town will always be more than a temporary post in our lives.

My church pleases me. I am quite dreadfully spoiled for any blown-in-the-bottle kind of a job. If I've got to preach (and it seems that I must for a while yet) I'd rather do it here. It means a good deal to me to be assured of a steady crowd rain or shine, not to be responsible for the administration of a lot of church activities, not to care one limpid damn about the raising of budgets. I have told you that I have days when I feel I have amply done my bit in this whole enterprise and would gladly sneak off in a corner and pretend, at least, to retire. But I can't do it yet. So here we go for another long ten months haul. I must begin thinking tomorrow what I am to preach about next Sunday. And every Tuesday morning from now until the middle of next July the same dilemma will face me.

But my Gosh! Shouldn't I be reasonably satisfied with things as is. How infinitely worse if I had no job.

Bessie and Ginger toil steadily on in the dressmaking business of getting the child ready to be married. I haven't seen my wife without her mouth full of needles and basting threads for ten days. I've a notion to retire and let her keep me with her needle.

January 7, 1932

I had a few strong words to say about the Pope last Sunday night, apropos of his proposal to the Protestants. We had a bumper house, and the Gazette gave me two and a half columns next morning. I am now getting mail from local fans and critics, plus a lot of boobs who fail to sign their names. These last, however, I am not required to reply to; so that helps relieve my bill for stamps. All in all, the thing has been pretty well accepted and I do not expect assassination, expulsion or any calamity. I had an anonymous letter of a single line—"You talk too much."

I agree with the fellow, and if he had signed his name I would write him and tell him that he is smarter than his bad penmanship gives him credit for. I do talk too much, and I'm so tired of talking that I could lie right down in the big mud-puddle out in front of our apartment and cry aloud.

A.O. Dawson and I had lunch today and attempted to figure out what relationship we are now that he is my daughter's father-in-law. We came to no conclusions but that the arrangement is entirely satisfactory. I grow increasingly fond of him. Today I half expected him to suggest that I tone down some of my pulpit statements, but there was nary a hint from him. The old boy is a good sport.

Your pretty mama, the lazy little loafer, stayed home from Divine

Service last Sunday night so she could be all set with a delicious T-bone steak and f.f. potatoes when I returned from warning Israel against images and gluttony.

I presume she has told you she is renewing her French with much ardor. She has a tooter now, a handsome, dapper Swiss gentleman with a cute little goatee. I am thinking of raising one myself in the event he seems to be too popular.

MARGARET
BLENNERHASSETT

F OR THE DURATION of her adult life, scandals and innuendo,
sexual and political, loitered around Margaret Blennerhassett
(c. 1773-1842) like tabloid journalists vulturing near a courtroom.

She was born Margaret Agnew, the daughter of a man known
universally in the reference books as the Lieutenant-Governor of the
Isle of Man, an otherwise nameless Mr. Agnew. What the reference
books do not mention is the first sensational fact of her life: she also
had a mother who became her sister-in-law; in other words, in 1796,
Margaret Agnew married her mother's brother, Harman Blennerhassett, a man thirteen years her senior.

The marriage was not only illegal, it was blasphemous and
malodorous to the society in which they lived. Instant, albeit quite
wealthy pariahs, they sailed for the New World, undoubtedly
hoping that with each mile forward their conjugal history would
dissipate behind them as surely as smoke leaving a ship's funnel.

One can only imagine their disappointment in discovering that
the Brahmins of New York and Philadelphia were as equally disap-
proving of the liaison as the British Establishment; the couple left
their brief, consecutive residences in those cities and purchased a relatively large island in the Ohio River. To this day, it keeps the name
Blennerhassett Island. There they built a mansion renowned in several states for the splendour of its architecture and the magnificence

of its holdings, and settled into what they must have assumed would be a bucolic idyll worthy of Virgil.

Then, in May 1805 they were visited by Aaron Burr. Burr remains a notorious figure in American history. He marched as an officer with Benedict Arnold into Canada for the attack on Quebec in 1775-76. He feuded openly with George Washington when few dared to cross the first President. In the election of 1800, he sought the Presidency himself, and it is a measure of his charisma (and his deft exploitation of Tammany Hall) that he came second only to Thomas Jefferson. At the time, the runner-up in the presidential elections was made Vice-President, so that at the age of forty-four, Burr had reached the near-apex of American political life. If his ascent had been rapid, his descent was an avalanche, such was its impact and speed.

Intriguingly described as "one of the most remarkable and one of the darkest specimens of moral obliquity" Vice-President Burr, not content with mere argument, challenged his most vexatious political opponent, Alexander Hamilton (the man on the American ten-dollar bill) to a duel: pistols at dawn. Burr, the better shot, killed the popular Hamilton, but also, with the same successful bullet, despite his colossal ambition, stupidly killed all hope of a future in legitimate politics.

Deprived of any chance to be leader of his country, Burr decided to establish a new nation, with himself as President, by armed invasion and the capture of part of Texas and probably northern Mexico. Not by coincidence, on his way to the southwest, he dropped in to visit the Blennerhassetts at their island home. Like Rasputin, his mental dominance of the couple was nearly immediate and complete; originally an overnight visitor, he stayed for months, convincing Harman Blennerhassett to part with much of his fortune to subsidize the illegal invasion of Texas and Mexico. Not content with Blennerhasset's money, Burr also convinced Margaret Blennerhassett, it seems from discreet references made at the time, to become his lover. In the autumn of 1806, Burr finally left the Blennerhassetts to begin his invasion of Mexico. However, not long after his departure, he was betrayed by one of his confederates, and President

Jefferson ordered him—and all those associated with him—arrested and charged with treason. Rather belatedly, Harman Blennerhassett seems to have realized the implications of his hospitality, and he fled his island home accompanied by his wife, abandoning almost all of their material goods. Their flight was unsuccessful. Blennerhassett was arrested. He was also acquitted; his infantile gullibility must have been painfully obvious to even hostile jurors. During their absence from the island, the Blennerhassetts learned that everything they owned there had been looted or burned.

Forced to earn a living for the first time in his life, Blennerhassett bought slaves and a thousand acres in Mississippi hoping to create a thriving cotton plantation. That endeavour failed. He tried other business ventures. They failed. His money dwindled precariously and, in desperation, he approached the Governor General of Canada, Charles Lennox, the Duke of Richmond, an old classmate, begging him for a position on the bench. The Duke asserted a position could be found, so the Blennerhassetts moved to Montreal in 1819 where, with the influence of his patron, Harman was quickly admitted to the Bar. It was while in Montreal that Margaret Blennerhassett appears to have started writing poetry.

Her husband left Montreal in 1822, travelling to London to seek the judgeship he felt was owed to him but which he had not yet received. Unfortunately, Lennox had died and, bereft of a champion, Blennerhassett was denied a place on the bench. He chose to stay in Europe, but his wife remained in Montreal for at least two more years, and perhaps many more. She joined her husband in Guernsey possibly just prior to his death in 1831, and returned to the United States in 1842, hoping to augment her meagre finances by obtaining restitution from the American government for the loss of her island home. Ironically enough, the lawyer who pressed her case was the eminent statesman Henry Clay who, earlier in his political career, perhaps more than any other American, had pressed for the invasion of Canada in the War of 1812. Clay won the case for Margaret Blennerhassett, but she died, probably penniless, before any monies were paid.

Margaret Blennerhassett published only one book of poetry, and that was in Montreal in 1824. *The Widow of the Rock*, not one of the seminal texts of the English language, is concerned largely with the lady's rancour over her lost chattel and lost possibilities. But the following poem from the book is included here partly because, as with Samuel Butler's "A Psalm of Montreal", its genesis was occasioned by economic hardship in Canada. It is also a curio because it would seem to be the first English language poem set in Canada published by a female literary visitor.

TO A HUMMING-BIRD

(The first seen by the Author in Canada)

Little bird why thus visit my bower?
  Like its owner 'tis desolate all,
The guest that but seeks the gay flower,
  At the bower of pleasure should call.

The hum of thy gossamer wing
  In the summer's short triumph display'd,
More welcome than thousands that sing
  Unmark'd in the thick southern shade.

Go—go never more to return,
  To the climes of the south fly away;
There mayst thou still fearless sojourn,
  Nor winter thy flutt'rings betray.

ANONYMOUS

THE IRISH, Welsh, Chinese, and citizens of Bristol, England (among other claimants) all have legends maintaining that their sailors made landfalls in Canada long before John Cabot in 1497. But despite the best efforts of archaeologists, after a century of serious searching, the only documented pre-Cabot, non-aboriginal encounters with Canada remain those of the Vikings.

There is a common but false belief that the Viking sagas are nothing more than stenographic transcriptions of oral lays popular among the Dark Age masses of northern Europe. In fact, scholarly opinion is unanimous in declaring that the sagas are polished texts composed with as much deliberation and with as much varying artistry as co-extant Continental medieval poetry: inspired by oral history, yes, but very much written, very much composed by professional authors. Their creation coincides with the rise in popularity of the Christian faith in the Nordic nations in the eleventh century; indeed, it was the Church which fostered the writing of sagas, both to diminish the allure of corporeal pleasures diverting the laity's attention from the proper study of God, and to supplement the then pitiful vehicles available for education.

Two of the many surviving Icelandic sagas deal specifically with the Norse landings on these shores: the *Greenlanders' Saga* and *Eirik's Saga*. Both accounts concur on the main points: circa 1000 A.D., blown far off-course, Viking pioneers sighted (but did not alight on) a strange new country. The winds then changed, and they were able to regain their original course, sailing home. Soon, though, tantalized by what they had glimpsed, they inspired their compatriots to join them in voyages of exploration to the new found land.

The two tales disagree, however, on who made the sighting, who organized the first planned voyage and on the personalities of the participants. The two sagas differ, as well, in their level of literary sophistication. *Greenlanders' Saga* was penned early in the discipline's history whereas *Eirik's Saga* is now seen to be a sophisticated literary reworking of the earlier text. The best estimate for the composition of *Eirik's Saga* is 1230-80; the *Greenlanders' Saga* is thought to date from a century earlier.

For professional historians and geographers, these two stories are agonizingly inexact. But just as Shakespeare was guided—but not enslaved—by formal history in writing his Roman plays, so too did the anonymous scribes of the sagas rudder and steer against the winds of history—using it when helpful, but not afraid to tack against it to tighten narrative and find truth.

The discovery in the 1960s of a semipermanent Norse settlement dating to the eleventh century at L'anse aux Meadows in northern Newfoundland confirmed the essence of the Vinland stories, but has left many questions unanswered. Foremost amongst these is why, after three decades of concentrated searching by archeologists, have no other Norse sites been discovered in Canada? Which begs the corollary question: why, having discovered such a seemingly attractive land, rich in natural vines, wheat and wood, commodities patently scarce in Greenland and Iceland, did the Norse not stay? Recent discoveries of what seem to be Viking artifacts on Ellesmere and Baffin Islands hint at centuries-long trade between the native populations of Canada and the Norse, but whether this means that trading networks were wider than previously believed or more dramatically, that the Vikings sailed throughout Canada's Arctic, remains to be determined. Disagreement still reigns even over which current North American names correspond to those cited by the saga-writers, although most commentators today believe that

"Helluland" is Baffin Island, that "Markland" is the area of Labrador (and Newfoundland) near L'anse aux Meadows, and that "Vinland" equals the shores of the lower St. Lawrence River.

Academic enquiry has now moved from asking if the Vikings were ever here, to asking why they left. Contributing to the Viking demise may have been the smallness of the originating community; even at its height in the 1300s, the Greenland community numbered no more than seven thousand, so the Canadian population, as an outpost of the Greenland settlements, is likely to have been much smaller, and may not have reached sufficient critical mass to survive. In addition, the Earth cooled significantly in the fourteenth century, probably enough to push, with the inevitability of a glacier, all hope of practical farming off the Greenland land mass. Under such climatic stress, the Greenlanders may well have preferred to return to the Nordic lands of their ancestors rather than the terra incognita of Canada. And, of course, as the following extract sadly demonstrates, European encounters with Canadian natives were too often nasty, brutish and motivated by the newcomer's greed for land.

It remains a compelling but little heralded irony of our history that the final Norse encounter with Canada most likely took place about the same time that John Cabot sailed, for the first time, into Canadian waters, and landed at a Canadian cove, probably not far from L'anse aux Meadows.

The following excerpt from *Eirik's Saga* was translated from the Old Norse by Magnus Magnusson and Herman Pálsson.

from EIRIK'S SAGA

Karlsefni goes to Vinland

There were great discussions at Brattahlid that winter about going in search of Vinland where, it was said, there was excellent land to be had. The outcome was that Karlsefni and Snorri Thorbrandsson prepared their ship and made ready to search for Vinland that summer.

Bjarni Grimolfsson and Thorhall Gamlason decided to join the expedition with their own ship and the crew they had brought from Iceland.

There was a man named Thorvard, who was Eirik the Red's son-in-law.

There was another man named Thorhall, who was known as Thorhall the Hunter; he had been in Eirik's service for a long time, acting as his huntsman in summer, and had many responsibilities. He was a huge man, swarthy and uncouth; he was getting old now, bad-tempered and cunning, taciturn as a rule but abusive when he spoke, and always a trouble-maker. He had not had much to do with Christianity since it had come to Greenland. He was not particularly popular, but Eirik and he had always been close friends. He went with Thorvald and the others because he had considerable experience of wild regions.

They had the ship that Thorbjorn Vifilsson had brought from Iceland, and when they joined Karlsefni there were mostly Greenlanders on board. Altogether there were 160 people taking part in this expedition.

They sailed first up to the Western Settlement, and then to the Bjarn Isles. From there they sailed before a northerly wind and after two days at sea they sighted land and rowed ashore in boats to explore it. They found there many slabs of stone so huge that two men could stretch out on them sole to sole. There were numerous foxes there. They gave this country a name and called it *Helluland*.

From there they sailed for two days before a northerly wind and sighted land ahead; this was a heavily-wooded country abounding with animals. There was an island to the south-east, where they found bears, and so they named it *Bjarn Isle;* they named the wooded mainland itself *Markland.*

After two days they sighted land again and held in towards it; it was a promontory they were approaching. They tacked along the coast, with the land to starboard.

It was open and harbourless, with long beaches and extensive sands. They went ashore in boats and found a ship's keel on the headland, and so they called the place *Kjalarness.* They called this stretch of coast *Furdustrands* because it took so long to sail past it. Then the coastline became indented with bays and they steered into one of them.

When Leif Eirikson had been with King Olaf Tryggvason and had been asked to preach Christianity in Greenland the king had given him a Scottish couple, a man called Haki and a woman called Hekja. The king told Leif to use them if he ever needed speed, for they could run faster than deer. Leif and Eirik had turned them over to Karlsefni for this expedition.

When the ships had passed Furdustrands the two Scots were put ashore and told to run southwards to explore the country's resources, and to return within three days. They each wore a garment called a bjafal, which had a hood at the top and was open at the sides: it had no sleeves and was fastened between the legs with a loop and button. That was all they wore.

The ships cast anchor there and waited, and after three days the Scots came running down to the shore; one of them was carrying some grapes, and the other some wild wheat. They told Karlsefni that they thought they had found good land.

They were taken on board, and the expedition sailed on until they reached a fjord. They steered their ships into it. At its mouth lay an island around which there flowed very strong currents, and so they named it *Straum Island.* There were so many birds on it that one could scarcely set foot between their eggs.

They steered into the fjord, which they named *Straumfjord;* here they unloaded their ships and settled down. They had brought with them livestock of all kinds and they looked around for natural produce. There were mountains there and the country was beautiful to look at, and they paid no attention to anything except exploring it. There was tall grass everywhere.

They stayed there that winter, which turned out to be a very severe one; they had made no provision for it during the summer, and now they ran short of food and the hunting failed. They moved out to the island in the hope of finding game, or stranded whales, but there was little food to be found there, although their livestock throve. Then they prayed to God to send them something to eat, but the response was not as prompt as they would have liked.

Meanwhile Thorhall the Hunter disappeared and they went out to search for him. They searched for three days; and on the fourth day Karlsefni and Bjarni found him on top of a cliff. He was staring up at the sky with eyes and mouth and nostrils agape, scratching himself and pinching himself and mumbling. They asked him what he was doing there; he replied that it was no concern of theirs, and told them not to be surprised and that he was old enough not to need them to look after him. They urged him to come back home with them, and he did.

A little later a whale was washed up and they rushed to cut it up. No one recognized what kind of a whale it was, not even Karlsefni, who was an expert on whales. The cooks boiled the meat, but when it was eaten it made them all ill.

Then Thorhall the Hunter walked over and said, "Has not Redbeard [Thor] turned out to be more successful than your Christ? This was my reward for the poem I composed in honour of my patron, Thor; he has seldom failed me."

When the others realized this they refused to use the whalemeat and threw it over a cliff, and committed themselves to God's mercy.

Then a break came in the weather to allow them to go out fishing, and after that there was no scarcity of provisions.

In the spring they went back to Straumfjord and gathered supplies, game on the mainland, eggs on the island, and fish from the sea.

Karlsefni sailed south along the coast, accompanied by Snorri and Bjarni and the rest of the expedition. They sailed for a long time and eventually came to a river that flowed down into a lake and from the lake into the sea. There were extensive sandbars outside the river mouth, and ships could only enter it at high tide.

Karlsefni and his men sailed into the estuary and named the place *Hope* (Tidal Lake). Here they found wild wheat growing in fields on all the low ground and grape vines on all the higher ground. Every stream was teeming with fish. They dug trenches at the high-tide mark, and when the tide went out there were halibut trapped in the trenches. In the woods there was a great number of animals of all kinds.

They stayed there for a fortnight, enjoying themselves and noticing nothing untoward. They had their livestock with them. But early one morning as they looked around they caught sight of nine skin-boats; the men in them were waving sticks which made a noise like flails, and the motion was sunwise.

Karlsefni said, "What can this signify?"

"It could well be a token of peace," said Snorri. "Let us take a white shield and go to meet them with it."

They did so. The newcomers rowed towards them and stared at them in amazement as they came ashore. They were small and evil-looking, and their hair was coarse; they had large eyes and broad cheekbones. They stayed there for a while, marvelling, and then rowed away south round the headland.

Karlsefni and his men had built their settlement on a slope by the lakeside; some of the houses were close to the lake, and others were farther away. They stayed there that winter. There was no snow at all, and all the livestock were able to fend for themselves.

Then, early one morning in spring, they saw a great horde of skin-boats approaching from the south round the headland, so dense that it looked as if the estuary were strewn with charcoal: and sticks were being waved from every boat. Karlsefni's men raised their shields and the two parties began to trade.

What the natives wanted most to buy was red cloth; they also wanted to buy swords and spears, but Karlsefni and Snorri forbade that. In exchange for the cloth they traded grey pelts. The natives took a span of red cloth for each pelt, and tied the cloth round their heads. The trading went on like this for a while until the cloth began to run short; then Karlsefni and his men cut it up into pieces which were no more than a finger's breadth wide; but the Skraelings paid just as much or even more for it.

Then it so happened that a bull belonging to Karlsefni and his men came running out of the woods, bellowing furiously. The Skraelings were terrified and ran to their skin-boats and rowed away south round the headland.

After that there was no sign of the natives for three whole weeks. But then Karlsefni's men saw a huge number of boats coming from the south, pouring in like a torrent. This time all the sticks were being waved anti-clockwise and all the Skraelings were howling loudly. Karlsefni and his men now hoisted red shields and advanced towards them.

When they clashed there was a fierce battle and a hail of missiles came flying over, for the Skraelings were using catapults. Karlsefni and Snorri saw them hoist a large sphere on a pole; it was dark blue in colour. It came flying in over the heads of Karlsefni's men and made an ugly din when it struck the ground. This terrified Karlsefni and his men so much that their only thought was to flee, and they retreated farther up the river. They did not halt until they reached some cliffs, where they prepared to make a resolute stand.

Freydis came out and saw the retreat. She shouted, "Why do you flee from such pitiful wretches, brave men like you? You should be able to slaughter them like cattle. If I had weapons, I am sure I could fight better than any of you."

The men paid no attention to what she was saying. Freydis tried to join them but she could not keep up with them because she was pregnant. She was following them into the woods when the Skraelings closed in on her. In front of her lay a dead man, Thorbrand Snorrason, with a flintstone buried in his head, and his sword beside him. She snatched up the sword and prepared to defend herself. When the Skraelings came rushing towards her she pulled one of her breasts out of her bodice and slapped it with the sword. The Skraelings were terrified at the sight of this and fled back to their boats and hastened away.

Karlsefni and his men came over to her and praised her courage. Two of their men had been killed, and four of the Skraelings, even though Karlsefni and his men had been fighting against heavy odds.

They returned to their houses and pondered what force it was that had attacked them from inland; they then realized that the only attackers had been those who had come in the boats, and that the other force had just been a delusion.

The Skraelings found the other dead Norseman, with his axe lying beside him. One of them hacked at a rock with the axe, and the axe broke; and thinking it worthless now because it could not withstand stone, they threw it away.

Karlsefni and his men had realized by now that although the land was excellent they could never live there in safety or freedom from fear, because of the native inhabitants. So they made ready to leave the place and return home....

RICHARD HENRY DANA, JR.

RICHARD HENRY DANA (1815-1882) was born in Cambridge, Massachusetts, of a father with the same name. Both men were writers and lawyers, the elder Dana a poet, his son the author of the American classic novel *Two Years Before the Mast*. Before completing his undergraduate degree, and because of illness and poor eyesight, Dana was advised, according to the best medical practice of the time, to take a long trip at sea. He served a low rating on a ship bound round the Horn for California. Appalled by the treatment he witnessed of the common sailor, Dana later wrote his famous novel largely in an effort to reform naval law. Upon his return to America, his seafaring done, he finished his legal studies and began a law practice specialising in maritime matters. Most commentators describe his practice as lucrative, but Van Wyck Brooks maintained that Dana "alienated all his paying clients" by his diligence for the welfare of the impoverished. He was also renowned, and vilified, for his attacks against slavery.

Dana, despite his familiarity with the sea, rarely travelled, either abroad or within America. Yet, despite his wander-abstinence, our country held sufficient allure that he managed an impressive five trips to Canada.

The first was a vacation in Nova Scotia in 1842. Excerpted below is a passage from his *Journal* for the period, illuminating not only because it is one of the earliest foreign literary descriptions of Halifax and other Nova Scotian centres, but because its subtext is unwittingly revealing.

The second trip to Canada, in the summer of 1845, involved the standard tourist views of Niagara Falls and environs, coupled with a flying visit to Toronto. This visit was distinguished, however, by a very un-Victorian decision to strip nude at the cataract: "I went down from the path & stood at the lowest point, where the driving of the water was just short of being past endurance. Took off all my clothes, when under the sheet, and made a complete bath of it."

His third visit was another vacation in Halifax, of three weeks' duration. However, his fourth sally to Canada was a fortnight's ramble in August 1853 to the increasingly popular triad of Montreal, Quebec and the Saguenay. As James Doyle has noted in his authoritative study of American literary writing about this country,

> Like Thoreau, who preceded him over much of this route three years earlier, Dana had very little comparative experience against which to measure the landscape and society of French Canada. As a result, his journal of the trip is filled with the enthusiastic exclamations of a wide-eyed neophyte on his first visit to an exotic civilization. Unlike Thoreau, however, Dana found very little to criticize about French Canada; his "Boston Brahmin" sensibilities inclined him to view the ostensibly ordered and efficient aristocratic society of Quebec City with approval.

Dana was better informed about this nation than any other American imaginative writer of the nineteenth century. Proof of this can be seen from his remarks made during his fifth and final Canadian circuit, a visit which saw him spend five months in Halifax as chief counsel to the American side of the Fisheries Commission, a tribunal held in 1877 to resolve American fishing rights within Canadian territorial waters.

Dana had been informed early in 1876 by the US President,

Ulysses S. Grant, that he was going to be the American Ambassador to Britain, an honour Dana greatly coveted. Despite having failed earlier in a run for Congress, Dana believed that he was made for "great things" in either politics or diplomacy, and that the appointment to the ambassadorship was an overdue acknowledgement of his, what were to him, obvious talents. Unfortunately, the US Senate failed to ratify his appointment (one Senator dismissing Dana as "One of those damn literary fellers"). As a sop, Dana was asked by the White House to deliver the case of the United States before a tribunal meeting in Halifax to deal with American and British grievances arising from previous free trade treaties and extant duties and embargoes. The tribunal was composed of three commissioners: a Briton (allegedly representing Canada's position), an American, and an ostensibly neutral chairman, a Belgian agreed upon by both sides. Disappointed as he must have been, Dana refused to sulk at this seemingly minor appointment and applied his extraordinary advocate's skills to the case. But as his unintentionally amusing letters from Halifax indicate (regarding the American commissioner, Ensign Kellogg), the case was lost even before it started:

> I must speak freely in strict confidence. He has been worse than useless. I have some notion that his powers (so to speak) are diminished by years of sloth and heavy feeding. Whether anything serious has happened to him, I do not know. I have never been able to get from him anything that could be called conversation; and when we have spoken about the case, I was never satisfied whether he understood it or not. His first public appearance was at a dinner given to us by the Bar, at which he made two speeches, the last volunteered. The effect was about an equal proportion of wonder and amusement. They were polite about it, but evidently thought he was a strange fish. The only explanation not impeaching his intellect was an excess of champagne. At a dinner given by M. Doutre he volunteered a speech, where none was expected, which was worse than that at

the Bar dinner. It caused us great mortification. Just before the decision, at a dinner by Sir A. Galt [the British-Canadian tribunal commissioner] he volunteered another speech, which was so distressing to us that the dinner broke up somewhat prematurely to save us the risk of another.... He complained that we did not address ourselves to him. We felt it to be true, for he was a great deal in a semi-somnolent state....

In a letter to his son, Dana further reported that, "it was on one of these dinners that the American member stumbled over Sir Alexander Galt's name, and called him 'Sir Harker Dandy' and 'Sir Harker Dardy' ... in addition to that Mr. [Kellogg's] clothing was untidy, his general appearance slovenly, and he was careless and forgetful in his tobacco-chewing."

To its gargantuan shock, the United States lost the case; Britain and Canada were awarded almost all that they asked for, and the USA was forced to pay Everest-sized damages. Dana's attendance at the tribunal marked his last encounter with Canada.

The following extract from a much earlier time shows Dana to be both ingenuous in some matters, sharp in others, and occasionally affected by the dominant prejudices of his day. One can only assume that the descriptions and tales of Canada taken from his personal journal kept during this 1842 trip are honestly related. In this particular excerpt, Dana, embarking from Boston, recounts his first experiences of the marine joys of Halifax, his impressions of the Nova Scotia coast, his encounters with a ghost town—and his secret rendezvous with a prostitute.

———————————————

from THE JOURNAL OF RICHARD HENRY DANA, JR.

July 16th [1842]. Saturday. Being completely worn down by fatigue from warm weather and hard work, determined to make a trip to Halifax, solely to change the scene, to get away from the care and toil of business, to relax my mind completely and to get upon salt water once more.

Set sail, or made steam at 5 p.m. in the steam ship *Caledonia* bound to Halifax and Liverpool. S. being quite well, and her mother and an excellent servant with her, I can leave without much anxiety.

Baggage on board, business left with Ned and Mr. Peck, fine afternoon, a noble vessel filled with passengers and we are off for Halifax....

No sooner had we got outside of the light house and the cool, salt night wind of ocean come over us than I felt myself a new creature. It was damp and a little foggy, but I staid on deck until nearly one o'clock on Sunday morning, walking to and fro, snuffing up the breeze and opening my whole system to its invigorating influence. I was on deck again before sun rise and walked deck until breakfast time, which was nine o'clock. At break-fast I had a terrific appetite and ate more than I have at any meal for months. I was the last that left the table.

At ten and a quarter a.m. a bell rang and the passengers were invited and the crew ordered into the cabin, where the captain, there being no clergyman of the Episcopal or Presbyterian Churches on board, read the service. The cabin was well filled and the company were attentive and responded in a proper and apparently devout manner. The rule of the boats is that if there is a clergyman of the established Churches of England or Scotland on board, he shall be invited to perform the services, and if not, that the captain shall read the service of the Church of England. This rule met with a good deal of opposition from the different dissenting sects in England and from the numerous independent sects in our own country; but seems to me to be a very necessary one. Before it was adopted every man calling himself a clergyman, of whatever denomination, creed, ordination, (and usually the most fanatical and extreme were the most forward) claimed a right to conduct religious services and to harangue the passengers upon their favorite topics. Universalists, Transcendentalists, Quakers,—Anti Slavery agents with their local and temporary topics—every description of wild-fire Western preachers who called themselves clergymen, whatever their creed or ordination,—nay, even Mormonites and Matthias men, had equal claims. In this state of things the captains found it difficult and embarrassing to make a choice, and there was no safety as to the doctrines, mode of service and address or the topics of preachers. Dissatisfaction arose among the passengers and the Sabbath turned into a day of dissention and ill feeling. Admitting the Episcopalian and Presbyterian clergy threw in the great body of the British Protestant preachers, and gave the surety that the man who officiated would be who had been ordained by a responsible body of men, bound look after his conduct, and who at least professed and who [would] not dare to preach against a well established Christian creed. The services of these two churches are, also, such as very few Christians cannot conscientiously and profitably join it. Such being the case, the present arrangement can be admitted to be, at least, the lesser evil.

On this day, the service being a regular order of the Governors of the company, connected with the national government, was treated with respect by all, and there being no motive for party-spirit or dispute, the day was passed in quietness and decorum.

On Monday morning, we were off Cape Sable, and before noon were going up Halifax harbour....

July 18th. Monday morning. Write to dear S. from my state room in order to send by the *Arcadia* which we hoped to find in Halifax. Going up the harbour Mr. Lyell said the country appeared very much like that about many of the Norwegian harbours,—rocks, pines and cedars. It is certainly a noble harbour, capacious, deep, well protected, and little affected by the tide. The fogs and the rocks a few miles below the mouth on the sea shore, are the only drawbacks. Mr. Young points out to us the York Redoubt, Georgia's Island, the citadel crowning and commanding the whole town and harbour, the North West arm and the Bedford Basin. Strange appearance of men carrying coal on their backs in large bags and red coats upon the wharf. Young sends us to Coblinty's Hotel, and a great mistake we have made of it. I am put into a large dancing hall capable of accommodating two hundred couples, with a niche screened off for a bed, wash stand, etc. There is no clerk or office to go to, no keeper to attend to you, but the chamber maid, an ignorant, stupid old woman, with a beard, gives you your room and you must hunt up a negro boy to do all you want done. "Mr. Cosey", the most popular and efficient of the negro waiters is tractable and can be driven into some attention to his duty but all the others are beyond hope.... Walked down to the wharf to take leave of the *Caledonia*. Shook hands with Capt. Lott, Sheridan, Adams and their set, and with my N.Y. radical friend whose name is Felix Argonti. The *Arcadia* is not in.

Return to the Hotel and dress for dinner. Dine at six, in English style. Most of the boarders are young men of business, in merchandise or the professions, and they come home at about half past five, and appear at table dressed for the evening, in light vests, dress coats, etc. The meal is made a comfortable and social one, as the business of the day is over.

After dinner, put off my dining dress, put on my blue loose trousers rough jacket and glased cap, and set out for a cruise about the town. Engage a boat for fishing tomorrow, and a boy to get bait and lines and to tend the boat. At nine go up to the barracks of the Sixty-ninth to hear the tattoo. All the drums and fifes of the garrison, and two or three bugles, are assembled on the parade in front of the barracks, and when the clock strikes, the bugles play a call and then the drums and fifes with the octave flute and triangle play for about half an hour favorite national tunes. The "Blue bells of Scotland" was played tonight in a way I never heard before and which I fear I shall never get out of my head. The whole concludes with "God save the Queen", accompanied by a roll of all the drums in the garrison at the end of each stave. The effect upon a stranger is very imposing. I cannot help recognizing the grandeur of the English name and nation. Here, three thousand miles from home, across the Ocean, are banded together in strictest discipline and perfect efficiency a corps of a thousand men, who are but a handful compared with that great army which is garrisoning half the world. At the same hour of the night, the tattoo is beating and the drums rolling, and "God save the Queen" is playing in the midst of English bayonets and nerving British hearts in China, in India, at the Southern Cape, in the Mediterranean, in the Pacific, and across half of North America! Webster's figure of the British morning drum beat, comes most forcibly upon the mind. An Englishman feels that he belongs to the greatest nation that ever existed upon the globe. Who can blame him or dispute him. It is a nation to be proud of. She has been the salt of the earth and the Israel of the Christian faith for the last four centuries.

Tuesday. July 19th. (The regiments at Halifax are the Sixty-fourth, Sixty-ninth and Seventy-sixth.) On the parade at ten a.m. to see the guard mounted. A fine hand and a good show of about two hundred men. At eleven, went fishing at the narrows of Bedford basin. Had two boys with me to tend the head sails and cut the bait. There are no rocks or flats, so that I could manage my own boat. Caught about a dozen cod and haddock, and put back for town about five o'clock. Was to dine at Mr. Young's at six. The wind came out ahead and we did not reach the wharf until that hour. Hurried up to the hotel and with great expedition got to Mr. Y's door at a quarter before seven....

July 20. Wednesday. Parade again at ten. About noon started off with Mr. Codman on horseback to Cole Harbour, about six miles

distant. Delightful ride there and back. Country very green. Dined
at six. In the evening put on my rough clothes again and strolled off
towards the barracks to hear the tattoo. While there, saw two girls
accosting men for bad purposes. I was struck with the manner of
one of them. She looked very young, had rather an interesting face
and could not muster the impudence necessary for her calling. The
girl with her went [boldly] up to the men, but this one kept behind
and seemed to be new in her calling. Observing that I was watching
them, and mistaking me in the twilight for a sailor or some rowdy
(from my dress) they came towards me, and the elder solicited me in
a very forward manner. I turned her off, but looked full into the face
of the other and her eye fell. I walked away and watching them from
some distance, saw that their relative conduct was the same. I felt a
sudden interest in the younger girl, and knowing that I was a
stranger and was completely disguised for the light there then was,
went up to the girls and beckoned the younger one to follow me.
Thinking it to be in the way of her trade she followed me, and the
other said nothing. I walked until I was hidden from view by the
side of a fence in a lane and then called the girl to me. I told her at
once that I did not want her in the way of her calling but wished to
say a word to her. I then in a careless manner opened my coat to
show her that I had the dress of a gentleman, and she saw by my
voice and man[ner] that I was different from what they supposed,
and she answered me very respectfully. I told her plainly and at once
that I knew what she was, what her life was and had been, and asked
her if she knew what she was fast going to. She made no reply; but
looked down. I then set before her in as kind and affectionate a manner as I could, the end which inevitably awaited her. I told her that
she would fall from step to step, would become diseased and in time
a burden upon the persons who kept [her] and then would be left to
die a miserable death of neglect, suffering and remorse. She was a
good deal affected, the tears stood in her eyes, and after a time she
said she knew it all. I then asked her how she came into that situation. Finding, from something she said, that she supposed me to
belong to Halifax, I let her go on in the error, thinking that she

would be more careful to tell me no more than the true story. She
told me her name, the name and occupation of her father and where
he lived. She said her mother died when she was fourteen and left
her father with herself and two younger brothers. The brothers were
put into the almshouse and bound out to trades. She could not go to
the almshouse and begged her father to take a room and she would
keep it for him; but her father was rather intemperate and refused to
do it, and she went out to service. A boy of about sixteen, the son of
a baker, (whom she mentioned as a person I must know) attended to
her and in time, being left without helps or advisors, he had his way
with her. This was discovered before long, and the person she lived
with turned her away, without any effort to save. She could not get
another place as she had no certificate of character. In this difficulty
she went to her father, who turned her away with contempt. One of
her brothers had gone to sea, and the other was too small to help her.
At this trying time she was invited to the house of a washer-woman
and went there to work. This was a bad house, and she fell into a set
of the lowest girls of the town, and was soon out in the streets in the
manner I saw her:—Such was her story. I could not but believe it,
partly because, taking me for a resident, she referred to so many
sources from which I could easily learn its falsity, if it were false, and
partly from its probability. Had she been seduced by a man of wealth
or gentility she would have been passed about as a kept mistress, for
she was very good looking, but having been turned loose upon the
town where she was well known for an affair with a poor lad, she
naturally fell thus early into the lowest walks of her calling.

I asked her if she ever went to church? She answered—"It would
only be making a mock of it, Sir, to go to church and then go right
away and do bad again." I found that her parents were Catholics and
that she had been baptised by Father Laughlan, the priest who usually attended upon the poor. I then told her to go to him, and tried
to encourage her that he might get her a place and that she might in
time regain her respectability, being young, and find herself in a
decent situation in the world. I told [her] that girls in her situation,
if taken away at once, had been reformed, had married respectable

men and found themselves happy and comfortable, instead of dying in misery and despair. She said she had thought often of this but that all were against her where she lived and would not permit her to leave and that no one had encouraged her. She promised me that she would see Father Laughlan the next day and would do all she could to get away. I gave her some money and told her to keep away from men, and asked her if she could not—"God knows", said she, seriously, and as though she was speaking her whole mind. "I never saw any pleasure in it." She then told me what her life was, of the dreadful death of one of the girls in the house, and seemed completely stirred up to extricate herself from it.

I then told her that I was a stranger and married, and that I had spoken to her from what I observed of her with the other girl and from a desire to do her good. I said that I should be at the same place the next night, and that if she was sincere and went to the priest, and wished to tell me so, I should be glad to hear it; but that she might do as she chose, and, as I should go away the day after never to return, if she did not do as she promised, she need not meet me, and I should never know more of her. This left her perfectly at liberty to do as she chose.

I had left her but a few minutes and was going down a street near South barracks when I saw a crowd rushing up the street with cries of "down with him", "kill him", "knock him over" etc., and saw a soldier running for his life toward the barrack gate. One man brought him a blow by the side of the head which knocked him down, and two or three more struck him as he fell. Some money fell from his pocket, upon the stones of the gutter and the men stopping to pick it up, the soldier got upon his feet, looked round a moment as though bewildered, and then ran for his life toward gate, calling out "By the Holy ghost"—"Oh, dear ! Oh, dear !" as though half stunned and in pain. The mob was too near the barracks to pursue him. I followed and saw him go in, and in an instant there was cry of "Serjeant of the guard!" "Picket, fall in!" etc., and in a minute more a dozen soldiers of the picket for the night, dressed in their long gray coats and high cloth caps with muskets in hand and bayonets fixed, headed by their serjeant, rush from the gate in the direction from which the crowd came. They overtook another soldier who had been beaten and who went with them to point out the men. In five minutes the picket returned with three or four prisoners, rowdyish looking fellows, whom they put in the watch house. I went to the scene of the row, and there saw about half a dozen houses, in each of which a fiddle, with tambourines or triangles, was playing, and a crowd of the lowest description, both males and females were going [in] and out. A decently dressed man standing near told me that this street, between the two barracks, on the hill, was the nest of the brothels and dance-houses, and that dancing went on here every night. Buttoning up my coat and pulling my cap over my face, I went into the largest of these houses. The door was open and people passed in and out as they chose. The entry terminated in an oblong room with low and black walls, sanded floor and closely barred shutters, used as a dancing hall. At one end was a platform holding two chairs upon which the fiddle and triangle player sat. At the other end was the bar, at which the bloated, red faced master of the house sold the glasses of rum, brandy and wine to the girls and their partners. In the middle of the room, in an arm chair, sat the old harridan, the "mother" of the house, with a keen wicked eye, looking sharp after the girls and see-ing to it that they made all the men dance and pay the fiddler and treat them at the bar after each dance. There were about a dozen girls, nearly all of whom were dancing, and the average number of men in the room at a time was from twenty to thirty. Having looked with sufficient disgust and horror at the old creatures who con-ducted the orgies and made gain out of this dreadful trade, I turned my attention to the girls, and after carefully watching them singly for some time, looking in their faces, for many of them came up and spoke to me as they did to others, and hearing them talk, I can sin-cerely say that there was not one of them who would not, to my mind, excite only loathing and pity in the breast of any but a man as degraded as they. Indeed, I asked myself several times—Can any man be in such a state as to have intercourse with these creatures? There was almost a certainty of disease, for every one of them looked broken down by disease and strong drink. The chance of a man's becoming diseased by connexion with them would certainly be ten to one with each of them. Then, with the exception of two or three who seemed coarse and hardened, they were such pitiable objects. One of them came up and spoke to me,—the best looking at a distance. She had bright cheeks, though thin, good features, and black hair curling in ringlets from the top of her head. When she came close to me, the marks of degradation were plain upon her. The skin was tight to her bones, her chest was fallen in, her eyes were wild and sparkling partly from liquor, but with dark lines and cavities under them, every sign of health, natural animation and passion had left her, and with a wasted form, hectic and fallen cheek, glassy eyes, and a frisette fastened to her head, she looked like a painted galvanized corpse. Her breath too was strong of brandy, and she was partly stupefied with drink. With the exception of two or three thick set, clumsy, coarse featured, pug-nosed and pock-marked Irish wenches, who seemed in good keeping, this poor girl was a fair specimen of the company. She is an instance of the effect of such a life upon those who have been handsome and in better circumstances, while those who have been coarse and vulgar and but little better than harlots from earliest life, brought up in vice, often retain their robustness, even when diseased. Black and white, too, were mixed up together, and the girl I have described had been dancing with a sooty fellow in a sailor's hat and duck trousers torn at the knees, probably the cook of some merchant vessel.

Having staid as long as I dared to without either dancing or going to the bar, or attracting notice, I slipped out and went into the next house. This was smaller and more filthy, and there were only two or three white girls of the lowest description among half a dozen black girls or women for some of them seemed quite advanced. There was very vulgar and rough work here, two or three drunken sailors and a good deal of horse-play. One of the girls kicked a man in the back not much below the shoulders while they were dancing and there was a good deal of swearing and hard talking. I was glad to slip out soon after I came in; but as it was one of the girls saw me going out and sprang towards me and got me by the arm, but I pulled my arm away from her and jumped through the narrow entry into the street. Fearing some of [the] drunken men might follow, and having no weapon of defense,—not even a cane—I stood under the shadow of the opposite building until I saw there was no pursuit.

Determined to see the whole of this new chapter in the book of life I went into a third and a fourth house, in which the scenes varied between the two first I had seen, neither quite so bad as the second, and neither superior to the first.

It being now eleven o'clock, having seen fair specimens of the life of Halifax Hill, and most other such places on the globe, I presume, and having got through in safety, I walked slowly home to my hotel. The two adventures I had met with so possessed my mind that I lay awake for hours. Poor Kitty Morricay! (for that is her name) are you coming to such a dreadful end as this? Will you end your days among the negroes and outcasts on the hill? What a dreadful fate has society ordered for a single fault in a woman! No pity! No repentance can help her! No return! Yet this must be God's order, and it is necessary. No lesser terrors would guard female virtue.

How unjust, too, the world is! Fanny Ellsler, or any other admired successful strumpet, though her whoredoms are a part of the history of Europe, and notorious as the death or birth of a crowned head,—will be applauded and followed after and the world sees nothing but her grace and the "poetry of motion"; but if to vice is added poverty and misfortune, the virtue of the world is stern and has no eye for pity. What will probably be the eternal condition of the people I have seen tonight?—immortal souls,—made in God's image, living by his grace and power!

Prayed earnestly and I trust sincerely, that God would touch the heart of the poor girl and save her from such an end.

July 21st. Thursday. Parade at ten, and went fishing immediately afterward. Before I went fishing, called at a tract and bible store to get a book that might be of use to poor Kitty, intending to give it to her that evening if she came to the place appointed. A short story, setting before her her life and its end, and which would stir up her religious feelings might be of use to her. I found no one in attendance but a woman, and I could neither find such a book myself nor describe it to her,—so I left the shop.

The Bedford basin where I sailed is the most remarkable sea-bay I was ever in. The harbour passes Halifax town like a wide river, and then, about two miles above the town, after narrowing in a little, it spreads out into this large, deep, irregular basin, surrounded by well wooded shores, but little affected by the tide, without flats or rocks, and containing, I was told, fourteen square miles of anchorage! It is the most complete sailing ground for boats and small vessels that can be imagined, and is at the same time large and deep enough to hold the whole British navy. This great head of water above the town, flowing in and out with the tides, and itself supplied by springs, small rivers and creeks, keeps the harbour deep and prevents any danger of its filling up. It would be almost impossible for a hostile force to get up into this basin, as there is but one passage way into it. The ride round the basin is said to be quite beautiful.

After fishing at the narrows some time I sailed about the basin in all directions, having a fine breeze. There were several other boats and small vessels there at the same time. Coming back, towards night, I sailed close under the lee of two sloops of war, just arrived from the West Indies,—the *Race Horse* and *Volage*, both with yellow fever on board. The old frigate *Pyramis* lay at her moorings, used as a receiving ship.

After dinner learned that Mr. Wm. Young had sent his servant with a horse for me to take a ride. Wrote a note to thank him.

Towards nine sauntered along in my boating dress towards the South Barracks. It began to rain and the tattoo was played within the gates. I went into the garrison by permission, and for a few minutes it rained quite heavily. When the music was over it had stopped raining but was cloudy. It was nearly half an hour later than the time I had agreed to meet the poor girl, and the rain would have kept her away, I was quite sure, or she would have gone away thinking I would not come,—even if she meant to come at all. I felt quite sure that she would not come unless she had been to her priest, for I had told her that I would call on the priest and speak to him about her, and thus she would suppose I would find her out. I passed along the parade and down the street, but saw no one. Returning I thought I saw some one at a distance, and walked back again slowly. Looking behind me I saw a figure coming toward me, and walking slowly on it overtook me, and it was she. I walked aside and she followed me. I asked her what she had to tell me, and she told me she had been to Father Laughlan that morning early, and he treated her kindly, remembered her family, and told her to come the next day and he would try to aid her. (This she told me, before knowing that I had not been to see the priest, as I told her I might.) She said he asked her how she came to think of reforming, and she told him how it happened, and that a gentleman who was a stranger had spoken to her and sent her to him. I told her that I had tried to get a book for her, and she said she could read easily and wished to have it. I told her, too, that I expected to go away the next day or the day after, and that if it should not be until the day after, I would meet her in the same place the next night and give her the book. I made her promise to read it [and] to keep it, and said that if she reformed and became happy and comfortable, the book would be a remembrance, and if she did not—still to keep it, and it might some day be of use to her. All this she promised, and seemed very much affected. I told her I had a wife at home to whom I should tell her story, and who would feel for her. She asked when I should come back. I told her probably never; but added that I had friends here who would inform me, if her efforts succeeded. I did not think it safe to let her know my name. I told her that if I did not meet her the next night, she might be sure that it was because I had gone away. She promised to be there. I once more set before her the certainty of the fate that awaited her, and drew the best picture of the chances in case she changed, and left her.

July 22. Friday. This morning learned that the steamer *Saxe Gothe*, the one I was to go in for St. John, was to sail at noon. I felt regret that I could not keep my appointment, for I wished to do all I could for the poor creature, and I feared that the discouragement of not seeing me might put her back.

I wrote a notice to Father Laughlan, describing the case and enclosing a sum of money with which I asked him to purchase a book and give to her of a kind which I mentioned, and commended her to his pastoral care, and requested him to let me know in case any good was accomplished for her....

Took leave of Halifax, its citadel, its barracks, the basin, the York redoubt, as we went down the harbour. The object of my visit had been answered. I had cleared my mind completely from business and cares, and by complete relaxation, with out door exercises, had restored the healthful and active tone of my system. I had refused all invitations to public places, to dinners, parties etc., and none of us delivered our letters of introduction, for we found that we could not go a fishing all day, and then sunburnt, tired and blackened, dress for a party in the evening. I had resolutely kept from books, and although I had books in my trunk and many leisure hours yet I made a principle of not looking at them, and loafed or walked about the streets or slept instead. Every morning before breakfast I had walked either over the citadel, which is the grandest fortification I ever saw, with a fine commanding situation, or to the Government House, or barracks....

We were no sooner round the point, and out upon the deep sea than the wind blew very heavily, and a violent sea arose.... After tea and about ten p.m. we touched at Lunenburgh and landed and took off a few passengers. At nine, I thought of poor Kitty Morricay. Did she wait for me? I hope she was not discouraged in her effort by my not returning.

July 23. Saturday. Arrived at Liverpool about seven a.m. As we were to stay an hour, went ashore and walked through the town. The town is built upon a single street running by the side of the river, winding along, and the houses have pretty garden spots before or by the side of them, and are painted, neat and comfortable in appearance. It is quite a pretty village of about two thousand inhabitants, I should judge....

Stood out again to sea, bound for Shelburne. About three o'clock stood up Shelburne Bay. This bay is said to be the best in Nova Scotia, being very extensive, deep and surrounded by well wooded country in many parts. The town of Shelburne is situated at the extreme end of the bay, and presents a remarkable instance of decay. It was founded by a large company of royalists who fled from the United States at the breaking out of the war of '75, and who selected this site on account of the excellence of the harbour. Here they built a town, planted farms, built vessels and engaged largely in privateering, the carrying trade and other modes of active industry by land and sea. There being a good deal of wealth among them the town was handsomely built and large capital was embarked and set in motion. For many years the town grew and flourished; but the general peace which followed the battle of Waterloo, threw it upon its regular legitimate resources for trade in times of peace; and from that time the downward progress of the place has been uninterrupted. The reasons for this were that it has no back country to support it and for which it would be the natural market and seaport, for it is situated at the end of the peninsula of Nova Scotia, with Halifax above it to cut off its [trade], and because it lies so far up the bay that it is little used as a port of supplies, or a fishing station, In fact, the world seems to have given it the go-by, entirely. With as beautiful a harbour as the face of the globe can show, and with large capital to assist it, it stands as a warning to all who disregard the regular course of things in the affairs of men and attempt to counter-act it by particular and local efforts. As we steamed slowly up the bay the captain of the boat told me that its shores had once been lined with beautiful farms, and that the forlorn unpainted houses which stood here and there without a fence near them or any signs of cultivation, and used as the dwellings of fishermen, were once the abodes of substantial farmers who tilled their acres, supplied the town and sent their produce to other countries. He said, too, that as fast as the older and more wealthy men died off or left, their houses were taken to pieces, exported and put up again in other places. And that in this way all the best part of the town had been gradually moved off. This accounted for the fact that in a town which had diminished to one quarter of its size within twenty years there should be no ruinous large houses. Throughout this wide sheet of water, spreading out like a large inland lake, not a sail nor a moving craft was to be seen. Had we been its discoverers we could not have gone over in more perfect stillness. As we drew nigh the town we saw a single vessel, a little fishing schooner lying at anchor off the wharves, while rotting by the side of the wharves, themselves decaying as rapidly, lay two small vessels, condemned for old age. We rang our bell as we made fast to the wharf, and its echoes awaked the dead stillness about us like the fire bell at night. The persons who came down to the wharf were children or old women. I believe but one or two men came, and they seemed decrepit, and laid on the shelf. As [we] were to stay here a half hour, I went ashore to walk about this singular place. As the captain had told me, there was not a large house in the town: they had all been moved off, and the cellars under them had gradu- ally filled up and been grown over with grass. The streets could not be distinguished except by the lines of houses, as carriage way and side walk were alike grown over with grass. Not a vehicle of any description was in motion, nor was there the sound of a blacksmith's hammer nor of the carpenter's axe in the place, but the dead stillness of a Jewish Sabbath reigned over the whole region. Excepting the inimitable accumulation of images of decay in the last chapter of Ecclesiastes, and part of Burke's description of the Carnatic, I know of nothing in descriptive literature which the sight of this place called to my mind. The doors were indeed shut in the streets, the pitcher broken at the fountain and the wheel broken at the cistern. As we walked through the deserted streets, carefully laid out at right angles, hardly a person rose up at the footsteps of strangers, and half a dozen men, strangers, walking about on a Saturday afternoon, hardly drew a face to the window, or brought a boy or girl to the door. No trade or occupation of industry of any description seemed to be carried forward, nor was there a house of entertainment or a shop in the entire settlement. In one window we observed some thread, papers of pins and a few weather stained articles placed, but the door step was almost inaccessible, and there seemed to be no one in the room.

The ringing of the second bell called us aboard and we cast off from this paralyzed village without having landed or taken on board a single passenger. The captain said he should represent to the company the expense and waste of time in coming up this long bay, and see if they would not dispense with these formal visits.

The dress of the people we saw was very antiquated and strange, and the stillness of the place seemed to have crept over the spirits of the inhabitants. I should hardly have been surprised had I been told that the children were deaf and dumb.

The bay looked beautifully as we steamed down it, towards sunset, and we rounded the point and were out upon the Ocean before nightfall.

FREDERICK
SWARTWOUT
COZZENS

F REDERICK S. COZZENS (1818-1869), like Richard Henry Dana,
was another mid-Victorian visitor to Nova Scotia. Whereas his
compatriot explored the province from Halifax south, Cozzens
explored the northern half—and wrote, in *Acadia: Or, A Month
With The Blue Noses*, about his explorations with far more wit than
Dana. With this book, Cozzens has written one of the funniest
books about Canada and Canadians ever penned by a foreigner.

Like his father, Cozzens was a prominent merchant in New York
City. At twenty-one he entered the family business full time, and in
short order made their store one of the leading wine shops in the
area. From his budding years, however, Cozzens had wanted to be a
writer, and he became a regular contributor of humorous essays and
poems to the leading literary magazines of the day. His most famous
book, *The Sparrowgrass Papers* (1856), a collection of very comical
sketches delineating the problems faced by a city man who moves to
the country, enjoyed broad praise and even wider currency.

At the height of his literary fame, apparently in June 1856, he
found himself stranded in Nova Scotia, his original goal of visiting
Bermuda by way of Halifax having been scuppered by the disappear-
ance of the vessel that was to take him to the Shakespearian isle.

Some travellers might have dreaded this misfortune, but not Cozzens. In fact, one of the charms of his book is the wonderful air of optimism at the prospect of discovering new land and new people. His constant references to Longfellow and *Evangeline* are totally ironic; despite the title of his book, he scarcely visits the villages of the Acadians, shows no particular urgency to do so in his perambulations throughout the province, and most of his references to Acadia are similar to those that any city sophisticate might make when entering a renowned Romantic literary landscape: one eye is awake for learned reference, the other is crescented with an eyebrow raised in bemused reserve.

In fact, near the end of his book, Cozzens has the temerity to make some negative comments about the inadequacy of *Evangeline vis-à-vis* the reality of the horror of the history of the Acadians:

> Much as we may admire the various bays, and lakes, and inlets, promontories, and straits, the mountains and woodlands of this rarely-visited corner of creation—and, compared with it, we [Americans] can boast of no coast scenery so beautiful—the valley of Grand Pré transcends all the rest in the Province. Only our valley of Wyoming, as an inland picture, may match it, both in beauty and tradition. One has had its Gertrude, the other its Evangeline. But Campbell never saw Wyoming, nor has Longfellow yet visited the shores of the Basin of Minas. And I may venture to say, neither poet has touched the keynote of divine anger which either story might have awakened.

Throughout the latter part of the book, Cozzens misses no opportunity to remind his American readers of the unforgivable and principal role that American soldiers played in the deracination of the Acadians. And again, he chastises Longfellow for not confronting the unsavory part played by Americans in the violation of this pacific precinct—but politely, for both Cozzens and Longfellow were contributors to *Knickerbocker Magazine*, the nineteenth century equivalent of today's *New Yorker*:

I feel as if the whole wrongs of the French Province concentrated here, as in the last drop of its life blood, no tender dream of pastoral description, no clever veil of elaborate verse, can conceal the hideous features of this remorseless act, this wanton and useless deed of New England cruelty. Do not mistake me, dear reader. Do not think that I am prejudiced against New England. But I hate tyranny—under whatever disguise....

Given the overwhelming popularity of Longfellow's poem when Cozzens was writing, and given that he sent an unsolicited copy of his book to Longfellow, he displays with these tangential criticisms either awesome arrogance, or a shrewd, mature sense of the recipient's generosity. Regardless, Longfellow seems to have enjoyed the book, and replied on July 7, 1859:

My Dear Sir,
    Many thanks for "Acadia," and the pleasant, friendly words you say therein of "Evangeline." It is an extremely interesting volume—both witty and wise, and I am sure will be a very successful one.... Hoping the result of your "Month among the Blue Noses" may be as the Spaniards say "Health and Pistareens" *salud y pesetas*—I remain, Yours truly, Henry W. Longfellow.

Like many American travellers to Canada, Cozzens is forced into tumult by the conjunction of the familiar with the contradictory. At times he wants to scream—at the heavens, then at the locals—for the failure to show Yankee ingenuity in exploiting the superb natural resources evident about him. He takes a deep breath, however, recovers his artfully lost composure, and commends the locals for possibly having the native genius to let things be. In this, he displays the sensibility of a contemporary traveller, rather than a Victorian. No better example of this can be found than his visit to Bras d'Or Lake in Cape Breton, alone with a coach and driver:

Yet it was a stately ride, that by the Bras d'Or; in one's own coach, as it were, traversing such old historic ground. For the very name, and its associations, carry one back to the earliest discoveries in America, carry one back beyond Plymouth Rock to the earlier French adventurers in this hemisphere; yea, almost to the times of Richard Crookback; for on the neighboring shores, as the English claim, Cabot first landed, and named the place *Prima vista,* in the days of Henry the Seventh, the "Richmond" of history and tragedy....

Well, well, ancient or modern, there is not a lovelier ride by white-pebbled beach and wide stretch of wave. Now we roll along amidst primeval trees, not the evergreens of the sea-coast, but familiar growths of maple, beech, birch; and larches, juniper or hacmatack—imperishable for ship craft. Now we cross bridges, over sparkling brooks, alive with trout and salmon, and most surprising of all, pregnant with *water-power.* "Surprising," because no motive-power can be presented to the eye of a citizen of the young republic without the corresponding thought of "Why not use it!" And why not, when Bras d'Or is so near, or the sea-coast either, and land at forty cents an acre, and trees are closely set, and as lofty, as ever nature planted them? Of a certainty, there would be a thousand saw-mills screaming between this and Canseau if a drop of Yankee blood had ever fertilized this soil.

Well, well, perhaps it is well. But yet to ride through a hundred miles of denationalized, highcheeked, red, or black-headed Highlandmen, with illustrious names, in breeches and round hats, without pistols or feathers, is a sorry sight. Not one of these McGregors can earn more than five shillings a day, currency, as a laborer. Not a digger upon our canals but can do better than that; and with the chance of *rising.* But here there seems be no such opportunity. The colonial system provides that every settler shall have a grant of about one hundred and twenty acres, in fee, and free. What then? The Government fosters and protects him. It sends out annually choice stocks of cattle, at a nominal price; it establishes a tariff of duties on foreign goods, so low that the revenue derived therefrom is not sufficient to pay the salaries of its officers. What then? The colonist is only a parasite with all these advantages. He is not an integral part of a nation; a citizen, responsible for his franchise. He is but a colonial Micmac, or Scotch Mac; a mere sub-thoughted irresponsible exotic, in a governmental cold grapery. By the great forefinger of Tom Jefferson, I would rather be a citizen of the United States than *own* all the five-shilling Blue Noses between Sydney and Canseau!

As we roll along up hill and down, a startling flash of sun-light bursts forth from the dewy morning clouds, and touches lake, island, and promontory, with inexpressible beauty. Stop, John Ormond, or drive slowly; let us enjoy *dolce far niente.* To hang now in our curricle upon this wooded hill-top, overlooking the clear surface of the lake, with leafy island, and peninsula dotted in its depths, in all its native grace, without a touch or trace of hand-work far or near, save and except a single spot of sail in the far-off, is holy and sublime.

While he is generally favourable to Thomas Haliburton, and is a true admirer of Joseph Howe, Cozzens could, on occasion, be obnoxious in his literary judgements. Here is Cozzens with his nose in the air in Halifax, puffed with American swagger:

Yonder among the embowering trees is the residence of Judge Haliburton, the author of "Sam Slick." How I admire him for his hearty hostility to republican institutions! It is natural, straightforward, shrewd, and, no doubt, sincere. At the same time, it affords an example of how much the colonist or satellite form of government tends to limit the scope of the mind, which under happier skies and in a wider intelligence might have shone to advantage.

But these asides, and his intermittent displays of the racial assumptions of his era, are no more blemishing of his portrayal than is craquelure on an old painting. He was not afraid to be impressed, even when the impression diminished some recollection of his homeland. Almost every chapter of his book has at least one rapturous description of landscape or townsite, and several are the times he compares some Nova Scotian vista with America, only to find the Canadian superior. His description of Canso is especially flattering (and includes an inherent knock against the barbaric ignorance of the Yankee immigrant coach-driver nicknamed Ear-rings):

> As we approach Canseau the landscape becomes flat and uninteresting; but distant ranges of mountains rise up against the evening sky, and as we travel on towards their bases they attract the eye more and more. Ear-rings is not very communicative. He does not know the names of any of them. Does not know how high they are, but has heard say they are the highest mountains in Nova Scotia. "Are those the mountains of Canseau?" Yes, them's them. So with renewed anticipations we ride on towards the strait "of unrivalled beauty," that travellers say "surpasses anything in America."
>
> And, indeed, Canseau can have my feeble testimony in confirmation. It is a grand marine highway, having steep hills on the Cape Breton Island side, and lofty mountains on the other shore; a full, broad, mile-wide space between them; and reaching from end to end, fifteen miles from the Atlantic to the Gulf of St. Lawrence. As I took leave of Ear-rings, at Plaister Cove, and wrapped myself up in my cloak in the stern-sheets of the row-boat to cross the strait, the full Acadian moon, larger than any United States moon, rose out of her sea-fog, and touched mountain, height, and billow, with effulgence. It was a scene of Miltonic grandeur. After the ruined walls of Louisburgh, and the dark caverns of Sydney, comes Canseau, with its startling splendors! Truly this is a wonderful country.

Indeed, Cozzens was so enamoured of Nova Scotia that he opened his book with exhorting prose one expects to find in a travel brochure. Unlike a brochure writer, however, he has some fun with the geographical ignorance of his American readers:

It is pleasant to visit Nova Scotia in the month of June. Pack up your flannels and your fishing tackle, leave behind you your prejudices and your summer clothing, take your trout pole in one hand and a copy of Haliburton in the other, and step on board a Cunarder at Boston. In thirty-six hours you are in the loyal little province, and above you floats the red flag and the cross of St. George. My word for it, you will not regret the trip.

That the idea of visiting Nova Scotia ever struck any living person as something peculiarly pleasant and cheerful, is not within the bounds of probability. Very rude people are wont to speak of Halifax in connection with the name of a place never alluded to in polite society—except by clergymen. As for the rest of the Province, there are some vague rumours of extensive and constant fogs, but nothing more. The land is a sort of terra incognita. Many take it to be part of Canada, and others firmly believe it is somewhere in Newfoundland.

A sense of how unconventional Cozzens could be for his time may be had from an aside he utters while preparing to read the story of the Acadian heroine Marie de la Tour:

There is nothing more captivating in literature than the narrative of some heroic deed of woman. Very few such are recorded; how many might be, if the actors themselves had not shunned notoriety and "uncommended died," rather than encounter the ordeal of public praise? Of such the poet has written:

Full many a flower is born to blush unseen,
And waste its sweetness on the desert air.

Of such, many have lived and died, to live again only in fiction; whereas their own true histories would have been greater than the inventions of authors. We read of heroes laden with the "glittering spoils of empire," but the heroic deeds of woman are oftentimes, all in all, as great without the glitter; without the pomp and pageantry of triumphal procession; without the pealing trumpet of renown. Boadicea, chained to the car of Seutonius, is the too common memorial of heroic womanity.

Always surprisingly unprepossessing for his period, Cozzens bid farewell to Nova Scotia with this decorous, diplomatic adieu: "If the salient features of the province have sometimes appeared to me, a stranger, a trifle distorted, it may be that my own stand-point is defective."

In the following excerpt, Cozzens, in the company of an English immigrant named Picton, having just explored Louisbourg and its ghosts, encounters taciturn locals, and smiles indulgently over other escapades.

---

from ACADIA: OR, A MONTH WITH THE BLUE NOSES

On Sunday the wind is still ahead, and Picton and I determine to abandon the "Balaklava." How long she may yet remain in harbor is a matter of fate; so, with brave, resolute hearts, we start off for a five-mile walk, to visit McGibbet, the only owner of a horse and wagon in the vicinity of Louisburgh. Squirrels, robins, and rabbits appear and disappear in the road as we march forwards. The country is wild, and in its pristine state; nature everywhere. Now a brook, now a tiny lake, and "the murmuring pines and the hemlocks." At last we arrive at the home of McGibbet, and encounter new Scotland in all its original brimstone and oat-meal.

Some learned philosopher has asserted that when a person has become accustomed to one peculiar kind of diet, it will be expressed in the lineaments of his face. How much the constant use of oatmeal could produce such an effect, was plainly visible in the countenances of McGibbet and his lady-love. Both had an unmistakable equine cast; McGibbet, wild, scraggy, and scrubby, with a tuft on his poll that would not have been out of place between the ears of a plough-horse, stared at us, just as such an animal would naturally over the top of a fence; while his gentle mate, who had more of the amiable draught horse in her aspect, winked at us with both eyes from under a close-crimped frill, that bore a marvellous resemblance to a head-stall. The pair had evidently just returned from kirk. To say nothing of McGibbet's hat, and his wife's shawl, on a chair, and his best books on the hearth (for he was walking about in his stockings), there was a dry *preceese* air about them, which plainly betokened they were newly stiffened up with the moral starch of the conventi-cle, and were therefore well prepared to drive a hard bargain for a horse and wagon to Sydney. But what surprised me most of all was the imperturbable coolness of Picton. Without taking a look scarcely at the persons he was addressing, the traveller stalked in with an—"I say, we want a horse and wagon to Sydney; so look sharp, will you, and turn out the best thing you have here!"

The moral starch of the conventicle stiffened up instantly. Like the blacksmith of Cairnvreckan, who, as a *professor,* would drive a nail for no man on the Sabbath or kirk-fast, unless in a case of abso-lute necessity, and then always charged an extra sixpence for each shoe; so it was plain to be seen that McGibbet had a conscience which required to be pricked both with that which know no law, and the sixpence extra. He turned to his wife and addressed her in *Gaelic!* Then we knew what was coming.

Mrs. McGibbet opened the subject by saying that they were both accustomed to the observance of the Sabbath, and that "she didn't think it was right for man to transgress, when the law was so plain"—

Here McGibbet broke in and said that—"He was free to confess he had commeeted a great many theengs kwhich were a great deal worse than Sabbath-breaking."

Upon which Mrs. McG. interrupted him in turn with a few words, which, although in Gaelic, a language we did not understand, conveyed the impression that the way not addressing her liege lord in the language of endearment, and again continued in English: "That it was held sinful in the community to work or do anything o' the sort, or to fetch or carry even a sma bundle"—

"For kwich," said McGibbet, "is a fine ta be paid to the meenister, of five shilling currency"—

Here Picton stopped whistling a bar of "Bonny Doon," and nodded to me: "about a dollar of your money. We'll pay the fine."

"Yes," chimed in McGibbet, "a dollar"—and was again stopped by his wife, who raised her eyebrows to the border of her kirk-frill and brought them down vehemently over her blue eyes at him.

"Or to travel the road," she said, "even on foot, to say nothing of a wagon and horse."

"But," interrupted Picton, "my dear madam, we must get on, I tell you; I must be in Sydney to-morrow, to catch the steamer for St. John's."

At this observation of the traveller the pair fell back upon their Gaelic for a while, and in the meantime Picton whispered me: "I see; they want to raise the price on us: but we won't give in; they'll be sharp enough after the job by and by."

The pair turned towards us and both shook their heads. It was plain to be seen the conference had not ended in our favor.

"Ye see," said the gude-wife, "we are accustomed to the observance of the Sabbath, and would na like to break it, except—"

"In case of necessity; you are perfectly right," chimed in Picton! "I agree with you myself. Now this is a case of necessity; here we are; we must get on, you see; if we don't get on we miss the steamer to-morrow for St. John's—she only runs once a fortnight there—it's plain enough a clear case of necessity; it's like," continued Picton, evidently trying to corner some authority in his mind, "it's like—let me see—it's like a—pulling,—a sheep out of a ditch—a—which they always do on the Sabbath, you know, to a—get us on to Sydney."

Both McGibbet and his wife smiled at Picton's ingenuity, but straightway put on the equine look again. "It might be so; but it was clean contrary to their preenciples."

"I'll be hanged," whispered Picton, "if I offer more than the usual price, which I heard at Louisburgh was one pound ten, to Sydney, and the fine extra. I see what they are after."

There was an awkward pause in the negotiation. McGibbet scratched his poll, and looked wistfully at his wife, but the kirk-frill was stiffened up wit the moral starch, as aforesaid.

Suddenly, Picton looked out of the window. "By Jove!" said he, "I think the wind is changed! After all, we may get around in the 'Balaklava.'"

McGibbet looked somewhat anxiously out of the window also, and grunted out a little more Gaelic to his love. The kirk-frill relented a trifle.

"Perhaps the gentlemen wad like a glass of mill after thae long walk? and Robert" (which the pronounced Robbut), "a bit o' the corn-cake."

Upon which Robbut, with great alacrity, turned towards the bedroom, from whence he brought forth a great white disk, that resembled the head of a flour-barrel, but which proved to be a full grown griddle cake of corn-meal. This, with the pure milk, from the cleanest of scoured pans, was acceptable enough after the long walk.

We had observed some beautiful streams, and blue glimpses of lakes on the road to McGibbet's, and just beyond his house was a larger lake, several miles in extent, with picturesque hills on either side, indented with coves, and studded with islands, sometimes stretching away to distant slopes of green turf, and sometimes reflecting masses of precipitous rock, crowned with the spiry tops of spruces and fir. Indeed, all the country around, both meadow and upland, was very pleasing to the sight. A low range of hills skirted the northern part of what seemed to be a spacious, natural amphitheatre, while on the south side a diversity of highlands and water added to the whole the charm of variety.

"You have a fine country about you, Mr. McGibbet," said I.

"Ay," he replied.

"And what is it called here?"

"We ca' it Get-Along!" said Robbut, with an intensely Scotch accent on the "Get."

"And yonder beautiful lake—what is the name of that?" said I, in hopes of taking refuge behind something more euphonious.

"Oh! ay," replied he, "that's just Get-Along, too. we don't usually speak of it, but when we do, we just ca' it Get-Along Lake, and it's not good for much."

I thought it best to change the subject. "Do you like this as well as the oat-cake?" said I, with my mouth full of the dry, husky provender.

"Nae," said McGibbet, with an equine shake of the head, "it's not sae fellin."

Not so filling! Think of that, ye pampered minions of luxury, who live only upon delicate viands; who prize food, not as it is useful, but as it is tasteful; who can even encourage a depraved, sensual appetite so far as to appreciate flavor; who enjoy meats, fish, and poultry, only as they minister to your palates; who flirt with spring-chickens and trifle with sweetbreads in wanton indolence, without a thought of your cubic capacity; without a reflection that you can live just as well upon so many square inches of oatmeal a day as you can upon the most elaborate French kickshaws; nay, that you can be elevated to the level of a scientific problem, and work out your fillings, with nothing to guide you but a slate and pencil!

"Then you like oatmeal better than this?" said Picton, soothing down a husky lump, with a cup of milk.

"Ay," responded McGibbet.

"And you always eat it, whenever you can get it, I suppose?" continued Picton, with a most innocent air.

"Ay," responded McGibbet.

"I should think some of you Scotchmen would be afraid of contracting a disease that is engendered in the system by the use of this sort of grain. I hope, Mr. McGibbet," said Picton, with imperturbable coolness, "you keep clear of the bots, and that sort of thing, you know?"

"Kwat?" said Robbut, with the most startled, horse-like look he had yet put on.

"The gasterophili," replied Picton, "which I would advise you to steer clear of, if you want to live long."

As this was a word with too many gable-ends for Robbut's comprehension, he only responded by giving such a smile as a man might be expected to give who had his mouth full of aloes, and as the conversation was wandering off from the main point, addressed himself to Mrs. McG. in the vernacular again.

"We would like to obleege ye," said the lady, "if it was not for the transgression; and we do na like to break the Sabbath for ony man."

"Although," interposed Robbut, "I am free to confess that I have done a great many thing worse than breakin' the Sabbath."

"But if to-morrow would do as well," resumed his wife, "Robbut would take ye to Sydney."

To this Picton shook his head. "Too late for the steamer."

"Or to-night; I wad na mind that," said thy pious Robbut, "*if it was after dark,* and that will bring ye to Sydney before the morn."

"That will do," said Picton, slapping his thigh. "Lend us your horse and wagon to go down to the schooner and get our luggage; we will be back this evening, and then go on to Sydney, eh? That will do; a ride by moonlight;" and the traveller jumped up from his seat, walked with great strides towards the fire-place, turned his back to the blaze, hung a coat-tail over each arm, and whistled "Annie Laurie" at Mrs. McGibbet.

The suggestion of Picton meeting the views of all concerned, the diplomacy ended. Robbut put himself in his Sunday boots, and hitched up a spare rib of a horse before a box-wagon without springs, which he brought before the door with great complacency. The traveller and I were soon on the ground-floor of the vehicle, seated upon a log of wood by way of cushion; and with a chirrup from McGibbet, off we went. At the foot of the first hill, our horse stopped; in vain Picton jerked at the rein, and shouted at him: not a step further would he go, until Robbut himself came down to the rescue. "Get along, Boab!" said his master; and Boab, with a mute, pitiful appeal in his countenance, turned his face towards saltwater. At the foot of the next hill he stopped again, when the irascible Picton jumped out, and with one powerful twitch of the bridle, gave Boab such a hint to "get on," that it nearly jerked his head off. And Boab did get on, only to stop at the ascent of the next hill. Then we began to understand the tactics of the animal. Boab had been the only conveyance between Louisburgh and Sydney for many years, and, as he was usually over-burdened, made a point to stop at the up side of every hill on the road, to let part of his freight get out and walk to the top of the acclivity with him. So, by way of compromise, we made a feint of getting out at every rise of ground, and Boab, who always turned his head around at each stopping-place, seemed to be satisfied with the observance of the ceremony, and trotted gaily forward. At last we came to a place we had named Sebastopol in the morning—a great sharp edge of rock as high as a man's waist, that cut the road in half, over which we lifted the wagon, and were soon in view of the bright little harbor and the "Balaklava" at anchor. Mr. McAlpin kindly gave quarters to our steed in his out-house, and offered to raise a signal for the schooner to wend a boat ashore. As he was Deputy United States Consul, and as I was tired of the red-cross of St. George, I asked him to hoist his consular flag. Up to the flag-staff truck rose the roll of white and red worsted, then uncoiled, blew out, and the blessed stars and stripes were waving over me. It is surprising to think how transported one can be sometimes with a little bit of bunting!

And now the labor of packing commenced, of which Picton had the greatest share by far; the little cabin of the schooner was pretty well spread out with his traps on every side; and this being ended, Picton got out his travelling-organ and blazed away in a *finale* of great tunes and small, sometimes fast, sometimes slow as the humor took him. After all, we parted from the jolly little craft with regret: our trunks were lowered over the side; we shook hands with all on board; and were rowed in silence to the land.

I have had some experience in travelling, and have learned to bear with ordinary firmness and philosophy the incidental discomforts one is certain to meet with on the road; but I must say, the discipline already acquired had not prepared me for the unexpected appearance of our wagon after Picton's luggage was placed in it. First, two solid English trunk's of sole-leather filled the bottom of the vehicle; then the traveller's Minie-rifle, life preserver, strapped-up blankets, and hand-bag were stuffed in the sides: over these again were piled my trunk and the traveller's valise (itself a monster of straps and sole-leather); then again his portable secretary and the hand-organ in a box. These made such a pyramid of luggage, that riding ourselves was out of the question. What with the trunk and the cordage to keep them staid, our wagon looked like a ship of the desert. To crown all, it began to rain steadily. "Now, then," said Picton, climbing up on his confounded travelling equipage, "let's get on." With some difficulty I made a half-seat on the corner of my own trunk; Picton shouted out at Boab; the Newfoundland sailors who had brought us ashore, put their shoulders to the wheels, and away we went, waving our hats in answer to the hearty cheers of the sailors. It was down hill from McAlpin's to the first bridge, and so far we had nothing to care for, except to keep a look-out we were not shaken off our high perch. But at the foot of the first hill Boab stopped! In vain Picton shouted at him to get on; in vain he shook rein and made a feint of getting down from the wagon. Boab was not intractable, but he was sagacious; he had been fed on that sort of chaff too long. Picton and I were obliged to humor his prejudices, and dismount in the mud, and after one or two feeble attempts at a ride, gave it up, walked down hill and up, lifted the wagon by inches over Sebastopol, and finally arrived at McGibbet's, wet, tired, and hungry. That Sabbath-broker received us with a grim smile of satisfaction, put on the half-extinguished fire the smallest bit of wood he could find in the pile beside the hearth, and then went away with Boab to the stable. "Gloomy prospects ahead, Picton!" The traveller said never a word.

Now I wish to record here this, that there is no place, no habitation of man, however humble, that cannot be lighted up with a smile of welcome, and the good right-hand of hospitality and made cheerful as a palace hung with tile lamps of Aladdin!

McGibbet, after leading his beast to the stable, returned, and warming his wet hands at the fire, grunted out; "It rains the nicght."

"Yes," answered Picton, hastily, "rains like blue blazes: I say, get us a drop of whisky, will you?"

To this the equine replied by folding his handy one o'er the other with a saintly look. "I never keep thae thing in the house."

"Picton," said I, "if we could only unlash our luggage, I have a bottle of capital old brandy in my trunk, but it's too much trouble."

"Oh! na," quoth Robbut with a most accommodating look, "it will be nae trouble to get to it."

"Well, then," said Picton, "look sharp, will you?" and our host, with great swiftness, moved off to the wagon, and very soon returned with the trunk on his shoulder, according to directions.

"But," said I, taking out the bottle of precious fluid, "here it is, corked up tight, and what it to be done for a cork-screw?"

"I've got one," said the saint.

"I thought it was likely," quoth Picton, dryly; "look sharp, will you?"

And Robbut did look sharp, and produced the identical instrument before Picton and I had exchanged smiles. Then Robbut spread out three green tumblers on the table, and following Picton's lead, poured out a stout half-glass, at which I shouted out, "Hold up!" for I thought he was filling the tumbler for my benefit. It proved to be a mistake; Robbut stopped for a moment, but instantly recovering himself, covered the tumbler with his four fingers, and, to use a Western phrase, "got outside of the contents quicker than lightning." Then he brought from his bed-room a coarse sort of worsted horse-blanket, and with a "Ye'll may-be like to sleep an hour or twa?" threw down his family-quilt and retired to the arms of Mrs. McG. Picton gave a great crunching blow with his boot-heel at the back-stick, and laid on a good supply of fuel. We were wet through and through, but we wrapped ourselves in our travelling blankets like a brace of clansmen in their plaids, put our feet toward the niggardly blaze, and were soon bound and clasped with sleep.

At two o'clock our host roused us from our hard bed, and after a stretch, to get the stiffness out of joints and muscles, we took leave of the Presbyterian quarters. The day was just dawning: at this early hour, lake and hill-side, tree and thicket, were barely visible in the grey twilight. The wagon, with its pyramid of luggage, mowed off in the rain, McGibbet walking beside Boab, and Picton and I following after, with all the gravity of chief mourners at a funeral. To give some idea of the road we were upon, let it be understood, it had once been an old *French* military road, which, after the destruction of the fortress of Louisburgh, had been abandoned to the British Government and the elements. As a consequence, it was embroidered with the ruts and gullies of a century, the washing of rain, and the track of wagons; howbeit, the only traverse upon it in later years were the wagon of McGibbet and the saddle-horse of the post-rider. "Get-Along" had a population of seven hundred Scotch Presbyters, and therefore it will be easy to understand the condition of its turnpike.

Up hill and down hill, through slough and o'er rock, we trudged, for mile after mile. Sometimes, beside Get-Along Lake, with its grey, spectral islands and woodlands; sometimes by rushing brooms and dreary farm-fields; now in paths close set with evergreens; now in more open grounds, skirted with hills and dotted with silent, two-penny cottages. Sometimes Picton mounted his pyramid of trunk-leather for a mile or so of nods; sometimes I essayed the high perch, and holding on by a cord, dropped off in a moment's forgetfulness, with the constant fear of waking up in a mud-hole, or under the wagon-wheels. But even these respites were brief. It is not easy to ride up hill and down by rock and rut, under such conditions. We were very soon convinced it was best to leave the wagon to its load of sole-leather, and walk through the mud to Sydney. After mouldy Halifax and war-torn Louisburgh the little town of Sydney is a pleasant rural picture. Everybody has heard of the Sydney coal-mines: we expected to find the miner's finger-marks everywhere; but instead of the smoky, sulphurous atmosphere, and the black road, and the sulky, grimy, brick tenements, we were surprised with clean, white, picket-fences;

and green lawns, and clever, little cottages, nestled in shrubbery and clover. The mines are over the bay, five miles from South Sydney. Slowly we dragged on, until we came to a sleepy little one-story inn, with supernatural dormer windows rising out of the roof, before which Boab stopped. We paid McGibbet's kirk-fine, wagon-fare, and his unconscionable charge for his conscience, without parleying with him; we were too sleepy to indulge in the luxury of a monetary skirmish. A pretty, red-cheeked chamber maid, with lovely drooping eyes, showed us to our rooms; it was yet very early in the morning; we were almost ashamed to get into bed with such dazzling white sheets after the dark-brown accommodations of the "Balaklava;" but we did get in, and slept; oh! how sweetly! until breakfast at one!

"Twenty-four miles of such foot-travel will do pretty well for an invalid, eh, Picton?"

"All serene?" quoth the traveller, interrogatively.

"Feel as well as ever I did in my life," said I, with great satisfaction.

"Then let's have a bath," and, at Picton's summons, the chambermaid brought up in our rooms two little tubs of fair water, and a small pile of fat, white napkins. The bathing over, and the outer men new clad, "from top to toe," down we went to the cosy parlor to breakfast; and such a breakfast!

I tell you, my kind and gentle friend; *you*, who are now reading this paragraph, that here, as in all other parts of the world, there are a great many kinds of people; only that here, in Nova Scotia the difference is in spots, not in individuals. And I will venture to say to those philanthropists who are eternally preaching "of the masses," and "to the masses," that here "masses" can be found—concrete "masses," not yet individualized: as ready to jump after a leader as a flock of sheep after a bell-wether; only that at every interval of five or ten miles between place and place in Nova Scotia, they are apt to jump in contrary directions. There are Scotch Nova Scotians even in Sydney. Otherwise the place is marvellously pleasant.

ZANE GREY

S NOBS dismiss Zane Grey (1875-1939) as a writer of Westerns of
no literary consequence. They are wrong to do so. While his is
certainly no threat to the positions of James Joyce or Gustave
Flaubert in the pantheon of authors, Zane Grey is, nonetheless, a
writer whose books have remained in print for almost a century. He
is also a writer who has been and continues to be read by millions of
people—a feat no writer of mere ephemera could hope to attain.

Technically, he made several innovations in the genre of the
Western. With *The Light of the Western Stars*, for example, he
became the first author to tell a Western from the woman's perspective. And from their first creation his novels, while never forgetting
that their first obligation was to plot, showed an almost modern
respect for the mystical power of Nature. Given, then, the bear-trap
strong connection between his name and the Western novel, many
readers are surprised to discover that his finest prose is set, not in the
dusty plains of cowboys and tumbleweed, but in the game-fishing
waters of Nova Scotia.

Grey was born in Zanesville, Ohio and dreamed of becoming a
writer from his earliest days as a boy angling in nearby streams.
However, the impulse to get what has been termed "a real job" led
him to study dentistry and open a practice in New York. His earliest
books, feeble counterfeits of Cooper's Leatherstocking tales, sold
poorly. It was not until he made his first visit to the West in 1907

(to Arizona—by horse for much of the distance) that the possibilities of writing about that region of America became evident. Months later, he returned to New York, and wrote both documentary accounts of what he had seen, and imaginative tales about the innocent young Easterner who travels to the West and there has a rite of passage leaving him wiser, braver, better. With *Riders of the Purple Sage* (1912) he had his first bestseller, and had found a formula for his fiction which would last him a lifetime and lead to sales estimated at a heart-stopping 130 million copies.

While the formula was making him lots of money, it was susceptible to fatigue. During the Depression, for instance, sales of his new books lagged far behind those which he had written two decades before. Indeed, despite the newspaper serials and Hollywood cliffhangers based on his books, his buyers seemed increasingly to be young adults. So, in order to maintain the expensive lifestyle to which he had grown accustomed (the expense caused mainly by his fondness for hugely exorbitant fishing expeditions) he chose, much against his finer instincts, to lend his talent and his name to a comic strip featuring Sergeant King of the Royal Canadian Mounted Police.

An American talent agent named Stephen Slesinger had urged Zane Grey and his son Romer Grey to exploit the elder Grey's name and fame with a "Western" strip for the Sunday funny pages. On the understanding that he would not have to write most of the material, Zane Grey agreed. While the evidence is elusive, it would seem that it was Zane Grey rather than Slesinger who chose both the subject and the name of the subject of the comic. For example, by this time, Grey had been visiting Nova Scotia for fishing expeditions for at least twenty years, and undoubtedly had gathered a visitor's knowledge of Canadian politics. Hence, as a wry joke to be understood best by Canadians, Zane Grey named his Mountie "King" and the Mountie's boss was named "McKenzie". William Lyon Mackenzie King, known usually as just "Mackenzie King", had been, and would again be the Prime Minister of Canada for much of Grey's adult life.

The goodly Mountie created by Zane Grey made his first appearance on February 17, 1935 as a Sunday colour strip for King Features

Zane Grey wrote the narrative outline for the first adventure of *King of the Royal Mounted* (February 1935), and lent his name to this comic strip. Initially King ran only in the funny pages of the Sunday newspapers throughout North America. He proved so successful so quickly that a daily strip (in black and white) of his exploits was soon added by most newspapers. The strip endured for two decades in both formats, and inspired a popular series of Big Little Books for the young adult market and a series of comic books, of which this is a typical cover.

Syndicate. He proved so popular so quickly that a daily strip was added in March 1936. The series lasted until March 1955. Although Zane Grey may have written the complete text for only the first adventure, he is believed to have created the plots for all of these Mountie comics, leaving the writing of the dialogue for the remaining episodes to his son, Romer.

Canada is the setting for all of Sergeant King's escapades. While the tales were supposed to be contemporary (in one episode King foils the nefarious plans of a Nazi U-Boat off the coast of British Columbia) the unrolling of the action in places such as the Yukon or the Saskatchewan prairies gave the impression that the noble hero was a man from an earlier, nobler age, when men were men, and good and bad were clearly defined.

The Mountie, the Canadian settings, and the poverty of "his" writing in *King of the Royal Mounted* were all new for Zane Grey, but apart from their place in the history of comics and their slight value as amusing *divertissements* for Canadians, the Canadian strips are not the Canadian publications for which Zane Grey should be remembered. More commendable, as least as far as the quality of the writing is concerned, is his only short story set entirely in Canada. "The Great Slave" was published in his *Tappan's Burro And Other Stories* (1923) and relates the story of the founding of a tribe of Indians in northern Alberta and the Great Slave Lake region of the Northwest Territories. Contemporary critics may find the story insufferably patronizing but given the era of its genesis the tale is sympathetic if not empathetic with the native view. The following brief extract tells of a young chief's first use of a rifle. The paragraphs betray both the strengths and weaknesses of the story: there is fine natural description, obviously inspired by the author's researches from his own hunting trips; but there is also a sense of natives as noble savages, Greek gods with but a darker complexion:

> Siena stood alone upon the bank, the wonderful shooting stick
> in his hands, and the wail of his frightened mother in his ears.
> He comforted her, telling her the white men were gone, that he

was safe, and that the prophecy of his birth had at last begun its fulfillment. He carried the precious ammunition to a safe-hiding place in a hollow log near his wigwam and then he plunged into the forest.

Siena bent his course toward the runways of the moose. He walked in a kind of dream, for he both feared and believed. Soon the glimmer of water-splashes and widening ripples, caused him to crawl stealthily through the ferns and grasses to the border of a pond. The familiar hum of flies told him of the location of his quarry. The moose had taken to the water, driven by the swarms of black flies, and were standing neck deep, lifting their muzzles to feed on the drooping poplar branches. Their wide-spreading antlers, tipped back into the water, made the ripples.

Trembling as never before, Siena sank behind a log. He was within fifty paces of the moose. How often in that very spot had he strung a feathered arrow and shot it vainly! But now he had the white man's weapon, charged with lightning and thunder. Just then the poplars parted above the shore, disclosing a bull in the act of stepping down. He tossed his antlered head at the cloud of humming flies, then stopped, lifting his nose to scent the wind.

"Naza!" whispered Siena in his swelling throat.

He rested the shooting stick on the log and tried to see over the brown barrel. But his eyes were dim. Again he whispered a prayer to Naza. His sight cleared, his shaking arms stilled, and with his soul waiting, hoping, doubting, he aimed and pulled the trigger.

Boom!

High the moose flung his ponderous head, to crash down upon his knees, to roll in the water and churn a bloody foam, and then lie still.

"Siena! Siena!"

Shrill the young chief's exultant yell pealed over the listening waters, piercing the still forest, to ring back in echo from Old Stoneface. It was Siena's triumphant call to his forefathers, watching him from the silence.

The herd of moose plowed out of the pond and crashed into the woods, where, long after they had disappeared, their antlers could be heard cracking the saplings.

But far beyond this romantic Western material, it is his descriptions of game-fishing in Canada for which Zane Grey deserves attention, and a wider readership beyond those who are subscribers to *Field and Stream*.

As his wealth increased, so too did Grey's ability to indulge his fishing mania. His first trip abroad seems to have been in 1913 when he and his brother, in the company of a renowned American sportfisherman, travelled to Nova Scotia to sport-fish the banks along the Canadian coast. Not long after this voyage, Grey wrote that his attraction to fishing was less for the thrill of the kill and much more for the transcendental communion he was allowed to have with the sea:

> As a man and a writer who is forever learning, fishing ... is tempered by an understanding of the nature of primitive man, hidden in all of us, and by a keen reluctance to deal pain to any creature. The sea and the river and the mountain have almost taught me not to kill except for the urgent needs of life.

Such ethereal thinking, however, did not stop him from fishing for large game all over the world; he haunted the best waters of the Caribbean, Pacific, Indian Ocean, New Zealand and Australia looking for ever larger trophies, ever more difficult species.

One of his stops was in British Columbia. In the late summer of 1919 he finally yielded to temptation: "For more years than I can remember I [had] been hearing wonderful fish stories about Campbell River, Vancouver Island." Accompanied by his brother and a fishing buddy, Zane Grey, travelling from Vancouver to Nanaimo ("a quaint little old English town"), slowly worked his way to the then very remote fishing camp at Campbell River. While en route he noted with revulsion the clear-cutting of forests and wrote later,

"Everywhere were blackened burned-over timber slashes hideous to me." Closer to his destination, he began to relish the change in terrain:

> The forest was magnificent, the richest, greenest, most verdant I had ever seen. The cedars and firs, massive and straight, stood far apart, and towered over the jungle of underbrush which consisted largely of broad-leaved maples. It seemed impenetrable. How wet and glistening and darkly green! This was a country of rain, of fertility. Vines and creepers matted the underbrush.
>
> In the heart of this woodland, a few miles up from the settlement, the Campbell River plunged into a canyon, making a waterfall that matched the beauty of the surroundings.

Grey found the fishing for tyee salmon to be challenging but not sublime. In fact, he seems to have found the water more forbidding than its inhabitants:

> One of the most striking features at Campbell River was the sound of the water out in the channel. It must have been a rip tide. All I could see was a roughened line of tiny whitecaps. But the sound was menacing. It did not resemble the moaning of the sea across a bar, nor the low sullen roar of river rapids, but it gave me a deep and haunting thrill. Nearly all the time, and especially at night, I was aware of this strange, weird murmur of chafing waters. It held a cold note of the northland. It suggested the contending tides of the dark green Arctic seas. Not a welcome sound for any angler!

At the conclusion of his account of this trip, Grey gave his opinion of the tyee, a "great northern fish. He is a magnificent, versatile fighter, strong, fast and enduring." This last word gave him pause however, for with uncanny prescience, Grey predicted the decline of Pacific salmon stocks at the hands of unscrupulous commercial fishermen using nets: "But I should add—the tyee, unless the netting is stopped, will soon be a memory. Like the sockeye, he is fast disappearing in the track of commercialism."

As his knowledge of fishing increased, he shared his learning and observations with his readers, penning more than one hundred informed articles for various periodicals, several of the articles forming the bases for his nine substantial books on the subject of angling. Of fellow scribblers, he could count the discerning Ernest Hemingway among the fans of his piscatorial writing. By 1929, Zane Grey was widely regarded as the finest fisherman on the planet, for in that year alone he held eleven world records. He later received what is perhaps the ultimate accolade for the compleat angler: marine biologists, in his honour, gave his name to a Linnaean designation for a species of sailfish: *Isiophorus greyi*.

Yet it was to Nova Scotia that he returned more than any other foreign fishing spot. Indeed, his visits seem to have been almost annual from 1913 onwards. The most significant visit took place in 1924 when he chose, for the first time, to fish for one of the strongest animals in the sea: the giant tuna.

On an earlier trip, he had met Captain Laurie Mitchell, an English immigrant to Canada and expert guide, and the two men became friends for life. It was Mitchell who whetted Grey's appetite for the relatively new sport of tuna fishing, and Mitchell who alerted Grey to the imminent sale of a Lunenberg schooner that Grey had admired for years. The boat was no dory: from bow to stern she was almost two hundred feet, with a beam of thirty-five feet and three huge masts. Grey bought her instantly, had her fittings modernized, and then he re-christened her *Fisherman*. For five years he sailed the world's oceans in this boat, but the formidable running costs were too much even for an author as wealthy as he, and five years later, he sold her with regret.

Zane Grey's account of his 1924 tuna expedition makes compelling reading even for those who would rather watch a faucet drip than dangle a fishhook in water. In the following excerpt, Zane Grey describes his preparations for the tuna hunt, accompanied by his son, Romer, and by his brother, known affectionately by the initials

R.C. This excerpt omits the descriptions of tuna hooked but not landed, but ends with Grey's riveting account of his capture of the largest fish ever landed, to that time, by rod and reel alone.

Some sense of the thrill that these waters held for Grey can be had by noting his description of his first sight of a giant tuna in the waters of Nova Scotia: "Of all the fish sights I had ever seen, this one was the greatest."

---

from TALES OF
SWORDFISH AND TUNA

It seemed a far cry from Avalon, California, to Liverpool, Nova Scotia. And at the beginning of the best swordfish time on the Pacific, to leave for the doubtful pursuit of giant tuna off the Atlantic coast was something extremely hard to do. Had I not made plans a year ahead, I probably would have taken the easy course of postponement...

An angler should not mind the discomforts of travel, weather, and crowds, but while these things are omnipresent, he has to think pretty hard of clear swift shady streams and limpid lakes and the cool heaving sea in order to convince himself that he is a rational being.

My plans of several years' development and a year of fixed purpose made it impossible to give up this Nova Scotia trip or regard it in any way except with thrilling zest.

Captain Laurie Mitchell of Liverpool, Nova Scotia, had inspired me to this undertaking. He had fought between fifty and sixty of these giant tuna, and had succeeded in catching one, the largest on record, seven hundred and ten pounds. This fish dragged him nine miles out to sea, and halfway back. It measured ten-and-one-half feet and was as large round as a barrel. J.K.L. Ross, another Canadian angler, who lives at St. Ann's Bay, has caught several of these great mackerel, all from four to six hundred pounds in weight. He, too, has lost at least seventy-five. Two others of these fish have been caught by an English angler, Mitchell Henry; and these few comprise the total that have ever been landed.

The game was a new one, with no very satisfactory method of pursuing it yet devised. Its possibilities seemed most remarkable. Its difficulties appeared almost as insurmountable as broadbill swordfishing, though a great difference existed between these two strenuous types of angling.

I determined to go as fully equipped as was possible, and to try out the Nova Scotia method of fishing from a skiff, and also what I called a mixture of Florida and California methods....

At Yarmouth we encountered heavy fog, and to me it was like meeting an old friend from across the continent. Long before we ran into this lowering silver bank of fog I could smell it. Probably all fogs are alike. Surely they are all cool, wet, silent, strange, mysterious; and they hide everything from the sight of man. It is a fear-inspiring sensation to go driving over the sea through a dense fog. The foghorns, the whistles, the bell buoys all have a thrilling, menacing sound.

Here we disembarked and took a train, without being able to see what the port looked like. Some ten miles on we ran out of the fog into bright sunshine, and I found the Province of Nova Scotia to be truly of the northland, green and verdant and wild, dotted with lakes and areas of huge gray rocks, and low black ranges covered with spruce, and rivers of dark clear water.

As we progressed these characteristics enhanced. What welcome relief to eyes seared by sight of barren desert and hot cities! The long grass, the wild flowers, the dense thickets of spruce, the endless miles of green were a soothing balm.

Liverpool proved to be six hours' journey from Yarmouth, and turned out to be the very prettiest little town I ever visited. The houses were quaint and of an architecture unfamiliar to me, very inviting to further attention. Everywhere were huge trees, maples, ash, locusts, and they graced ample yards of luxuriant green. A beautiful river ran through the town, and picturesque fishing smacks lined its shores.

We were met by Captain Mitchell, and also my two boatmen, who had come on in advance. My party included my brother R.C. and my boy Romer and an Arizonian named Jess Smith. Out of these three I hoped to have a good deal of fun, besides the considerable help they could give.

We spent that afternoon unpacking our innumerable bags and grips and in trying out the Florida launch on the river. Bob King and Sid Boerstler, mv boatmen, found out a good deal that did not suit them; and as often before, their incomparable value to me manifested itself....

That evening we went down to the dock to see the native fishermen come in and unload their catch for the market. Docks are always fascinating places for me. This one appeared especially so. The brown river ran between green banks, with farms and cottages on the west side, and low rising piny hills beyond. On the town side a line of old weather-beaten storehouses stood back from the plank dock. You did not need to be told that Liverpool was a fisherman's town and very old. The scent of fish, too, was old, almost overpoweringly so. Two small schooners were tied up to the dock, the *Ena C.* and the *Una II.* What beautiful names are given to Englishwomen and flowers and boats! One of these small ships, a two-master, had a crew of six, sturdy brown seamen, clad in rubber overalls. They had been out three days and had a catch of sixteen thousand pounds, codfish, halibut, and two swordfish. I surely had a thrill at sight of the broadbills. These were small fish compared with most I had seen during June and July on the Pacific. The codfish averaged twenty to thirty pounds. They had a number of halibut, several over two hundred pounds.

This schooner, with its weather-and-service-worn appearance, its coils of heavy hand-line, its skiffs dovetailed into one another, its rope and barrels and paraphernalia scattered about on the deck, and the deep hold from which the fishermen were pitchforking cod out on the dock, and the rude pulpit built out over the bowsprit, from which swordfish were ironed—all these held great interest and curiosity for me, filling me with wonder about the exploits of these brave simple men who lived by the sea, and emphasizing again the noble and elemental nature of this ancient calling.

We inquired to find out if any tuna had been seen lately. Several weeks ago, they told us, tuna had been plentiful in the bays and inlets. They had come with the first run of herring. But none had been seen lately. The first run of herring was earlier than usual. A big season was expected. Sometime round the middle of August the great mass of herring would arrive. These were the species that spawned along this shallow Nova Scotia shore. They were larger than the present fish. The schools of tuna followed them. We were a little early.

We engaged two natives to accompany us—Pence to run the large launch, and Joe to make himself generally useful. Both men knew the coast and all the fishermen.

Next morning we were up before five, and on the water in half an hour. When we turned the corner of high land, where the quaint white lighthouse stood, and I saw down the widening bay, I was charmed. The shore lines were rugged clean boulders that merged into the dark spruce forest. As we glided down the bay I saw green and black hills rising to a considerable height, and here and there white or gray cottages shone in the sunlight. Toward the mouth of the bay we entered the zone of the nets. They were stretched all along the shore, and the bobbing floats could be seen everywhere, from a quarter to a half mile out. We discovered several traps, which were likewise nets, but operated differently from the gill-nets. These had circles and lines of corks on the surface, marking the trap, and long wings leading off to each side. Captain Mitchell explained that the fishermen had just begun to put in their traps, and that around these the tuna would come and stay, and that was where there was the best chance of hooking one.

We ran up to one boat, to which two fishermen were hauling

their gill-net. I saw herring shining in the water and being picked out of the net by the fishermen. We bought a bushel of them for chum and bait. This variety of herring was a beautiful little fish, nearly a foot long, shaped somewhat like a trout, only with smaller head, and colored brilliantly, dark green on the back, silver underneath; with sides that glowed opalescent. We proceeded along these nets, to a point opposite Western Head, a bold cape jutting out, and asked all the fishermen if they had discovered any tuna. But no one had seen any for over a week.

Then we ran outside the bay, round a picturesque lighthouse, into the ocean. I was amazed at the smooth, calm sea. R.C. and I could not believe our eyes. Was this the Atlantic? The gray old stormy sea we had fought so long? Captain Mitchell assured us that it was and that we would see many such fine days in this latitude. There was no swell. The water scarcely moved. The coast line appeared to be wonderfully indented by bays and coves and inlets, and marked by beautiful islands, dark with spruce, and bold headlands, rugged and gray. Low clouds of fog shone white in the sun. We ran through some of them, and between islands, and along the shore for fifteen miles to a place called Cherry Hill. Off this point Captain Mitchell had won his memorable fight with his 710-pound tuna. We met and talked with several net fishermen, none of whom had seen any fish that day. So we ran out a few miles, and then circled back toward Western Head. We sighted some schools of pollack feeding on the surface, but no other kind of fish. The sea remained tranquil all day, and when we entered the bay again, late in the afternoon, there was only a gentle ripple on the water. Then we ran in, and so ended our first day, August 1st.

That night we heard of tuna having been seen ten miles west, at Port Mouton, and decided to go there next day. We made the same early start. The day equaled the one before, and the shore line proved remarkably beautiful. High wooded hills, green slopes, gray rough banks, rose above the sea. We wound, at length, in between gemlike islands, where the channels were calm and clear, and the round bays like glass, and the sandy beaches burned white in the sunlight. Port Moulton was a little fishing village with gray weather-worn houses facing the sea. We landed at a dock where fishermen were unloading tons of herring. Many of these were being salted in barrels for lobster bait. It was a crude, primitive place, singularly attractive with the weather-beaten huts, boats, docks, its bronzed fishermen, its air of quaint self-sufficiency. We were told that tuna had been seen two days before off the island and eastward from the nets. There was a wreck that marked the locality. The leader of this fisherman squad talked interestingly:

"Our methods are crude," he said. "We have no money to buy proper equipment. We could do ten times as much. Herring fishing is but in its infancy. The supply is enormous and inexhaustible. The sea is a gold mine."

I agreed with him about the sea being a treasure house, but I could not believe the supply of herring inexhaustible. I had seen the bluefish, the menhaden, the mackerel, the white sea bass and alba-core, all grow scarce where once they had been abundant. Herring, however, may be different. I heard of schools twenty miles in extent. In fact, I received an impression of the marvelous fecundity and vitality of this species. The whole south shore of Nova Scotia lived by the herring.

These fishermen called the tuna by the name of albacore. That was a surprise to me, for they certainly are not albacore. Horse-mackerel and tunny are two other names, characteristic of the Jersey shore and of the Mediterranean.

We found the place to which we had been directed, off a wild and lonely shore, where the ocean boomed and a great iron steamer, bro-ken in the middle, gave grim evidence of the power of the sea in storm. The current was swift here. We anchored, and tried chum-ming for a few hours. But we raised no tuna. The wind came up strong and on the run back we sent the spray flying. The air grew chill. When the sun went under clouds I felt quite cold, despite my warm woolen clothes; and I was glad to get back.

Next day was Sunday. The Nova Scotians keep the Sabbath. They do not fish on the seventh day of the week. I am afraid they made me feel ashamed of my own lack of reverence. More and more we Americans drift away from the Church and its influence. Perhaps that is another reason for our lawlessness, our waning home life, our vanishing America. I should never forget that some of Christ's disciples were fishermen, and since then all fisher folk have been noted for their simplicity and faith. Liverpool was to awaken in me something long buried under the pagan self-absorption of life in the United States. When I was a boy I had to go to Sunday school and to church. It made me unhappy. I never could listen to the preacher. I dreamed, mostly of fields, hills and streams, of adventures that have since come true. As I grew older, and learned the joys of angling, I used to run away on Sunday afternoons. Many a time have I come home late, wet and weary after a thrilling time along river or stream, to meet with severe punishment from my outraged father. But it never cured me. I always went fishing on Sunday. It seemed the luckiest day. I do not consider it wrong. But I shall respect the custom of the Nova Scotians and stay quietly in the hotel on that day. Full well I know there will come a Sunday when the tuna will run into the bay and smash the water white....

Later we drove over to Lockeport to make inquiries there. The run of herring had slackened. The best ground at this time was between Blue Island and Western Head, and this was the place about which R.C. had been told. I was informed that a week ago one fisherman had reported a huge tuna round his net every morning. It was very tame and would just about eat out of his hand. In size it was twice as large as any seen thereabouts for some time. This was happening some six or eight miles from us, and we did not know. What an opportunity! But it seemed ungracious of me to want so much. One of an angler's weaknesses is to yearn to be in two places at the same time. I have never yet discovered any way to accomplish this. On thinking it over, however, I put this down as a natural eagerness to see more of these great tuna, and not as a dissatisfaction. The game is very hard. I would not want it otherwise. It would not be a real test of an angler to catch some of these wonderful fish without great expense, labor, discomfort, and agony.

Sunset was a flare of red and gold, herald of a fair to-morrow. During twilight I watched several nighthawks wheeling to and fro over a swale back of the wharf. The tide was low and this hollow had only a little water. Flies or gnats of some kind must have been hovering over this particular spot. The birds flitted like streaks across the shadowy space, out over the bare bank, and all around. They came within a few feet of me, so near that I could see the white spots on their drab wings. Wonderful, graceful, eerie creatures! They did not make the slightest noise as they cut the air. They darted, whirled, flitted, infinitely faster than swallows. The irregular flight was owing to their pursuit of the gnats. They would swoop low along the ground, like an arrow, then suddenly dart upward, poise an instant, and shoot on again. As a boy I had been mystified by these strange birds. In Ohio we called them bull-bats, and they greatly resembled whippoorwills.

It struck me that I had almost forgotten my propensity to wait and watch for wild creatures. But these huge giant mackerel fish had obsessed my mind. I had forgotten that we had seen three deer on our way here. They were almost yellow, viewed against the bright wet green background, and the largest deer I had ever seen. Indeed I thought, when I sighted the first one, that it was a cow moose. But when it moved, leaping across the bank, I at once recognized that it was a buck deer. The Arizona deer are a blue-gray at this season; and these red-gold species were strikingly new and beautiful to us.

Before I turned in for the night I sat awhile in the dark over by the bridge over the cut where the tide ran in and out. It was a lonely place and a quiet hour. I heard katydids up in the woods. Lonesome and weird, they reminded me of October—of the melancholy autumn nights at Lackawaxen. Then, as if this was not enough, a frog began to boom his croaky song. He seemed to be aware of the cold and that he could not much longer bemoan the death of summer.

At three-forty-five I awoke the boys. It was cold. The moon shone with a pale brightness over the bay. There was no wind. The sea swelled in calm and peaceful movement, without any wash. The morning star burned white and large in the east, and Orion showed pale by comparison.

We had our meager breakfast, and before five o'clock were on our way down the bay. Daylight came soon. The sky was softly gray, with an open space low down in the east where the blue was kindling. Presently the gray tinged to pink and then to red. All around us the broad bay gleamed mistily, like a moving jeweled medium, and the clouds in the west took on golden crowns.

At five-thirty the sun burst up over the black forest ridge, too dazzling for my gaze. It blanched the water and caused the moon to dim. I climbed up on the bow and held to the towrope. We had reached a point between Gull Rock and Blue Island where the great swells came heaving in. How wonderful to rise on them, high and higher! We would shoot down the far slope, gliding like an arrow. Those moments were full of reward. The break of day was fair, promising. Sea and land welcomed the sun. What joy there seemed in the hour, alone there on this isolated bay, seeing and feeling the everyday life of the native fisherman!

Only two boats were sighted here between the islands, and they reported few herring in the nets and no sign of tuna. We ran on round Gull Rock, out into the open sea. Here the swells lifted us seemingly on hills of sunglazed water. The surf pounded on the gray rocks. Gulls screamed and wheeled around and over us, and the snowy white-breasted gray-backed terns welcomed us as if they remembered how we had dispensed manna on the waters.

I saw seven boats between Gull Rock and Shelberne Lighthouse, but they were really beyond the mouth of the bay. We approached them. Herring showed plentifully in their nets. "They've come back," said one fisherman. Another informed us no tuna had yet been sighted. We bought our usual quantity of bait, and asked the men to wave to us if anyone saw a tuna. In one boat there were two men and a boy, a bright-faced lad, very curious about us. I asked him how the herring were running.

"Pretty good. We've got several bushel out of three nets. And we have eight more nets to pick."

"Have you seen any tuna?" I asked.

"Not yet. But yesterday there were six around our boat all the time we hauled. I hit one with an oar. He was a big fellow. I'd like to see you hook him."

I knew by the way he smiled at me that he could anticipate nothing but disaster for me.

"Well, if you see one this morning you wave your cap," I told him. "Perhaps you will have some fun watching me."

We proceeded then toward the end of the net zone, where our other boat had halted. Suddenly I saw R.C. and Captain Mitchell waving to us.

"Hook her up, Cap!" I shouted.

"Shore there's somethin' doin'," remarked Bob.

It did not take many moments for us to reach the boat. R.C. yelled and pointed. I turned to see two net-boats near at hand, and a fisherman in one of them waved to us, at the same time throwing herring overboard. Instantly a boiling swirl appeared on the water just where the herring had alighted.

"Say, did you see that?" queried Bob, turning his sharp blue glance at me.

We sped over to this boat, and Bob lifted the net-buoy out of the water and up on our bow.

"Big albacore here," said the fisherman. "He's taken two herring. I saw his head and his eye."

"Thanks for waving to us," I replied. He was a tall lean chap, dark and weather-beaten, and as he stood there in his old boat, holding the net in his hands, with fish scales shining all over his rubber clothes, I paid him a silent tribute. There is something great about fishermen who live by the sea. His boat was a low-lying launch, black with age, wet as if it had been under water. The engine box was situated in the middle. I saw scattered herring on the floor, an old oar, and a net-scoop, and several round baskets, low and flat, and ready to fall apart. All this I took in with one swift glance.

Then I threw my bait overboard, and let it drift away and sink until I could not see the end of the leader. Sid had stopped the engines. Bob was already grinding chum. I coiled fifteen feet of line on the stern, and held it in my hand, while I straddled my rod, and gazed into the beautiful green depths with fascinated eyes. I was looking to see the tuna show again. Something would happen soon, but I hardly thought I would have a bite. We all expected to see the fish come up to take one of the herring the fisherman threw out.

R.C. and Captain Mitchell and Romer stood on the deck of the other boat just outside the zone of nets, and they were observing us. The morning, the place, the situation seemed perfect for some extraordinary adventure. I felt it. Three of the fishermen's boats were near us, one just a few yards away. The men had stopped work to watch us, very curious, jovial, and with goodnatured unconcealed doubt. They thought I was in for an albacore bite—and broken tackle.

Suddenly I felt a strong slow tug. The line slipped through my hand.

"He's got it!" I called. I flashed a quick glance at R.C. He waved. His sharp eyes had seen the line pay out. All the coiled line slipped overboard. I sat down, and stripped off several yards more. It was a slow sweeping movement of line. When it straightened out I jerked with all my weight and strength. The response was a tremendous downward pull on my rod. My arms cracked. My body, braced as it was by my feet against the boat, lurched over hard. Sid had the engines roaring and the launch moving. The fishermen cheered us. My line slipped off the big reel. But it did not fly off, as in the former runs. This tuna showed no lightning-swift movements at the onset. What was worse, however, he ran straight inshore toward a net. He took about two hundred feet of line before we got going satisfactorily after him. We were not saying anything. If I had spoken I could have voiced only fears. The excitement of the strike had not left me. Besides that, I had a horrible expectancy of some sure and quick calamity.

The tuna sheered just short of the net. Probably he ran to it and turned. Then he headed toward another. In fact we were hemmed in on three sides by nets. They were all within two hundred yards.

"He'll go out to sea. Don't worry," yelled Bob.

As my tuna had headed straight for another net I could not accept Bob's optimistic assertion. The action of the fish was not slow, yet it did not compare with that of the first runs of the others. We even gained a little line. When I was about to give way to despair the tuna sheered abruptly to the right. This brought our launch toward another net—the third. We had headed back almost toward the boats and the spot where I had hooked him. Hope revived in me. He might be looking for a place to get out to sea.

As good fortune would have it this tuna made another swerve away from a net, and found the lane that led out to open water. I had to whoop.

"What'd I tell you!" shouted Bob. "He didn't want to run in them nets any more than we wanted him to."

Sid bent a beaming red face upon me. "What's your legs wabbling for?" he queried. Indeed my legs were shaking, especially the right one. My knees seemed to have no bones or muscles in them. No feeling! I had not observed this proof of unusual agitation until Sid called my attention to it. But it was an old affection, not experienced for long, and it returned with a vigor and familiarity calculated to make up for absence.

The tuna got up speed; still he did not compel us to race after him. He took a couple of hundred yards of line before we regulated our pace to his. And instead of heading out to sea he took a straight course across the mouth of East Jordan Bay. It was three or four miles wide. The nets to our left were close to Gull Rock, and we soon passed them. All seemed clear sailing now. My feelings underwent change and I felt as strong as a horse. I worked so hard that the boys expressed some little fear that I might break him off.

"No danger!" I declared. "It's the lightning-swift runs that scare me. This fellow acts different. He swims deep and doesn't change his pace. But, oh, he's heavy!"

"Reckon he's a buster," observed Bob. "Suppose you try to lead him out to sea."

Whereupon we got the tuna on our port side, and while Sid

edged the launch quarteringly out to sea I hauled strenuously on the rod. I lost line. Then we changed our course until I had recovered it, and tried over again. For all I could tell I did not budge him an inch from the bee line he had taken toward Blue Island. When we had covered three miles or more, and were slowly approaching the ragged black reefs reaching out from this island, I began to grow alarmed. Captain Mitchell and R.C., following us within hailing distance, waved and yelled for us to turn the fish out to sea.

"Turn this fish!" I yelled. "Ha! Ha!"

When we arrived within a half mile of the point of Blue Island we abandoned any hope of heading the tuna out to sea. He was well inside the reef now, and he might be turned up the bay.

"Boys, we'll take a chance," I decided. "If he means to go for the rocks we'll have it out with him."

Bob shook his head dubiously. He was plainly worried. Sid showed more signs of perturbation. This magnificent tuna fishing had some features not calculated to be good for one's heart.

"Run up on him," I ordered.

We closed in on the fish, and I hauled and reeled in line until we were perhaps less than two hundred feet from him. Then I shut down on the drag and set determinedly to the task ahead. The setting of this angling adventure was something on a tremendous scale, consistent with the nature of this giant tuna fighting. The south side of Blue Island showed its naked black teeth wreathed in white. Already we were lifted on the ground swells that heaved us slowly and gracefully. We were riding hills of green water. Even the fear that had begun to grip me could not wholly kill my mounting exhilaration.

Bob stood in the bow, like a mariner searching ahead for reefs. He made a strong figure standing there, his sharp-cut profile expressing courage and intelligence.

"Shore we'll stay with him," he said. "I'm not worryin' aboot hittin' a reef. It's the line that bothers me. If it touches a rock—snap!"

"I'll go so far and no farther," replied Sid, stubbornly.

"But, man, you've got two engines heah, an' a boat followin'" expostulated Bob. Then they argued while I toiled on that irre-sistible tuna. I had begun to sweat, perhaps from fright as much as exertion. For it was cold sweat! But the time and place lent me more strength than I had ever possessed before. I bent the big Murphy hickory double. I put arms, shoulders, back, and weight, with all the bracing power in my legs, into united effort to work slowly up to my limit. No sudden violence would have changed that fish. It would only have broken the tackle. My plan was to keep at him slowly and hard, all the time.

When we were a quarter of a mile off the end of the island, with my tuna heading straight in, the situation narrowed down to the cli-max. I had no thought then of the dramatic side of it. But I was filled with emotions freed by this struggle and the hazard, and the physical things impossible not to see and hear and feel.

Blue Island seemed a mountain, green on top, black at the sea line, a bleak jagged precipitous shore against which the great swells burst ponderously. The white spray shot high. I saw the green swells rise out of the calm sea and move in with majestic regularity, to crash and boom into white seething ruin. Then the water falling and run-ning back off the rocks sounded like the rapids of a river. The feel of the sea under me was something at that moment to take heed of. If I had not been hooked to what must be a gigantic tuna, I would have grown panic-stricken.

"So far and no farther!" called out Sid.

"You'll do as I tell you," I replied, sharply.

"All right. If we smash it won't be my fault. I can swim!" he said.

"Swim! It'd sure do you a lot of good heah," retorted Bob. "But I'm tellin' you we're safe. The big boat is just behind. Captain Mitchell is out in the skiff. Let's stay with this son-of-a-gun. He must be some fish!"

"Boys, I feel him slowing up," I called out, eagerly. "He's bumped into the bottom."

"Work all the harder then," advised Bob.

I gazed behind me to see Captain Mitchell perhaps a hundred feet from us, and beyond him the big launch rode the swells. R.C.

stood in the bow. Romer waved from the deck. I could hear his shrill wild cry above the roar of the surf. Whatever else the moment held, it surely was full of stinging excitement.

We reached a point perhaps a hundred yards from the shore. It seemed closer because of the thunder of water and the looming rocks. The reef on the point stood out to our right, beyond us. Far to our left another reef extended out. Low, sharp, ugly rocks showed at times, cutting the white water.

"It's now or never," I yelled to the boys. "This is no fun. But we're in it. Now let's do the right thing, and still hang.... Sid, edge her off a little. We'll head him out of here or break him off."

Still I did not mean to break the tuna off. I could trust that line so long as it did not touch a rock. Putting on the small drag, something I had never done before and screwing the larger one tighter, I increased my exertions. I determined to turn that tuna. Somehow I had not shared the opinion of the boys that the fish had gone inshore to cut off on the rocks. I pulled until at the end of every sweep I saw red. Gradually the line slipped off the reel. Gradually the launch worked her bow out from the shore. Gradually the tuna responded to the great strain put upon him. Of course the elastic rod and the perfect reel saved the line from parting. It slipped off the drags just short of the breaking point. All I had ever learned in swordfishing, about the limit of tackle strength and the conserving of muscular force, came into play here. Had I not had such long experience the task here would have been hopeless. It was a terrific fight. We dared not go any closer to where the swells smashed in green-white mounds on the rocks. I did not seem to be conscious of weakness, but I was of strain. Never had I subjected my body to such concerted and sustained effort. When I heard Bob yelling I knew we were turning the fish, though I could not hear what he said. The roar was almost deafening. Our launch glided and rose, glided on and fell, with easy motion. The violence of the seas was all inshore. Across my taut line, that sang like a telephone wire in cold wind, I saw the notched noses of the black rocks, the white seething rise and fall of foamy waves, the angry curl and break, the short spurts of water. Beyond the reef tumbled the breakers along the inside of the island. Never had a given point in my angling experiences seemed so unattainable. Only a few hundred yards! How slowly we moved! Could I last it out? I had begun that climax of this part of the fight within two hundred feet of my fish. As I worked I had lost line until over seven hundred feet were off the reel. The more feet out the more pressure on the line! It looked like a wet fiddle string and it twanged off my thumb and flipped a fine spray into my face. But hopeful indications were not wanting. The launch was not outside the danger zone, beyond the end of the reef, even if we ran straight. But the tuna had been turned broadside to the shore. That sustained me. What I had gained I would not surrender. I held to that slow, ponderous, terrific regularity of heave and wind. My sight grew dim. My heart seemed about to crack. My breast labored. My back had no sensation. I could no longer feel the bind of the leather harness.

There seems no limit to human endurance. Always I could hang on a moment longer. And I held on until my tuna rounded the end of the reef. Bob whooped the glorious news. Then I released the drags and lowered my rod to rest on the barrel of bait in front of me. Bob had stacked cushions on it. What unutterable relief! I seemed numb all over. I heard the line running off the reel, and also the accelerated working of the engines.

"Careful—slow—till I—get my breath," I panted.

"Shore. Let him have line. He's runnin' to his funeral now," shouted Bob.

The din of the surf subsided. Where dark rocks and white waves had obstructed my vision I now saw with clearing sight the wide shining waters of the bay and the beautiful forested shore line. My tuna took four hundred yards of line, with our launch going fairly fast, while I was recovering myself. Then I approached further work gradually. In half an hour I had all the line we wanted back on the reel, and we were four miles farther up the bay.

Here the large boat, with R.C. and Romer and Captain Mitchell gayly industrious with cameras of all kinds, cruised round us and up alongside.

"Must be a whopper!" yelled Romer. "Don't work too hard, Dad. Don't let him get away. Don't give him any rest."

Impossible as it was to follow so much varied advice, it struck me as being sound. I recovered surprisingly, considering the effort I had made, and soon got down to hard work again. This tuna had somehow inspired me with a conviction that he was bigger than the others. I must not spare anything. How strange it was to feel him at the end of my line, to know he was monstrous, almost unconquerable, to realize that he was indeed a tuna, though I had not had one glimpse of him. He swam deep. He never made a wave on the surface. While I fought him to the best of my reduced strength he towed the launch. Oftener and oftener Sid threw out the clutches. Then he shut off one engine entirely.

"Shore that'll take the sap out of him," declared Bob.

We seemed to be a ruthless combination of skill, cunning, experience, and strength, equipped with special instruments, all for the destruction of that poor luckless tuna. The incongruity, the unfairness of it struck me keenly. Why did I do this sort of thing? I could not answer then any more than at other times when the vexatious problem had presented itself—always at the extreme moments of the struggle. Afterward, when I asked myself the same queries, I could answer them to my satisfaction. But just then the sport seemed inhuman and unjustifiable. The psychological changes an angler goes through while fighting a fish adversary vastly his superior, the capture of which seems a vital thrilling need, are varied and extreme, some swift as flashes of emotion, and others long drawn out and compelling.

"That's a big fish," observed Bob for the twentieth time. He said it meditatively and seriously, as if talking only to himself. Bob was always thinking fish.

My tuna had developed into a more important possibility than that of the first one. I was intensely curious to have a look at him and bewailed his deep-fighting temper. He crossed the bay with us, rather close to the Two Sisters, the only reefs in the upper waters of this harbor, and if he had turned in their direction we would have had more serious work cut out for us. But he passed by them and turned again toward the sea. This was eminently satisfactory. He took us back down the bay straight for Gull Rock. Three more miles of stubborn flight! When we got within a mile of the nets off the rock we all agreed that it was high time for us to contest this flight back toward the open sea. The brunt of such contest fell upon me. So we fought it out right there in that wide space of deep water, and I was the vanquished one. In the end I had to give in to him and let him tow us, while I confined my efforts to turning him from a straight course.

The bay here was as smooth as a mill pond, waved only by gentle swells. My tuna came up. What a wave he pushed ahead of him! Then he roared on the surface, showing first his sickle dorsal fin, then his black wide tail, then the blue bulge of his back, round as a huge tree trunk, and at last his magnificent head, out of the water to his eyes.

"Oh! Oh!" bawled Sid, wildly.

"Some socker!" ejaculated Bob. "I said he was a big fish."

To me he seemed enormous, supremely beautiful and unattainable. He flashed purple, bronze, silver-gold. When he went under he left a surging abyss in the water, a gurgling whirlpool. This sight again revived me. I was a new man, at least for a little while. I turned that tuna round. I pulled the launch toward him. I held him so that he towed us stern first. In short I performed, for the time being, miraculous and hitherto unknown feats of rod endurance. I would cheerfully have walked overboard into the sea for that fish. All the same, he took us gradually toward the nets.

"They don't worry me none," said Bob, seeing my growing anxiety and dismay. "We'll go under or cut through. I was afraid of nets at first. But one end of them is free. It drifts with the tides. We can go through a dozen nets. Just you hand it to that tuna and never worry aboot nets."

Nevertheless I did worry, and I worked to the extent of all left in me. If I had not been able to slow him up, turn him from side to side, I could not have found the heart to keep it up. Many times he swerved to the surface, raising a wave that thrilled me every time I saw it. It was not a wave, but a swell. Next to that the boils that rose to the surface never ceased to fascinate me. These were new in my experience. They came when he was swimming along deep, and they would rise to the surface as far as a hundred feet behind him. They were swirls, eddies, powerful circles beginning with a small radius, and spreading until they were whirlpools six feet in diameter. More than any other single detail these breaks on the surface impressed me with the extraordinary tail power of these tuna.

I got the double line over the reel—lost it—won it back again—watched it slip away once more—heaved and wound it in—again, again, again, until my thumbs stung through gloves and stalls and my wrists and arms were pierced by excruciating pains. Still I heaved on. The ring in the wire leader came out of the water and spun round. How the leader vibrated! Bob leaped on the bow and reached for it. One last supreme effort! It took all I had left. Bent and tense, with bursting heart and failing sight, I got that leader to Bob's eager hand. When the strain was released I fell back, spent and shaking, hot and wet, absolutely all in, and most assuredly conscious of the worst beating ever given to me by a fish. I was thoroughly whipped, and so exhausted that my nerve wavered.

But seeing Bob hang to the leader reinspirited me, and so roused my thrilling wonder and speculation that I forgot my pangs. Bob would not let go. The great fish rolled and soused on the surface, thumping the water heavily. He too was tired. He could just wag his tail. But the effect of that wag pulled the launch round and round. Sid was helping to make it spin by running the engines full reverse and working the wheel. The tuna had his head toward us, and he was almost within reach of a gaff. We had to back and go round with him to keep him from going under us. Bob would haul in six or eight feet of the leader, then lose it a little at a time. I stood up the better to see. The tuna rolled on his side. And then I had my most electrifying shock. He looked as wide as a door and as long as the boat. His color was a changing blaze of silver, gold, amber, purple, and green. He seemed at once frightful and lovely, fierce and pitiful, a wild creature in the last act of precious life.

Then he changed these tactics. Righting himself, he sheered ahead and with fin out of the water he began to tow the launch. I could not see plainly. But it was evident that he could not swim otherwise than in a circle. The launch was dragged round at a fairly rapid rate, as if it were at the mercy of a strong eddy. Finally the tuna pulled the leader through Bob's hands, so that he was holding by the double line.

"Let go, Bob!" I shouted. "I'll work the leader back."

"But we'll shore have that all to do over again," objected Bob.

"No matter. Let go. I know it's tough, when you had him so near."

Bob did as he was bidden, and again the issue lay between the tuna and me. If I was weaker, so was he. I held him on the double line, so that only a few inches slipped off the reel. And he towed the launch around precisely the same as when Bob had held the leader. He came up about forty feet away, a little to the right of our bow, and turned on his side. Pale green, wonderful shield-like shape! He was fast weakening, and that recalled my vanished strength. I thumbed the reel-drag tight as I dared, and with left gloved hand I held to the line. It cut through glove and burned my palm. But I held him. Strangely, we were all quiet now. We had seen him close. I could not look up to see where our other boat was, but I heard the beat of its engine and the cries of my faithful comrades. I could see only the shining oval fish-shape, sailing, gliding like a specter under the smooth surface. The bow of the boat and Bob's crouched form showed in the tail of my eye.

"That fish's a lost fawn-skin," yelled Bob. His quaint mode of speech and Southern twang had never struck me more forcibly. And I shared his conviction about the tuna. I felt that he was beaten. Letting go of the line, I set to heaving on the rod and whirling the reel. I could hold him, move him, drag him.

"Grab the leader, Bob," I shouted. "Sid, get ready to jump for the gaff."

A few powerful pulls brought the leader to Bob. He held it. The magnificent fish creature rolled and gaped on the surface. Bob drew on the leader, inch by inch at first, then, when he got the tuna coming, foot by foot, until he was close to the bow, head toward us, swimming on his side while Sid backed the boat. When I gave the word Sid threw out the clutch, leaped over the engine box, and grasping the gaff he leaned far over—and lunged back. The detachable gaff pole came loose, leaving the rope in Sid's hands, but the pole hit him hard over the head. He yelled lustily, as mad as if one of us had done it with intent. I could not see the tuna now, but I heard him begin to splash and pound, harder, faster, until the water flew above us and I could scarcely see Bob.

"Did he make a good job of it?" I yelled, fearfully.

"Shore. We got him. An' I'll have a rope round his tail in a jiffy," replied Bob.

That gave me license to sit down and let go of the rod, so suddenly a burden. The other boat came up and we were hailed and cheered. Captain Pence waved the British flag. Presently Bob had the tuna safely lassoed and tied to our stern, where the ponderous thumps from a mighty tail splashed water over me.

"Three hours an' ten minutes!" exclaimed Bob, consulting his watch.

"Seemed a year to me," I replied, but I did not tell them then how that tuna had punished me.

"Well, let's go home," spoke up Sid, brightly. "The little launch and the big tackle sure are the dope."

"Wal, where do we all come in?" drawled Bob.

It took us nearly two hours to tow our catch back up the bay to the breakwater. Every time I looked at him I was sure he grew larger in my sight. When we reached the wharf our eager comrades almost fell overboard to see that fish.

We rigged up three poles with block and tackle, and prepared to haul the tuna up on the wharf. I told Captain Mitchell that I had beaten his world record of 710 pounds. I had no way of knowing, yet somehow I felt absolutely sure of it.

"I hope you have," replied Mitchell, studying the blue-and-silver monster lying in the water.

The men had a hard time hauling the fish up, and as he came

more and more into sight his enormous size grew manifest. Moreover, for me there was something appallingly beautiful about him. At last they had him high enough to lower on the wharf. Then I was mute! I could not believe my own sight.

"What a grand tuna!" ejaculated Captain Mitchell, in heartfelt admiration and wonder. "Indeed you have beaten my record.... Old man, I congratulate you. I am honestly glad."

They all had something fine to say to me, but I could not reply. I seemed struck dumb by the bulk and beauty of that tuna. My eyes were glued to his noble proportions and his transforming colors. He was dying!, and the hues of a tuna change most and are most beautiful at that time. He was shield-shaped, very full and round, and high and long. His back glowed a deep dark purple; his side gleamed like mother-of-pearl in a lustrous light; his belly shone a silver white. The little yellow rudders on his tail moved from side to side, pathetic and reproachful reminders to me of the life and spirit that was passing. If it were possible for a man to fall in love with a fish, that was what happened to me. I hung over him, spellbound and incredulous.

"Well, I always said it was coming to you," averred R.C., and I gauged his appreciation by his tone and the significance of his words.

The native fishermen who lived near the breakwater came down to see the tuna. I was most eager to get their point of view. Frank Sears had been there for fifteen years and had been recommended to me as a man of integrity and intelligence. One of his men had fished for herring along that coast all his life. These fishermen had seen thousands of albacore, as they called the tuna. They walked round him, from one side to the other, and the more they gazed the keener were my thrills and anticipations.

"Biggest albacore I ever saw," said Sears, at length. "He's got a small head. He's all body, and big and thick clear down to his tail. We have shipped over two hundred albacore to the markets and have had hundreds in the traps and weirs. But that's the biggest I ever saw. You might fish for ten years and never see another like it."

Zane Grey, one of the best sport fishermen in the world, stands beside the giant tuna he caught by rod and reel in the waters of Nova Scotia in 1924. The fish weighed 758 pounds and at the time was considered a world record. "Of all the fish sights I had ever seen," wrote Grey, "this was the finest."

Photo courtesy of Loren Grey.

Sears's man was even more gratifying. "I can say the same. He'll go over eight hundred pounds. Fish are my business and I'm not given to overestimating.... You certainly must have caught the big one that's been seen around Western Head for a month or more."

When I exhibited my tackle to these fishermen their interest and amaze knew no bounds. They could hardly believe so huge and powerful a fish, the kind that had often smashed their boats, gone through net and weir, could have been held and subdued on that little line. In truth the thirty-nine-thread line did look small, but its strength was mighty.

My tuna was eight feet eight inches in length, six feet four inches in girth. His head measured two feet and five inches in length. Yet Sears had called his head small. He weighed 750 pounds.

Perhaps my son's remark pleased me most of all:

"Sure is some fish! Biggest ever caught on a rod, by anybody, any kind of a game fish.... And I was here to see you lick him, Dad!"

Mr. Sears signed an affidavit for me, substantiating his statements above, and Captain Mitchell wrote another for me as follows:

EAST JORDAN, NOVA SCOTIA, August 22, 1924
To ANYONE IT MAY CONCERN:

This is to certify that I was one of the eight men who saw Mr. Zane Grey's 758-pound tuna fought, landed, and weighed. It broke my record tuna weight, 710 pounds, which I have held for some years. And I confirm the statement made by Sears and the native fishermen here.

(Signed) CAPTAIN LAURIE D. MITCHELL.

That evening there was a rather pale and threatening sunset. The bay became as calm as a mill pond. But before dark a slight ripple moved from the southeast and a damp wind followed it. Then a ring appeared round the moon. We were in for more weather.

And the next day it rained. Moreover, although it rained hard all day it did not really get started until night. Then there was a deluge. We passed a most uncomfortable night....

It rained hard that night. And next day was dismal, wet, dark. Toward evening the wind increased and the rain beat. When I went to bed it was pouring. About one o'clock I was awakened by the shaking of the house and the roaring of wind. A storm had burst upon us. I could not go back to sleep. Indeed, in an hour I did not want to. The lights went out, so that the whole place was in total darkness. I lay listening to the lash of rain, the roar of wind, the crash of breaking branches and falling trees. And presently I realized that it was a hurricane. I remembered then that I had seen the dock lined by fishing smacks which had run in that day. But surely all boats and ships had not made some safe port. I knew that somewhere out there in the roaring ebony blackness mariners and fishermen were at the mercy of the elements.

I lay awake until dawn, when the fury of the storm abated. It had lasted four hours and had been the worst in my experience. When I went out I found the streets almost impassable for wires and fallen trees. Much damage had been done. I walked down to the park, where the little lighthouse stood, and there I gazed out over the bay toward the open sea.

A pale sun was rising. The black clouds were sweeping away before a shifting wind. On the reefs great combers were breaking, green and white. The cold bright Atlantic Ocean! I did not on the moment feel any love for it. It cleared off and the day became fine, with a brisk northwest breeze.

Not until next day did we learn much of what a fearful storm it had been. Then tales of wrecked ships and missing men came in, all the way from Halifax to the Bay of Fundy. That jagged shallow shore, cut like the teeth of a saw, and the fiercest driving sea seen for years, had exacted a frightful toll of loss and life. I read of several wonderful rescues by shore fishermen, one particularly filling me with awe and reverence for the single fisherman who at terrible risk of his life had saved the crew of a trawler. And it is the modern trawlers that are driving the shore fishermen out of business. How heroic, such a man! But somehow it is good to know. This storm made clearer to me the lives of these fishermen. I understood then the quiet lean faces, the pondering brows, the sad eyes, the lack of something that I might call joy of life. For them life was as hard as the relentless sea. It made them pay....

On the way back to Liverpool Bay we passed a stormbattered fishing smack, returning from the banks. She certainly showed scars of struggle with the hurricane. We learned, later, that one man had been lost overboard. Two schooners came into Lunenburg that day, with flags at half mast, and both captains reported loss of life and much damage in the worst storm of their sea experience. A number of fishing schooners had not yet been heard from. Assuredly some of them had been lost. It struck me to the heart, the tragedy of these fishermen's lives. Yet they are not hardened. They are serious seafaring folk, religious and simple in their lives, as indeed are most men who live in the open and fight the elements. I could not help but try to picture in mind the fury of the storm, the black night, and the terrible white horses of the sea, crashing over the vessels and carrying away boats, spars, and men. These heroic fishermen faced death every time they left home. And some of them had met it. Man overboard! Perhaps he was not even missed in the grim wild moment. But he knew! When he was swept away into the black night, on the crest of a crashing wave, he knew his doom. How tremendous and sickening to think of, and yet how splendid! He was washed overboard. He would swim and fight for his life, as a brave man, when all the time he would know. Surely he would pray. There would be thought of home, wife, children.... And then—!

On Sunday morning I arose early and went out for a walk. It was a quiet, peaceful, beautiful morning. The streets were deserted. Not a sign of life! I walked to the park at the end of the street, and sat near the lighthouse, facing down the bay.

At once I was struck with the remarkable tranquillity and repose of the scene. Never had I seen such an unruffled surface of water. It was like silk. Only at the shoals near the beach did any motion show, and that was a gentle, almost indistinguishable swell. The bay shone a dark pearl-gray color, mirroring the clouds. Had it not been for the dark-green rugged shores stretching away to the east, and the lighthouse marking the headland, there would not have been any telling sea and sky apart. Not a breath of wind I How strange that seemed after the recent hurricane! It was only another mood of the inscrutable ocean. Almost I loved it then. But I could not forget. I think the ocean fascinates me, draws me, compels me, but not with love. By listening intently I caught a faint low roar of surf far outside the headlands, and then the moaning of the whistle buoy, and at last the melancholy ring of a bell buoy. The spell of the scene gripped me and was difficult to explain. There was no sign of sunrise, though the hour was long past. A pale purple bank of cloud rose above the dim horizon line. Toward the south it broke and lightened, until a clearer space shone with some hue akin to rose and pearl. The whole effect seemed one of lull before a storm, and I was reminded that another hurricane had struck off the Virgin Islands and was reported traveling north. While I sat there, watching, listening, feeling, a strong desire to return to Nova Scotia at some future time moved me to vow that I would. It was indeed a far cry from California. Nevertheless I found myself planning another trip to this land of spruce forests and rock-lined streams of amber water, to this wild storm-bound coast with its beautiful bays and coves, its thundering reefs and lonely gale-swept headlands.

NATHANIEL HAWTHORNE

THE AUTHOR of the classic novels *The Scarlet Letter* and *The House of the Seven Gables* was aesthetically engrossed by the American species of Puritan culture, and its powerful hold over the social life of his country. So, while it would be foolish to make claims that Canada played a large part in Hawthorne's imaginative life, the country did appear regularly in his correspondence, and played an uncelebrated role in both his fiction and non-fiction over several years.

As a young man, Nathaniel Hawthorne (1804-1864) made wide-ranging trips with an uncle who worked as a horse-trader, trips that, from the internal evidence of his letters home, probably included stays in Quebec. These were followed by solo trips across the north-western United States, perhaps because travel provided a means to disguise his solitary nature. His widowed mother had adopted a life of odd behaviour and unconventional seclusion, reinforcing in her son a tendency to withdrawal. He attended Bowdoin College in Brunswick, Maine where he was a classmate of Henry Wadsworth Longfellow, the poet, who was to become a lifelong friend.

After graduation, he made annual walkabouts lasting several weeks, but the documentation from his early twenties is sparse, and only with the rarest exceptions can scholars be certain as to his exact itineraries. That he may have toured parts of Canada circa 1830 might be inferred from his reading at that time. In 1829, for example, he borrowed two titles from the Salem, Massachusetts Athenaeum which are suggestive, but no more: *The Natural and Civil History of the French Dominions in North and South America* by Thomas Jefferys, and *A Journal: or Full Account of the Late Expedition to Canada* by Hovenden Walker.

We do know that he travelled to Detroit in 1830, probably taking the same Lake Erie route followed (at approximately this time) by Harriet Martineau, Captain Marryat, and William Cullen Bryant. On June 28, 1832, he wrote to a correspondent about another, aborted excursion:

> I was making preparations for a northern tour, when this accursed Cholera broke out in Canada. It was my intention to go by way of New York, and Albany to Niagara, from thence to Montreal and Quebec, and home through Vermont and New Hampshire. I am very desirous of making this journey on account of a book by which I intend to acquire an (undoubtedly) immense literary reputation, but which I cannot commence writing till I have visited Canada.

Three months later, in a letter to his mother from Vermont, he indicated a continuing desire to enter Canada, but the fear of plague dissuaded him from going to the Province of Quebec. The projected book, believed to be titled *The Itinerant Storyteller* was never completed, although small sections of it survive in manuscript.

After the adventures of 1832, he began writing stories, first published in a periodical called *The Token*, which were later collected in 1837 as *Twice-Told Tales*, his first important book. Unfortunately the collection went largely unnoticed by the public, and he spent the next decade toiling as an editor and journalist. It was as a journalist that he wrote about Canada for the first time. In the February 1835 issue of the *New England Magazine*, he published an article "My Visit to Niagara," a personal essay wherein he congratulates himself for not rushing to see the cataract upon disembarking from the train, for he was "loathe to exchange the pleasures of hope for those of memory." Thanks to a dated Niagara souvenir, we know the date of the visit which inspired this account: September 28, 1832.

Initially, Hawthorne is disappointed in the Falls, but gradually he comes to accept their wonder on their own terms rather than on his unreal expectations. It is the sight and roar of the Canadian falls, in particular, which awaken in him a sense of the glory of nature:

> The last day I was to spend at Niagara, before my departure for the far west, I sat upon Table Rock. This celebrated station did not now, as of old, project fifty feet beyond the line of the precipice, but was shattered by the fall of an immense fragment, which lay distant on the shore below. Still, on the utmost verge of the rock, with my feet hanging over it, I felt as if suspended in the open air. Never before had my mind been in such perfect unison with the scene.... But when the beholder has stood awhile, and perceives no lull in the storm, and considers that the vapor and the foam are as everlasting as the rocks which produce them, all this turmoil assumes a sort of calmness. It soothes while it awes the mind.

In 1836, Hawthorne began editing the monthly *American Magazine of Useful and Entertaining Knowledge*, and one of his first contributions of prose to the journal was an article, "An Ontario Steam-Boat," possibly the earliest description by a *litterateur* of the squalor and penury of the poorest immigrants to Canada. Hawthorne's view of these early Canadian settlers is oddly aloof and almost clinical; his descriptions of their actions and demeanour disturbingly resemble more those of a scientist neutrally describing phenomena rather than an artist depicting woe and affliction. The essay is also significant because it contains a line wherein Hawthorne laments the refusal of Canadians to feel one with Americans, a point he was to make more than once later in his life:

> The Steam-boats on the Canadian lakes, afford opportunities for a varied observation of society. In the spacious one, on board

which I had embarked at Ogdensburgh, and was voyaging westward, to the other extremity of Lake Ontario, there were three
different orders of passengers;—an aristocracy in the grand
cabin and ladies saloon; a commonalty in the forward cabin;
and, lastly, a male and female multitude on the forward deck,
constituting as veritable a Mob, as could be found in any country. These latter did not belong to that proud and independent
class among our native citizens, who chance, in the present generation, to be at the bottom of the body politic; they were the
exiles of another clime—the scum which every wind blows off
the Irish shores—the pauper-dregs which England flings out
upon America. Thus, within the precincts of our Steam-boat—
which indeed was ample enough, being about two hundred feet
from stem to stern—there were materials for studying the characteristics of different nations, and the peculiarities of different
castes. And the study was simplified, in comparison to what it
might have been in a wider sphere, by the strongly marked dis-
tinctions of rank that were constituted by the regulations of the
vessel. In our country at large, the different ranks melt and mingle into one another, so that it is as impossible to draw a decided
line between any two contiguous classes, as to divide a rainbow
accurately into its various hues. But here, the high, the middling,
and the low, had classified themselves, and the laws of the vessel
rigidly kept each inferior from stepping beyond his proper lim-
its. The mob of the deck would have infringed these immutable
laws, had they ventured abaft the wheels, or into the forward
cabin; while the honest yeomen, or other thrifty citizens, who
were the rightful occupants of that portion of the boat, would
have incurred both the rebuke of the captain and the haughty
stare of the gentry, had they thrust themselves into the department of the latter. Here, therefore, was something analogous to
that picturesque state of society, in other countries and earlier
times, when each upper class excluded every lower one from its
privileges, and when each individual was content with his allot-
ted position, because there was no possibility of bettering it.

I, by paying ten dollars instead of six or four, had entitled myself to the aristocratic privileges of our floating community. But, to confess the truth, I would as willingly have been any where else, as in the grand cabin. There was good company, assuredly;—among others, a Canadian judge, with his two daughters, whose stately beauty and bright complexions made me proud to feel that they were my countrywomen; though I doubt whether these lovely girls would have acknowledged that their country was the same as mine. The inhabitants of the British provinces have not yet acquired the sentiment of brotherhood or sisterhood, towards their neighbors of the States....

The scene on the forward deck interested my mind more than any thing else that was connected with our voyage. On this occasion, it chanced that an unusual number of passengers were congregated there. All were expected to find their own provisions; several, of a somewhat more respectable rank in life, had brought their beds and bedding, all the way from England or Ireland; and for the rest, as night came on, some sort of litter was supplied by the officers of the boat. The decks, where they were to sleep, was not, it must be understood, open to the sky, but was sufficiently roofed over by the promenade-deck. On each side of the vessel was a pair of folding doors, extending between the wheels and the ladies' saloon; and when these were shut, the deck became in reality a cabin. I shall not soon forget the view which I took of it, after it had been arranged as a sleeping apartment for at least, fifty people, male and female.

A single lamp shed a dim ray over the scene, and there was also a dusky light from the boat's furnaces, which enabled me to distinguish quite as much as it was allowable to look upon, and a good deal more than it would be decorous to describe. In one corner, a bed was spread out on the deck, and a family had already taken up their night's quarters; the father and mother, with their faces turned towards each other on the pillow, were talking of their private affairs; while three or four children, whose heads protruded from the foot of the bed, were already

asleep. Others, both men and women, were putting on their
night-caps, or enveloping their heads in handkerchiefs, and laying aside their upper garments. Some were strewn at random
about the deck, as if they had dropped down, just where they
had happened to be standing. Two men, seeing nothing softer
than the oak-plank to stretch themselves upon, had sat down
back to back, and thus mutually supporting each other, were
beginning to nod. Slender girls were preparing to repose their
maiden-like forms on the wide, promiscuous couch of the deck.
A young woman, who had a babe at her bosom, but whose husband was nowhere to be seen, was wrangling with the steward
for some better accommodation than the rug which he had
assigned her. In short, to dwell no longer upon the particulars of
the scene, it was, to my unaccustomed eye, a strange and sad
one—and so much the more sad, because it seemed entirely a
matter of course, and a thing of established custom, to men,
women, and children. I know not what their habits might have
been, in their native land; but since they quitted it, these poor
people had led such a life in the steerages of the vessels, that
brought them across the Atlantic, that they probably swept
ashore, far ruder and wilder beings than they had embarked; and
afterwards, thrown homeless upon the wharves of Quebec and
Montreal, and left to wander whither they might, and subsist
how they could, it was impossible for their moral natures not to
have become woefully deranged and debased. I was grieved,
also, to discern a want of fellow-feeling among them. They
appeared, it is true, to form one community, but connected by
no other bond than that which pervades a flock of wild geese in
the sky, or a herd of wild horses in the desert. They were all
going the same way, by a sort of instinct—some laws of mutual
aid and fellowship had necessarily been established—yet each
individual was lonely and selfish. Even domestic ties did not
invariably retain their hallowed strength....

Still, the general impression that I had received from the
scene, here so slightly sketched was a very painful one. Turning

away, I ascended to the promenade deck, and there, paced to and fro, in the solitude of wild Ontario at nightfall. The steersman sat in a small square apartment, at the forward extremity of the deck; but I soon forgot his presence, and ceased to hear the voices of two or three Canadian boatmen, who were chatting French in the forecastle.

Having little luck in finding an audience for his *Tales*, and finding journalism unrewarding, Hawthorne turned to the creation of stories for children as a means of making money and placating his muse. Using the device of a fictional chair, passed on from generation to generation, Hawthorne intended to convey to children the entire history of Canada and the United States. He found the task too confining for a single volume so he produced three books in quick succession: *Grandfather's Chair* (1840); *Famous Old People* (1841); and *Liberty Tree* (1841). Unfortunately for Hawthorne, yet again, the sales were poor—primarily because his telling of history is more suited to an adult's ear than a child's. Children can grasp the main elements of his alleged juveniles, but the larger issues and the nuances escape their notice in the same way that they can only vaguely comprehend the subtext of *Gulliver's Travels*. Despite the packaging in the children's book format, the trilogy is better consumed by a grown audience.

Just two months after the publication of *Famous Old People* (which contains a brief history of the Acadians), Hawthorne went for dinner to the home of his friend Henry Wadsworth Longfellow, in the company of a man called Horace Conolly. Conolly was the first to tell Hawthorne the legend of an Acadian bride who, although long separated from her husband, spent years searching for him. Hawthorne decided, that try as he might, he could not do justice to the legend. So he exhorted Longfellow instead to deal with it in verse. Acadians, especially, are glad he did so, for the result was Longfellow's most famous poem, *Evangeline*.

By the the middle of the nineteenth century, Hawthorne's fortunes were waxing: his best novels were garnering impressive reviews and sales, and his political connections helped him to obtain the consul-generalship of Liverpool in England. The novelist, his wife, and his Boston publisher Ticknor set sail for Britain, stopping in Halifax en route. Mrs. Hawthorne described their enchantment with the city:

Steamer *Niagara*, July 8, 1853

This morning at one o'clock we left Halifax; and we are now careering on to England on a lovely summer sea, with summer air. Yesterday it was very cold. We entered the harbour of Halifax at eleven last night, and Mr. Hawthorne and Mr. Ticknor and I remained on deck to see all we could by the light of the stars and lamps. The blue lights that were burned on the prow and on shore kindled up the rigging and fine ropes in the forepart of the vessel, and against the black-blue sky they looked like spun glass, glittering and white and wholly defined.... The salute of four cannon greeted the Queen's dominions, and Mr. Ticknor said that two were for my husband. There was no fog, which is very uncommon, for the fogs usually delay the steamers in entering and leaving the harbor.... I wished to go towards the gangway of the steamer, in and out of which many people were passing (for we landed fourteen and received seventeen, I believe); and behold! my husband pressed on to the pier and on and on up into the streets of Halifax, till I was quite alarmed, and feared we should not get back. But I have really been to Halifax now! ... I was very sorry not to see Halifax by day, or at least by moonlight, though it was very picturesque by starlight and torchlight.

Hawthorne's final and without doubt most telling reference to Canada came in a letter he wrote, after he was settled again in America, to an old friend, Henry Bright of England. Writing to congratulate him on his forthcoming marriage, Hawthorne, depressed by the lurk of Civil War in the United States, wrote on December 17, 1860:

Why should not you spend the honeymoon, and a month or two more, in a trip to America? If you come soon enough, you will have the pleasure (and I know it would be a great one, to your wicked English heart) of seeing the Union in its death-throes, and of triumphing over me in revenge for all the uncivil things I used to say about England and her institutions. How queer, that the rotten old patchwork of your Constitution should be so likely to outlast all our brand-new contrivances! Well, I am ashamed to say how little I care about the matter. New England will still have her rocks and ice, and I should not wonder if we become a better and a nobler people than ever heretofore. As to the South, I never loved it. We do not belong together; the Union is unnatural, a scheme of man, not an ordinance of God; and as long as it continues, no American of either section will ever feel a genuine thrill of patriotism, such as you Englishmen feel at every breath you draw.

Don't you think England (if we petition her humbly enough) might be induced to receive the New England States back again, in our old Provincial capacity? What a triumph that would be! Or perhaps it would be a better scheme to arrange a kingdom for Prince Alfred by lumping together Canada, New England, and Nova Scotia. Those regions are almost homogeneous as regards manners and character and cannot long be kept apart, after we lose the counterbalance of our Southern States. For my part, I should be very glad to exchange the South for Canada, though I have not quite made up my mind as to the expediency of coming either under the Queen's sceptre or Prince Alfred's. But if any such arrangement takes place, I shall claim to be made a peer for having been the first to suggest it.

Meanwhile (unless you wish to see me indicted for high treason, or tarred and feathered by lynch law) it will be as well to keep these speculations secret.

The following excerpt from *Famous Old People* (1841) contains a reference to the Acadians which may have been one of Hawthorne's prods to Longfellow, urging him to write the Evangeline story in verse. The excerpt is interesting, as well, for its description of the valorous death of General Wolfe, a recounting rare among American writers of this period.

---

from FAMOUS OLD PEOPLE

Among all the events of the Old French War, Grandfather thought that there was none more interesting than the removal of the inhabitants of Acadia. From the first settlement of this ancient province of the French, in 1604, until the present time, its people could scarcely ever know what kingdom held dominion over them. They were a peaceful race, taking no delight in warfare, and caring nothing for military renown. And yet, in every war, their region was infested with iron hearted soldiers, both French and English, who fought one another for the privilege of ill treating these poor harmless Acadians. Sometimes, the treaty of peace made them subjects of one king, sometimes of another.

At the peace of 1748, Acadia had been ceded to England. But the French still claimed a large portion of it, and built forts for its defense. In 1755, those forts were taken, and the whole of Acadia was conquered, by three thousand men from Massachusetts, under the command of General Winslow. The inhabitants were accused of supplying the French with provisions, and of doing other things that violated their neutrality.

"These accusations were probably true," observed Grandfather; "for the Acadians were descended from the French, and had the same friendly feelings towards them, that the people of Massachusetts had for the English. But, their punishment was severe.

The English determined to tear these poor people from their native homes, and scatter them abroad."

The Acadians were about seven thousand in number. A considerable part of them were made prisoners, and transported to the English colonies. All their dwellings and churches were burnt, their cattle were killed, and the whole country was laid waste, so that none of them might find shelter or food in their old homes, after the departure of the English. One thousand of the prisoners were sent to Massachusetts; and Grandfather allowed his fancy to follow them thither, and tried to give his auditors an idea of their situation.

We shall call this passage of the story of

The Acadian Exiles

A sad day it was for the poor Acadians, when the armed soldiers drove them, at the point of the bayonet, down to the sea-shore. Very sad were they, likewise, while tossing upon the ocean, in the crowded transport vessels. But, methinks, it must have been sadder still, when they were landed on the Long Wharf, in Boston, and left to themselves, on a foreign strand.

Then, probably, they huddled together, and looked into one another's faces for the comfort which was not there. Hitherto, they had been confined on board of separate vessels, so that they could not tell whether their relatives and friends were prisoners along with them. But, now, at least, they could tell that many had been left behind, or transported to other regions.

Now, a desolate wife might be heard calling for her husband. He, alas! had gone, she knew not whither, or perhaps had fled into the woods of Acadia, and had now returned to weep over the ashes of their dwelling. An aged widow was crying out, in a querulous, lamentable tone, for her son, whose affectionate toil had supported her for many a year. He was not in the crowd of exiles; and what could this aged widow do, but sink down and die? Young men and maidens, whose hearts had been torn asunder by separation, had hoped, during the voyage, to meet their beloved ones at its close. Now, they began to feel that they were separated forever. And, perhaps, a lonesome little girl, a golden-haired child of five years old, the very picture of our little Alice, was weeping and wailing for her mother, and found not a soul to give her a kind word.

Oh, how many broken bonds of affection were here! Country lost!—friends lost!—their rural wealth of cottage, field and herds, all lost together! Every tie between these poor exiles and the world seemed to be cut off at once. They must have regretted that they had not died before their exile; for even the English would not have been so pitiless as to deny them graves in their native soil. The dead were happy; for they were not exiles!

While they thus stood upon the wharf, the curiosity and inquisitiveness of the New England people would naturally lead them into the midst of the poor Acadians. Prying busy-bodies thrust their heads into the circle, wherever two or three of the exiles were conversing together. How puzzled did they look, at the outlandish sound of the French tongue! There were seen the New England women, too. They had just come out of their warm, safe homes, where everything was regular and comfortable, and where their husbands and children would be with them, at night-fall. Surely, they could pity the wretched wives and mothers of Acadia! Or, did the sign of the cross, which the Acadians continually made upon their breasts, and which was abhorred by the descendants of the Puritans—did that sign exclude all pity?

Among the spectators, too, was the noisy brood of Boston school-boys, who came running, with laughter and shouts, to gaze at this crowd of oddly dressed foreigners. At first they danced and capered around them, full of merriment and mischief. But the despair of the Acadians soon had its effect upon these thoughtless lads, and melted them into tearful sympathy.

At a little distance from the throng, might be seen the wealthy and pompous merchants, whose ware-houses stood on Long Wharf. It was difficult to touch these rich men's hearts; for they had all the comforts of the world at their command; and when they walked abroad, their feelings were seldom moved, except by the roughness of the pavement, irritating their gouty toes. Leaning upon their gold headed canes, they watched the scene with an aspect of composure. But, let us hope, they distributed some of their superfluous coin among these hapless exiles, to purchase food and a night's lodging.

After standing a long time at the end of the wharf, gazing seaward, as if to catch a glimpse of their lost Acadia, the strangers began to stray into the town.

They went, we will suppose, in parties and groups, here a hundred, there a score, there ten, there three or four, who possessed some bond of unity among themselves. Here and there was one, who, utterly desolate, stole away by himself, seeking no companionship.

Whither did they go? I imagine them wandering about the streets, telling the townspeople, in outlandish, unintelligible words, that no earthly affliction ever equalled what had befallen them. Man's brotherhood with man was sufficient to make the New Englanders understand this language. The strangers wanted food. Some of them sought hospitality at the doors of the stately mansions, which then stood in the vicinity of Hanover Street and the North Square. Others were applicants at the humbler wooden tenements, where dwelt the petty shopkeepers and mechanics. Pray Heaven, that no family in Boston turned one of these poor exiles from their door! It would be a reproach upon New England—a crime worthy of heavy retribution—if the aged women and children, or even the strong men, were allowed to feel the pinch of hunger.

Perhaps some of the Acadians, in their aimless wanderings through the town, found themselves near a large brick edifice, which was fenced in from the street by an iron railing, wrought with fantastic figures. They saw a flight of red free-stone steps, ascending to a portal, above which was a balcony and balustrade. Misery and desolation give men the right of free passage everywhere. Let us suppose, then, that they mounted the flight of steps, and passed into the Province House. Making their way into one of the apartments, they beheld a richly clad gentleman, seated in a stately chair, with gilding upon the carved work of its back, and a gilded lion's head at the summit. This was Governor Shirley, meditating upon matters of war and state, in Grandfather's chair!

If such an incident did happen, Shirley, reflecting what a ruin of peaceful and humble hopes had been wrought by the cold policy of the statesman, and the iron hand of the warrior, might have drawn a deep moral from it. It should have taught him that the poor man's hearth is sacred, and that armies and nations have no right to violate it. It should have made him feel, that England's triumph, and increased dominion, could not compensate to mankind, nor atone to Heaven, for the ashes of a single Acadian cottage. But it is not thus that statesmen and warriors moralize....

"Alas..." said Grandfather, "the exiles grew old in the British provinces, and never saw Acadia again. Their descendants remain among us, to this day. They have forgotten the language of their ancestors, and probably retain no tradition of their misfortunes. But, methinks, if I were an American poet, I would choose Acadia for the subject of my song."

And now, having thrown a gentle gloom around the Thanksgiving fireside, by a story that made the children feel the blessing of a secure and peaceful hearth, Grandfather put off the other events of the Old French War till the next evening.

Accordingly, in the twilight of the succeeding eve, when the red beams of the fire were dancing upon the wall, the children besought Grandfather to tell them what had next happened to the old chair....

As Grandfather's chair had no locomotive properties, and did not even run on castors, it cannot be supposed to have marched in person to the Old French War.

... in 1759, Sir Jeffrey Amherst was appointed commander-in-chief of all the British forces in America. He was a man of ability, and a skillful soldier. A plan was now formed for accomplishing that object, which had so long been the darling wish of the New Englanders, and which their fathers had so many times attempted. This was the conquest of Canada.

Three separate armies were to enter Canada from different quarters. One of the three, commanded by General Prideaux, was to embark on Lake Ontario, and proceed to Montreal. The second, at the head of which was Sir Jeffrey Amherst himself, was destined to reach the river St. Lawrence, by the way of Lake Champlain, and then go down the river to meet the third army. This last, led by General Wolfe, was to enter the St. Lawrence from the sea, and ascend the river to Quebec. It is to Wolfe and his army that England owes one of the most splendid triumphs, ever written in her history.

Grandfather described the siege of Quebec, and told how Wolfe led his soldiers up a rugged and lofty precipice, that rose from the shore of the river to the plain, on which the city stood. This bold adventure was achieved in the darkness of night. At day-break, tidings were carried to the Marquis de Montcalm, that the English army was waiting to give him battle on the plains of Abraham. This brave French general ordered his drums to strike up, and immediately marched to encounter Wolfe.

He marched to his own death. The battle was the most fierce and terrible, that had ever been fought in America. General Wolfe was at the head of his soldiers, all while encouraging them onward, received a mortal wound. He reclined against a stone, in the agonies of death; but it seemed as if his spirit could not pass away, while the fight yet raged so doubtfully. Suddenly, a shout came pealing across the battle-field—"They flee! they flee!"—and, for a moment, Wolfe lifted his languid head "Who flee?" he inquired. "The French," replied an officer. "Then I die satisfied!" said Wolfe, and expired in the arms of victory.

"If ever a warrior's death were glorious, Wolfe's was so!" said Grandfather; and his eye kindled, though he was a man of peaceful thoughts, and gentle spirit. "His life-blood streamed, to baptize the soil which he had added to the dominion of Britain! His dying breath was mingled with his army's shout of victory!"

"Oh, it was a good death to die!" cried Charley, with glistening eyes.

"Was it not a good death, Lawrence?"

Lawrence made no reply; for his heart burned within him, as the picture of Wolfe, dying on the blood-stained field of victory, arose to his imagination; and yet, he had a deep inward consciousness, that, after all, there was a truer glory than could thus be won.

"There were other battles in Canada, after Wolfe's victory," resumed Grandfather; "But we may consider the Old French War as having terminated with this great event. The treaty of peace, however, was not signed until 1763. The terms of the treaty were very disadvantageous to the French; for all Canada, and all Acadia, and the Island of Cape Breton, in short, all the territories that France and England had been fighting about, for nearly a hundred years—were surrendered to the English."

"So, now, at last," said Lawrence, "New England had gained her wish. Canada was taken!"

"And now there was nobody to fight with, but the Indians," said Charley.

WILLIAM COBBETT

T O DESCRIBE William Cobbett (c. 1762-1835) as principally a journalist is to be factually accurate, and yet wildly off the mark, for he was one of the greatest pamphleteers in the history of the language, a curmudgeonly exposer of pretense, a holder of political opinion as firm as a pendulum, and a life-long enemy of establishment bunk. At a time when the Romantics held sway in Britain, he produced English prose of such muscularity that it swaggered like a well-built lifeguard, proud of its own vigour. It is salient to remember that for G.K. Chesterton Cobbett was "the noblest English example of the noble calling of the agitator," and that Carlyle classed Cobbett's writing with Walter Scott's:

> Cobbett also as the John Bull of his country, strong as the rhinoceros, and with singular humanities and genialities shining through his thick skin, is a most brave phenomenon. So bounteous was nature to us when British literature lay all sprawling in Werterism, Byronism, and other sentimentalism, tearful or spasmodic nature was kind enough to send us two healthy men, of whom she might still say not without pride, "These also were made in England: Such limbs do I still make there."

By his own account, Cobbett ran away from his farming home in England to join the army. A year later, in 1785, he arrived with his regiment (the Fifty-fourth of Foot) in Halifax, Nova Scotia, a vision of horror he describes with especial relish:

> When I first beheld the barren, not to say hideous, rocks at the entrance of the Harbour, I began to fear that the master of the vessel had mistaken his way; for I could perceive nothing of that fertility that my good recruiting Captain had dwelt on with so much delight.
>
> Nova Scotia had no other charm for me than that of novelty. Every thing I saw was new: bog, rocks and stumps, mosquitos and bull-frogs. Thousands of captains and colonels without soldiers, and of squires without stockings or shoes.

Within a few weeks of arrival, the newly-arrived soldiers moved to New Brunswick where they were charged with the relatively light task of guarding the boundary between Canada and America. Fond of righteously dispensing unsolicited advice to the young, Cobbett, in his *Emigrant's Guide*, talked of his early Canadian years as if he were Adam toiling in an odd paradise:

> For I actually saw the colony of New Brunswick begun to be settled; I almost saw the axe laid to the stem of the first tree that was felled; I saw wild woods and river banks turned into settlements; I had to assist in cutting down trees, and in peeling off bark, to make sheds to live under before we had any covering other than the sky....

British North America, however, is not a destination he recommends to the emigrant. His portrayal is witheringly discouraging:

> The English colonies in North America consist of Lower and Upper Canada, New Brunswick, Nova Scotia, Newfoundland, and Prince Edward's Island. These form an immense extent of country; but with the exception of a small part of Canada, and here and there a little strip of land in New Brunswick, which

have been pre-occupied, the whole is wretchedly poor: heaps of rocks covered chiefly with fir-trees. These countries are the offal of North America.... People who know nothing of the matter frequently observe that the United States will *take* our American colonies one of these days. This would be to act the wise part of a thief, who should come and steal a stone for the pleasure of carrying it about. These miserable colonies, the whole of which do not contain, army, blacks, and all, a population equal to that of the single state of New York, are fed, with the exception of Canada, chiefly by food brought from the United States ... even green peas ... are carried from the United States to regale the petty sovereigns who strut in that country.... These are no countries to go to: a small part of Canada might become pass-able; but even there, the government and the state of dependence are such, that no sensible man will hesitate for a moment between that country and the United States.... In short, the choice lies between the country which has to send for green peas to another country, and the country in which the green peas grow: I am for the latter....

William Cobbett was clearly extraordinarily ambitious for his class, and within a year of enlisting he had been promoted to Corporal and made clerk of the regiment. Willing to do anything legal for advancement, he soon discovered that the officers were happy, as long as they won credit for the labour, to let him do most of the administrative work of the regiment, and much else besides.

He was not oblivious to the exploitation. A blatant example arose when his superiors in Canada had not bothered to institute a new drill procedure (although they had been ordered to do so). When notice was received that inspectors of the drill were presently due to arrive from Britain, the officers, desperate, called on Cobbett for assistance:

When the time came for the annual review, I, then a Corporal, had to give lectures of instruction to the officers themselves, the

Colonel not excepted, and for several of them, if not all of them, I had to make out, upon large cards which I bought for the purpose, little plans of the position of the regiment, together with lists of the words of command, which they had to give in the field…. There was I at the review … confounded in the ranks amongst other men, while those who were commanding me to move my hands or my feet, thus or thus, were, in fact, uttering words which I had taught them; and were, in everything except mere authority, my inferiors, and ought to have been commanded by me. It was impossible for reflections of this sort not to intrude themselves; and, as I advanced in experience, I felt less and less respect for those whom I was compelled to obey.

By the following year, Cobbett had been promoted to Regimental Sergeant-Major over the heads of at least thirty other sergeants. At this echelon, he came into daily contact with the inadequacy—if not outright bestial stupidity—of the officer corps, and it was this education in Canada in the perfidy of rank, and the abuse of class privilege, which fixed in him a life-long determination never to yield to upper class arrogance or patrician dismissal.

Clearly, Cobbett was not afraid of egotism. Again and again, he was intransigent because he knew he was right, and while his pigheadedness would later cause him much trouble, it was in the Maritimes of Canada that he learned to recognize the conduct of power, recognize who leveraged control:

I had a very delicate part to act with those gentry; for, while I despised them for their gross ignorance and their vanity, and hated them for their drunkenness and rapacity, I was fully sensible of their power. My path was full of rocks and pitfalls; and, as I never disguised my dislikes, or restrained my tongue, I should have been broken and flogged for fifty different offences, had they not been kept in awe by my inflexible sobriety, impartiality and integrity, by their consciousness of their inferiority to me, and by the real and almost indispensable necessity of the use of

William Cobbett's life as a non-commissioned officer aroused the satirical impulses of the legendary British caricaturist James Gilray. In a series of lampoons, Gilray mocked Cobbett's self-aggrandizement. Two of Gilray's prints, of which this is one, depict Cobbett in the Maritime provinces confronting the bovine stupidity of his superior officers. Regrettably, not a single Canadian art institution holds a copy of either print. Photo courtesy of the Thomas Fisher Rare Book Library, University of Toronto.

my talents. They, in fact, resigned all the discipline of the regiment to me, and I very freely left them to swagger about and get roaring drunk.

It was also in Canada that Cobbett started to write well. In both senses of the word. His punctiliousness about grammar was legendary: he practiced his prose every day through a variety of regimental studies and orders, and he was vain about his handwriting. Years later, he was to publish a bestseller: *A Grammar of the English Language* which he crowed had sold more than fifty thousand copies "without ever having been mentioned by the old shuffling bribed sots called Reviewers." Regarding a major study of the military readiness of Nova Scotia and New Brunswick, he would later boast:

> As was the case with everything that I meddled with, it was done in so clear, correct, and, in point of penmanship, so beautiful a manner that, I have been told, the Duke of Kent, when he afterwards became Commander-in-Chief of those provinces, had it copied, and took away the original as a curiosity.

Later in his life, he denounced the British Government's ostrich policy of encouraging the poor to emigrate to the colonies, especially Canada; he felt it was only moral to confront and rectify the problems of the poor at their source, in Britain. He had already seen what happened to soldiers, cashiered and encouraged to stay in Canada rather than return to England:

> But the best way of showing what must be done in such a case, is to show what actually was done, when this government colonized New Brunswick, which country is, in my opinion, one of the best colonies for purposes of this sort that belongs to His Majesty's Dominions.... I was in the province not long after the colonizing began.... I know, therefore, something about the manner in which a government colonizes. The distance

which the people had to go was a mere trifle. The expense of this was very little. Then the settlers were far from being poor. They were soldiers, who had gone through a war, or they were able Yankee farmers.... Yet they had provisions (pork, flour, butter, peas and rice) found them for four years. They had blankets found them to a liberal extent. They were supplied with tools, nails and other things.... And though they were not more than twenty thousand, the suffering among them after the four years was very great.... Is it likely that each settler cost the country less than fifty pounds? There was a provision store for them which served afterwards as a barrack for four hundred men.

His opinion of Prince Edward Island was as low as his feelings for his superior officers. Quite when he was in that province is unknown, but his duties often took him far afield from the regimental fort near Saint John. Again, referring to Scottish emigration to Canada, he wrote:

Those that are poor and cannot pay their passage, or can rake together only a trifle, are going to a rascally heap of sand and rock and swamp called Prince Edward Island, in the horrible Gulf of St. Lawrence; but when the American vessels come over with Indian corn and flour and pork and beef and poultry and eggs and butter and cabbages and green peas and asparagus, for the soldier officers and other tax eaters that we support upon that lump of worthlessness—for the lump itself bears nothing but potatoes—when these vessels come ... the sensible Scotch will go with them to the United States for a dollar a head, till at last not a man of them will be left but the bed-ridden. These villainous colonies are held for no earthly purpose but that of giving money to the relations and dependents of the aristocracy.... Withdraw the English taxes, and except in a small part of Canada, the whole of these horrible regions would be left to the bears and the savages in the course of a year.

After six years in New Brunswick, Cobbett returned to Britain in September 1791. Shortly thereafter, he married Anne Reid whom he had met in New Brunswick in 1787. He loved her deeply for the duration of his life, and her fortitude and stability while chaos maelstromed around them inspired him, year after year, to praise of her person bordering on poetry.

In the same year that he had met his wife, he discovered widespread criminal fraud by the quartermaster of the New Brunswick regiment. "This, the old sergeants told me, had been the case for many years; and, they were quite astonished and terrified at the idea of my complaining of it. This I did, however, but the reception I met with convinced me that I must never make another complaint 'till I got safe to England." Emboldened by his Canadian experience, in 1792 in England he delivered allegations of corruption against the British Army to the Secretary of War, Sir George Yonge. (Toronto's main thoroughfare was named Yonge Street, after this same Secretary, by Governor John Graves Simcoe, coincidentally in the same year as Cobbett's charges.) Not surprisingly, in a coverup, the authorities claimed that Cobbett lacked sufficient evidence to support his slanders; the military establishment circled its wagons, and he was forced to flee to France (chosen not only because of its proximity, but because he had learned French while stationed in Acadia).

While he was in exile, loudly-delivered indelicate remarks about the French soon forced him to abscond to the USA. Once there, though, he felt compelled to write pro-British pamphlets and tirades against the blackguards he alleged were rife throughout the American regime. Adopting the suitably prickly *nom-de-plume* of Peter Porcupine, he also became much hated in the new republic. Hounded out of America, he returned to a forgiving Britain. In 1802 he founded the *Political Register*, one of the earliest daily newspapers in the world, immensely popular and influential with the working class. True to character, he was sentenced, in 1810, with no hint of irony from the judge, to two years in jail, merely for publishing his criticisms of the length and severity of military prison sentences.

His income fluctuated wildly during the first two decades of the century due to his sudden, often forced departures for refuge abroad, and infinite libel actions (for and against). One of his fiscal plunges forced him to sell his profitable reporting of parliamentary debates to another printer; had this not been the case, we would quote today from Cobbett—rather than Hansard.

Cobbett published in his lifetime dozens of books and dozens, possibly hundreds, of pamphlets on a shameless variety of topics, many of which he was poorly qualified to discuss. (Whether this ignorance was key to his later election to the House of Commons is unclear; it may be false to apply the standards of today's MPs to those of an earlier time.) In 1834 he had dinner with fellow rebel, journalist and soul-mate William Lyon Mackenzie when the latter was in London seeking amends and vindication for the wrongs done to taxpayers by the ruling gentry in Upper Canada. The dinner seems ripe with possibilities yet to be exploited by Canadian dramatists.

This outrageous, endearing iconoclast was, in the opinion of Canadian writer Douglas Fetherling, "one of those figures who, by temperament, always took the other side of every important issue of the day.... He was not simply an antagonist of the prevailing establishment but a questioner of the very idea of establishment.... [He was a] maverick who seems to represent the best in journalism even when at his frequent worst." For Chesterton, Cobbett was an awkward hero, often askew in his indignant pronouncements, yes, but so deserving of respect for his prose: "Conventional writers use heavy words so lightly; and he used light words so heavily; every homely word like a hatchet."

Despite his unhappiness with Canada as a destination for emigrants, and his seeming dismissal of the land as little more than rocks, trees and snow, Canada remains the country where his character was shaped. His later blindness to its influence on his life should not distract us from recollecting that in Canada he gained advancement, independence, a wife, maturity, fluency in French, and a New World delight in tweaking the nose of Old World authority.

The following, just one of many comments he made on Canada,

is from his typically hortatory book *Advice to Young Men, and (Incidentally) to Young Women in the Middle and Higher Ranks of Life*, published in 1829. It is a remarkably honest document, detailing his pangs of love, and the temptations to the human heart to cheat.

———————————

from ADVICE TO YOUNG MEN

When I first saw my wife, she was thirteen years old, and I was within about a month of twenty-one. She was the daughter of a sergeant of artillery, and I was the sergeant-major of a regiment of foot, both stationed in forts near the city of St. John, in the province of New Brunswick. I sat in the same room with her for about an hour, in company with others, and I made up my mind that she was the very girl for me. That I thought her beautiful is certain, for that I had always said should be an indispensable qualification; but I saw in her what I deemed marks of that sobriety of conduct of which I have said so much, and which has been by far the greatest blessing of my life. It was now dead of winter, and, of course, the snow several feet deep on the ground, and the weather piercing cold. It was my habit, when I had done my morning's writing, to go out at break of day to take a walk on a hill at the root of which our barracks lay. In about three mornings after I had first seen her, I had, by an invitation to breakfast with me, got up two young men to join me in my walk; and our road lay by the house of her father and mother. It was hardly light, but she was out on the snow, scrubbing out a washing-tub. "That's the girl for me," said I, when we had got out of her hearing. One of these young men came to England soon afterwards; and he, who keeps an inn in Yorkshire, came over to Preston, at the time of the election, to verify whether I were the same man. When he found that I was, he appeared surprised; but what was his surprise when I told him that those tall young men whom he saw around me were the sons of that pretty little girl that he and I saw scrubbing out the washing-tub on the snow in New Brunswick at daybreak in the morning!

From the day that I first spoke to her, I never had a thought of her ever being the wife of any other man, more than I had a thought of her being transformed into a chest of drawers; and I formed my resolution at once, to marry her as soon as we could get permission, and to get out of the army as soon as I could. So that this matter was at once settled as firmly as if written in the book of fate. At the end of about six months, my regiment, and I along with it, were removed to Frederickton, a distance of a hundred miles up the river of St. John; and, which was worse, the artillery was expected to go off to England a year or two before our regiment! The artillery went, and she along with them; and now it was that I acted a part becoming a real and sensible lover. I was aware that, when she got to that gay place Woolwich, the house of her father and mother, necessarily visited by numerous persons not the most select, might become unpleasant to her, and I did not like, besides, that she should continue to work hard. I had saved a hundred and fifty guineas, the earnings of my early hours, in writing for the paymaster, the quartermaster, and others, in addition to the savings of my own pay. I sent her all my money before she sailed; and wrote to her, to beg of her, if she found her home uncomfortable, to hire a lodging with respectable people: and, at any rate not to spare the money, by any means, but to buy herself good clothes, and to live without hard work, until I arrived in England; and I, in order to induce her to lay out the money, told her that I should get plenty more before I came home.

As the malignity of the devil would have it, we were kept abroad two years longer than our time, Mr. Pitt (England not being so tame then as she is now) having knocked up a dust with Spain about Nootka Sound. Oh how I cursed Nootka Sound, and poor brawling Pitt too, I am afraid! At the end of four years, however, home I came, landed at Portsmouth, and got my discharge from the army by the great kindness of poor Lord Edward Fitzgerald, who was then the major of my regiment. I found my little girl a servant of all work (and hard work it was), at five pounds a year, in the house of a Captain Brisac; and, without hardly saying a word about the matter, she put into my hands the whole of my hundred and fifty guineas unbroken!

[No man has] any right to sport with the affections of a young woman, though he stop short of positive promises. Vanity is generally the tempter in this case; a desire to be regarded as being admired by the women: a very despicable species of vanity, but frequently greatly mischievous, notwithstanding. You do not, indeed, actually, in so many words, promise to marry; but the general tenor of your language and deportment has that meaning; you know that your meaning is so understood; and if you have not such meaning; if you be fixed by some previous engagement with, or greater liking for, another; if you know you are here sowing the seeds of disappointment; and if you, keeping your previous engagement, or greater liking, a secret, persevere, in spite of the admonitions of conscience, you are guilty of deliberate deception, injustice, and cruelty: you make to God an ungrateful return for those endowments which have enabled you to achieve this inglorious and unmanly triumph; and if, as is frequently the case, you glory in such triumph, you may have person, riches, talents to excite envy; but every just and humane man will abhor your heart.

There are, however, certain cases in which you deceive, or nearly deceive, yourself; cases in which you are, by degrees and by circumstances, deluded into something very nearly resembling sincere love for a second object, the first still, however, maintaining her ground in your heart; cases in which you are not actuated by vanity, in which you are not guilty of injustice and cruelty; but Cases in which you, nevertheless, do wrong: and as I once did a wrong of this sort myself, I will here give you a history of it, as a warning to every young man who shall read this little book; that being the best and, indeed, the only atonement that I can make, or ever could have made, for this only serious sin that I ever committed against the female sex.

The Province of New Brunswick, in North America, in which I passed my years from the age of eighteen to that of twenty-six, consists, in general, of heaps of rocks, in the interstices of which grow the pine, the spruce, and various sorts of fir-trees, or, where the woods have been burned down, the bushes of the raspberry or those of the huckleberry. The province is cut asunder lengthwise by a great river, called the St. John, about two hundred miles in length, and, at half-way from the mouth, full a mile wide. Into this main river run innumerable smaller rivers, there called creeks. On the sides of these creeks the land is, in places, clear of rocks; it is, in these places, generally good and productive; the trees that grow here are the birch, the maple, and others of the deciduous class; natural meadows here and there present themselves; and some of these spots far surpass in rural beauty any other that my eyes ever beheld; the creeks abounding towards their sources in waterfalls of endless variety, as well in form as in magnitude, and always teeming with fish, while water-fowl enliven their surface, and wild-pigeons, of the gayest plumage, flutter, in thousands upon thousands, amongst the branches of the beautiful trees, which sometimes, for miles together, form an arch over the creeks.

I, in one of my rambles in the woods, in which I took great delight, came to a spot at a very short distance from the source of one of these creeks. Here was everything to delight the eye, and especially of one like me who seems to have been born to love rural life, and trees and plants of all sorts. Here were about two hundred acres of natural meadow, interspersed with patches of maple-trees in various forms and of various extent; the creek (there about thirty miles from its point of joining the St. John) ran down the middle of the spot, which formed a sort of dish, the high and rocky hills rising all round it, except at the outlet of the creek, and these hills crowned with lofty pines: in the hills were the sources of the creek, the waters of which came down in cascades, for any one of which many a nobleman in England would, if he could transfer it, give a good slice of his fertile estate; and in the creek, at the foot of the cascades, there were, in the season, salmon, the finest in the world, and so abundant, and so easily taken, as to be used for manuring the land.

If nature, in her very best humour, had made a spot for the express purpose of captivating me, she could not have exceeded the efforts which she had here made. But I found something here besides these rude works of nature; I found something in the fashioning of which man had had something to do. I found a large and well-built log dwelling-house, standing (in the month of September) on the edge of a very good field of Indian corn, by the side of which there was a piece of buckwheat just then mowed. I found a homestead, and some very pretty cows. I found all the things by which an easy and happy farmer is surrounded; and I found still something besides all these, something that was destined to give me a great deal of pleasure and also a great deal of pain, both in their extreme degree; and both of which, in spite of the lapse of forty years, now make an attempt to rush back into my heart.

Partly from misinformation, and partly from miscalculation, I had lost my way; and, quite alone, but armed with my sword and a brace of pistols, to defend myself against the bears, I arrived at the log-house in the middle of a moonlight night, the hoar frost covering the trees and the grass. A stout and clamorous dog, kept off by the gleaming of my sword, waked the master of the house, who got up, received me with great hospitality, got me something to eat, and put me into a feather-bed, a thing that I had been a stranger to for some years. I, being very tired, had tried to pass the night in the woods, between the trunks of two large trees, which had fallen side by side, and within a yard of each other. I had made a nest for myself of dry fern, and had made a covering by laying boughs of spruce across the trunks of the trees. But unable to sleep on account of the cold; becoming sick from the great quantity of water that I had drunk during the heat of the day, and being, moreover, alarmed at the noise of the bears, and lest one of them should find me in a defenceless state, I had roused myself up, and had crept along as well as I could. So that no hero of Eastern romance ever experienced a more enchanting change.

I had got into the house of one of those Yankee Loyalists, who, at the close of the revolutionary war (which, until it had succeeded, was called a rebellion), had accepted of grants of land in the King's Province of New Brunswick; and who, to the great honour of England, had been furnished with all the means of making new and comfortable settlements. I was suffered to sleep till breakfast time, when I found a table, the like of which I have since seen so many in the United States, loaded with good things. The master and mistress of the house, aged about fifty, were like what an English farmer and his wife were half a century ago. There were two sons, tall and stout, who appeared to have come in from work, and the youngest of whom was about my age, then twenty-three. But there was another member of the family, aged nineteen, who (dressed according to the neat and simple fashion of New England whence she had come with her parents five or six years before) had her long light-brown hair twisted nicely up, and fastened on the top of her head, in which head were a pair of lively blue eyes, associated with features of which that softness and that sweetness, so characteristic of American girls, were the predominant expressions, the whole being set off by a complexion indicative of glowing health, and forming, figure, movements, and all taken together, an assemblage of beauties, far surpassing any that I had ever seen but once in my life. That once was, too, two years agone; and, in such a case and at such an age, two years, two whole years, is a long, long while! It was a space as long as the eleventh part of my then life. Here was the present against the absent: here was the power of the eyes pitted against that of the memory: here were all the senses up in arms to subdue the influence of the thoughts: here was vanity, here was passion, here was the spot of all spots in the world, and here were also the life, and the manners and the habits and the pursuits that I delighted in: here was everything that imagination can conceive, united in a conspiracy against the poor little brunette in England! What, then, did I fall in love at once with this bouquet of lilies and rose? Oh! by no means. I was,

however, so enchanted with the place; I so much enjoyed its tranquillity, the shade of the maple trees, the business of the farm, the
sports of the water and of the woods, that I stayed at it to the last
possible minute, promising, at my departure, to come again as often
as I possibly could; a promise which I most punctually fulfilled.

Winter is the great season for jaunting and dancing (called frol-
icking) in America. In this province the river and the creeks were the
only roads from settlement to settlement. In summer we travelled in
canoes; in winter in sleighs on the ice or snow. During more than
two years I spent all the time I could with my Yankee friends; they
were all fond of me: I talked to them about country affairs, my evident delight in which they took as a compliment to themselves: the
father and mother treated me as one of their children; the sons as a
brother; and the daughter, who was as modest and as full of sensibility as she was beautiful, in a way to which a chap much less sanguine
than I was would have given the tenderest interpretation; which
treatment I, especially in the last-mentioned case, most cordially
repaid.

It is when you meet in company with others of your own age that
you are, in love matters, put most frequently to the test, and exposed
to detection. The next-door neighbour might, in that country, be
ten miles off. We used to have a frolic sometimes at one house and
sometimes at another. Here, where female eyes are very much on the
alert, no secret can long be kept; and very soon father, mother,
brothers, and the whole neighbourhood looked upon the thing as
certain, not excepting herself, to whom I, however, had never once
even talked of marriage, and had never even told her that I loved her.
But I had a thousand times done these by implication, taking into
view the interpretation that she would naturally put upon my looks,
appellations, and acts; and it was of this that I had to accuse myself.
Yet I was not a deceiver; for my affection for her was very great: I
spent no really pleasant hours but with her; I was uneasy if she
showed the slightest regard for any other young man; I was unhappy
if the smallest matter affected her health or spirits: I quitted her in
dejection, and returned to her with eager delight: many a time when

I could get leave but for a day, I paddled in a canoe two whole succeeding nights, in order to pass that day with her. If this was not
love, it was first cousin to it; for as to any criminal intention, I no
more thought of it in her case, than if she had been my sister. Many
times I put to myself the questions: " What am I at? Is not this
wrong? Why do I go?" But still I went.

Then, further in my excuse, my prior engagement, though carefully left unalluded to by both parties, was, in that thin population,
and owing to the singular circumstances of it, and to the great talk
that there always was about me, perfectly well known to her and all
her family. It was a matter of so much notoriety and conversation in
the province, that General Carleton (brother of the late Lord Dorch-
ester) who was the Governor when I was there, when he, about fifteen years afterwards, did me the honour, on his return to England,
to come and see me at my house in Duke Street, Westminster, asked,
before he went away, to see my wife, of whom he had heard so much
before her marriage. So that here was no deception on my part; but
still I ought not to have suffered even the most distant hope to be
entertained by a person so innocent, so amiable, for whom I had so
much affection, and to whose heart I had no right to give a single
twinge. I ought, from the very first, to have prevented the possibility
of her ever feeling pain on my account. I was young, to be sure; but I
was old enough to know what was my duty in this case, and I ought,
dismissing my own feelings, to have had the resolution to perform it.

The last parting came; and now came my just punishment! The
time was known to everybody, and was irrevocably fixed; for I had to
move with a regiment, and the embarkation of a regiment is an
epoch in a thinly settled province. To describe this parting would be
too painful even at this distant day, and with this frost of age upon
my head. The kind and virtuous father came forty miles to see me,
just as I was going on board in the river. His looks and words I have
never forgotten. As the vessel descended, she passed the mouth of
that creek, which I had so often entered with delight; and though
England, and all that England contained, were before me, I lost
sight of this creek with an aching heart.

On what trifles turn the great events in the life of man! If I had received a cool letter from my intended wife; if I had only heard a rumour of anything from which fickleness in her might have been inferred: if I had found in her any, even the smallest, abatement of affection; if she had but let go any one of the hundred strings by which she held my heart: if any of these, never would the world have heard of me. Young as I was; able as I was as a soldier; proud as I was of the admiration and commendations of which I was the object; fond as I was, too, of the command, which, at so early an age, my rare conduct and great natural talents had given me; sanguine as was my mind, and brilliant as were my prospects: yet I had seen so much of the meannesses, the unjust partialities, the insolent pomposity, the disgusting dissipations of that way of life, that I was weary of it: I longed, exchanging my fine laced coat for the Yankee farmer's homespun, to be where I should never behold the supple crouch of servility, and never hear the hectoring voice of authority again; and, on the lonely banks of this branch-covered creek, which contained (she out of the question) everything congenial to my taste and dear to my heart, I, unapplauded, unfeared, unenvied and uncalumniated, should have lived and died.

THOMAS HUGHES

RARE is the book which has remained in print without interruption since its first appearance more than one hundred and thirty years ago, but *Tom Brown's School Days* (1857) by Thomas Hughes is a novel which has never lost its popularity. Indeed, its influence continues to reverberate because most North Americans, even today, think life at a private boy's school in England is lived much as it was portrayed by Hughes in his famous novel.

Thomas Hughes (1822-1896) was born near London and was soon enrolled at Rugby where he came under the sway of one of the most remarkable educators of the nineteenth century, Dr. Thomas Arnold. Headmaster at Rugby from 1827-42, Arnold instituted what were then regarded as radical changes into the traditional curriculum: higher mathematics, modern languages and modern history, for example, were added to the orthodox study of the classics. Independence of mind was fostered, and sacrifice of ego for the good of the group a goal he much encouraged.

As important for his charges, however, was Thomas Arnold's charismatic preaching in Rugby chapel. Here he delivered homilies espousing a new vision of Christianity, one that later evolved into Christian Socialism. Still later it came to be called "muscular Christianity", one that gloried in the body rather than its shame, and saw in the meld of physical labour, principled social welfare and a Christian ethos the ideal of Jesus' teaching. Thomas Arnold's influence can certainly be seen in the writings of his son, Matthew Arnold, and there are tinges of it in the writings of his granddaughter, Mrs. Humphry Ward. Without doubt, the charisma of Thomas Arnold and the magnetic attraction of his ideals appealed to Thomas Hughes. So it is no accident that Thomas Arnold is depicted heroically in the famous tale of young Tom Brown at Rugby. Ironically, it was only when Thomas Hughes's own son, aged eight, was preparing to enter school for the first time that Hughes turned to writing fiction. He wanted a literary vehicle in which to honour the pedagogical labour of Dr. Arnold, and a means of alerting a wide public to the personal values which Thomas Hughes believed were essential to the meaningful Christian life. *Tom Brown's School Days* was an instant bestseller: more than five large printings were made in less than seven months and the book made so much money that Hughes was able to subsidize social experiments, large and small, in which he was personally interested. The large experiments would eventually nearly bankrupt him.

Hughes entered Oriel College, Oxford in 1842 and his years there, while undistinguished scholastically, were lived to the full and later provided raw material for his third and final novel, *Tom Brown at Oxford* (1861). Upon graduation, he pursued legal studies and was called to the Bar in 1848, the same year in which he founded the movement known formally as Christian Socialism, with, among others, Charles Kingsley, the noted novelist. While their formal organization soon disintegrated, Hughes continued to lead his personal life according to religious socialist principles, directing his attention and energies to the problems of the working class, and the elimination of barriers leading to the betterment of that class. He was elected to Parliament in 1865, kept his seat for nine years, was made a Queen's Counsel in 1869, and was then appointed to the bench as County Court Judge in 1882.

Unlike many of his compatriots in the British Establishment, Hughes was an outspoken supporter of the North during the American Civil War. His opposition to slavery was vehement, and his interest in the United States stemmed not only from his involvement in the American civil conflict, but with that nation's apparently class-less economy and proudly democratic instincts. It was an interest that was also to make him aware of Canada as something other than colonial fodder, a place different from the USA, but one that offered unique attractions to the working class emigrant from England.

Hughes was, by the standard of the day and by his own inclination, a peripatetic soul. With nine children, however, his funds for unrestricted roving abroad were limited. So to augment his resources he arranged with the *Spectator* to publish his "letters" from foreign places, the articles later published in book form as *Vacation Rambles* (1895).

His first visit to North America came as his fame was high and still arcing upward. A long correspondence with James Russell Lowell, the renowned Boston author and abolitionist, had included several invitations from Lowell to visit the States, and in August 1870, during a lengthy Parliamentary recess, Hughes set sail on the *Peruvian* to experience in the flesh what until then he had only read about. While his ultimate destination was the USA, Hughes arrived first in Canada and his descriptions of the country border on the rapturous. Even before landing, he was impressed by the hundreds of immigrants, travelling steerage, intending to settle, with high hopes, in Canada and he spent most of his voyage caring for and preaching to them.

Once he entered Canadian waters, a scintillating tone enveloped his letters home:

> [We] entered the strait between Newfoundland and Labrador. By the time we had done breakfast we were running close by a huge iceberg, like a great irregular wedding cake, except near the water, where the colour changed from sugary white into the most delicious green. There were nine other icebergs in sight to the north, and a number of others round us, just showing above the water, one like a great ichthyosaurus creeping along the waves, or a white bear with a very long neck. Had we gone on last night it would have been a perilous adventure. Soon afterwards we

sighted the *North American*, a companion ship belonging to the same Company, running some miles in front of us to the north. We had a most exciting race, coming abreast of her about twelve, and communicating by signals. Then we drew ahead, and shall be in Quebec nearly a day before her. Then we played shovel-board on deck, the air getting more balmy every minute as we drew out of the ice region. We had a grand gathering of emigrants amid-ships, and sung hymns, "Jesus, lover of my soul," and others, with a few words from G—, the busy parson, who has recovered from his long sea-sickness at last, and is a famous fellow.... We are well in the Gulf of St. Lawrence, and all going as well as possible.

It was while on board the *Peruvian* that Thomas Hughes met the Canadians to whom he refers in the excerpt printed below. He reported to his wife that he was "much pleased with the specimens of Canadians whom we have on board. There are some twenty of them, with their wives, daughters, and small boys. They are a quiet, well-informed, pleasant set of men, and ready and pleased to talk of their country and her prospects." As he enters the debouch of the St. Lawrence River, the contrasts delight him:

Last night we danced on deck till nearly eleven under the most lovely soft moon I have ever seen. This morning we are running up the St. Lawrence along the southern bank, the northern being dim in the extreme distance. There is a long continuous range of hills covered entirely with forest, except just along the water's edge, where it has been cleared by the French-Canadian settlers. They live along the shore, too close, I should say, to the water line for comfort; but as their chief occupation is fishing, I have no doubt they have good reasons for their selection. There is scarcely a quarter of a mile for the last twenty or thirty miles, I should say, in which there is not a cottage, but the villages are far between. The people are a simple, quiet folk, living just as their fathers lived, happy, clean, contented, and stationary. This last quality provokes the English of Upper Canada dreadfully, who complain that the French make everything they require at home, and buy nothing whatever which contributes to the revenue of the Dominion except a little cheap tea. However, there is much to be said for the Frenchmen, and I am very glad that our English people have constantly before them the example of such a self-sufficing and unambitious life.

Hughes had never before experienced a river as grand as the St. Lawrence, but its immensity impressed him more than just topographically:

Nothing could have brought the startling contrast of the old and the new world so vividly home to me as this steaming literally day after day up the stream, and finding it still at seven hundred miles from the mouth two miles broad, with anchorage for the largest ships that float.... [I] scuffled up on deck in my trousers and fur coat to find myself in the most perfect moonlight rounding the last point below Quebec. Then up went three rockets, and as we slacked our speed at the side of the wharf right opposite the citadel, two guns were fired and the voyage of the *Peruvian* was over. My packing was all done, so while the vessel was being unladen I went quietly to bed again and slept for another two or three hours amid all the din. Between six and seven I turned out again and had a good breakfast on board, after which came leave-takings, and then those of us who were not going on by train and were ready to start, went on board a little tug ferryboat and were paddled across to Quebec. I have sent a small map to show you how the land lies. Our ferry-boat took us over from Port Levi to the quay just under the citadel along the line I have dotted, and we at once chartered two carriages to visit the falls of Montmorency, to which you will see a line drawn on the map and which is about six miles from Quebec. Oh, the air! You know what it is when we land at Dieppe, or at Brussels, or Aix. Well, all that air is fog, depressing wet blanket compared to this Canadian nectar. I really doubt whether it would not be almost worth while to emigrate merely for the exquisite pleasure of the act of living in this country.

After a day of seeing the standard sights of Quebec and environs, and enjoying them thoroughly, Hughes set forth for Montreal, finding almost everything he encountered different from what he had known, and exciting. Landing in Montreal on August 17, 1870, he allowed himself to be swept up in the high life of the city, the guest of some of the wealthiest Canadians of the day, including George Stephen and Sir Hugh Allan. More than any other foreign literary visitor to Victorian Montreal, Thomas Hughes gives the reader such a sense of the daily life in the streets—smells, tastes, temperatures, and delights—that reading his descriptions is akin to savouring a daguerreotype of a long-disappeared cityscape.

In the evening we went on board the great river steamer, and came away all night up the St. Lawrence to Montreal. There were one thousand passengers on board, every one of whom had an excellent berth—mine was broader and lighter than that on the *Peruvian*. We were not the least crowded in the splendid saloon (some 150 feet long), and the open galleries running all round the ship in two tiers. I preferred the latter, though there was music, Yankee and Canadian, in the saloon, and spent my evening till bedtime out in the stern gallery looking at the most superb moonlight on the smooth water you can conceive. We had a small English party there, and there were half a dozen constantly changing groups round us. The girls have evidently much more freedom than at home, at least more than they had in our day— two or three would come out with as many young men, and sit round in a ring. The men lighted cigars, and then they would all set to work singing glees, songs, or what not, and chaffing and laughing away for half an hour perhaps, after which they would disappear into the saloon. There was a regular bar on board at which all manner of cool drinks were sold. We tried several, which I thought, I must say, very nasty, especially brandy-smash.

After a most comfortable night I awoke between five and six as we were nearing Montreal. The city is very fine, the river still two miles broad, an ocean steamer drawing twenty feet and more of water able to lie right up against the quay.

S—, a friend of Sir J. Rose's, a great manufacturer here, whom I had taken to the "Cosmopolitan," was in waiting on the landing-place, and took us at once up to his charming house on the hill (the mountain they call it) at the back of the city. He is a man of forty-three or forty-four; his wife a very pleasant woman, a little younger, and adopted daughter, Alice (a very sweet girl of nineteen, just home from an English school), form the whole family. I can't tell you how kind they are and how perfectly at home they have made us. After breakfast we went down to see the city, got photographed with the rest of the above-named Peruvians, had a delicious lunch of fried oysters at a luncheon shop kept by a Yankee, washed it down with a drink called John Collins, a pleasant, cold, weak, scented kind of gin and water. Sir Geo. Cartier and Sir Fras. Hincks, two of the present Government, both of whom I had met in England, came to dinner, also Holton the leading senator of the Opposition, and the two young Roses, one bringing his pretty young wife, and we had a long and very interesting political talk afterwards. Nothing could have suited me better, as there are many points of Canadian politics I am very anxious to get views on. We didn't get to bed till twelve-thirty, so I had no time to write. On Wednesday we saw more of the city, which I shan't attempt to describe till I can sit by you with photographs and explain, lunched at the Club, of which we have been made honorary members, with a large party of merchants and other big folk, and then at three were picked up by Mrs. S—, who drove us up the river to a place called Lachine, past the rapids (see Canadian boat-song), "The rapids are near and the daylight's past." Lachine gets its queer name from the first French Missionaries who started up the St. Lawrence to get to China, and for some unaccountable reason thought they had reached the flowery land when they got to this place, so settled down and called it China. The air was still charming, but the sky was beginning to get less bright, and Mrs. S—and A—agreed that there must be a forest burning somewhere. And so it proved, for in a few hours the whole sky was covered with a smoke-cloud, light but not depressing, like our fogs, but still so dense that we could scarcely see across the river. We got back in time for dinner, to which came Colonel Buller, now commanding the Rifles here; Hugh Allan, the head of the great firm of ship-owners to whom the Peruvian and all the rest of the Allan Line packets belong; and several young Canadians. It was very pleasant again, and again I got a heap of information on Canadian subjects from Allan…. [Montreal] isn't the least like an English or indeed any European town, the reason being, I take it, that it has been built with the necessity of meeting extremes of heat and cold, which we never get. Except in the heart of the city, where the great business streets are, there are trees along the sides of all the thoroughfares—maples, which give real shade, and are in many places indeed too thick, and too near the houses for comfort I should say—as near as the plane-tree was to our drawing-room window at 33. This arrangement makes walking about very pleasant to me, even when the thermometer stands at ninety degrees in the shade as it did yesterday. Then instead of a stone foot-pavement you have almost everywhere boards, timber being the most plentiful production of the country. Walking along the boards in the morning you see at every door a great lump of ice, twenty pounds weight or so, lying there for the maid to take in when she comes out to clean. This is supplied by the ice merchants for a few shillings a year. The houses are square, built generally of a fine limestone found all over the island (Montreal is an island thirty-six miles long by nine wide), and have all green open shutterblinds, which they keep constantly shut all day, as in Greece, to keep out the heat, and double windows to keep out the cold. The roofs are generally covered with tin instead of tiles or slates, and all the church steeples, of which there are a very large number, are tinned, as you remember we saw them in parts of Austria and Hungary. There are magnificent stores of dry goods, groceries, etc., but scarcely any shop in our sense. No butcher, milkman, greengrocer, etc., calls at the door, and the ladies have all to go down to the market or send there. Nothing can be better than the living, but Mrs. S— complains that it is very hard work for *haus fraus*, and I have heard Lady R— say the same thing. This house is in one of the shaded avenues on the slopes of the mountain, two miles I should say from the market. Mrs. S— drives down every market-day and buys provisions, market-days being twice a week, but the stalls are open on other days also, so that if a flood of company comes in on the intermediate days, the anxious housewife need not be absolutely done for. The living is as good as can be, not aspiring to first-rate French cookery, but equal to anything you find in good English houses. Prices are very reasonable except for fancy articles of clothing etc. Furs, which you would expect to find cheap, are at least as high as in London, and R— made an investment in gloves for which he paid six shillings a pair. The city is the quietest and best-behaved I ever was in. We dined at the mess of the Sixtieth Rifles last night, and walked home through the heart of the city at ten-thirty. Every one had gone to bed, apparently, for there wasn't a light in fifty houses and we literally met no one—not half a dozen people certainly in the whole distance. Altogether I am very much impressed with the healthiness of the life, morally and physically, and can scarcely imagine any country I would sooner start in were I beginning life again.

Hughes finished his week in the province of Quebec as the guest of Hugh Allan at the latter's grand country house on Lake Memphremagog, south of Montreal on the border with Vermont. While clearly enjoying the luxury of his accommodation, Hughes briefly observed the other half and how they lived. He ended his stay in Canada in the most spectacular manner possible, beneath the flames of the aurora borealis:

After leaving Montreal we travelled I should say for from thirty to forty miles through reclaimed country, dotted with French villages and the homesteads of well-to-do farmers. Then we gradually slipped into half-cleared woods, and then into virgin forest. Presently we came across a great block of the forest on fire, but in broad daylight the sight is not the least grand, though unpleasant from the smoke, and melancholy from the waste and mischief which the fires do. I think I told you in my last that the forests about Ottawa, the capital of the Dominion, were all fire last week. The fire became so serious that great fears were entertained for the town, the militia and volunteers were called out, and a special train with fire-engines was sent up from Montreal. Scores of poor settlers were in the streets, having with difficulty escaped with their lives, and last of all several wretched bears trotted out of the burning woods into the town. The fire we passed through was not at all on this scale, and didn't seem likely to get ahead. There were the marks of fires of former years on all sides in these forests. Tall stems by hundreds, standing up charred and gaunt out of the middle of the bright green maple underwood, which is fast growing up round them, and in a very short time makes the tangle as thick as ever. Before long we came to small clearings of from three to four acres, on each of which was a rough wooden shanty, with half a dozen wild, brown, healthy-looking children rolling and scrambling about it, and standing up in their single garments to cheer the train. On these plots the trees had all been felled about two feet from the ground, and the brushwood cleared away, and there were crops of Indian corn, oats, or buckwheat growing all round the stumps. Then we came to plots which had been occupied longer, where the shanty had grown into a nice-sized cottage, with a good-sized outhouse near. Here all the stumps had been cleared, and the plot divided by fences, and three or four cows would be poking about. Then we came to a fine river and ran along the bank, passing here and there sawmills of huge size, and stopping at one or two large primitive villages, gathered round a manufactory. In short, in the day's run we saw Canadian life in all its phases, ending with a delicious twelve miles' run up the lake in Mr. Allan's steam yacht, with the whole sky flickering with Northern lights....

Despite the fact that he spent less than a month in Canada, Thomas Hughes later became one of the most perspicacious of the many British commentators on Canada. Having seen both nations of North America, he was convinced that Canada was to be preferred by the emigrant from the United Kingdom, because it offered the democratic freshness of the new world while yet providing emotional links with the mother country. Indeed, Hughes arranged, while on the continent, for his eldest son to immigrate to western Canada to take up farming.

But more than this, more than any other creative writer up to that point who had visited the nation, Hughes *thought* about Canada, ruminated at length about its present and its future, and for the rest of his life cared about its health and its status as an independent country. His contemplation focussed on Canada as Canada, not on Canada as a senior colony or source of raw material for the Old Country, or some other patronizing, astigmatic perception.

No doubt his position as a liberal member of parliament kept him abreast, far more than his fellow Britons, of the nuances of political developments throughout the Empire, especially in the oldest Dominion. But his analysis of Canada's political future, part of which is printed below, is the result of more than haphazard conversations with business tycoons or Canadian members of parliament encountered on the fly.

Rather, his studies are mature analyses of a complicated country, showing affection for its polyglot nature, and a nervy vision of the independence of its spirit.

The following excerpt is taken from Hughes' long introduction to the *Guide Book to the Canadian Dominion Containing Full Information for the Emigrant, the Tourist, the Sportsman, and the Small Capitalist* by Harvey Philpot, published in London, England in

1871. Mr. Philpot's contribution is the standard fare; Mr. Hughes' contribution is not.

Given how little time he was actually in Canada, and given that the nation was but three years old when he penned the following remarks, his speculations are uncannily intelligent, exceptional in their accuracy, disturbingly prescient, relevant today to the point of eeriness and—perhaps most refreshingly—only proportionately respectful.

---

from GUIDE BOOK TO THE CANADIAN DOMINION

British North America is in a period of crisis and transition, feeling about like one awakening out of sleep, and scarcely yet conscious of the new powers and responsibilities which have been silently maturing and gathering, within and around him. The Dominion, in two words, cannot remain as she is, and it is well that her own children, and those who mean to become so, and the two great countries of her blood, her mother and elder sister—in short, that all who are interested in her future, should make this fact thoroughly clear to themselves.

It is now just four years (March 29, 1867) since, in compliance with the expressed wishes of the provinces of Canada, Nova Scotia, and New Brunswick, the Imperial Parliament passed the Act known as the British North America Act, for the purpose of "federally uniting" those great colonies "into one Dominion under the Crown, with a constitution similar in principle to that of the United Kingdom." This Act establishes the constitution of the Dominion of

Canada, and was intended practically to bind the whole of the provinces into one nation. It has accomplished its object to an extent which has astonished Englishmen, and which many of the lending statesmen and public writers of the Dominion are apparently unable to recognize, or unwilling to admit. In fact the work of unification has been done so rapidly and thoroughly that the Act of 1867, and the Constitution which rests on it are already obsolete (or "played out," to use the more expressive trans-Atlantic phrase). We may regret that this should be so, or rejoice, as our political and natural temperaments sway us; but there the fact remains, amongst the more pressing that England has to deal with. Many of us who voted for the Act of 1867 did it with open eyes, and a distinct recognition that, if the experiment of confederation should succeed, and so soon as it should succeed, one of two issues became inevitable for the Dominion, independence, or a more intimate and equal union with the mother country.

The experiment of confederation has now succeeded, and, at one bound, Canada has become a great power, from whatever point of view you like to look....

Take enterprize. Thirty years ago the St. Lawrence was not navigable above Quebec for vessels of more than three hundred tons burthen. Now the channel has been made perfectly safe for ocean steamers, and you see the vessels of the Allan Line lying by the quays of Montreal. The Welland Canal, the Grand Trunk Railway, and the Tubular Bridge over the St. Lawrence, as notable works as any the world can yet show, may perhaps fairly be placed to a great extent to the credit of the mother country. But this Allan Line of ocean steamers, the most numerous in the world, is the product of Canadian energy and Canadian capital. The same may be said of the woollen manufactures of the Dominion, which are more than holding their own already against the best goods which Leeds and Bradford can turn out. If we prefer the test of general prosperity as evidenced by the wealth of the country, an even more startling state of things meets us. There are more people in the Dominion in proportion to population than any other country in the world who are worth

$1000. Such results speak for themselves as to the character of the people, who are as enterprizing and thrifty as any branch of the English-speaking race. They are already far more numerous, and more united than the thirteen colonies were at the declaration of Independence ninety-five years ago. It is idle to suppose that they can any longer be kept in leading strings....

And so we get back again to the consideration of the alternatives from which we started. Is the House to be a semi-detached one? Well, there are many persons, both at home and in Canada who answer Yes, unreservedly. The Canadian press, with a few exceptions, is exceedingly angry when the contrary theory is mooted. The word "independence" acts on them like a red flag on a bull. They shut their eyes, down with their heads, and go at it. They seem to wish to burk all discussion of the question, treating it as though the time for argument had passed, all endeavouring to fix the stigma of "disloyalty," the most odious and offensive of all accusations to a Canadian, on any one who will insist on looking the crisis fairly in the face.

But meantime what do they advocate in the place of independence, for not one of them, so far as I know, believes that the Constitution of 1867 can stand. Imperial Federation will probably be the answer, and the name, no doubt, has a grand sound. Other races, we are told, are grouping themselves together, according to their nationalities, and it is monstrous that the English race alone should be allowed to split up. But in the first place one has to admit that there is no question of splitting up....

For there is no question that the English people are anxious to keep the connection, if it can be done in any way which will be acceptable to the Colonies, and not burthensome to the mother country. The Colonies, it would seem, and before all the eldest of them, the Dominion of Canada, are at present as anxious as the mother country. Apart from and below all question of the commercial advantage to them of forming part of the Empire, there is a strong appreciation of the sentimental value of British citizenship, which, whatever clever writers of articles and essays may say in its disparagement, is not a possession to be lightly cast aside.

Such a connection with the mother country as would leave the Dominion the entire mistress of her own destinies, and give her the power to declare formally her absolute independence at any moment, seems to be the only hopeful alternative hitherto proposed for entire separation at a very early date. But after all would not absolute independence be better for her, and for England? In looking at this question her relations with the United States should be the first consideration, as her future prosperity and development depends upon the terms upon which she lives with the great neighbour, whose boundary line runs now side by side with hers to the Rocky Mountains, and, on the accession of British Columbia to the Dominion, will extend side by side to the seaboard of the Pacific.

Let us first clear away, if possible, one of the wildest notions which has ever found serious advocates at home, or in the Colony, that, if England were to retire, the United States, if they could not annex or absorb Canada by peaceful means, would do so by a war of aggression. One has hardly patience to argue with those who entertain such fears. Their case rests on the assumption that Brother Jonathan is a fool, and no one who has any regard for the value of time will care to argue this point. From a somewhat large and intimate acquaintance with American politicians, and with the periodical political literature of the United States, I venture to say, that there is no leading man, and no leading journal in the Union, which has ever seriously put forward such a proposal. A very large majority of Americans believe that the union of Canada with the United States is only a question of time. A majority, not so large, but still I think considerable, are quite willing that their Government should use any means at their disposal, short of hostilities, to hasten the day when British North America will range itself under the stars and stripes.... But, with the exception of Butler, and three or four politicians of his stripe, there is, I repeat, no man of recognized position in politics, who dare, even for election purposes, to advocate the conquest of Canada. The American people are anxious to get half a dozen free states of the best old northern type into the Union, as a set off in the direction of permanence, stability, steadiness, against the thinly-veiled sullen disloyalty of the Southern whites, and the restless ferment of the *colluvies gentium* as it settles down on the great west. They do not want another group of Carolinas and Georgias on their northern frontier, smarting under the humiliation of defeat, and ready at any moment to make common cause with the South for the destruction of an Union, which would be to them, not the symbol of Freedom, but of conquest. I omit all consideration of the chances of defeat in an invasion of a country, so hardy, vigorous, and prosperous as the Dominion. Whether practicable or not in a military sense, it's just the one impossible issue. The attempt would be forbidden, at once by the highest conscience, and the shrewdest self-interest, of the Amerrican people.

I think we may safely start then with two assumptions, that the United States will accept the independence of Canada as a satisfactory fulfillment of the Monroe doctrine and that Canada has her own future in her own power, and has only her own interests to consider in determining what that future shall be.

Perhaps the strongest argument for independence, pure and simple, is, that in this way only can the Canadian statesmen and people be made to feel the full responsibility of their own acts and words. So long as the present connection with England continues, the temptation of shifting that responsibility will be overwhelming, and what has been grotesquely called the "national policy" (or, in other words, irritating speech and retaliatory tariffs), is not likely to be abandoned by the Dominion.... Self-reliance is the soundest foundation for national manliness and moderation; and any alliance or connection, however advantageous or honourable, which hinders its full development, should be abandoned. I am sure that Englishmen will unhesitatingly acquiesce in this view. England wants, before all things, to see Canada a nation; if in alliance with herself so much the better, but in no sense dependent on her. If she cannot rise to the full stature of a nation while even one of the old ropes remains, let the last drop gently into the water by the side of the vessel, and wish her God speed! But if there is no danger whatever of forcible, is there not a strong likelihood of peaceable annexation of Canada to the United

States? Undoubtedly there is such a likelihood. At present there is no material inducement to Canada to join the Union. Taxation is heavier in the States, and their fiscal policy is opposed to that of the Dominion. But the war debt is fast disappearing, and the free trade movement is gaining strength, as the recent repeal of the protective duties on coal and salt shows. Whenever the United States assimilate their tariff to that of the Dominion—which is a revenue tariff, with a wide free list of raw materials—the pinch will come. If at that time, which is nearer than people generally expect, Canadian statesmen are still half awake, drifting along purposeless, with a constant sidelong or backward glance to England, the great Republic will most probably absorb them. If, on the other hand, the Dominion is then practically self-reliant, and independent, the result will probably be, a Zolverein or Customs Union between the two countries—a commercial but not a political union, in which England might not be included but which in any case would be greatly to her advantage, and enormously increase her present exports to North America.

But in any case would not annexation be disastrous, and humiliating to England? I answer, why should it be? It will not be disastrous to us commercially, if it cannot (as I hold) take place until the United States assimilate their tariff to the Canadian. It will not be disastrous politically to us, as it will throw a vast English vote into the party struggles of the Union. It will not be humiliating, for England will have done her part by the Dominion, and started her eldest child in the world with a single eye to her advancement and prosperity, and no nation can be humbled which has done its duty to the best of its power.

At the same time I must own that in one sense I think it would be a misfortune, not specially to England, but to Christendom. The world, and more particularly the new world, wants variety and colour. If Canada is annexed she becomes an undistinguishable unit in a vast confederation, already too uniform, constantly tending, in spite of their marvellous material prosperity, to a deeper and more colourless uniformity.

I would not for a moment deny that one of the best and strongest characteristics of our time is a craving for union, amongst nations, churches, people, but there is a good and a bad way of reaching it. I doubt whether union reached by the lion swallowing the lamb in all lands, and the big fish the little ones in all ponds, is what we ought to work or pray for.

It seems to me that it would be better for the United States themselves to have a kindred nation by their side, with a character and history of its own, and institutions as free as, but not identical with, theirs.

The traditions of the Dominion and the States have been for a century not only distinct, but to some extent antagonistic.... If Canada should be absorbed, the tradition of her national life will be rudely severed, and she and the world will be by so much the poorer. There are likely to be too few chances of welcoming a new member into the sisterhood of nations, and I own I should be sorry to see this one lost.

On the other hand, if so it must be, the sight of a whole continent confederated under one Government, but needing very little government of any kind, will be an excellent lesson to the old world. One would prefer to see Canada independent, and the three English speaking powers knit together in an alliance which might keep peace over at least half the globe. But whether she shall stand alone, or merge in the Union, her future can scarcely fail to be a noble one, for she carries within herself all the elements of healthy and beneficent prosperity. Her people are a brave, hard-working, simply-living folk, contact with whom freshens up and braces the spirit of the wanderer from the old world, as the superb climate does his body. Her soil teems with wealth for the worker, coal, iron, sulphates, oils, copper; her vast forests are of the finest timber; the motive power lying almost unused in her inland waters, is probably the cheapest and best in the world. Plenty and comfort are in all her borders, and nowhere (as yet at any rate) are there signs of the corruption and feebleness, which cling and fester round the huge accumulations of material wealth, raising problems which weigh so heavily on the brain, if they do not daunt the heart, of the bravest and truest men in older lands.... There is a career for every one with a pair of hands, and the will to use them diligently. There are no bad times in the Dominion "except for wastrels," and for them there can be no good times anywhere that I know of, either in the old world or the new.

KHUSHWANT SINGH

O<small>NE OF INDIA'S</small> most eminent, and certainly most popular authors began his literary career not in India, but in Canada.

With the Partition of India in 1947, Kushwant Singh (b. 1915) lost his house and his job in Lahore, and, anxious to earn a living for himself and his new bride, he applied for a job with the Indian Ministry of External Affairs, a department eager to fill the hundreds of foreign postings now necessary because of independence. To his surprise, he was given the job of Information Officer at the High Commission in London, one of the most prestigious posts available. Unfortunately, the position was short-lived; a victim of rivalries at the ambassadorial level, Singh, within a few months of his arrival, was punished with a transfer to Ottawa:

> In Ottawa my boss was my wife's uncle, H. S. Malik of the Indian Civil Service. He was a great golfer and a party man, who disdained to mix with anyone except heads of state, ministers, and the rich. He spent more time on the golf course and at diplomatic receptions than in the office. In any event, there was very little for us to do. I began to write short stories, cultivate writers, poets, and editors of literary journals. It was in Canada that my literary efforts first appeared in print in the *Canadian Forum*, *Saturday Night*, and *Harper's*. Although I soon fell out

with my High Commissioner, I made deep and abiding friend-
ships with many Canadians. I travelled across the length and
breadth of the country, went skiing in winter, hiking in the
Rockies in summer, and saw the autumn light maple forests on
fire. Canada remains my favourite country.

Despite the fact that he had been in Canada only six months, Singh
was transferred back to London, although his Canadian excursion
stood him in good stead. After the war, London was bereft of hard
liquor, but as a diplomat, Singh had "come back from Canada with
several crates of premium scotch." In an autobiographical sketch
written decades later, Singh recalled wryly how the abundance of his
Canadian booze—and his house parties where London literati
drank it apparently without the usual British reserve—no doubt
abetted the fine critical reception of his first book of stories, *The
Mark of Vishnu.*

Twenty years after his first trip to Canada, Khushwant Singh was
invited to give one of the Noranda Lectures at Expo '67 in Montreal.
At the beginning of his Expo address, Singh reminisced flatteringly
about his first impressions of Canadians and their land:

I first came to this country twenty years ago—soon after India
had attained independence and had become an equal partner
with Canada in the Commonwealth. I was sent here as Press
and Cultural Attaché charged with the duty of selling my
country's politics, culture, and way of life to the Canadians. I
did this to the best of my very limited ability along channels
open to diplomatic missions. I bombarded your newspapers
and broadcasting stations with press handouts. Little notice
was taken of my handouts by either your press or your radio. I
went on extensive tours and addressed Masons, Rotarians,
Lions, Elks, and other groups. Even as I orated, drooping heads
made me conscious of how little my audiences were taking
from me. And being a diplomat, with a generous entertainment
allowance, I let liquor flow like the waters of the holy Ganga.

This, I need hardly say, went down better with the Canadians than either my handouts or my speeches. Nevertheless, I proved to be a very poor salesman for my country. After a six-month trial in Canada, I was transferred to London and then fired.

The reason of my failure was simple. In the political jargon of the times, I had allowed myself to be *brainwashed* by the Canadians. So eager was I to know all I could about Canada that in the months that I spent here I read little besides Canadian literature, saw few pictures except those made by the National Film Board of Canada, and refused to go to concerts unless they were performed by Canadian orchestras. I made a large number of friends ranging from elder statesmen to poets, painters, journalists, and tradesmen. I played tennis and bathed and skied with Canadians: twenty years ago I could do all these things. There were many Canadian homes I began to call my own. I ate, drank, danced, and flirted with Canadians: twenty years ago I could do that too....

On my side it was a deep emotional involvement with this country and its peoples. Ever since, in my home in India, seldom does an evening pass when I have not tried to paint your native maple—redder than it is during fall. Though in the intervening long summers and winters I have wandered over many lands in many climes and lived among diverse races—black, brown, yellow, and white—I remain as convinced as I was twenty years ago that there is no country in the world as beautiful as Canada, and there are no people in the world nicer than the Canadians.

To me, coming back to Canada is like coming back to my spiritual home. Canada quickened in me the impulse to appreciate the best there is in life; the ability to perceive beauty in things that are beautiful; the ability to love people who are lovable. It was in Canada that the desire to write came upon me. It was in Canada that I first saw my name in print. I owe more to this country and its people than I can put in words.

Many among you will be embarrassed by this kind of soppy sentimentalism. Well, I am a soppy sentimentalist.

Singh made two other visits to Canada. One was occasioned by research for a monumental and much-praised history of Sikhs and Sikhism published in two volumes in the 1960s by Princeton and Oxford. He examined the previously undocumented Sikh communities in Vancouver and environs, connecting their histories to those on the west coast of the United States. The other trip, made in 1975, to conduct research on wildlife conservation, took him to Ottawa, Montreal, the James Bay Hydro-Electric Project and Vancouver. His fourteen-page account of this latter trip was published in 1978 in *Around the World With Khushwant Singh*. In this volume his interviews and comments are directed at the home market and are largely restricted to observations on recent Indian and Pakistani immigrants.

The following short story appeared in Singh's first collection of tales, published in 1950, the collection based on his experiences in Lahore and Ottawa. While "When Sikh Meets Sikh" may have the faults of any neophyte professional fiction, its humour, like a silver fibre through a sari, is typical of the insouciance which threads through all his work. While reading it, one is sobered by the reflection that racial insensitivities in Toronto have a longer history than generally supposed.

WHEN SIKH MEETS SIKH

When a Sikh meets another Sikh they both say "Sut Sree Akal," which means simply "God is truth." More frequently one starts loudly proclaiming "Wah guru jee ka Khalsa," which means "The

Sikhs are the chosen of God," and the other joins him in completing it even more loudly with "Wah guru jee kee Fateh"—"And victory be to our God." The latter form of greeting is fast gaining in popularity at the expense of the former. The reason for this is obvious. Just saying God is truth is as pointless as the European habit of referring to the time of the day and prefixing it as good. The other form goes further. It expresses both a truth and a hope. That the Sikhs are the chosen of God is something no Sikh has any doubt about—the Guru himself called them the Khalsa or the elect. And what could be more fitting than wishing victory to one's god all the time!

Although the Sikhs themselves rightly believe that they are the elect, there are other races who consider themselves chosen, other nations which call themselves A1, and sects which style themselves the salt of the earth. As a matter of fact, in India itself other communities belittle the Sikhs as an odd people and have lots of stories making fun of them. Sikhs ignore these jests and have a lordly sort of superiority which they express in their day-to-day vocabulary. Thus all clean-shaven people are *Kirars,* which literally means cowards, or *Sirghassas,* which means bald-because-of-beating-on-the-head. A Sikh refers to himself as equal to a hundred and twenty-five thousand, or simply as an army.

Sikhs are not just a crude fighting type. Despite the many Victoria and Military Crosses they have won on the field of battle, they are essentially a peace-loving people. They were virtually the first community to prove the efficacy of passive resistance as a political weapon (and, paradoxically, also the first to organize a planned insurrection against British rule). The one thing which really marks them out is their spirit of pioneering. Although they number little over four million, there is hardly a country in the world without a Sikh—except perhaps Saudi Arabia and, now, Pakistan. There are Sikh sentries, policemen and taxi-drivers in all countries from Northern China to Turkey. There are Sikh farmers and artisans in Australia, South Africa, United States, Canada, and the countries of South America. There are Sikh doctors, pedlars and fortune-tellers in every country of Europe.

There is nothing racial or hereditary about the professions the Sikhs choose. A farmer in the Punjab may become a money-lender in Bombay, a carpenter in East Africa, a picker of fruit in California, or a lumber-jack in Canada. If necessary, he can train a troupe of love-birds to pick out cards telling fortunes to matelots in Marseilles—or just look more oriental himself and read ladies' hands at fun fairs. If all that fails, he can exploit his fine physique and cash in on feats of endurance. This brings me to the story of my meeting with Narinjan Singh—a farmer in the Punjab, a domestic servant in Shanghai, a fruit picker in San Francisco, an accountant in Vancouver, and an all-in wrestler in Toronto. I met him in Toronto.

For several days I had read his name in the papers and on hoardings. He was apparently quite a figure in the Canadian wrestling world and was due to fight someone called Mazurki, a Pole who also acted in the films. Narinjan Singh was known as Nanjo the Villain, Mazurki as Iron Mike. It seemed to be an important fight. In any case, Nanjo promised to be an interesting character. So I went to the auditorium.

The Maple Leaf Garden Auditorium was packed with nearly twenty thousand Canadian men, women and children. When I tuned up to buy my ticket a couple of burly Mounted Policemen came up to me and said in a friendly way: "You be careful." They escorted me to my seat and one of them stood by in the gangway.

After the preliminary bouts the microphone blared forth: "Attention please, attention please. We now come to the last fight, between Nanjo Singh of India and Iron Mike Mazurki of Hollywood, California. Time—twenty minutes. Umpire—Steve Berman."

A tremendous applause went up as the tall, lanky Pole walked down the gangway. He bowed to his admirers and entered the ring, followed by scores of autograph hunters. A minute later came the Indian, in a yellow turban and green dressing gown. The crowd hissed and booed. Unconcerned with the reception, he clambered into his corner, took off his turban and knelt in prayer—Moslem fashion towards Mecca. Then he unrobed. He was a short, squat man with brown bulging muscles, and a broad hairy chest. The umpire spoke to them in the centre of the ring. Then the fight started.

Nanjo was certainly the "top cad" in the Canadian wrestling world. He was also an excellent actor. A Sikh, he turned to Mecca as the Canadians thought he should. He rudely pushed away autograph hunters and hit a couple of youngsters who made faces at him. In the ring he dug his fingers in his adversary's eyes, pulled his hair and bit him. In fact, he broke all the rules of wrestling and everyone saw him break them barring the umpire (who was not supposed to notice).

"This is all phoney, you know," my neighbour informed me. "Actually, Nanjo is as meek as a lamb. Nice guy once you get to know him."

They all knew it was phoney, but it did not prevent them getting hysterical. When Nanjo twisted Mazurki's arms they shared the Pole's agony with sympathetic "No! No's!" When Mazurki had Nanjo squirming under him they yelled: "Kill the nigger." So it went on for full fifteen minutes.

"Five minutes to go" announced the loudspeaker.

My neighbour braced himself and nudged me. "Now the phoney ends and the fight begins."

In a trice the Indian flung the lanky Pole, who had been sitting on his chest for the last five minutes, sprawling on the canvas. With a murderous yell he pounced upon Mazurki, caught the man's head between his thighs and twisted his arms behind his back. This was his famous "cobra hold." It squashed the head and strangled the victim at the same time. There was a petrified silence in the arena.

A raucous voice rang out: "Mar dey Saley ko." Enthusiastically I joined my solitary countryman with a loud "Mar dey." There was a shower of empty cigarette cases, paper balls and silver paper on my head and twenty thousand voices roared: "Shut up."

My neighbour was nervous. "You better look out—people get a little worked up, you know." The Mountie came close to me and warned me: "Better keep quiet, mister, if you want to go home."

The crowd rose from their seats and clustered round the ring. A woman ran up and put the lighted end of her cigarette on the Indian's ankle. But Nanjo wouldn't let go his victim. The police

rushed in to get the spectators back in their seats and formed a cor-
don round the wrestlers. For some time Mazurki struggled and
groaned, then he gave up. The referee stopped the fight and held
aloft Nanjo's hand as the victor. The crowd booed and hissed and
made towards him. Half-a-dozen stalwart Mounties surrounded the
wrestler and hustled him into his dressing room.

A quarter of an hour later, when the crowd had dispersed and it
looked safe enough for a bearded and turbaned Indian to venture
forth, I made for Nanjo's dressing room to collect some facts of his
life. In the over-heated, stuffy room there were more than a dozen
hulking masses of fat and flesh—Toronto's leading heavyweights.
They were the best of friends. Nanjo and Mazurki were pounding
each other's bellies with friendly blows and being obscenely intimate—"You son-ov-a-gun," "You son-ov-a-bitch," and so on.

Nanjo saw me and a broad smile lit his face.

"Holy mackerel—see who's here—feller from my own country."

I introduced myself and shook several sweaty hands. Nanjo's
vocabulary of English words came to an end with "Jeezez it's good to
see you." Then he broke into pure rustic Punjabi.

"I could floor the lot of them, but my manager won't let me. I
have to lose. I have to act as a bad man and am often disqualified for
fouling. What can I do?" Then with a characteristically Indian gesture he slapped his stomach. "All for the belly. But when I have made
enough I will show you what I can do. I'll floor the incestuous sister-
sleepers. The whole bloody lot of them. Then I will go back to
Hoshiarpur and till the land. I want to show my village to my wife."
He looked round the crowded room and shouted for his wife. A
buxom blonde with a broad grin that bared several gold teeth
emerged from the ring of wrestlers and greeted me with a loud
"How dyedo" and vigorous chewing of gum.

"She's a Sikh now. Her name is Mahinder Kaur. I've taught her
some Punjabi. Baby, tell the gentlemen what I taught you."

The blonde spat out her chewing gum.

"Wah guru jee ka Khalsa."

"Wah guru jee kee Fateh."

GAETANO DONIZETTI

FOREIGN OPERAS rarely mention Canada or Canadians. So it is always a surprise to learn that even Mozart refers fondly to our land in his opera *Così fan tutte*. A famous aria from that opera uses the name of Canada again and again.

Another opera, *La Cambiale di Matrimonio*, an *opera buffa* in Italian by Rossini, is the only opera by a composer of the standard repertoire which employs a Canadian in any crucial way. But *Rita*, written by Gaetano Donizetti (1797-1848) in the summer of 1841, is a charming one-act opera where Canada plays a tangential but important role.

Sadly, Donizetti never heard his own creation. The music scholar William Ashbrook explains why, as well as the origins of the work in Paris:

> Donizetti happened to meet Gustave Vaez [a journeyman librettist whose real name was the mouth-filling Jean-Nicolas-Gustave van Nieuvenhuysen] on the street one day and begged him for a one-act subject, simply to keep himself occupied. Vaez was happy to oblige. The upshot of this chance encounter was *Rita*, a one-act work consisting of eight numbers connected by spoken dialogue. Within a week the score was complete, even to the orchestration. Since apparently Crosnier, the Director of the

Opera-Comique, rejected it, Donizetti started arrangements to have it translated into Italian so that it might be produced at the Fondo in Naples, but the death of Barbaja in October 1841 apparently put an end to that scheme. The still unperformed score of *Rita* was among Donizetti's effects when he died, but it had to wait a dozen years before it was finally produced; appropriately, its premiere took place at the theatre it had been originally designed for—the Opera-Comique.

Rita, one of the main characters, is, unknowingly, a bigamist who exhorts the women in the audience to find happiness by marrying a stupid man. Her first husband, Gasparo, a wife-beater, was, she believed, drowned at sea. Her second husband, Beppe, is, in turn, constantly nagged and boxed about the ears by the domineering Rita and, but for his own timidity, he would have left long ago. The sub-title of the opera is *The Battered Husband*.

Alas for the heroine, Gasparo, hearing a rumour that Rita has died, returns after many years to announce that, far from being dead, he has been abroad in Canada, and has found a Canadian girl whom he wishes to marry. In order to do so, however, in light of Rita's very healthy and continued existence, he must have his original banns annulled and his marriage certificate rescinded.

Given that each man is trying to foist Rita onto the other, the opera-goer is served a delicious permutation on the two gallants-fighting-over-the-girl story: the two men do fight, but only over who can be rid of her. Rita, misconstruing, believes Beppe is standing up for her and finally for himself, so her initial affection for him, long dormant, is rekindled. The short tale concludes happily ever after when Gaspar convinces Beppe that Rita would make him, Beppe, a happy man after all. We last see Gasparo as he sets sail for Canada to live happily ever after with his *Canadienne*.

The opera was rarely performed in the years immediately following its premiere on May 7, 1860, but in recent decades it has enjoyed a substantial revival. The following translation is by Dr. Francesca

Valente, the Director of the Italian Cultural Institute, Toronto, with the assistance of the editor.

---

from RITA

Scene Four

Bortolo, Beppe. Gasparo, coming from the main street, with a suitcase in his hand. He speaks with a foreign accent.

GASPARO *Buon giorno!* Do you own this hotel?

BEPPE At your service.

GASPARO I'm thirsty.

BEPPE Please, have a seat.

GASPARO I don't think a seat will quench my thirst.

BEPPE Bortolo, some wine.

GASPARO Two glasses.

BEPPE Two glasses.

GASPARO What the hell are you rubbing your face for?

BEPPE Oh, it's nothing, just an itch.

GASPARO No it's not. You look as if someone … maybe some guy tried to….

BORTOLO (*pouring the wine*) Some guy? I'd like to see him! Dream on! It was his wife …

GASPARO Your wife! And you allow that … A wife who hits him … That's an outrage. In a well-arranged marriage, it is the husband who hits the wife, Russian-style. I was in Russia, and I've made a study of conjugal customs. Try it with your wife and both of you will be satisfied. To tell you the truth, I am a married man myself—in fact, I've had two wives....

BEPPE Dessert?

GASPARO You bet! I'm sure she would have adored me if I hadn't been called away to my ship (I'm a man of the sea) on the very night of my wedding. I embarked at once, and sailed many leagues until a storm arose and caused the ship to sink; I was captured by cannibals. But luckily they had already dined. And then one day I landed in Canada.

BEPPE Canada?

GASPARO Yes, Canada, where I took up farming and made lots of money. But one day, I learned from a sailor who had recently emigrated to Canada that I was left a widower. So, after an absence of eight years I have come back to my village to get the death certificate of my wife because I intend to marry one more time.

BEPPE, BORTOLO *(together)* What? Again?

GASPARO Naturally. To a fantastic Canadian girl—a real animal— waiting for me to return to give me her heart and her fortune, and I guarantee that things will go just like the day of my other wedding—Russian-style. It is the only reasonable system....

ALEISTER CROWLEY

A LEISTER CROWLEY (1875-1947) wrote a lot of verse but he was not a very good poet. Nonetheless, he remains in print, and continues to be popular with those interested in "New Age" material, the history of theosophy, and the darker aspects of cabbalistic magic. He was a self-proclaimed expert in the diabolical; indeed, was fond of boasting that he was the "Beast from the Book of Revelation" and "the wickedest man in the world". Along with Yeats, he was a key member of the Order of the Golden Dawn, a legendary branch of theosophy. He might, to be lenient, be regarded as a precursor of Stephen King and other writers of commercial horror fiction.

In 1906, he travelled across Canada and, as the following excerpt from his autobiography displays with charming clarity, he hated the experience.

from THE CONFESSIONS
OF ALEISTER CROWLEY

I was in some doubt as to whether to go to America via Honolulu or by the northern Pacific route to Vancouver. I longed to see Oahu again, and yet I felt it a sort of duty to cover fresh ground. While I hesitated, fate decided.

The last berth for San Francisco via the Sandwich Islands was sold over my head. Alas!—had I only known! A quarter of an hour's delay caused me to miss what might have been the most dramatic moment of my life. The ship I should have sailed by left Honolulu in due course and fetched up four days later outside the Golden Gate—to find San Francisco a raging flower of flame.

I sailed on April 21st by *The Empress of India*, took a flying glance at Japan and put out into the Pacific.

> A savage sea without a sail,
> Grey gulphs and green aglittering.

We never sighted the slightest suggestion of life all the way to Vancouver, twelve days of chilly boredom, though there was a certain impressiveness in the very dreariness and desolation. There was a hint of the curious horror that emptiness always evokes, whether it is a space of starless night or a bleak and barren waste of land. The one exception is the Sahara Desert where, for some reason that I cannot name, the suggestion is not in the least of vacancy and barrenness, but rather of some subtle and secret spring of life.

Vancouver presents no interest to the casual visitor. It is severely Scotch. Its beauties lie in its surroundings.

I was very disappointed with the Rockies, of which I had heard such eloquent encomiums. They are singularly shapeless; and their proportions are unpleasing. There is too much colourless and brutal base; too little snowy shapely summit. As for the ghastly monotony of the wilderness beyond them, through Calgary and Winnipeg right on to Toronto—words fortunately fail. The manners of the people are crude and offensive. They seem to resent the existence of civilized men; and show it by gratuitous insolence, which they mistake for a mark of manly independence. The whole country and its people are somehow cold and ill-favoured. The character of the mountains struck me as significant. Contrast them with the Alps where every peak is ringed by smug hamlets, hearty and hospitable, and every available approach is either a flowery meadow, a pasture pregnant with peaceful flocks and herds, or a centre of cultivation. In the Rockies, barren and treeless plains are suddenly blocked by ugly walls of rock. Nothing less inviting can be imagined. Contrast them again with the Himalayas. There we find no green Alps, no clustering cottages; but their stupendous sublimity takes the mind away from any expectation or desire of thoughts connected with humanity. The Rockies have no majesty; they do not elevate the mind to contemplation of Almighty God any more than they warm the heart by seeming sentinels to watch over the habitations of one's fellow men.

Toronto as a city carries out the idea of Canada as a country. It is a calculated crime both against the aspirations of the soul and the affections of the heart. I had been fed vilely on the train. I thought I would treat myself to a really first-class dinner. But all I could get was high-tea—they had never heard the name of wine! Of all the loveless, lifeless lands that writhe beneath the wrath of God, commend me to Canada! (I understand that the eastern cities, having known French culture, are comparatively habitable. Not having been there I cannot say.)

THEODORE DREISER

THEODORE DREISER (1871-1947) had only two encounters with Canada, one real, one imaginary—both disastrous.

The real encounter took place in Toronto in September 1942. Dreiser had accepted an invitation to speak, during World War II, to a public affairs group known as the "Toronto Town Forum". He wanted to speak about the pressing need to open a second front in Europe in order to relieve German pressure on Russia. Given the modesty of the speaking fee offered, it is more accurate to say that he really came to Toronto in order to spend time with a Toronto woman (pseudonymously called Sylvia Bradshaw in Dreiser biographies) with whom he had had happy and intimate relations earlier in the year in his home town of Los Angeles.

Soon after Dreiser arrived and checked into the Royal York Hotel, he conducted amiable interviews in his room with some local reporters. But the organizers of his speech, sensing a bigger pay-day, gambled and chose to postpone his address by one night, asking Dreiser to conduct further interviews with the press. The delay was to prove lamentable.

The next morning, Dreiser met with several reporters *en masse*, including Margaret Aitken, a reporter for the *Toronto Telegram*, who also happened to be the niece of Lord Beaverbrook. With hindsight, it is clear that Dreiser was set up for a fall.

His left-wing perceptions of the War, his unqualified support for

Russia, and his loud belief in the innate corruption of European cap-
italism were views extensively reported and widely known long
before his arrival in Toronto. But there seems no doubt that having
in his grasp, so to speak, the actual progenitor of such views stimu-
lated the self-righteousness of both Beaverbrook, a shameless Anglo-
phile, and of the arch-Tory paper, the *Telegram*.

Dreiser would later recount that shortly after he began his
remarks to the journalists, he was interrupted by Margaret Aitken
with several, he felt, provocative questions. Succumbing to her good
looks, he lowered his guard and made comments which would
haunt him for the rest of his life. Later, in the USA, he could not
deny the accuracy of her quotations, merely their context.

On the afternoon of September 21, 1942, the *Telegram* hit the
streets with a major story headlined "ABUSE FOR BRITAIN
DREISER'S CONTRIBUTION TO ANGLO-US AMITY". The article
began, "Toronto citizens will be addressed by a man tomorrow night
who stated today that he 'would rather see the Germans in England
than the damn snobs now there.' Theodore Dreiser, American
author of German parentage, was the sponsor to these sentiments."
The article continued, "Should Russia go down to defeat, I hope the
Germans invade England.... Churchill has no intention of opening
a second front. He's afraid the Communists will rule the world. So
he does nothing except send thousands of Canadians to be slaugh-
tered at Dieppe. He didn't send any English. They stay at home and
do nothing. Nothing." Further similar intemperate remarks (recall
these were the darkest days of World War Two for the Allies) completed the newspaper story whose intent, it would seem clear, was to
make Dreiser look like a Nazi sympathizer.

The response from the public was volcanically quick and ferocious. Police were sent by the dozens to the hotel, ostensibly to protect Dreiser from mob attack. City Council went into emergency
session to discuss the matter. There was little debate; a motion calling for the police to "take such action as is necessary to prohibit Mr.
Theodore Dreiser from addressing any public meeting in this city,"
was easily and quickly passed.

The Minister of Justice in Ottawa, Louis St. Laurent, without speaking to Dreiser, or checking the veracity of the newspaper report, issued a nation-wide order chilling in its fury and breadth:

> Theodore Dreiser shall not, until further order, anywhere in Canada, make any speech or address any public meeting or make any statement with the intention that the same shall be made public by means of the public press or otherwise, and no proprietor or other person having charge of any public hall or other meeting place shall permit Theodore Dreiser to address any public meeting thereat.

St. Laurent further ordered the RCMP to follow Dreiser's movements, and began investigating avenues by which he could be quickly deported—or even be interned for the duration.

Initially slow to appreciate the danger of his position, Dreiser (and Sylvia Bradshaw) finally decided to leave town promptly. To avoid the police, they fled via the back stairs of the Royal York and caught the next train to Detroit—not at Union Station where they feared the Mounties might be waiting, but at the suburban Sunnyside Station. A telegram ordering the train to halt reached the conductor just as they were about to cross into Michigan. But the conductor (by some accounts an Irishman antipathetic to the British and so sympathetic to the plight of Dreiser) pretended not to have received the halt-order in time, and had the train cross the border.

Once across, Dreiser and Bradshaw checked into a Port Huron hotel. Dreiser signed the hotel register, "T.H. Dresser and wife," a gesture and condition coolly similar to a scene in the novel excerpted below—a novel written half a century earlier.

Following his Toronto experience, Dreiser was vilified by the American press for what instantly became known around the world as his "Toronto speech." Even more hurtfully to him, he was assailed by writers he admired. He soon suffered a heart attack. Bitter to the end of his life, he chose never again to make public political statements.

Dreiser's "other" encounter with Canada was second-hand, hence

EXIT MR. DREISER

JACK CANUCK: "And this for your second front!"

Editorial cartoon in *The Telegram* (Toronto) of September 23, 1942 demonstrating Canada's reaction to Theodore Dreiser's purported desire that Hitler should invade Britain. Dreiser had been invited to give a public lecture on the need to open a second front in the war in Europe, but because of remarks to the press, quoted out of context, his speech was cancelled, and he had to flee the country in disgrace.

imaginary. As a boy of fifteen in Chicago, his family had been scandalized by the elopement of his eldest sister, Emma. The Dreisers, devout Catholics, were horrified not only by the manner of the daughter's departure, but by the fact that she fled Chicago in the arms of a thief: L.A. Hopkins. Hopkins had been a trusted clerk of a noted "eating and drinking establishment", with access to large sums. But in February 1886, he robbed his employers of $3,500 and, with his inamorata, escaped by train. The couple headed immediately for Canada because Hopkins believed there was no extradition treaty with the States. Their destination was Montreal, a city which Hopkins seems to have visited before.

The heist was sensationally reported in the Chicago papers. Although the Dreiser name was never actually cited, news of the daughter's involvement must have been widely known to the Dreiser friends and neighbours. Even though Hopkins eventually returned most of the money, and Theodore's sister abandoned Hopkins to pursue her own career in New York, the infamy and humiliation of the incident so stuck with Theodore Dreiser that when he came to write his first novel, he chose to render loosely into fiction this family-shaming story of his sibling. The resulting book is considered a classic of American letters: *Sister Carrie*.

The realism of his fiction and his refusal to condemn the fleeing woman as a shameless hussy apparently disconcerted the wife of Abner Doubleday, Dreiser's publisher; indeed, she regarded the novel as obscene. Although the book was contracted for, because of Mrs. Doubleday's rancour, the house made little effort to promote or sell it. As a result, the novel sold poorly, and the rumours of its obscenity were sufficiently widespread in prudish America to nearly kill Dreiser's journalism career, if not the young man himself. "Magazines for which he had written previously, now refused to accept his articles.... Alone, he took a $1.25-a-week room and lived on bread and milk. His weight dropped to 130 pounds.... In desperation he sought the East River to drown himself" But treatment at a hospital brought him back to health; soon he would write a series of novels that would make him a titan in American letters.

So Dreiser's contacts with Canada, while brief, were poignant, certainly zesty. The Canadian connections serve almost as bookends to his life: his first novel, his last (attempted) public speech.

The following excerpt is taken from the authoritative edition of *Sister Carrie* recently published by the University of Pennsylvania. This edition restores material cut deliberately by censorious editors and accidently by typists and typesetters, including, oddly, several paragraphs describing Canada and Montreal.

---

from SISTER CARRIE

By noon the train rolled into Detroit and he began to feel exceedingly nervous. The police must be on his track by now. They had probably notified all the police of the big cities, and detectives would be watching for him. He remembered instances in which defaulters had been captured. Consequently, he breathed heavily and paled somewhat. His hands felt as if they must have something to do. He simulated interest in several scenes without which he did not feel. He repeatedly beat his foot upon the floor.

Carrie noticed his agitation, but said nothing. She had no idea what it meant or that it was important.

He wondered now why he had not asked whether this train went on through to Montreal or some Canadian point. Perhaps he could have saved time. He jumped up and sought out the conductor.

"Does any part of this train go to Montreal?" he asked.

"Yes, the next sleeper back does."

He would have asked more but it did not seem wise, so he decided to inquire at the depot.

The train rolled into the yards, clanging and puffing.

"I think we had better go right on through to Montreal," he said to Carrie. "I'll see what the connections are when we get off."

He was exceedingly nervous but did his best to put on a calm exterior. Carrie only looked at him with large, troubled eyes. She was drifting mentally, unable to say to herself what to do.

The train stopped and Hurstwood led the way out. He looked warily around him, pretending to look after Carrie. Seeing nothing that indicated studied observation, he made his way to the ticket office.

"The next train for Montreal leaves when?" he asked.

"In twenty minutes," said the man.

He bought two tickets and Pullman berths. Then he hastened back to Carrie.

"We go right out again," he said, scarcely noticing that Carrie looked tired and weary.

"I wish I was out of this all," she exclaimed gloomily.

"You'll feel better when we reach Montreal," he said.

"I haven't an earthly thing with me," said Carrie, "not even a handkerchief."

"You can buy all you want as soon as you get there, dearest," he explained. "You can call in a dressmaker."

Carrie said nothing and Hurstwood breathed easy. He saw no detectives anywhere.

Now the crier called the train ready and they got on. Hurstwood breathed a sigh of relief as it started. There was a short run to the river and then they were ferried over. They had barely pulled the train off the ferry boat when he settled back with a sigh.

"It won't be so very long now," he said, remembering her in his relief. "We get in the first thing in the morning."

Carrie scarcely deigned to reply.

"I'll see if they haven't got on a dining car," he added. "I'm hungry."

To the untraveled, territory other than their own familiar heath is invariably fascinating. Next to love it is the one thing which solaces and delights. It is a boon to the weary and distressed, the one thing, which, because of its boundless prodigality of fact and incident, causes the mind to forget. Not even wounded love can long wander to and fro amid new scenes without in a measure forgetting its wound. The things to see are too important to be neglected, and mind, which is a mere reflection of sensory impressions, succumbs to this flood of objects. It is so busy storing new ideas that there is scarcely any time for old ones. Thus lovers are forgotten, sorrows laid aside, death hidden from view. There is a world of accumulated feeling back of the trite dramatic expression—"I am going away." To the untraveled, that is the only equivalent for love lost—the one partial compensation, the thing which, if it cannot restore, can make us forget. Let us not forget therefore that Carrie, the untraveled, was traveling.

As she looked out upon the flying scenery, she almost forgot that she had been tricked into this long journey against her will, and that she was without the necessary apparel for traveling. She quite forgot Hurstwood's presence at times, and looked away to lonely farm houses and cosy cottages in villages with wondering eyes. It was an interesting world to Carrie. Her life had just begun. She did not feel herself defeated at all. Neither was she blasted in hope. The great city held something, she knew not what. Possibly she would come out of bondage into freedom—who knows? Perhaps she would be happy. These were thoughts, which in the thinking raised her above the level of the erring. She was saved in that she was hopeful.

Hurstwood conversed some with her after leaving Detroit, but as the day waned, both grew weary and slept. By eight-thirty the porter began to let down the berths, and by nine many were retired. Hurstwood was the first to suggest that she retire early. After she had gone he went forward to smoke a cigar but found no comfort. Before long he sought his berth, and so the night was passed.

The following morning the train pulled safely into Montreal and they stepped down, Hurstwood glad to be out of danger, Carrie wondering at the novel atmosphere of the northern city. Long before, Hurstwood had been here, and now he remembered the name of the hotel at which he had stopped. As they came out of the main entrance of the depot, he heard it called anew by a busman.

"We'll go right up and get rooms," he said to Carrie, moving with her toward the welcoming busman.

Carrie acquiesced and he helped her in. The bus drove through streets radically different from those of Chicago to the large hotel, which they entered by the ladies' way.

"Sit down a moment," said Hurstwood as they reached the little waiting room. "I'll go and see about the room."

Carrie, however, preferred to walk about and look at the few pictures on the walls.

At the clerk's office Hurstwood swung the register about while the clerk came forward. He was thinking what name he would put down. With the latter before him, he found no time for hesitation. The name he had seen out of the car window came swiftly back. It was pleasing enough. With an easy hand he wrote "G. W. Murdoch and wife." It was the largest concession he felt like making to necessity. His initials he could not spare.

"Anything on the second floor with a bath?" he asked.

The clerk studied his list.

"Yes, number eleven."

"Let me see it," he said.

A boy was called and he went to look. For a wonder it was eminently satisfactory, being decorated in dark green, with furniture to match, and having three outside windows. He kept the key and went down for Carrie.

"I think I've got a suitable room for you," he said quietly.

Carrie also liked it. She was soothed by the simple, decorative treatment of the place. She felt at once that he had secured her a lovely chamber.

"You have a bath there," said he. "Now you can clean up when you get ready."

Carrie went over and looked out the window, while Hurstwood looked at himself in the glass. He felt dusty and unclean. He had no trunk, no change of linen, not even a hair brush.

"I'll ring for soap and towels," he said, "and send you up a hair brush. Then you bathe and get ready for breakfast. I'll go for a shave and come back and get you, and then we'll go out and look for some clothes for you."

He smiled goodnaturedly as he said this.

"All right," said Carrie. She sat down in one of the rocking chairs, while Hurstwood waited for the boy, who soon knocked.

"Soap, towels and a pitcher of ice water."

"Yes, sir."

"I'll go now," he said to Carrie, coming towards her and holding out his hands, but she did not move to take them. "You're not mad at me, are you?" he asked softly.

"Oh, no," she answered, rather indifferently.

"Don't you care for me at all?"

She made no answer but looked steadily toward the window.

"Don't you think you could love me a little?" he pleaded, taking one of her hands, which she endeavoured to draw away. "You once said you did."

"What made you deceive me so?" asked Carrie.

"I couldn't help it," he said. "I wanted you too much."

"You didn't have any right to want me," she answered, striking cleanly home.

"Oh, well, Carrie," he answered, "here I am. It's too late now. Won't you try and care for me a little?"

He looked rather worsted in thought as he stood before her.

She shook her head negatively.

"Let me start all over again. Be my wife from today on."

Carrie rose up as if to step away, he holding her hand. Now he slipped his arm about her and she struggled, but in vain. He held her quite close. Instantly there flowed up in his body the all-compelling desire. His affection took an ardent form.

"Let me go," said Carrie, who was folded close to him.

"Won't you love me?" he said. "Won't you be mine from now on?"

Carrie had never been ill-disposed toward him. Only a moment before she had been listening with some complacency, remembering her old affection for him. He was so handsome, so daring.

Now, however, this feeling had changed to one of opposition, which rose futilely. It mastered her for a moment, and then, held close as she was, began to wane. Something else in her spoke. This man to whose bosom she was being pressed was strong, he was passionate, he loved her and she was alone. If she did not turn to him—accept of his love, where else might she go? Also the physical claims its own. Her resistance half-dissolved in the flood of his strong feeling.

"Won't you love me a little?" he asked. "I'll start over. Won't you own that you love me?"

Carrie was relaxing her struggle. She found him lifting her head and looking into her eyes. What magnetism there was, she could never know. His many sins, however, were for the moment all forgotten.

He pressed her closer and kissed her, and she felt that further opposition was useless.

"Will you marry me?" she asked, forgetting *how.*

"This very day," he said with all delight.

Now the hall boy pounded on the door, and he released his hold upon her regretfully.

"You get ready now, will you?" he said. "At once."

"Yes," she answered.

"I'll be back in three-quarters of an hour."

Carrie, flushed and excited, moved away, as he admitted the boy.

Below stairs he halted in the lobby to look for a barbershop. For the moment he was in fine feather. His recent victory over Carrie seemed to atone for much he had endured during the last few days. Life seemed worth fighting for. The eastward flight from all things customary and attached seemed as if it might have happiness waiting at the end of it. The storm showed a rainbow, at the end of which might be a pot of gold.

He was about to cross to a little red and white striped bar which was fastened up beside a door, when a voice greeted him familiarly. Instantly his heart sank.

"Why hello, George, old man," said the voice. "What are you doing down here?"

Hurstwood was already confronted and recognized his friend Kenny, the stock broker.

"Just tending to a little private matter," he answered, his mind working like the keyboard of a telephone station. This man evidently did not know—he had not read the papers.

"Well, it seems strange to see you way up here," said Mr. Kenny genially. "Stopping here?"

"Yes," said Hurstwood uneasily, thinking of his handwriting on the register.

"Going to be in town long?"

"No, only a day or so."

"Is that so. Had your breakfast?"

"Yes," said Hurstwood, lying blandly. "I'm just going for a shave."

"Won't come have a drink?"

"Not until afterwards," said the ex-manager. "I'll see you later. Are you stopping here?"

"Yes," said Mr. Kenny, and then turning the word again added, "How are things out in Chicago?"

"About the same as usual," said Hurstwood, smiling genially.

"Wife with you?"

"No."

"Well, I must see more of you today. I'm just going in here for breakfast. Come in when you're through."

"I will," said Hurstwood, moving away. The whole conversation was a trial to him. It seemed to add complications with every word. This man called up a thousand memories. He represented everything he had left. Chicago, his wife, the elegant resort—all these were in his greeting and inquiries. And here he was in this same hotel, expecting to confer with him, unquestionably waiting to have a good time with him. All at once the Chicago papers would arrive. The local papers would have accounts in them this very day. He forgot his triumph with Carrie in the possibility of soon being known for what he was, in this man's eyes, a safe-breaker. He could have groaned as he went into the barber-shop. He decided to escape this friend and stay with Carrie to seek a more secluded hotel.

Accordingly, when he came out, he was glad to see the lobby clear, and hastened toward the stairs. He would get Carrie and go out by the ladies' entrance. They would have breakfast in some more inconspicuous place.

Across the lobby, however, another individual was surveying him. He was of a commonplace Irish type, small of stature, cheaply dressed and with a head that seemed a smaller edition of some huge ward politician's. This individual had been evidently talking with the clerk, but now he surveyed the ex-manager keenly.

Hurstwood felt the long range examination and recognized the type. Instinctively he felt that the man was a detective, that he was being watched. He hurried across, pretending not to notice, but in his mind were a world of thoughts. What would happen now? What could these people do? He began to trouble concerning the extradition laws. He did not understand them absolutely. Perhaps he could be arrested. Oh, if Carrie should find out. Montreal was too warm for him. He began to long to be out of it.

Carrie had bathed and was waiting when he arrived. She looked refreshed—more delightful than ever, but reserved. Since he had gone she had resumed somewhat of her cold attitude toward him. Love was not blazing in her heart. He felt it and his troubles seemed increased. He could not take her in his arms; he did not even try. Something about her forbade it. In part his opinion was the result of his own experiences and reflections below stairs.

"You're ready, are you?" he said kindly.

"Yes," she answered.

"We'll go out for breakfast. This place down here doesn't appeal to me very much."

"All right," said Carrie.

They went out and turned into the main street, but at the corner the commonplace Irish individual was standing, eyeing him. Hurstwood could scarcely refrain from showing that he knew of this chap's presence. The insolence in the fellow's eye was galling. Still they passed, and he explained to Carrie concerning the city. Another restaurant was not long in showing itself, and here they entered.

"What a queer town this is," said Carrie, who marvelled at it solely because it was not like Chicago.

"It isn't as lively as Chicago," said Hurstwood. "Don't you like it?"

"No," said Carrie, whose feelings were already localized in the great western city.

"Well, it isn't as interesting," said Hurstwood.

"What's here?" asked Carrie, wondering at his choosing to visit this town.

"Nothing much," returned Hurstwood. "It's quite a resort. There's some pretty scenery about here."

Carrie listened but with a feeling of unrest. This city did not appeal to her. There was much about her situation which destroyed the possibility of appreciation.

"We won't stay here long," said Hurstwood, who was now really glad to note her dissatisfaction. "You pick out your clothes as soon as breakfast is over and we'll run down to New York soon. You'll like that. It's a lot more like a city than any place outside Chicago."

He was really planning to slip out and away. He would see what these detectives would do—what move his employers at Chicago would make—then he would slip away—down to New York where it was easy to hide. He knew enough about that city to know that its mysteries, and possibilities of mystification, were infinite.

The more he thought, however, the more wretched his situation became. He saw that getting here did not exactly clear up the ground. The firm would probably employ detectives to watch him—Pinkerton men or agents of Mooney and Boland. They might arrest him the moment he tried to leave Canada. So he might be compelled to remain here months, and in what a state! His heart revolted at it. Nothing in Montreal appealed to him. It was comparatively small—comparatively provincial. Worst of all it was not Chicago—and now that he was threatened with long separation from that place and his daily duties and greetings, the misery of it became great. He began to feel the first faint touches of nostalgy—as old and experienced as he was.

After breakfast he went with Carrie to several large dry goods stores and waited while she ordered a number of things. Young as she was, Carrie had already a fund of experience to draw upon.

Thrown thus upon her own responsibility in the matter of selecting clothing, she arose and met the occasion with admirable determination. Her selection was altogether good, because while following her feelings, she had not forgotten the advice of Mrs. Hale. She selected with fair rapidity and finally came away.

"Got all you want?" asked Hurstwood.

"All I need just now," answered Carrie.

At the hotel Hurstwood was anxious and yet fearful to see the morning papers. He wanted to know how far the news of his criminal deed had spread. So he told Carrie he would be up in a few moments, and went to secure and scan the dailies. No familiar or suspicious faces were about, and yet he did not like reading in the lobby, so he sought the main parlour on the floor above and, seated by a window there, looked them over. Very little was given to his crime, but it was there, several "sticks" in all, among all the riff-raff of telegraphed murders, accidents, marriages and other news items from out the length and breadth of the land. He wished deeply, as he read, that all his eyes followed were not true. He wished half sadly that he could undo it. Every moment of his time in this far-off abode of safety but added to his feeling that he had made a great mistake. There could have been an easier way out, if he had only known.

He left the papers before going to the room, thinking thus to keep them out of the hands of Carrie.

"Well, how are you feeling?" he asked of her. She was engaged in looking out of the window.

"Oh, all right," she answered.

He came over and was about to begin a conversation with her when a knock came at their door.

"Maybe it's one of my parcels," said Carrie.

Hurstwood opened the door, outside of which stood the individual whom he so thoroughly suspected.

"You're Mr. Hurstwood, are you?" said the latter with a volume of affected shrewdness and assurance.

"Yes," said Hurstwood calmly. He knew the type so thoroughly that some of his old familiar indifference to it returned. Such men as these were of the lowest stratum welcomed at the resort. He stepped out and closed the door.

"Well, you know what I am here for, don't you?" said the man confidentially.

"I can guess," said Hurstwood softly.

"Well, do you intend to try and keep the money?"

"That's my affair," said Hurstwood grimly.

"You can't do it, you know," said the detective, eyeing him

"Look here, my man," said Hurstwood authoritatively. "You don't understand anything about this case, and I can't explain to you. Whatever I intend to do I'll do without advice from the outside. You'll have to excuse me."

"Well, now there's no use of your talking that way," said the man, "when you're in the hands of the police. We can make a lot of trouble for you, if we want to. You're not registered right in this house, you haven't got your wife with you and the newspapers don't know you're here yet. You might as well be reasonable."

"What do you want to know?" asked Hurstwood.

"Whether you're going to send back that money or not."

Hurstwood paused and studied the floor.

"There's no use explaining to you about this," he said at last. "There's no use of your asking me. I'm no fool, you know. I know just what you can do and what you can't. You can create a lot of trouble if you want to—I know that all right, but it won't help you to get the money. Now, I've made up my mind what to do—I've already written Hannah and Hogg, so there's nothing I can say. You wait until you hear more from them."

All the time he had been talking, he had been moving away from the door, down the corridor, out of the hearing of Carrie. They were now near the end where the corridor opened into the large general parlour.

"You won't give it up?" said the man.

The words irritated Hurstwood greatly. Hot blood poured into his brain. Many thoughts formulated themselves. He was no thief. He didn't want the money. If he could only explain to Hannah and Hogg, maybe it would be all right again.

"See here," he said, "there's no use my talking about this at all. I respect your power all right, but I'll have to deal with the people who know."

"Well, you can't get out of Canada with it," said the man.

"I don't want to get out," said Hurstwood. "When I get ready, perhaps there'll be nothing to stop me for."

He turned back and the detective watched him closely. It seemed an intolerable thing. Still he went on and into the room.

"Who was it?" asked Carrie.

"A friend of mine from Chicago."

The whole of this conversation was such a shock, that coming as it did after all the other worry of the past week, it sufficed to induce a deep gloom and moral revulsion in Hurstwood. What hurt him worst was the fact that he was being pursued as a thief. He began to see the nature of that social injustice which sees but one side, often but a single point in a long, cumulative tragedy. All the newspapers noted but one thing, his taking the money. How and wherefore were but in differently dealt with. All the complications which led up to it were unknown. He was accused without being understood.

What began to take clearest form in his mind was the fact that he did not want to keep the money. It was a wretched piece of business, the taking of it, and he did not care to keep it. Besides, if he retained it, he sold for a paltry sum all his connections with the past—his rights, privileges and desires. If he kept it, he bought nothing but suffering and the necessity to sneak about in by-ways and secret places. He would be watched some day he would be caught. Canada would be his only refuge and it was cold, different, un-American. Already he missed the clang and clatter of Chicago life. The absence of the show and shine of the resort was telling deeply upon his spirits.

Sitting in his room with Carrie the same day, he decided to send the money back. He would write Hannah and Hogg, explain all and then send it by express. Maybe they would forgive him. Perhaps they would invite him back. He would make good the false statement he had made about writing them. Then he would leave this peculiar town.

IVOR GURNEY

G IVEN that more than sixty thousand Canadians were casualties in World War One, the dearth of literary praises by foreign writers for—even acknowledgement of—the bravery of our soldiers is yet one more proof that if Canadians do not bother to write their own history, no one else will—at least in a manner befitting its majesty.

A rare and delightful exception to this deficiency is the following poem by Ivor Gurney (1890- 1937), an English poet best known for his verses inspired by the Great War. Gurney was a private on the western front from 1915; in 1917 he was gassed and wounded at Passchendaele. Treated for, and cured of his physical wounds in Edinburgh, the war succeeded in exacerbating his fragile mental health, and from 1922 until his death he was a patient at the London Mental Hospital. During his lifetime, he published just two books of poetry, although these were of sufficient merit to gain him the spirited support of Vaughn Williams, Edmund Blunden and Walter de la Mare. After his death, however, hundreds of his poems were found—poems suggesting, sadly, that his mental condition may not have been so severe as to deserve a lifetime's confinement in an institution for the insane.

In Gurney's poem, there is no stink of Kiplingesque imperialism, no unctuous gratitude from the motherland at the colonials' willingness to be cannon-fodder. Nor is there the rage we associate with the better-known, younger war poets of that period. As the renowned English poet (and acclaimed Gurney editor) P.J. Kavanagh has remarked,

Whereas the other war poets (Owen, Sassoon and so on) reacted against the war rhetoric of their elders with indignation and tell us truths we ought to have guessed, Gurney gives us pictures we would not have imagined: the gentleness of his first reception in the front line, the effect of a clarinet played in the trenches. It is the poetry of a particularized, not a generalized, humanity, of the flesh and nerves rather than of the intellect.

CANADIANS

We marched, and saw a company of Canadians,
Their coats weighed eighty pounds at least, we saw them
Faces infinitely grimed in, with almost dead hands
Bent, slouching downwards to billets comfortless and dim.
Cave dwellers last of tribes they seemed, and a pity
Even from us just relieved, much as they were, left us.
Lord, what a land of desolation, what iniquity
Of mere being, of what youth that country bereft us;
Plagues of evil lay in Death's Valley, we also
Had forded that up to the thighs in chill mud,
Gone for five days then any sign of life glow,
As the notched stumps or the grey clouds we stood
Dead past death from first hour and the needed mood
Of level pain shifting continually to and fro.
Saskatchewan, Ontario, Jack London ran in
My own mind; what in others? these men who finely
Perhaps had chosen danger for reckless and fine,
Fate had sent for suffering and dwelling obscenely
Vermin-eaten, fed beastly, in vile ditches meanly.

WILLIAM
CULLEN BRYANT

T HE AMERICAN POET and editor William Cullen Bryant (1794-
1878) was introduced to the joys of good writing through the
vast library of his wealthy father. His earliest poems, deeply influenced by the English Romantic poets, took Nature as their subject,
and like a good Romantic, he published his first book at the age of
fourteen. Bryant practised law up to the age of thirty-one, but it was
the poetry he published during the 1820s that made his name known
throughout America. In 1829, he became Editor-in-Chief of the
New York Evening Post, a position of eminence he was to hold for a
remarkable five decades more. Towards the end of his journalism
career, ever the poet, he translated the complete works of Homer
into blank verse.

His friend, the American novelist Richard Henry Dana, suggested to Bryant that Bryant's travel articles written for the *Evening
Post* should be gathered into a book. Initially, he was reluctant to do
this, regarding the writing as ephemeral, written for the imperma-
nence of a newspaper. But spurred by G.P. Putnam, who offered to
publish the tome as *Letters of a Traveler*, Bryant, in 1850, assembled
fifty-three reports, ranging over Europe and North America.

One of these accounts describes in detail his 1846 voyage by
steamer through Lakes Erie, St. Clair, Huron and Michigan. It con-
stitutes some of the earliest descriptions of Canada by an American

writer who is also a major literary figure. There is, in these articles, as in many of his travelogues, an aloofness of tone, a lack of desire—or perhaps inability—to embrace, to mingle fully with the people and the places visited. But his affection for the natural world draws him, sometimes despite himself, into Canada, and an awareness that the Great Lakes divide two very different countries.

---

from LETTERS OF A TRAVELER

To the *Evening Post*

> Steamer *Oregon*, Lake Michigan
> July 25, 1846.

Soon after passing the flats described in my last letter, and entering the river St. Clair, the steamer stopped to take in wood on the Canadian side. Here I went on shore. All that we could see of the country was a road along the bank, a row of cottages at a considerable distance from each other along the road, a narrow belt of cleared fields behind them, and beyond the fields the original forest standing like a long lofty wall, with its crowded stems of enormous size and immense height, rooted in the strong soil—ashes and maples and elms, the largest of their species. Scattered in the foreground were numbers of leafless elms, so huge that the settlers, as if in despair of bringing them to the ground by the axe, had girdled them and left them to decay and fall at their leisure.

We went up to one of the houses, before which stood several of the family attracted to the door by the sight of our steamer. Among them was an intelligent-looking man, originally from the state of

New York, who gave quick and shrewd answers to our inquiries. He told us of an Indian settlement about twenty miles further up the St. Clair. Here dwell a remnant of the Chippewa tribe, collected by the Canadian government, which has built for them comfortable log-houses with chimneys, furnished them with horses and neat cattle, and utensils of agriculture, erected a house of worship, and given them a missionary; "The design of planting them here," said the settler, "was to encourage them to cultivate the soil."

"And what has been the success of the plan?" I asked.

"It has met with no success at all," he answered. "The worst thing that the government could do for these people is to give them every thing as it has done, and leave them under no necessity to provide for themselves. They chop over a little land, an acre or two to a family; their squaws plant a little corn and a few beans, and this is the extent of their agriculture. They pass their time in hunting and fishing, or in idleness. They find deer and bears in the woods behind them, and fish in the St. Clair before their doors, and they squander their yearly pensions. In one respect they are just like white men, they will not work if they can live without."

"What fish do they find in the St. Clair?"

"Various sorts. Trout and white-fish are the finest, but they are not so abundant at this season. Sturgeon and pike are just now in season, and the pike are excellent."

One of us happening to observe that the river might easily be crossed by swimming, the settler answered: "Not so easily as you might think. The river is as cold as a well, and the swimmer would soon be chilled through, and perhaps taken with the cramp. It is this coldness of the water which makes the fish so fine at this season."...

We now proceeded up the river, and in about two hours came to a neat little village on the British side, with a windmill, a little church, and two or three little cottages, prettily screened by young trees. Immediately beyond this was the beginning of the Chippewa settlement of which we had been told. Log-houses, at the distance of nearly a quarter of a mile from each other, stood in a long row beside the river, with scattered trees about them, the largest of the forest, some girdled and leafless, some untouched and green, the smallest trees between having been cut away. Here and there an Indian woman, in a blue dress and bare-headed, was walking along the road; cows and horses were grazing near the house; patches of maize were seen, tended in a slovenly manner and by no means clear of bushes, but nobody was at work in the fields. Two females came down to the bank, with paddles, and put off into the river in a birch-bark canoe the ends of which were carved in the peculiar Indian fashion. A little beyond stood a group of boys and girls on the water's edge, the boys in shirts and leggings, silently watching the steamer as it shot by them. Still further on a group of children of both sexes, seven in number, came running with shrill cries down the bank. It was then about twelve o'clock and the weather was extremely sultry. The boys in an instant threw off their shirts and leggings, and plunged into the water with shouts, but the girls were in before them, for they wore only a kind of petticoat which they did not take off, but cast themselves into the river at once and slid through the clear water like seals.

This little Indian colony on the edge of the forest extends for several miles along the river, where its banks are highest and best adapted to the purpose of settlement. It ends at last just below the village which bears the name of Fort Saranac, in the neighborhood of which I was shown an odd-looking wooden building, and was told that this was the house of worship provided for the Indians by the government....

We were soon upon the broad waters of Lake Huron, and when the evening closed upon us we were already out of sight of land. The next morning I was awakened by the sound of rain on the hurricane deck. A cool east wind was blowing. I opened the outer door of my state-room and sniffed the air which was strongly impregnated with the odor of burnt leaves or grass, proceeding, doubtless, from the burning of woods or prairies somewhere on the shores of the lake. For mile after mile, for hour after hour, as we flew through the mist, the same odor was perceptible; the atmosphere of the lake was full of it.

"Will it rain all day?" I asked of a fellow-passenger, a Salem man, in white cravat.

"The clouds are thin," he answered; "the sun will soon burn them off."

In fact, the sun soon melted away the clouds, and before ten o'clock I was shown, to the north of us, the dim shore of the Great Manitoulin Island, with the faintly descried opening called the West Strait, through which a throng of speculators in copper mines are this summer constantly passing to the Sault Ste. Marie. On the other side was the sandy isle of Bois Blanc, the name of which is commonly corrupted into Bob Low Island, thickly covered with pines, and showing a tall light-house on the point nearest us....

To the *Evening Post*

Sault Ste. Marie,
August 13, 1846.

... At half-past seven the next morning we were on our way to the Sault Ste. Marie, in the little steamer *General Scott*. The wind was blowing fresh, and a score of persons who had intended to visit the Sault were withheld by the fear of seasickness, so that half a dozen of us had the steamer to ourselves. In three or four hours we found ourselves gliding out of the lake, through smooth water, between two low points of land covered with firs and pines into the west strait. We passed Drummond's Island, and then coasted St. Joseph's Island, on the woody shore of which I was shown a solitary house. There I was told lives a long-nosed Englishman, a half-pay officer, with two wives, sisters, each the mother of numerous offspring. This English polygamist has been more successful in seeking solitude than in avoiding notoriety. The very loneliness of his habitation on the shore causes it to be remarked, and there is not a passenger who makes the voyage to the Sault, to whom his house is not pointed out, and his story related. It was hinted to me that he had a third wife in Toronto, but I have my private doubts of this part of the story, and suspect that it was thrown in to increase my wonder.

Beyond the island of St. Joseph we passed several islets of rock with fir-trees growing from the clefts. Here, in summer, I was told, the Indians often set up their wigwams, and subsist by fishing. There were none in sight as we passed, but we frequently saw on either shore the skeletons of the Chippewa habitations. These consist, not like those of the Potawottamies, of a circle of sticks placed in the form of a cone, but of slender poles bent into circles, so as to make an almost regular hemisphere, over which, while it serves as a dwelling, birch-bark and mats of bulrushes are thrown....

To the *Evening Post*

Sault Ste. Marie
August 15, 1846.

... In the afternoon we engaged a half-breed and his brother to take us over to the Canadian shore. His wife, a slender young woman with a lively physiognomy, not easily to be distinguished from a French woman of her class, accompanied us in the canoe with her little boy. The birchbark canoe of the savage seems to me one of the most beautiful and perfect things of the kind constructed by human art. We were in one of the finest that float on St. Mary's river, and when I looked at its delicate ribs, mere shavings of white cedar, yet firm enough for the purpose—the thin broad laths of the same wood with which these are inclosed, and the broad sheets of birch-bark, impervious to water, which sheathed the outside, all firmly sewed together by the tough slender roots of the fir-tree, and when I considered its extreme lightness and the grace of its form, I could not but wonder at the ingenuity of those who had invented so beautiful a combination of ship-building and basket-work. "It cost me twenty dollars," said the half-breed, "and I would not take thirty for it."

We were ferried over the waves where they dance at the foot of the rapids. At this place large quantities of white-fish, one of the most delicate kinds known on our continent, are caught by the Indians, in their season, with scoop-nets. The whites are about to interfere with this occupation of the Indians, and I saw the other day a seine of prodigious length constructing, with which it is intended to sweep nearly half the river at once. "They will take a hundred barrels a day," said an inhabitant of the place.

On the British side, the rapids divide themselves into half a dozen noisy brooks, which roar round little islands, and in the boiling pools of which the speckled trout is caught with the rod and line. We landed at the warehouses of the Hudson Bay Company, where the goods intended for the Indian trade are deposited, and the furs brought from the northwest are collected. They are surrounded by a massive stockade, within which lives the agent of the Company; the walks are gravelled and well-kept, and the whole bears the marks of British solidity and precision. A quantity of furs had been brought in the day before, but they were locked up in the warehouse, and all was now quiet and silent. The agent was absent; a half-breed nurse stood at the door with his child, and a Scotch servant, apparently with nothing to do, was lounging in the court inclosed by the stockade; in short, there was less bustle about this centre of one of our most powerful trading-companies in the world, than about one of our farm-houses.

Crossing the bay, at the bottom of which these buildings stand, we landed at a Canadian village of half-breeds. Here were one or two wigwams and a score of log-cabins, some of which we entered. In one of them we were received with great appearance of deference by a woman of decidedly Indian features, but light-complexioned, barefoot, with blue embroidered leggings falling over her ankles and sweeping the floor, the only peculiarity of Indian costume about her. The house was as clean as scouring could make it, and her two little children, with little French physiognomies, were fairer than many children of the European race. These people are descended from the French voyageurs and settlers on one side; they speak Canadian

French more or less, but generally employ the Chippewa language in their intercourse with each other.

Near at hand was a burial ground, with graves of the Indians and half-breeds, which we entered. Some of the graves were covered with a low roof of cedar-bark, others with a wooden box; over others was placed a little house like a dog-kennel, except that it had no door, others were covered with little log-cabins. One of these was of such a size that a small Indian family would have found it amply large for their accommodation. It is a practice among the savages to protect the graves of the dead from the wolves, by stakes driven into the ground and meeting at the top like the rafters of a roof; and perhaps when the Indian or half-breed exchanged his wigwam for a log-cabin, his respect for the dead led him to make the same improvement in the architecture of their narrow houses. At the head of most of these monuments stood wooden crosses, for the population here is principally Roman Catholic, some of them inscribed with the names of the dead, not always accurately spelled.

Not far from the church stands a building, regarded by the half-breeds as a wonder of architecture, the stone house, *la maison de pierre*, as they call it, a large mansion built of stone by a former agent of the Northwest or Hudson Bay Company, who lived here in a kind of grand manorial style, with his servants and horses and hounds, and gave hospitable dinners in those days when it was the fashion for the host to do his best to drink his guests under the table. The old splendor of the place has departed, its gardens are overgrown with grass, the barn has been blown down, the kitchen in which so many grand dinners were cooked consumed by fire, and the mansion, with its broken and patched windows, is now occupied by a Scotch farmer of the name of Wilson.

We climbed a ridge of hills back of the house to the church of the Episcopal Mission, built a few years ago as a place of worship for the Chippewas, who have since been removed by the government. It stands remote from any habitation, with three or four Indian graves near it, and we found it filled with hay. The view from its door is uncommonly beautiful; the broad St. Mary lying below, with its bordering village and woody valley, its white rapids and its rocky islands, picturesque with the pointed summits of the fir-tree. To the northwest the sight followed the river to the horizon, where it issued from Lake Superior, and I was told that in clear weather one might discover, from the spot on which I stood, the promontory of Gros Cap, which guards the outlet of that mighty lake.

The country around was smoking in a dozen places with fires in the woods. When I returned I asked who kindled them. "It is old Tanner," said one, "the man who murdered Schoolcraft." There is great fear here of Tanner, who is thought to be lurking yet in the neighborhood. I was going the other day to look at a view of the place from an eminence reached by a road passing through a swamp, full of larches and firs. "Are you not afraid of Tanner?" I was asked. Mrs. Schoolcraft, since the assassination of her husband, has come to live in the fort, which consists of barracks protected by a high stockade. It is rumored that Tanner has been seen skulking about within a day or two, and yesterday a place was discovered which is supposed to have served for his retreat. It was a hollow, thickly surrounded by shrubs, which some person had evidently made his habitation for a considerable time. There is a dispute whether this man is insane or not, but there is no dispute as to his malignity. He has threatened to take the life of Mr. Bingham, the venerable Baptist missionary at this place, and as long as it is not certain that he has left the neighborhood a feeling of insecurity prevails. Nevertheless, as I know no reason why this man should take it into his head to shoot me, I go whither I list, without the fear of Tanner before my eyes.

JOSÉ MARÍA
HEREDIA

WILLIAM CULLEN BRYANT described Heredia's famous ode to Niagara as "the best which has been written about the Great American Cataract." While Canadians will decidedly challenge Bryant's claim that the Falls are an American cataract, few would contradict his literary assessment, despite the passage of nearly two centuries since the poem's composition. To this day, José María Heredia (1803-1839) is the only author whose presence at the Falls has been celebrated by the city authorities: his poem has been commemorated by a bronze plaque prominently placed near the Horseshoe Falls. This is a greater honour than it might first seem, in that more imaginative authors have been to Niagara, and have written about it, than any other geographical splendour on the continent.

Ironically, Heredia may never have seen the Falls. Following his flight when only twenty years old from his native Cuba to escape prosecution for alleged revolutionary activity, he moved first to Boston then later to New York City. It was there that he met Bryant, and the ensuing acquaintanceship inspired Bryant "to the further study of the literature of Spain and to [an] interest arguably in Latin America during the rest of his life."

Heredia's time in the States was marked by extreme poverty and ill health. While he may have travelled to Niagara, there is no record that he did so, and so his famous composition may have been inspired by the "idea" of the Falls rather than by their actual sighting.

A trip to Niagara was not foremost among his distractions while in exile, although during his American purgatory his legendary poem "Niagara" was published; he was also writing other, superb poems, and he was sentenced to death in absentia by a Cuban court.

Mexico, having recently won its independence, saw in Heredia a revolutionary hero, and generously offered him refuge and positions worthy of his erudition and standing. He accepted. However, hungry for his homeland, he returned briefly to Cuba for four months (1836-37) under a general amnesty, but continued to be appalled by that country's politics. He returned, heartbroken by Cuba, to Mexico. A mere two years later, Heredia died of tuberculosis at the chillingly early age of thirty-five.

Latin American literary critics regard Heredia as one their most important poets: he is prominent in every literary history, and there is unanimity in declaring him of the greatest importance as the first Romantic of Hispano-America. In Niagara Falls, Heredia saw the tumult of existence manifest. Philosophically, for him, the authority, indifference, health, rage and balm of Nature were all combined in what might be mischievously called the Canadian cataract; the river crashes in awesome disarray only to be reborn downstream, and these natural properties struck him as but metaphors not only for his own turbulent soul and feelings—but also for the political aspirations of his and other Latin American lands. Oppressed, he believed, by European imperialists wallowing in the delights of neo-classicism, Latin American countries could only be free if inspired by a natural ideal. Even the neo-classical painting and sculpture of Europe so admired by the colonials were oppressive because the European Academy alone dictated the standards of art, and even dictated who could show his or her work. This theory (more a notion than a theory) claimed legitimacy not by rational argument but more by subjective feeling, and the Romantic saw himself (in admirable melancholy) set apart from humanity, alone, often homeless, open to new sensation, and most importantly perhaps, a rebel.

Of particular interest to Canadians is Heredia's acknowledgement of—insistence on—the purity and hence superiority of the northern landscape and the Canadian relationship with Nature. Unsullied and strong, the Canadian, he implies, is free of the pollution, spiritual and otherwise, caused by mankind in the tropical countries.

Heredia quickly became known throughout the Spanish-speaking world as the "Singer of Niagara". His eponymous poem was, and is, widely studied by generation after generation of students throughout the Spanish-speaking world. They study the poem for its excellence, and as a paradigm of its period, shameless in its Romanticism. The translation below, published in 1827, was made by William Cullen Bryant in honour of his first meeting with Heredia.

———————

NIAGARA

My lyre! Give me my lyre! My bosom feels
The glow of inspiration. O, how long
Have I been left in darkness, since this light
Last visited my brow! Niagara!
Thou with thy rushing waters dost restore
The heavenly gift that sorrow took away.

Tremendous torrent! for an instant hush
The terrors of thy voice, and cast aside
Those wide-involving shadows, that my eyes
May see the fearful beauty of thy face!
I am not all unworthy of thy sight,
For from my very boyhood have I loved,
Shunning the meaner track of common minds,
To look on Nature in her loftier moods.

At the fierce rushing of the hurricane,
At the near bursting of the thunderbolt,
I have been touched with joy; and when the sea
Lashed by the wind hath rocked my bark and showed
Its yawning caves beneath me, I have loved
Its dangers and the wrath of elements.
But never yet the madness of the sea
Hath moved me as thy grandeur moves me now.

Thou flowest on in quiet, till thy waves
Grow broken 'midst the rocks; thy current then
Shoots onward like the irresistible course
Of Destiny. Ah, terribly they rage,—
The hoarse and rapid whirlpools there! My brain
Grows wild, my senses wander, as I gaze
Upon the hurrying waters, and my sight,
Vainly would follow, as toward the verge
Sweeps the wide torrent. Waves innumerable
Meet there and madden,—waves innumerable
Urge on and overtake the waves before,
And disappear in thunder and in foam.

They reach, they leap the barrier,—the abyss
Swallows insatiable the sinking waves.
A thousand rainbows arch them, and woods
Are deafened with the roar. The violent shock
Shatters to vapor the descending sheets.
A cloudy whirlwind fills the gulf, and heaves
The mighty pyramid of circling mist
To heaven. The solitary hunter near
Pauses with terror in the forest shades.

What seeks my restless eye? Why are not here,
About the jaws of this abyss, the palms—
Ah, the delicious palms,—that on the plains

Of my own native Cuba spring and spread
Their thickly foliaged summits to the sun,
And, in the breathings of the ocean air,
Wave soft beneath the heaven's unspotted blue?

But no, Niagara,—thy forest pines
Are fitter coronal for thee. The palm,
The effeminate myrtle, and frail rose may grow
In gardens, and give out their fragrance there,
Unmanning him who breathes it. Thine it is
To do a nobler office. Generous minds
Behold thee, and are moved, and learn to rise
Above earth's frivolous pleasures; they partake
Thy grandeur, at the utterance of thy name.

God of all truth! in other lands I've seen
Lying philosophers, blaspheming men,
Questioners of thy mysteries, that draw
Their fellows deep into impiety;
And therefore doth my spirit seek thy face
In earth's majestic solitudes. Even here
My heart doth open all itself to thee.
In this immensity of loneliness,
I feel thy hand upon me. To my ear
The eternal thunder of the cataract brings
Thy voice, and I am humbled as I hear.
Dread torrent, that with wonder and with fear
Dost overwhelm the soul of him that looks
Upon thee, and dost bear it from itself,—
Whence hast thou thy beginning? Who supplies,
Age after age, thy unexhausted springs?
What power hath ordered, that when all thy weight
Descends into the deep, the swollen waves
Rise not and roll to overwhelm the earth?

The Lord has opened his omnipotent hand,
Covered thy face with clouds, and given voice
To thy down-rushing waters; he hath girt
Thy terrible forehead with his radiant bow.
I see thy never-resting waters run,
And I bethink me how the tide of time
Sweeps to eternity. So pass of man—
Pass, like a noonday dream—the blossoming days
And he awakes to sorrow. I, alas!
Feel that my youth is withered, and my brow
Ploughed early with the lines of grief and care.

Never have I so deeply felt as now
The hopeless solitude, the abandonment,
The anguish of a loveless life. Alas!
How can the impassioned, the unfrozen heart
Be happy without love? I would that one
Beautiful, worthy to be loved and joined
In love with me, now shared my lonely walk
On this tremendous brink. 'Twere sweet to see
Her sweet face touched with paleness, and become
More beautiful from fear, and overspread
With a faint smile while clinging to my side.
Dreams,—dreams! I am an exile, and for me
There is no country and there is no love.

Hear, dread Niagara, my latest voice!
Yet a few years, and the cold earth shall close
Over the bones of him who sings thee now
Thus feelingly. Would that this, my humble verse,
Might be, like thee, immortal! I, meanwhile,
Cheerfully passing to the appointed rest,
Might raise my radiant forehead in the clouds
To listen to the echoes of my fame.

FRANÇOIS RENÉ, VICOMTE DE CHATEAUBRIAND

M OST PEOPLE, when they travel to a foreign land for the first time, are cautious in their ambitions. Not François René, vicomte de Chateaubriand (1768-1848). Held by most scholars and readers to be the finest French writer of his generation, and the progenitor of the Romantic era in France, he was inspired (by sloppily conceived descriptions of the Noble Savage uttered by philosophers) to travel to North America with two primary goals: to see for himself "real savages" and—difficult as this may be to credit, it is nonetheless true—to sail the Northwest Passage. Not least among his problems was the fact that at that time, the Northwest Passage had not yet been found.

During his travel to these shores, from July 10 to November 28, 1791, only one of his two goals was fulfilled, and scholarly doubt remains as to whether he travelled further north than Niagara Falls, such is the vagueness—no doubt deliberate—enveloping his description of his forays.

Like most Europeans, even to this day, visiting these shores for the first time, Chateaubriand grossly underestimated the size of the continent. Among his original plans was a colossal excursion that he described as if it were merely an afternoon's stroll, starting from the

Gulf of California: "From there, following the outline of the continent, and always in sight of the sea, I planned to continue north to the Bering Straits, to round the last cape of America, to go east along the shores of the polar sea, and to come back into the United States by Hudson Bay, Labrador, and Canada." Given the ease with which he felt this sojourn could be accomplished, one wonders why he didn't mention what he planned to do on the second day.

That he saw Niagara is certain because it was there that he fractured his arm in a foolish descent of the rock-face adjoining the Falls. It is also possible, but unlikely, that he glimpsed the upper Great Lakes. Because of specific references in his writing, we can be more certain that he beheld Lakes Ontario and Erie.

Another genius of French letters, André Maurois, was fascinated enough by Chateaubriand to write the latter's biography. Regarding Chateaubriand's final days in North America, Maurois is detailed:

> Our traveller did not persist in his plans, he contented himself with an expedition to Niagara, quite strenuous and adventurous enough. He chose a Dutchman for his guide, and dressed up as a forester, letting his hair and beard grow. Thus equipped, he made his way into the forests along untrodden paths towards the north. He soon came upon his first real "savages", a few Iroquois, with whom he went hunting. But he was not long in discovering that these natives did not at all resemble the literary picture the Philosophers had drawn of them. Of course, it was only too easy for the whites to corrupt these children of nature, but even without the whites they had their vices and passions, and were very far from the innocence that Rousseau attributed to any people untouched by civilization.... The primeval might of this uninhabited region taught him at every step that Nature, untrodden as yet by man, might well be innocent, but at the same time cruel and violent. The idyll gave place to grandiose brutality. His mind filled with new images of a Nature that would not allow itself to be trifled with. So even here the eighteenth century was coming to a close and

surrendering to a reality that forced mankind to acknowledge its power.

Ten years after his only trip to this continent, Canada figured significantly in the author's first novel, *Atala* (1801), the work which thrust him into the centre of French literary life with volcanic force. While much of the novel is set in the realm of the Natchez Indians of the United States, Chateaubriand felt compelled to end his book, despite its assault on the verisimilitude of the plot, at Niagara Falls—for so many European authors that perpetual symbol of the raw power of Nature and the New World. The fauna resident at his Niagara, however, are unlike any known to science, and include simian descriptions of wolverines that will astound, if not amuse, students of natural history:

> Soon we reached the edge of the cataract, whose mighty roar could be heard from afar…. The cataract is split into two branches, and bends in the form of a horseshoe. Between the two falls an island juts out, hollow underneath, and hanging with all its trees over the chaos of the waves. The mass of water hurtling down in the south curves into a vast cylinder, then straightens into a snowy sheet, sparkling iridescent in the sunlight. The eastern branch falls in dismal gloom, calling to mind some downpour of the great flood. A thousand rainbows arch and intersect over the abyss. As it strikes the shuddering rock, the water bounds back in foaming whirlpools, which drift up over the forest like the smoke of some conflagration. The scene is ornate with pine and wild walnut trees and rocks carved out in weird shapes. Eagles, drawn by air currents, spiral down into the depths of the chasm, and wolverines dangle by their supple tails from the ends of low-hanging branches, snatching the shattered corpses of elk and bears out of the abyss.

Atala was originally going to appear as part of a much larger work, a great tract intending to prove the superiority of the state religion of

France. *The Genius of Christianity* appeared, without *Atala* however, the following year (1802; *Atala* had been published in 1801) and its success was as prodigious as that of *Atala*, making Chateaubriand, almost overnight, the cynosure of French letters. Napoleon was so impressed by the work that he offered to its author several distinguished embassy postings, the postings gladly accepted.

Unlike *Atala*, the first draft of which was probably written in North America, thus accounting in part for its vague sympathy with the natives, *The Genius of Christianity* was composed later, circa 1798, while Chateaubriand sagged in anti-Revolution exile in England. During his residence in England he converted from the Nature philosophy of his youth to the formalities and dogma of Catholicism. So his attitude hardened to what he regarded as the heathenism of the natives.

In the same year that he published *Atala* (1801), Chateaubriand wrote and published a forty-page essay devoted to the just-published discoveries of the renowned Canadian explorer Alexander Mackenzie. *The Voyages ... to the Frozen and Pacific Oceans* won for Mackenzie a knighthood and massive admiration throughout the western world, especially in Europe. Given that Mackenzie did what Chateaubriand had hoped to do—and to Chateaubriand's chagrin Mackenzie had performed his feats of exploration at the very time when Chateaubriand had been in North America!—the latter might be forgiven had his essay on Mackenzie allowed some envy to creep into its tone. But the French author appreciated the immensity of Mackenzie's travails and of his accomplishment, and only in the last page does he lament a fate which denied him the glory, including the naming of a mighty river, now accruing to the famed explorer.

Detractors of Chateaubriand stone him for the sin of fibbing and for the sin of stealing facts and phrasings from other writers. These charges were leveled especially against his book *Travels in America*, written circa 1826. Whether literary plagiarism was even recognized as an offence in his day is moot, but his liberal borrowings from the writings of others (particularly travel accounts) is a venial peccadillo, surely, not a mortal sin.

For many years after his first visit Chateaubriand dreamed of returning to this continent. His notebooks replete with the minutiae of his future needs, he talked to friends of a journey to North America lasting up to nine years, his labours to be aided by three whites and three natives from the Six Nations—the same aboriginals who at their best had so impressed him and who had named him "the Man with the Long Beard".

The following passages from Chateaubriand's descriptions of Canada in *Travels in America*, typical of the Romantic Age, shamelessly amalgamate fact with fiction, and focus on the purity of the landscape, a Canadian vista wistfully described as still largely unpolluted by European humanity.

This excerpt is from the fine modern translation by Richard Switzer published by the University of Kentucky Press.

---

from TRAVELS IN AMERICA

The savages of Niagara Falls, in the English territory, were charged with guarding the frontier of Upper Canada in this area. They came before us armed with bows and arrows and kept us from passing.

I was obliged to send the Dutchman to Fort Niagara to get a pass from the commander before entering the territories under British domination; that tugged at my heart because I was thinking that France had formerly commanded in these lands.... I stayed for two days in the village of the savages. The manuscript offers here the draft of a letter I was writing to one of my friends in France. Here is that letter:

Letter Written from the Land of the Savages of Niagara: "I must tell you what happened yesterday morning with my hosts. The grass was still covered with dew; the wind was coming out of the forests heavy with perfume, the leaves of the wild mulberry were loaded with the cocoons of a kind of silkworm, and the cotton plants of the country, turning back their expanded capsules, looked like white roses.

The Indian women, busy with diverse tasks, were gathered together at the foot of a big red ash. Their smallest children were hung in nets in the branches of the tree: the breeze of the woods rocked those aerial cradles with an almost imperceptible movement. The mothers got up from time to time to see if their children were sleeping and if they had not been wakened by a multitude of birds singing and flitting about. This scene was charming.

We were seated at one side, the interpreter and I, with the warriors, seven of them; we all had large pipes in our mouths; two or three of these Indians spoke English. At a distance, young boys were playing; but in the course of their games, jumping, running, throwing balls, they spoke not a word. There were not to be heard the deafening cries of European children; these young savages bounded like bucks, and they were as mute as bucks are. A big boy of seven or eight, detaching himself from the group at times, would come to his mother to suck and then would return to play with his friends.

The child is never forcibly weaned; after feeding on other foods, he drains his mother's breast, like a cup drained at the end of a banquet. When the entire nation is dying of hunger, the child still finds in the maternal breast a source of life. This custom is perhaps one of the causes which prevent the American tribes from increasing as much as the European families.

The fathers spoke to the children and the children replied to the fathers. I had my Dutchman report the conversation to me. Here is what happened:

A savage about thirty years old called his son and suggested that he moderate his jumping; the child answered, "That is reasonable." And, without doing what the father told him, he returned to the game.

The grandfather of the child called him in turn, and said to him, "Do that"; and the little boy obeyed. Thus the child disobeyed his father, who asked him, and obeyed his grandfather, who ordered him. The father is almost nothing for the child.

The child is never punished; he recognized only the authority of age and of his mother. A crime considered frightful and unheard of among the Indians is that of a son rebellious to his mother. When she grows old, he feeds her.

As for the father, as long as he is young, the child gives him no consideration; but when he advances in life, his son honors him, not as a father, but as an old man, that is, as a man of good advice and experience.

This way of raising children in their full independence should make them prey to ill humor and caprice; however the children of the savages have neither caprice nor ill humor because they want only that which they can obtain. If it happens that a child cries for something that his mother does not have, he is told to go get that thing where he saw it; now, since he is not the stronger party and since he feels his weakness, he forgets the object of his desires. If the savage child obeys no one, no one obeys him: there lies the whole secret of his joy and his reason.

The Indian children do not quarrel, do not fight. They are neither noisy, annoying, nor surly; they have in their appearance something serious, like happiness, something noble, like independence.

We could not raise our youth this way; we would have to start by relieving ourselves of our vices; now we find it easier to shut them up in the hearts of our children, being careful only to keep these vices from being seen on the outside.

When the young Indian feels growing within him the taste for fishing, hunting, war, or politics, he studies and imitates the arts that he sees his father practicing. Then he learns to sew a canoe, braid a net, use the bow, the gun, the tomahawk, cut down a tree, build a hut, explain necklaces. What is an amusement for the son forms the father's authority: his right of strength and intelligence is thus recognized, and this right gradually leads him to the power of the Sachem.

The girls enjoy the same liberty as the boys: they do more or less as they wish, but they remain more with their mothers, who teach them the tasks of the home. When a young Indian girl has acted badly, her mother is content to throw some drops of water in her face and to say to her, "You dishonor me." This reproach rarely misses its effect.

Until noon we stayed at the door of the cabin; the sun had become burning hot. One of our hosts went toward the little boys and said to them, "Children, the sun will eat your heads, go and sleep." They all cried out, "That is so." And, an indication of their obedience, they continued to play after having agreed that the sun would eat their heads.

But the women got up, one showing *sagamite* in a wooden bowl, another a favorite fruit, a third unrolling a sleeping mat. They called the obstinate troop, joining to each name a word of tenderness. Immediately the children flew toward their mothers like a flock of birds. The women caught hold of them, laughing. With a certain amount of difficulty each one of them took her son away. Clasped in the maternal arms, each child was eating what had just been given him.

Farewell: I do not know if this letter written from the depths of the woods will ever reach you."

I went from the Indian village to the cataract of Niagara.... The Indian ladder that used to be there being broken, I determined, in spite of the protests of my guide, to reach the bottom of the falls down a rocky cliff about two hundred feet high. I ventured down. In spite of the bellowing of the cataract and the frightful abyss that boiled below me, I kept my head and reached a place about forty feet from the bottom. But here the smooth and vertical rock face no longer offered any roots or cracks for my feet. I hung full length by my hands, unable to go up or down, feeling my fingers opening bit by bit with the fatigue of holding up my body and seeing death as inevitable. There are few men who have spent in their lives two minutes as I counted them then, hanging over the abyss of Niagara. Finally my hands opened and I fell. By the most unbelievable luck, although I was on the bare rock, where I should have been broken to bits, I did not feel much pain; I was a half-inch from the abyss, and I had not rolled into it, but when the coldness of the water began to penetrate me, I realized that I had not come out unscathed, as I had first thought. I felt an unbearable pain in my left arm; I had broken it above the elbow. I signaled my guide, who was looking at me from above, and he ran to get some savages, who with a great deal of difficulty hoisted me up with birch ropes and took me to their camp.

That was not the only risk I ran at Niagara. When I arrived, I had gone to the falls holding my horse's bridle twisted around my arm. While I leaned over to look down, a rattlesnake stirred in the nearby bushes; the horse was frightened and reared back toward the abyss. I couldn't free my arm from the reins, and the horse, more and more frightened, dragged me after him. Already his front legs were going over the edge, and crouching on the edge of the abyss he held on only with the strength of his hind quarters. It was all over with me, when the animal, astonished by the new danger, made a new effort and by a kind of pirouette jumped back ten feet from the edge.

I had but a simple fracture of the arm: two splints, a bandage, and a sling sufficed to cure me. My Dutchman did not wish to go farther; I paid him off and he returned home. I made a new bargain with some Canadians of Niagara who had part of their family at Saint Louis of the Illinois, on the Mississippi....

HARRIET
MARTINEAU

WILLIAM WORDSWORTH, Thomas Carlyle, George Eliot, and Matthew Arnold were just some of the eminent guests at Harriet Martineau's summer house in the Lake District. Another visitor, Charlotte Brontë, described her hostess as "both hard and warm-hearted, abrupt and affectionate. I believe she is not at all conscious of her own absolutism." Brontë's portrait might serve to describe Martineau's entire life (1802-1876), in that it was a unique meld devoted, with varying degrees of sternness, to the careers of novelist, educator, social activist, translator, and journalist. In addition, Martineau was the author of a head-spinning variety of texts ranging from analyses of mesmerism to comments on how to keep cows. She deemed no subject unworthy of literary treatment.

Today, she is remembered and increasingly studied at universities especially for three books. Her novel, *Deerbrook*, is "her first and best novel, in which women's intellectual aspirations and bonds with each other are alike taken seriously."

The second, her *Autobiography*, was written in less than ninety days, so convinced was she that chest pains indicated her imminent death. It was not imminent. She lived a further twenty-one years without, apparently, feeling the need to update her memoirs; the *Autobiography* was published posthumously in 1877. For its frankness, assessments of her eminent colleagues in politics and the arts, and forthrightness in discussing the challenge of being both woman and writer the book has been called "one of the most important autobiographies by a woman to appear in the Victorian period."

The third title for which she is celebrated today, *Retrospect of Western Travel*, is the more enduring of two books born of a two-year trip to North America, 1834-36. Motivated by a desire to see the new world with her own eyes (she had no sense of smell, or taste, and her deafness had grown to the point that she needed a horn in order to hear) she travelled as widely as possible. During her travels throughout the United States she spoke frequently on behalf of the abolitionists, often at risk to her person.

Her preoccupations overseas were principally with the United States rather than Canada. However, her political and economic interests kept her abreast of broad developments in Canadian life. In spite of her spinsterish tsk-tsking, quoted below, at Canadian dawdling compared to American industry, Martineau was generally sympathetic to the Canadian viewpoint. As early as January 1838, back in Britain, she was writing with eerie perspicacity about the previous year's Rebellion in the Canadas:

> We are all uncomfortable about Canada. My own conviction is that the Canadians are mainly right; and that the government, both here and there, is unfathomably wrong. As a letter I have just received says, "What definition of a 'rebel' could be given which would not include Lord John Russell?" All agree that an amicable separation is possible, is *most* desirable: but nobody on the British side will stir to effect it, you will see. In our insolence and vanity we shall insult and despise the Canadians till we are head and ears in guilt towards them.

More than three decades later, she could still lament, "It frightens me to see the ignorant eagerness with which our people—Irish and English workfolk—are emigrating to the United States instead of our North American colonies while utterly unaware of the dearness of living in the United States, the crushing taxation … and the truly appalling hostility, daily aggravated, between capitalists and labourers."

Lord Durham, the man who recommended to the British parliament that Canada be given responsible government, was a friend of Martineau's. She comments in her *Autobiography* on her initial fears for the success of his duties overseas:

> One of the strongest interests of the year 1838 was Lord Durham's going out as Governor-General of the North American colonies.... I was concerned when I heard of his acceptance of the post, because the difficulties appeared all but insuperable at best.... He said himself that he felt "inexpressible reluctance" to undertake the charge: but his confiding temper misled him into trusting his political comrades.... In talking over the matter one day with our mutual friend, Lady Charlotte Lindsay, I did not conceal my regret and apprehension. She called one day, soon after, to tell me honestly that she had told Lord Durham, the night before, that I was not sanguine about his success. He questioned her anxiously as to my exact meaning; and she referred him to me. I had no wish to disturb him, now that it was too late, with my bad opinion of those in whose hands he was placing his fate: and I did not do so. I answered all his questions about Canada and the United States as well as I could.

Two points to note about the above are her ease of movement among the most important people of the day—and her shameless audacity in conveying information to Durham as if she were an old Canada hand. In fact, she spent no more than a week in the country, and that almost entirely within the environs of Niagara.

Following extensive travelling throughout the USA, Martineau concluded her visit to the continent with a journey over the lower half of the Great Lakes: "My last journey was with a party of friends, far into the west, visiting Niagara again, proceeding by Lake Erie [by boat] to Detroit ... to Chicago, and by the Lakes Michigan, Huron, and St. Clair [back to] Detroit." She was unimpressed by what would later become the City of Windsor. Looking from Detroit, she wrote, "The Canada side of the river looks dull enough from the city;

but I cannot speak from a near view of it, having been disappointed in my attempts to get over to it. One occasion, we were too late for the ferry-boat; and we never had time again for the excursion."

Unlike Bryant, Martineau seems never to have landed on the Canadian side during her final travels. In fact, the countryside north of Sarnia was, in 1836, for Martineau, little more than a mirage of savage beauty:

> Lake Huron was squally, as usual. Little remarkable happened while we traversed it. We enjoyed the lake trout. We occasionally saw the faint outlines of the Manitoulin Islands and Canada.... In twenty minutes, the sun gilded the fort, the woods, and the green, prairie-like Canada shore. On the verge of this prairie, under the shelter of the forest, an immense herd of wild horses were seen scampering, and whisking their long tails. A cloud of pigeons, in countless thousands, was shadowing alternately the forests, the lake, and the prairie.... It was a dark curtain lifted up on a scene of wild and singular beauty.

The following excerpt gives a sense of the tone with which she usually wrote and with which she conducted her affairs: clipped, earnest, yet ever alive to all about her.

---

from RETROSPECT OF
WESTERN TRAVEL

On consulting a good map, a little promontory may be seen jutting out into Lake Erie on the Canada shore, nearly opposite to Black

Rock. Perhaps it may be marked Fort Erie, for there Fort Erie stood.

A lady of Buffalo, who happens to be a good walker, proposed that she and I should indulge in a ramble to Fort Erie one fine day towards the end of October. She showed me that she was provided with stout boots, in case of our having to cross swampy ground; and she said she believed we might trust to getting some sort of a dinner on the Canada side, and might therefore go unencumbered with provisions.

After crossing the ferry at Black Rock we pursued our walk in a southwest direction, sometimes treading a firm sand and sometimes a greensward washed by the fresh waters of the lake. Though we were on British ground we were entertained by an American woman who lived on the lake shore close by the fort. She treated us with negus and cake while preparing to get a dinner for us, and amused us with accounts of how butter and eggs are smuggled into Buffalo from her neighborhood, these articles not being allowed to pass the custom-house. My eyes never rested on the Canada shore without my feeling how absurd it was that that poor country should belong to us, its poverty and hopeless inactivity contrasting, so much to our disgrace, with the prosperous activity of the opposite shore; but here was the climax of absurdity, the prohibition of a free traffic in butter and eggs! What a worthy subject of contention between two great nations, the one breaking the laws to provide Buffalo with butter and eggs, and the preventive force of the other exercised in opposition!

Our hostess was sewing when we went in, amusing herself meanwhile with snatches of reading from "Peter Parley," which lay open before her. She put away her work to cook for us, conversing all the while, and by no means sorry, I fancy, to have the amusement of a little company. She gave us tea, beefsteak, hot rolls and butter, honeycomb, and preserved plums and crab-apples. Immediately after dinner I went out to the fort, my friend promising to follow.

The thickness of the remaining fragments of the walls shows the fort to have been substantially built. It was held by the Americans to the last extremity in the war of 1814, and then blown up by a brave man to prevent its falling into the hands of the British. He remained alone in the fort to do the deed; and as I now beheld the desolation of the solitude in which it stands, I felt as if I could enter into what his feelings must have been on the last day of his life. At one moment all had been dead silence; and the next the windows in Buffalo were blown out by the explosion.

I sat alone beside a pool in the middle of the fort. Fragments of the building lay tumbled around, overgrown with tall grass, and bristling with shrubbery. Behind me was the grim forest, with the ruins of a single deserted house standing within its shadow. Before me lay the waste of waters, with gulls dipping and sailing. A single birch overhung the pool beside me, and a solitary snipe, which seemed to have no fear of me, vibrated on the top of a bulrush. I do not know that I was ever so oppressed with a sense of solitude; and I was really glad soon to see my friend standing on a pinnacle of the ruined wall, and beckoning me to come up....

It is not my intention to describe what we saw at Niagara so much as to relate what we did. To offer an idea of Niagara by writing of hues and dimensions is much like representing the kingdom of Heaven by images of jasper and topazes.

I visited the falls twice: first in October, 1834, in company with the party with whom we traversed the state of New York, when we stayed nearly a week; and again with Mr. and Mrs. F., and other friends, in June, 1836, when we remained between two and three days. The first time we approached the falls from Buffalo, the next from Lewistown and Queenstown.

I expected to be disappointed in the first sight of the falls, and did not relish the idea of being questioned on the first day as to my "impressions." I therefore made a law, with the hearty agreement of the rest of the party, that no one should ask an opinion of the spectacle for twenty-four hours. We stepped into the stage at Buffalo at half past eight in the morning on the 14th of October. At Black Rock we got out to cross the ferry. We looked at the green rushing waters we were crossing, and wondered whether they or we should be at the falls first. We had to wait some minutes for the stage on the Canada side, and a comely English woman invited us into her kitchen to warm ourselves. She was washing as well as cooking; and such a log was blazing under her boilers as no fireplace in England would hold. It looked like the entire trunk of a pine somewhat shortened. I could not help often wishing that some of the shivering poor of London could have supplies of the fuel which lies rotting in the American woods.

The road is extremely bad all the way from the ferry to the falls, and the bridges the rudest of the rude. The few farms looked decaying, and ill-clad children offered us autumn fruit for sale. We saw nothing to flatter our national complacency; for truly the contrast with the other side of the river was mournful enough. It was not till we had passed the inn with the sign of the "Chippeway Battle Ground" that we saw the spray from the falls. I believe we might have seen it sooner if we had known where to look. "Is that it?" we all exclaimed. It appeared on the left-hand side, whereas we had been looking to the right; and, instead of it being suspended in the air like a white cloud, as we had imagined, it curled vigorously up like smoke from a cannon or from a replenished fire. The winding of the road presently brought this round to our right hand. It seemed very near; the river, too, was as smooth as oil. The beginning of the Welland canal was next pointed out to me, but it was not a moment to care for canals. Then the little Round Island, covered with wood and surrounded by rapids, lay close at hand, in a recess of the Canada shore. Some of the rapids, of eight or ten feet descent, would be called falls elsewhere. They were glittering and foamy, with spaces of green water between. I caught a glimpse of a section of the cataract, but not any adequate view, before we were driven briskly up to the door of the hotel. We ran quickly from piazza to piazza till we reached the crown of the roof, where there is a space railed in for the advantage of the gazer who desires to reach the highest point. I think the emotion of this moment was never renewed or equalled. The morning had been cloudy, with a very few wandering gleams. It was now a little after noon; the sky was clearing, and at this moment the sun lighted up the Horseshoe Fall. I am not going to describe it. The most striking appearance was the slowness with which the shaded green waters rolled over the brink. This majestic oozing gives a true idea of the volume of the flood, but they no longer look like water.

We wandered through the wood, along Table Rock, and to the ferry. We sat down opposite to the American Falls, finding them the first day or two more level to our comprehension than the Great Horseshoe Cataract; yet throughout, the beauty was far more impressive to me than the grandeur. One's imagination may heap up almost any degree of grandeur; but the subtle colouring of this scene, varying with every breath of wind refining upon the softness of driven snow, and dimming all the gems of the mine, is wholly inconceivable. The woods on Goat Island were in their gaudiest autumn dress; yet, on looking up to them from the fall, they seemed one dust colour. This will not be believed, but it is true....

One morning we found an old man, between seventy and eighty years old, gazing from Table Rock. He was an American. Being on a journey, he had walked from Queenstown to see the falls. He quietly observed that he was ashamed to think there had been wars near such a place, and that he hoped the English and Americans were grown wiser now, and would not think of fighting any more. This came in echo of my thought. I had been secretly wishing that all the enemies in the world could be brought together on this rock; they could not but love as brethren.

An English family at the hotel seemed marvellously skilled in putting away all the good influences of the place. The gentleman was so anxious about where he should settle, so incessantly pettish, so resolutely miserable, as to bespeak the compassion of all the guests for the ladies of his family, one of whom told me that she had forgotten all about the falls in her domestic anxieties. As this gentleman found fault with everybody and everything, and ostentatiously proved that nothing could give him any pleasure, it was not surprising that the cataract itself failed to meet his approbation; yet I was not prepared for the question he put to me across the table, in the presence of both Canadians and Americans, whether I did not think the natives made a very silly fuss about the falls, and whether the

Falls of the Clyde were not much finer. Such are the persons by whom foreigners suppose themselves made acquainted with the English character. Such is the way in which not a few English study to mortify the inhabitants, and then come home and complain of American conceit. I told this gentleman that I perceived he was speaking of the rapids, and had not seen the falls.

We wished, while we were in the neighborhood, to obtain a glimpse of Lake Ontario, as we were not sure of being able to visit Canada at a future time. We took the opportunity of two of our party going northward, to accompany them as far as Queenstown seven miles off, where we intended to see Brock's monument, satisfy ourselves with the view from the top of it, and walk home through the woods in the afternoon. In the stage were an Irish gentleman and his wife. The lady amused me by the zeal with which she knitted all the way, just as if she were in a dark parlour in the Old Jewry; and the gentleman with some sentiments which were wholly new to me; for instance, he feared that the independence of the Americans made them feel themselves independent of God. This consequence of democratic government had not struck me before, and I never perceived any traces of its existence; but if it should occur, there will probably soon be an epidemic or a bad season to bring them to their senses again.

Before the door of the wretched, foul inn at Queenstown, we sorrowfully shook hands with our Prussian and Dutch companions, hoping to meet them again in the course of our travels; which, indeed, happened more than once. We provided ourselves here with cider, cakes, and sandwiches; i.e., beefsteak laid between thick dry bread. With this provision we ascended the hill to the foot of Brock's monument, and found the portress, an active little Irishwoman, waiting to let us in. She was delighted to meet ladies from the old country, and heartily invited us to spread our dinner in her cottage below. She told us all her affairs, and seemed unwilling to leave us when we told her we meant to stay a long while on the top of the monument, and would not detain her from her washtub, but would come down to her by-and-by. She and her husband have, for showing the monument, sixty dollars a season (that is, while the boats run), and all that they happen to take in the winter. They were soon to have a cottage built for them nearer the monument. When we went down to her cottage she had spread plates, knives, and pickles, and had her head full of questions and communications. She was grateful for a small payment for her trouble, and gave us the impression of her being a very amiable, contented person, whom we should like to see again.

Sir Isaac Brock fell at the battle of Queenstown, in October, 1812, near the base of this monument. It is 146 feet high and being built on a pretty steep hill, commands a fine view. To the left a prodigious sweep of forest terminates in blue Canadian hills. On the right is the American shore, at this time gaudy with autumn woods. There stands the village of Lewistown, with its winding descent to the ferry. At our feet lay Queenstown, its sordidness being lost in distance, and its long street presenting the appearance of an English village. The green river rushes between its lofty wooded banks; which suddenly widen at Queenstown, causing the waters to spread and relax their speed while making their way, with three or four bends, to the lake. We saw the white church of Niagara rising above the woods some miles off where the junction takes place; and beyond, the vast lake spreads its waters, gray on the horizon. There was life in this magnificent scene. The ferryboat was buffeted by the waves; groups were in waiting on either side of the ferry, and teams were in the fields. The Irishwoman was grieved that she had no telescope wherewith to enable us to see what was doing on the lake. She and her husband had provided one for the accommodation of visitors. Some travellers (English) had thrown it down from the top of the monument, and when she asked for payment only bullied her; and her husband had not been able to afford to get another.

After dinner we sat on the top of the precipitous wooded bank of the river, looking down into its green eddies, and watching the family of white birds which hovered far beneath us, but yet high over the stream. Meditating, as we were, that we were now sitting on the spot where the falls were pouring down their flood ages before Babylon was founded or the Greek Mythology had arisen out of the elements of universal conviction, it was not surprising that we had no thoughts to spare for the weather. We did not observe how the sky had been darkening. Two wagons driven by lads stopped in passing, and their drivers offered us seats to Niagara. We at first declined, being bent upon walking; but feeling heavy drops of rain at the moment, we retracted our refusal, and jumped into one of the vehicles. It was a mere box upon wheels; a barbarous machine, but of great service to us in the ensuing storm. Before we reached our hotel we were thoroughly wet, but had obtained a good deal of information from our driver about the condition of the Canadian settlers in the neighborhood. He was the son of a Canadian father and Scotch mother, who were doing well in the world, as he said the English settlers do who set the right way to work the land is not the best near the road; so that what is seen there is no fair specimen of the state of the settlers. The farms hereabout consist of about one hundred acres generally, and are all the property of the residents. Labourers live with the farmers, and receive, besides their board and lodging, about 120 dollars a year. A gentleman, a farmer and physician, from some distance, called on me one day when I was out, and left messages for me with one of our party. He said he wished me to see and do justice to Canada. People go, he believes, with wrong expectations, and so are disappointed. He, his wife and daughters, went, expecting ease and comfort, and they have found it; but they have not wealth and luxury. He declared that civility and cheerfulness would always command good manners and service. As I had no opportunity of "seeing and doing justice to Canada," I give this gentleman's testimony. It is very agreeable, and I do not doubt its justness.

E. M. DELAFIELD

E M. DELAFIELD (1890-1943) was a woman who wore many masks: the descendant of Royalists who fled to Britain following the French Revolution, she wrote five novels with Catholic themes, yet managed never to refer to her religion in interviews or public remarks. Furthermore, in several of her more popular satirical books she poked fun at bourgeois housewives pretending happiness and fulfilment while leading quiet lives of desperation, yet she herself endured a marriage distinguished by fraudulent contentment and domestic busyness. Even her name is a double remove from reality: she was the daughter of Count Henry de la Pasture, and was christened Edmée Elizabeth Monica; yet for publication, she half-anglicized her family name into her pseudonym: Delafield.

Some of her books remain in print after half a century. Today, she is most remembered for her five novels featuring a protagonist known as "The Provincial Lady". The series began in 1929 in response to a request from the early feminist magazine *Time and Tide* for material that would run over several issues. Delafield was a director of the magazine. Her lead character, writing in the first person singular, quickly became popular, in part because of the perspicacity of her observations, but also because Delafield had an unusually astute ear for dialogue. She shares this trait, of course, with many excellent authors, but what makes her writing extraordinary for its time is the technically adroit way in which she interweaves direct and indirect speech, peppering it with pinches of interior monologue. Part of the series' charm was also due to its contemporary setting at a time when Old Money was being forced to confront the realities of the Depression.

Delafield was never a brutally scathing critic. Her satire preferred the stiletto to the broadaxe. Today, her interest for most readers lies in the clarity of the reflection she mirrors of her time, and in her sense of humour. Her bestselling description of the struggles and challenges unique to women also make her compelling to feminist critics, one of whom points out that Delafield "reveals the frustrations, desires, evasions, and vanities through which women's complicity in their subjugation is exposed. For her, self-awareness is the strength by which women become shrewd critics of their society and responsibilities."

Following *Diary of a Provincial Lady* (1930) and *The Provincial Lady Goes Further* (1932) Delafield was invited to visit North America for the first time to give a brief series of lectures in 1933. Her fictionalized account of the trip was serialized in *Punch* (to which she was a frequent contributor) then appeared in book form in 1934 as *The Provincial Lady in America*. She visited New York, Washington, Boston, Chicago, Cleveland, and then made her first of two forays into Canada, at Toronto.

Her subsequent literary career was productive and certainly kept her in the public eye. She continued to write plays and much journalism, including feature articles on crime, particularly murder stories, from unusual angles. She also wrote two more novels featuring The Provincial Lady.

At the age of fifty-three, in the middle of a lecture at Oxford, she passed out, and died from cancer but a few weeks afterward.

from THE PROVINCIAL
LADY IN AMERICA

November 11th—Reach Toronto at preposterous hour of *5.55 a.m.* and decide against night-travelling once and for ever, day having actually started with Customs inspection considerably before dawn. Decide to try and see what I can of Canada and glue my face to the window, but nothing visible for a long while. Am finally rewarded by superb sun-rise, but eyelids feel curiously stiff and intelligence at lowest possible ebb. Involve myself in rather profound train of thought regarding dependence of artistic perception upon physical conditions, but discover in the midst of it that I am having a night-mare about the children both being drowned, and have dropped two books and one glove.

Colored porter appears with clothes-brush, and is evidently convinced that I cannot possibly present myself to Canadian inspection without previously submitting to his ministrations. As I feel that he is probably right, I stand up and am rather half-heartedly dealt with, and then immediately sit down again, no doubt in original collection of dust, and weakly present porter with ten cents, at which he merely looks disgusted and says nothing.

Train stops, and I get out of it, and find myself—as so often before—surrounded by luggage on strange and ice-cold platform, only too well aware that I probably look even more *dégommée* than I feel.

Canadian host and hostess, with great good feeling, have both turned out to meet me, and am much impressed at seeing that neither cold nor early rising have impaired complexion of my hostess. Find myself muttering quotation:

"Alike to her were time and tide,
November's snow and July's pride."

but Canadian host, Mr. Lee, says Did I speak? and I have to say No, no, nothing at all, and remind myself that talking aloud to oneself is well-known preliminary to complete mental breakdown. Make really desperate effort, decide that I am awake and that the day has begun—began, in fact, several hours ago—and that if only I am given a cup of very strong coffee quite soon, I shall very likely find myself restored to normal degree of alertness.

Mr. Lee looks kind, Mrs. Lee—evidently several years younger—is cheerful and goodlooking, and leads the way to small car waiting outside station.

This appears to me to be completely filled already by elderly lady in black, large dog, and little girl with pig-tails. These, I am told, are the near neighbors of the Lees. Should like to ask why this compels them to turn out at four o'clock in the morning in order to meet complete stranger, but do not, naturally, do so.

Explanation is presently proffered, to the effect that the Niagara Falls are only eighty miles away, and I am to visit them at once, and the little girl—Minnie—has never seen them either, so it seemed a good opportunity. Minnie, at this, jumps up and down the seat and has to be told to Hush, dear. Her mother adds that Minnie is very highly-strung. She always has been, and her mother is afraid she always will be. The doctor has said that she has, at nine years old, the brain of a child of fifteen. I look at Minnie, who at once assumes an interesting expression and puts her head on one side, at which I immediately look away again, and feel that I am not going to like Minnie. (This impression definitely gains ground as day goes on.) Mrs. Lee, on the other hand, earns gratitude almost amounting to affection by saying that I must have breakfast and a bath before anything else, and that both these objectives can be obtained on the way to Niagara.

I ask what about my luggage? and am told that a friend of some cousins living near Hamilton has arranged to call for it later and convey it to Mr. Lee's house. Am impressed, and decide that mutual readiness to oblige must be a feature of Canadian life. Make mental note to develop this theme when talking to Women's Institute at home.

At this point Minnie's mother suddenly asks What we are all here for, if not to help one another, and adds that for her part, her motto has always been: Lend a Hand. Revulsion of feeling at once overtakes me, and I abandon all idea of impressing the Women's Institute with the desirability of mutual good will.

Car takes us at great speed along admirable roads—very tight squeeze on back seat, and Minnie kicks me twice on the shins and puts her elbow into my face once—and we reach house standing amongst trees.

Is this, I civilly enquire of Mrs. Lee, her home? Oh dear no. The Lees live right on the other side of Toronto. This is Dr. MacAfie's place, where we are all having breakfast. And a bath, adds Mrs. L., looking at me compassionately. Dr. MacAfie and his wife both turn out to be Scotch. They receive us kindly, and Mrs. L. at once advocates the bathroom for me.

Bath is a success, and I come down very hungry, convinced that it must be nearer lunchtime than breakfast-time. Clock, however, declares it to be just half-past seven. Find myself counting up number of hours that must elapse before I can hope to find myself in bed and asleep. Results of this calculation very discouraging.

Breakfast, which is excellent, restores me, and we talk about America—the States very unlike Canada—the Dominions—life in Canada very like life in the Old Country—snow very early this year—and my impressions of Chicago World's Fair.

Minnie interrupts a good deal, and says Need she eat bacon, and If she went on a big ship to England she knows she'd be very sick. At this everybody laughs—mine very perfunctory indeed—and her mother says that really, the things that child says ... and it's always been like that, ever since she was a tiny tot. Anecdotes of Minnie's infant witticisms follow, and I inwardly think of all the much more brilliant remarks made by Robin and Vicky. Should much like an opportunity for retailing these, and do my best to find one, but Minnie's mother gives me no opening whatever.

Expedition to Niagara ensues, and I am told on the way that it is important for me to see the Falls from the *Canadian* side, as this is greatly superior to the *American* side. Can understand this, in a way, as representing viewpoint of my present hosts, but hope that inhabitants of Buffalo, where I go next, will not prove equally patriotic and again conduct me immense distances to view phenomenon all over again.

Am, however, greatly impressed by Falls, and say so freely. Mr. Lee tells me that I really ought to see them by night, when lit up by electricity, and Mrs. Lee says No, that vulgarises them completely, and I reply Yes to both of them, and Minnie's mother asks What Minnie thinks of Niagara, to which Minnie squeaks out that she wants her dinner right away this minute, and we accordingly proceed to the Hotel.

Buy a great many postcards. Minnie watches this transaction closely, and says that she collects postcards. At this I very weakly present her with one of mine, and her mother says that I am really much too kind—with which I inwardly agree. This opinion intensified on return journey, when Minnie decides to sit on my lap, and asks me long series of complicated questions, such as Would I rather be an alligator who didn't eat people, or a man who had to make his living by stealing, or a tiny little midget in a circus? Reply to these and similar conundrums more or less in my sleep, and dimly hear Minnie's mother telling me that Minnie looks upon her as being just a great, big, elder sister, and always tells her everything just as it pops into her little head, and don't I feel that it's most important to have the complete confidence of one's children?

Can only think, at the moment, that it's most important to have a proper amount of sleep.

Mr. Lee's house is eventually attained, and proves to be outside Toronto. Minnie and her parent are dropped at their own door, and say that they will be popping in quite soon, and I get out of car and discover that I am alarmingly stiff, very cold, and utterly exhausted.

Am obliged to confess this state of affairs to Mrs. Lee, who is very kind, and advises bed. Can only apologise, and do as she suggests.

November 12th—Spend comparatively quiet day, and feel better. Host and hostess agree that I must remain indoors, and as it snows violently I thankfully do so, and write very much over-due letters.

Quiet afternoon and evening of conversation. Mr. Lee wants to know about the Royal Family—of which, unfortunately, I can tell him little except what he can read for himself in the papers—and Mrs. Lee asks if I play much Bridge. She doesn't, she adds hastily, mean on Sundays. Am obliged to reply that I play very little on any day of the week, but try to improve this answer by adding that my husband is very good at cards. Then, says Mrs. Lee, do I garden? No—unfortunately not. Mrs. Lee seems disappointed, but supposes indulgently that writing a book takes up quite a lot of time, and I admit that it does, and we leave it at that.

Am rather disposed, after this effort, to sit and ponder on extreme difficulty of ever achieving continuity of conversation when in the society of complete strangers. Idle fancy crosses my mind that Mr. Alexander Woollcott would make nothing of it at all, and probably conduct whole conversation all by himself with complete success. Wonder—still more idly—if I shall send him a postcard about it, and whether he would like one of Niagara.

November 12th *(continued)*—Main purpose of Canadian visit—which is small lecture—safely accomplished. Audience kind, rather than enthusiastic. Mrs. Lee says that she could tell I was nervous. Cannot imagine more thoroughly discouraging comment than this.

Mr. Lee very kindly takes me to visit tallest building in the British Empire, which turns out to be a Bank. We inspect Boardrooms, offices, and finally vaults, situated in basement and behind enormous steel doors, said to weigh incredible number of tons and only to be opened by two people working in conjunction. I ask to go inside, and am aghast when I do so by alarming notice on the wall which tells me that if I get shut into the vaults by accident I am not to be alarmed, as there is a supply of air for several hours. Do not at all like the word "several," which is far from being sufficiently specific, and have horrid visions of being shut into the vaults and spending my time there in trying to guess exactly when "several" may be supposed to be drawing to an end. Enquire whether anyone has ever been locked into the vaults, and if they came out mad, but Mr. Lee only replies no one that he has ever heard of, and appears quite unmoved by the idea.

Have often associated banking with callousness, and now perceive how right I was.

Evening is passed agreeably with the Lees until nine o'clock, when Minnie and parent descend upon us and we all talk about Minnie for about half-an-hour. Take cast-iron resolution before I sleep never to make either of the dear children subjects of long conversations with strangers.

(*Mem:* To let Robert know of this resolution, as feel sure he would approve of it.)

November 13th—Five o'clock train is selected to take me to Buffalo, and am surprised and relieved to find that I have not got to travel all night, but shall arrive in four-and-a-half hours. Luncheon party is kindly given in my honor by the Lees—Minnie not present, but is again quoted extensively by her mother—and I am asked more than once for opinion on relative merits of Canada and the United States. Can quite see that this is very delicate ground, and have no intention whatever of committing myself to definite statement on the point. Talk instead about English novelists—Kipling evidently very popular, and Hugh Walpole looked upon as interesting new discovery—and I am told by several people that I ought to go to Quebec.

As it is now impossible for me to do so, this leads to very little, beyond repeated assurances from myself that I should *like* to go to Quebec, and am exceedingly sorry not to be going there. One well-informed lady tells me that Harold Nicholson went there and liked it very much. Everybody receives this in respectful silence, and I feel that Harold Nicholson has completely deflated whatever wind there may ever have been in my sails.

Morale is restored later by my host, who takes me aside and says that I have been Just a breath of fresh air from the Old Country, and that I must come again next year. Am touched, and recklessly say that I will. Everyone says good-bye very kindly, and gentleman—

hitherto unknown—tells me that he will drive me to the station, as he has to go in that direction later. Minnie's mother heaps coals of fire on my head by telling me that she has a little present for my children, and is going just across the street to get it. This she does, and present turns out to be a Service revolver, which she thinks my boy may like. Can reply with perfect truth that I feel sure of it, and am fortunately not asked for my own reaction; or Robert's.

JOYCE CAROL OATES

W ITH THE EXCEPTION of Elizabeth Spencer, no author
currently regarded among the first rank of American literary
artists has lived in Canada as an adult for as long as Joyce Carol
Oates (b.1938). From 1968-78 she taught at the University of Windsor, making the border city her home. From this vantage, she continued to write the many novels, stories and poems for which she is
globally renowned. While her decade in Canada saw the introduction of our citizens and landscape into her work for the first time,
her Canadian decade arguably forced her to substantially modify her
perceptions of her own country—also for the first time. Ensconced
in a foreign land, albeit one a mere five minute drive away from the
States, she had the advantage of a broader perspective obtained by all
literary expatriates, yet she could maintain, unlike traditional exiles,
an immediate physical link to her homeland.

Violence and brutality, hallmarks of much of her fiction, may
seem extraordinary to some academic critics, but merely realistic
reflections of American society to more learned readers. The liti-
giousness, infatuation with guns, and ferocity of American culture,
so demarcating to Canadians as American national traits, are prevalent in one of Oates' most respected novels, *Wonderland* (1971). In
fact, the book ends in Toronto, the foreignness of the city so augmenting the American protagonist's sense of alienation from his

body, from the world, that his behaviour becomes irrational, the action nearly hallucinatory. For Jesse, the hero of *Wonderland*, it could be said of Canada as the early cartographers used to write of terra incognita, *here be monsters*.

Initially, Jesse brings to his Toronto visit a common American perception:

> Jesse could smell the coolness of the wind that blew from the lake, and he imagined that this city was more northerly, more pure, than the cities he had known in the United States.

The vitality of the downtown life also strikes him as odd:

> So this was Yonge Street!
>
> He walked headlong into odors of food, fumes, currents that were stale and intimate and welcoming. An open-air fruit market: a whiff of the tropics. A meat market with objects dangling inside, plucked and withered, headless. Scrawny little wings. The odor of blood and sawdust. And all the restaurants—the pizza diners, the coffee shops, the hamburger joints that were no more than single counters.... The street was noisy with music from competing record stores.

Just prior to diving into a sordid commune on Yonge Street to rescue his daughter, Jesse soon changes his mind about this new metropolis. Initially believing himself in a different kind of city, he reassesses: "This was Toronto: a city in a foreign country. But it seemed like any other city.... It did look like an American city after all."

Before the novel ends, he changes his mind yet again. In Toronto, after rescuing his child from an American, Manson-like maniac, Jesse meanders the city streets, totally lost, almost psychedelically distracted, conscious again only of the alien land, and his extrinsic sensations. The two stumble down to the Toronto docks, steal a small boat and drift into Lake Ontario, the father holding his dying daughter in his arms, a Canadian *pietà*. Even the final words of the novel may be an allusion to the order of Canadian society versus the chaos of American: "The boat drifted most of the night. Near dawn it was picked up by a large handsome cruiser, a Royal Mounted Police boat, a dazzling sight with its polished wood and metal and its trim of gold and blue."

Oates addressed Canada directly in two collections of stories: *The Hungry Ghosts* and the deftly titled *Crossing the Border*, deft because, as the allusions in *Wonderland* make clear, there are many borders crossed by humans that have nothing to do with immigration officers or flags. While some of the stories deal exclusively with American reactions to crossing frontiers, however frontier is defined, the following is Oates' most explicit tale concerned with the abutment of American and Canadian characteristics.

NATURAL BOUNDARIES

Renée, having lived so long in apartments, inside buildings shared with others, was struck by the novelty of living in a house—though only a rented house, and very small. And since it was on the river, she found herself staring out the back windows, sometimes for a half hour at a time, fascinated, transfixed by the movement of the river. *How quickly everything changed....*

There was nothing pretty about the Maynards' frame house or the rocky back yard or the scrubby beach, and nothing pretty about the river itself: yet everything seemed to her, in this setting, in the harsh overbright light of autumn, incredibly beautiful. She wondered if her personality were being altered, subtly. On the wide choppy river were flocks of mallards ... swimming, bobbing with the waves ... occasionally squawking loudly ... one morning there had been three Canada geese out there, swimming complacently, high regal heads and bills ... but they had flown away before Renée's husband got home from work, and he seemed amused rather than interested when she spoke excitedly of them, *how beautiful they are, and at the same time a little frightening ... something snakelike about the long necks and heads....*

The river was continually changing. The sky was continually changing: now clouding up, thick and gray and massive and depressing, now abruptly blue again, miraculously cleansed. And then the storm clouds would reappear. An hour of premature darkness ... the promise of rain ... then, once again, the sky would turn blue, and the clouds were far away, blown across the lake to the horizon, harmless. Renée liked this, the rapidity with which the day changed. It was something new to her.

In sunny weather there were many sailboats on the river. Most had white sails, but some were decked out with sails of blue and white stripes, or red and white stripes, one was a bright brave yellow ... and there were a number of powerboats, occasionally a large cabin cruiser from the yacht club on the American side of the river ... continual movement, motion. Freighters passed all day long. From east to west, bound for Lake Erie ... from west to east, bound for Lake Huron. And beyond. Some of the lakers were hardly more than decrepit barges, carrying automobiles or coal or steel ... some of the ocean vessels, from as far away as Japan, were handsome, gleamingly painted, their flags and insignia illuminated at night, proudly. Home alone much of the time, Renée stared at the slow-passing vessels, fascinated by their rough, functional beauty, which was different from the kind of beauty she had been taught to admire. She wondered who worked on those boats.... Did the workers ever gaze at the houses along the shore, at her house, perhaps, and wonder who lived there?

And the coast-guard helicopters that flew back and forth along the river—what missions had they?—why did they patrol so often?—were they ready to arrest people crossing the border illegally, by boat?—or were they merely wasting time, wasting fuel? The rotor blades were certainly loud. When one of the helicopters passed overhead, the thunderous choppy sound was deafening. Renée supposed she would eventually come to loathe it, but in the first months she found herself unaccountably excited by it. *Had something happened? Was something wrong? Was there danger? ...* So far as she knew there were no accidents on the river, no sailboats capsizing, no small rowboats turned over by the wash of the freighters. Practice rescue maneuvers took place once or twice a week along her stretch of the river, so she was able to watch the operation from her kitchen window, safe, knowing everyone to be safe. How orderly and logical it was, the rescue procedure: the helicopter with its enormous swordlike blades and its flashing red lights, descending slowly, almost in steps toward the boat, the roaring of its engines, the sudden dropping of the rope ladder ... It was an orderly, sane procedure, yet, watching it, Renée sometimes felt an accumulation of tension that was almost painful.

They were rehearsing, practicing for disaster.

She was watching the rescue maneuvers one morning in October, when the telephone rang. She continued to watch the boat and the helicopter, drifting downstream, powerful waves all around them—white-capped—and overhead the sky was battered with thick swollen-gray clouds—The telephone rang. She knew who it was; she would not answer it. From the east came one of the long rust-streaked barges with the words *Cleveland Cliffs* in white letters on its side ... by the time it had passed, the telephone had stopped ringing.

Of course she was flattered.

But also alarmed.

He had something to do with the river, this man, this stranger.

No: he had something to do with her loneliness.

She thought of him constantly though she did not love him; she did not love him. She did not even know him. Her husband worked in a hospital on the city's west side, some distance away, and Renée, though qualified to teach in public schools in the United States, was not qualified to teach in Canada … and she knew the futility of applying for a job, when unemployment figures were headlined nearly every evening in the newspaper…. It was a bad time, economically. A very bad time. She was temporarily unemployed but believed, vaguely, that she would find something to do before long. There was no hurry. Being a woman, she thought—ironically, but sincerely—that it did not matter quite so much, her being unemployed: to Evan, it would have been like death. But she did not mind. She was a "housewife."

Still, the loneliness of the house was sometimes disturbing. That it was *lonely* because she was *alone* made sense, intellectually; yet the experience of it was somehow a surprise. The silence of the house would at times seem to her sinister … the sound of the wind in the oaks and poplars, usually so soothing, at times sounded threatening, like whispers not audible enough to be heard … so that she was almost grateful for the noisy interruptions of the coast-guard helicopters or the jet airliners passing overhead. Then the telephone. But after the first several times, the *Hello? Yes? Yes, this is Renée,* she had stopped answering it … *I'd like to talk with you but I can't, I can't, I can't … please don't call me again.*

Sometimes she told Evan that she had to get out, *she had to get out of the house,* and it didn't matter where she walked: a few blocks up to the shopping area, or down to the library, or just on an aimless walk…. Surprised by her, irritated, Evan had not understood; he spoke as if she had somehow betrayed him. His work was exhausting—he was a laboratory technician, assisting a chemist who had a Canada Council grant for the year, who was lovingly and bitterly attached to his work, and expected Evan to stay in the laboratory all day long and after he left, to clean things up—doubly exhausting since the research was not Evan's, and he was forced to subordinate his interest to another man's. Evan didn't speak much about this problem, though Renée had the idea he thought about it constantly, and he seemed to expect her, at the house, at home, to be fully grateful for not having to work. His hands stained with chemicals, his fingernails ridged with something dark that no amount of soap and scrubbing could get out, he laughed sardonically at Renée and said, *Surprising to hear that—you did want to come here with me, didn't you?—or were you pretending?* She did not flinch and did not exactly defend herself—she had too much dignity to "defend" herself to anyone—explaining that she loved this place, this new life, and her loneliness was a trivial and temporary thing, which she wouldn't mention again.

Just to get out of the house: she walked a dozen or more blocks to the branch library, though she had books at home, and journals of Evan's she wanted to read.... *To get out of the house, to escape the telephone's ringing or the fact of it not ringing, to end her absurd obsessive thoughts about that man:* so she found herself up at the library several times a week, until the librarians began to recognize her, greet her by name. There, at the round table where popular magazines were piled, Renée might fully enjoy herself, absorbed in her reading, wasting time, scanning articles on travel, though they could not afford to travel, on frozen-food storage, though they could barely afford meat, gazing at full-page advertisements in the fashion magazine ... *STARTLING NEW LOOK FOR AUTUMN.... TWELVE MAKEUP "MAKE-OVERS" FROM BRITISH COLUMBIA....* Other articles purported to be more serious: *WILL CANADIAN-US RELATIONS TAKE A TURN FOR THE BETTER? ... NEW HOPE FOR ARTHRITIS SUFFERERS: MONTREAL RESEARCHER MAKES CAUTIOUS PREDICTIONS.... THE SHIFTING MORAL PERSPECTIVE: ADULTERY IN THE MIDDLE CLASS.*

She read about adultery in the middle class.

Reading these paragraphs in their logical unexcited order, seeing how the columns of print on glossy paper were sanely arranged to divide advertisements, to bracket recipes and occasional cartoons, she could see how superficial a subject it was. The mere fact that the word "adultery" might be used in this way, the lead article in the November *Woman's Journal* with graphs and statistics and quotations and small excited headlines, and all of it to sell copies of the magazine, to sell, sell, sell ... allowed Renée to see how ordinary it was, how unthreatening. What had it to do with her?—what had it to do with this man Karl?—certainly she was superior to it all, saved from it, from *it*, by the fact of being able to read about it. Still, she felt nervous, not wanting anyone to stroll past her as she sat at the table ... nervous as if she were already betraying her husband.

The Telford branch library was hardly more than one large room—the floors always polished, the librarians chattering quietly behind the desk, no rude noises, no upsets. Not many people came in during the day, and few sat down, as Renée did, to read. After three fifteen, students came in and things got noisy, so Renée usually left by then.... No, the very sanity of her surroundings would prevent her from making any mistakes: what was *passion*, what was *love*, what were emotions of any kind, in this setting?

The danger was back at her house, where she was alone.

She had met Karl Davies at a poetry reading two weeks before. He was one of the area poets, one of six people reading poems at a special program at the city's art gallery. Renée had received a flier in the mail, sent to occupant, *no admission charge, everyone welcome* ... and had known at once that she would go. It was certainly not a desperate act; she wasn't that lonely, really. And Evan was home in the evenings.

Long ago, Renée had come to terms with a part of herself. She was one of those people who admired worth in others, especially artistic worth, she was one of the followers, a member of an audience, grateful enough, yet sometimes rather baffled by the division of humanity into those "with talent" and those "without." She wondered if perhaps she were smaller-souled than artists, somehow less concentrated, less passionate. Yet she was more easily content; she was not a competitor, only an admirer. She wanted to admire. She considered it mature of herself, to have come to terms with her own lack of originality, and to be eager to admire it in others.

Why, that night, a feeling of resentment?—jealousy?

The reading was held in one of the gallery's wings. Folding chairs had been set up on the parquet floor, and about fifty people had come out. There was an emphasis on casualness: informality. Each of the poets read without strain, low-keyed, standing at a podium, leafing through papers without much concern for performing. Renée did not know if she cared for that; she wanted to idolize someone, after all.... Four men, two women. They were not remarkable people physically, though attractive enough, likable enough; one was especially nervous and ended his selections abruptly ... Renée had the idea he was a little drunk.... Karl Davies read last. The program must have been arranged in order to allow him to read last, since he was the best speaker—probably the best poet, though the poetry was so obscure that Renée could hardly judge. What she could understand was striking, some of it banal, but much of it was lost to her ... though she didn't mind, she didn't mind not understanding, as she usually did not understand music or art in any rational way. Karl Davies's voice was rather raw, seemingly untrained, yet very effective—very dramatic. He was about thirty-five years old, with black curly hair, thick eyebrows that nearly met over the bridge of his nose ... a powerful, pushing manner and bearing. He read some of the poems too rapidly, but his voice rang upon certain words, images, and Renée knew she would remember them. *Yes, he's good, that man is really good.* She sensed that the audience admired him very much, it was a performance well done, well done....

Coffee was served in an adjoining room. Renée noticed Karl Davies with a small group of people—friends of his, probably, one of them a woman who linked her arm through his, his wife?—yes, his wife—Renée could see her wedding band. Karl seemed still rather unusual, though he was shorter than Renée had imagined, and the way he spoke, laughed, tapped at his friends' arms showed that he too had been nervous. Though away from the podium he struck her, still, as being an extraordinary man.... Two of his children were there: a small boy, a girl of about seven. They were restless, dodging in and out of the crowd. The boy had Karl's dark curly hair and his mother's roundish, high-colored face. Renée, fascinated, stood alone and watched the Davieses and their friends ... now being joined by one of the women poets, a tall lanky girl in trousers, with a curtain of straight bronze-brown hair ... all of them laughing loudly, cheerfully. When Karl happened to glance over at her Renée did not even respond to his vague smile, since she had imagined she was invisible: she had become especially invisible, since moving to Canada.

He came over to her; he introduced himself. His manner was aggressive, overbearing, and whatever they said—she must have managed to congratulate him on his poetry, he must have asked her the usual rapid-fire questions *Are you new to the city? American? What does your husband do? Like it here?*—was afterward lost to her. She was intimidated by him. It had really startled her, his singling her out like this ... she was quick to laugh, embarrassed and girlish and honored and at the same time disturbed ... thinking that something was wrong, must be wrong. Around them people were milling, holding coffee cups and doughnuts. Karl was telling her about an informal group of people who liked poetry, some of them poets, some not, some associated with the university, some not ... they just enjoyed each other's company, since the city wasn't exactly a center of culture, as he said sardonically. Renée liked the city and had not compared it to any other city; she was grateful just to be here. But she stammered an agreement and he seemed to be left with the impression that she would join them sometime.

... *A fairly good turnout tonight, surprising,* Karl muttered.

Renée, twenty-six years old, with dark-red hair sometimes worn loose on her shoulders and sometimes drawn back into a knot, had the look, she supposed, of a university student: one of those tall, startled-looking, quite often very attractive girls whose bearing— both submissive and striking—make them popular with men of a certain type. Never extravagantly dressed, never ostentatiously "pretty," their appeal is almost intellectual: even their beauty, if they are beautiful, is an arrangement of facial bones, strong elegant cheekbones, strong graceful body. Renée's complexion was milky pale and freckled. Her forehead was rather wide, so she wore bangs to disguise it; her red-blond eyebrows were scant and light, making her eyes appear larger than they were. Her nose was small and ordinary. Her mouth was ordinary. She was convinced that her appearance was an ordinary one, and most of the time she didn't bother to exaggerate her good features—to outline her eyes in black or to paint her eyelids green or blue, as many of the girls here tonight had—so it always surprised her, it truly flattered her, when men approached her; *it must be for herself, herself alone.* Tonight Renée did feel pretty; she was flushed, excited. Karl spoke enthusiastically to her about a recent provincial grant that had come their way— "their" referring to his circle of poet friends, she assumed—that would subsidize readings in local high schools and in several institutions, a home for the blind, a home for elderly people, a halfway house for young people near the university, and as he spoke he leaned toward her, urgent, yet still casual, with his mannered informality, so that she lost the thread of his conversation and began to feel, uneasily, that this man had somehow recognized her ... there was a kind of agreement between them.... But she must have been imagining it. Only near the end of their conversation did he say something odd, meant to be amusing: *I can tell you're married, you couldn't not be married ... right? ... How do you like my son Jamie, the brat crawling under the table there, see him, about to surface by that lady's legs? ... that's how I looked at his age.*

Later, Renée wished she had drawn closer to Mrs. Davies, after Karl excused himself and returned to her and his friends ... she wished she had made an effort to see what the woman looked like, up close. *Evie,* her name was; Renée had overheard it. *Evie.* She was a pretty woman in her mid-thirties, though rather flush-faced—her cheeks reddened with the pleasure of conversation, of laughter— blond, the hair too severe, too short, for her plump face. She wore scarlet slacks and a silkish scarlet and green blouse.... The kind of woman everyone liked, and Renée herself would probably have liked her; she knew suddenly that she would never meet her. Renée watched the group, watched Karl with them, sliding his arm around his wife's shoulders ... and, without glancing back at Renée, he drifted with the group across the room, to meet someone else. Renée stared after them, her cup still in her hand, the coffee cold, thinking that it did not matter; it really did not matter.... *You couldn't not be married.*

He had nothing to do with her loneliness, or with the river out there, nothing to do with the infinitely changing sky and the waves that were now fierce and white-capped, now flattened, shallow, washing up on the beach. Yet when he telephoned her the first time, a few days after the reading, she stumbled with the telephone across the kitchen, as far as the cord would let her, to stare wildly out the window. She hardly heard what he was saying; she hardly heard her own hesitant, confused replies, *No I don't think so. No, really....* It was a shock, though she had been thinking of him. She had even endured a puzzling and possibly humiliating dream about him, which she could not quite remember. *No, Karl, really ... I ... I don't think so....* She laughed at her own timidity. He laughed also, nervously. She had the idea he was extremely nervous.... He forced himself to speak more casually, asking her fairly routine questions about how she and her husband liked living where they did: any discrimination against them, as Americans? ... he hoped not, he liked Americans, he identified with them, for some reason ... not with the government, of course, but with Americans ... that is, the Americans he ran into, here and in Toronto. They were rather like himself, he thought. Did she agree? ... Renée didn't know; she told him *Yes.* He was overbearing even when seemingly deferential. It must always be easier to agree with him, she thought. Always easier to agree.... Then he asked her what she did all day long: she hadn't a baby, eh? Somehow he knew she hadn't. Her body, her stance, the way she'd been standing there ... something about the tilt of the pelvis, he knew, he could tell ... she was certainly someone's wife, but not a young mother, was that right? ... Renée was too confused to be offended; she stared out at the river, not seeing it, aware of one of the barges edging into the corner of her vision, aware of something happening, something mysterious and alarming ... she stared out there, as if Karl were there.

Finally she told him, embarrassed, that she had to hang up.

Of course, of course, he said philosophically.

Yet he telephoned again that day, so late in the afternoon that Renée kept listening for the sound of Evan's car—their drive was gravel, and noisy—and felt how, if she heard it, she would put the receiver back at once. It would be an automatic reflex.... Karl apologized for bothering her. He knew it was rude, he knew it was absurd. His excuse, he explained, was to inform her of a foreign film series shown every Friday evening at the university ... he thought she might like it, the film being shown next was an early Bergman movie, was he correct, wouldn't she enjoy that? ... Then he laughed, he said that his excuse really was ... his real excuse was ... that he was at Leon's, did she know where that was? ... no? ... A tavern, a fish-and-chips place, really a kind of dive ... right on the river, adjoining a marina, he had the idea it wasn't far from where she lived.... Where did she live on the Drive, exactly?

Renée said she would talk to him another time ... her husband would be home in a few minutes, and....

Hey, I know I'm bothering you, upsetting you, Karl said. But he was cheerful. Behind him were muffled noises: occasionally someone laughed. *I realize that. The thing is ... the odd thing is.... I'm writing a poem for you, having a hard time with it, very frustrating, most of my stuff as you may have noticed is short and blunt and not exactly, you know, idealistic.... All I would like is your address, Renée, so that if I ever finish it I could mail it to you.*

When she did not reply, he laughed agreeably. He said he'd read it at the next poetry reading, then; hopefully she'd be there.... He mentioned a place, a date, a time. Hopefully she'd be there.

Renée could not remember what she said. She had the idea she said *Yes.*

But he must have discovered her address, since she received a letter from him the following week.

She seemed to hear, reading the five-page letter, his highly charged, nervous, yet casual voice: his handwriting was heavy, mostly block letters, he had used a felt-tip pen and had made whimsical slashes and curls and question marks and explanation points in the margins, as if he were writing to himself, daydreaming, a long

Lyric monologue. The letter began *Dear Renée (Maynard)* and was signed *Yours, Karl (Davies)*.

He began by apologizing again, underlining the word *Sorry!* several times. He told her he'd been born in Blenheim, in Ontario; that he'd traveled mainly in the northeastern part of the United States, and in New York State; that he'd lived in this city most of his adult life ... and though he mocked it, like everyone else, he really liked it here and had no interest in moving.... What he wanted to know was why *she* had come here. Why. Did it mean anything to her, had it meant anything to her. Only an accident, probably? He supposed so; only an accident.... But embarrassing as it was to him (and in parenthesis he said *It's good to be embarrassed, good for my ego, let the worst happen I deserve it*) he had the strange idea that, years ago, probably when he'd driven around summers with some friends, down into New York, years ago he must have seen her.... She had mentioned she was from New York City originally; he hadn't gone there, but perhaps ... was it possible ... was it possible he'd seen her somewhere else? ... He was not superstitious, he said; he disliked people who believed in astrology, omens, dreams, that kind of thing.... But, embarrassing as it was, he had to confess to her that seeing her face had reminded him of someone: a sense of *déjà vu*, very powerful, upsetting. And he was certain he had dreamed about her the night before the reading. She had appeared to him along with the word *separation* and somehow, magically, she had erased that word ... had caused it to vanish. He had not seen her face clearly, and yet somehow he had absorbed it.... It had been a disturbing dream, and he had remembered it when he woke. Now he apologized for having written so much for probably embarrassing her and wasting her time, but he was curious ... she didn't have to reply, of course ... he was curious about whether she had dreamed about him or seemed to recognize him or....

Renée let the letter fall on the kitchen table, her head spinning.

She did not usually remember her dreams; she shied away from thinking of them. That jumble of emotions, memories, visual fragments.... No, she had never taken any interest in them, she believed in a way that it was risky, to try to recollect too much, poking and probing into that part of one's consciousness. There was something in the dream life that was not human, not recognizable. What was "human" was tempered with a cold, relentless, sinister objectivity, as if viewed from an angle not experienced during the day; though confused and baffling, the dream world struck her as hideously truthful. Yet she did not remember dreams when she woke, only the aftermath of emotions stirred by them, and she never made any effort to recall them.

When Karl telephoned again, one morning a few days later, she thanked him for the letter but told him no, she hadn't dreamed of him, no, she was sorry, and it wasn't likely that he had ever met her ... and though she hoped to attend the next poetry reading she didn't feel she could talk to him much more, like this, because....

Right, he said at once. *I agree.*

She stopped answering the telephone.

She read clinical articles about "adultery"—scanning the quotations—women's remarks, *Mrs. S., Mrs. K.,* allegedly housewives responding honestly to the interviewers' prying questions, *Mrs. Y. of Toronto, Mrs. M. of....* She had the idea that the entire article was fiction; that the interviewer, a sociologist, had made everything up. For the view of marriage, love, family life, and of adultery itself advanced by the essay was peculiarly passionless: as if these events happened so easily, so mechanically! ... No, she could not believe. With one part of her mind she respected the statistics, of course. But she could not believe it was that easy; that these women, if they were "real," would not pay emotionally for their cheerful lightweight adventures.

IS TRADITIONAL MORALITY DYING?—DEAD?—OR IN HIBERNATION?

She stopped reading the articles, and now that the weather was colder, rainier, she stayed in the house, she occupied herself with repainting one of the bedrooms: there was much to do, since the house was in poor repair. One day someone knocked at the door. She knew it was Karl; she felt a rush of certainty that was physical, a charge that went through her entire body. A rapping at the door ... at the front door.... She knew it was Karl, and that she would let him in.

No, she would not let him in.

She had not gone to the October poetry reading; she had refused to think about it. At the same time she had been thinking, not quite consciously, that he would therefore come to her ... he *must* therefore come to her. But now that he had come and was knocking on the door, she would not let him in.

She was trembling. Panicked.... Found herself in the tiny bathroom, the door closed, even locked. He could not get her. Let him knock on the door, let him pound on it ... he could not get to her, she was safe. The young woman who watched her in the mirror was almost white-faced, the blood drawn out of her cheeks especially. Grotesque. Ugly. *If he should see her like this*—! She was wearing old clothes, paint-smeared. A smudge of yellow on her chin. Sallow-pale complexion, not pretty. She was not pretty now. She trembled, wondering if she would be sick to her stomach, wondering at the bravery other women possessed or said they possessed or were said to possess, that adultery should be so easy for them, life itself so easy.

She knew now that they lied.

One day, downtown, she was heading for the parking lot near the river, when she saw a man who resembled Karl. He was leaving Cole's, walking quickly. Alone. Karl himself, Karl Davies. It was a Saturday, streets were crowded, Renée had been walking near the buildings, on the inside of the sidewalk—she always gravitated inward, away from the curb—and Karl took the outside of the walk, not seeing her. They were going to pass within a few yards of each other. He wore sunglasses with metallic frames and lenses of a dark, greenish-beige, and was dressed as he had been at the poetry reading, in an open-collared blue shirt, a baggy colorless sweater, work trousers, canvas shoes. He was scanning the sidewalk, scanning faces absentmindedly; he seemed to glance at Renée, his eyes moving quickly and curiously behind the beige lenses.

Her hair was drawn back into a knot; she wore an old olive-green trench coat; her face felt very exposed.

… He glanced at her, he had seemed to glance at her. Yet he kept on walking. Evidently he had not seen her.

Renée kept on walking.

She knew he had seen her; he had looked right at her. Yet he had not recognized her…. Clutching a yellow and black bag from the store, Karl Davies on a Saturday, early afternoon, an attractive man of medium height, with black curly hair…. No, not really attractive. His face was bumpy in the white-glaring air. His hair was not black, really brown. And he had not recognized her.

Hello, Renée thought. *Hello,* good-bye.

After months of drought, rains were falling farther north, along the river. The river was rising. There might be floods: floods were excitedly predicted. Renée raked debris off the beach, a scarf tied tight around her head. If the telephone rang back at the house she could not hear it. If it didn't ring, she could not hear the silence.

"Hello," she would tell him. "I can't talk. Good-bye."

The river made a natural border. Across its choppy, rather ugly waters was the United States, looking like any dismal manufacturing city at this point—smokestacks, billowing black smoke, ragged puffs of white smoke, occasionally small figures that must have been human. "Renée Maynard" raked the beach and laughed to herself, thinking of how she must tell Evan about her experience, someday. How "Karl Davies" and "Renée Maynard" had almost come into existence, had almost confronted each other, yet had not. For some reason they had not. They had not even met. So "Renée" raked the beach, deftly, impatiently, and did not care at all about the flood warnings: let the river rise, let it flood. They were not going to leave their new home. She was not going to leave her life. "Renée" thought of how Renée would always be safe, no matter what.

RUDYARD KIPLING

R UDYARD KIPLING (1865-1936) enjoyed a popularity in his own lifetime few writers have savoured: his verse was memorized by millions of people who otherwise were uninterested in poetry; and he was the prevailing champion of imperialism in the decades when the British Empire was most globally powerful. While today, in the public imagination, he is regarded as a man who wrote mostly about England and India, in his own time his words about Canada were voluminous, and of import to both Canadians and the Empire puppet-masters in London. Indeed, he regarded Canada with a unique affection.

Kipling, although born in Bombay, received his primary and secondary school education in England. At age seventeen he returned to India to work as a journalist, but after a few years, years which included some success with poems and stories, he decided to settle in London in order to further his embryonic literary career.

In order to reach London, Kipling chose to proceed across the Pacific and then, at an extremely leisurely pace, across North America. He landed by ship in California where, even at this early age, he was feted at civic receptions held in his honour. But by June 1889, he found himself enjoying the San Francisco beer-halls, bucket-shops and poker-hells rather too much. He was not enjoying, however, the public spitting, the horrible hotels, and the loud, arrogant and apparently ceaseless American declarations of patriotism. At which

306

point "A voice inside me said 'Get out of this. Go north. Strike for Victoria and Vancouver. Bask for a day under the shadow of the old flag.'" So, travelling by train, he arrived in Vancouver on June 24, 1889. This tour marked his first visit—of at least seven—to Canada.

He stayed about a week in the area, and published his impressions as one of a series of travel essays, later issued as a book, *From Sea to Sea*. Kipling would always be pleased to cross the main North American international boundary, for he felt able to detect (with antennae sometimes more hopeful than sensitive) crucial differences between Canada and the States. On this first trip, for example, he noted:

> Vancouver three years ago was swept off by fire in sixteen minutes, and only one house was left standing. To-day it has a population of fourteen thousand people, and builds its houses out of brick with dressed granite fronts. But a great sleepiness lies on Vancouver as compared with the American town: men don't fly up and down the streets telling lies, and the spitoons in the delightfully comfortable hotel are unused; the baths are free and the doors are unlocked. You do not have to dig up the hotel clerk when you want to bathe, which shows the inferiority of Vancouver. An American bade me notice the absence of bustle, and was alarmed when in a loud and audible voice I thanked God for it.

Kipling so relished Vancouver's amenities that he let down his guard and seems to have been duped by a remittance man. Within a day or two of his arrival, and with large profits to be made from land speculation dancing in his head, Kipling bought two lots in the Mount Pleasant district of North Vancouver:

> He that sold it me was a delightful English Boy who, having tried for the Army and failed, had somehow meandered into a real-estate office, where he was doing well. I couldn't have bought it from an American.... All the Boy said was "I give you my word it isn't on a cliff or under water, and before long the

town ought to move out that way. I'd advise you to take it." And
I took it as easily as a man buys a piece of tobacco.

Unfortunately for Kipling, as he was to discover much later, despite
having paid property taxes for years, the "delightful English Boy"
apparently did not have clear title to the land. According to some
commentators, Kipling's total investment in Vancouver was lost.

During this same trip of 1889, he took a steamer to Victoria, at
that time a naval station which made a muted first impression on the
writer: "I found in that quiet English town of beautiful streets quite
a colony of old men doing nothing but talking, fishing and loafing
at the Club. That means that the retired go to Victoria." Moved by a
"lust for trout", Kipling also found time on the mainland to travel
seventy miles inland by Canadian Pacific ("cleaner and less stuffy
than the Pullman") to do some sportfishing before returning to
explore other parts of America.

Two months later, Kipling was still working his easterly way
through America, and by mid-August was close enough to Niagara
to make the, by now, almost compulsory pilgrimage to this shrine
for tourists. In an August 13th letter to a friend, Kipling confessed, "I
was not half as impressed as I ought to have been." This letter was
written from Toronto (which he visited briefly after Niagara Falls)
but the Ontario capital made even less of an impression, for in the
same letter he wrote not a word about the city.

By October 1889, Kipling finally arrived in Britain where his
career immediately soared. Among the many people he met was a
young American woman named Carrie Balestier, and in early 1892
they were married. As a wedding gift, Rudyard offered his bride a
honeymoon trip around the world, but, ever the professional writer,
he also arranged for various periodicals to publish his literary
sketches of the many places the couple were to visit.

The newlyweds sailed from England destined initially for Carrie
Balestier's hometown of Brattleboro, Vermont. After a week to catch
their breath, they set out at an unhurried pace for Winnipeg (via
New York and Chicago) in order to take the train across Canada to

Vancouver—from where they would catch the liner *Empress of India* for Japan. Kipling's would seem to be one of the first accounts by a literary man of travel across the prairies. In the following passage, he describes his happy entrance into Canada from Minnesota, then sketches with an eerie vocabulary the land that, in some parts, was still to see its first farmer:

There is more snow as we go north, and Nature is hard at work breaking up the ground for the spring. The thaw has filled every depression with a sullen gray-black spate, and out on the levels the water lies six inches deep, in stretch upon stretch, as far as the eye can reach. Every culvert is full, and the broken ice clicks against the wooden pier-guards of the bridges. Somewhere in this flatness there is a refreshing jingle of spurs along the cars, and a man of the Canadian Mounted Police swaggers through with his black fur cap and the yellow tab aside, his wellfitting overalls and his better set-up back. One wants to shake hands with him because he is clean and does not slouch nor spit, trims his hair, and walks as a man should. Then a custom-house officer wants to know too much about cigars, whisky, and Florida water. Her Majesty the Queen of England and Empress of India has us in her keeping. Nothing has happened to the landscape, and Winnipeg, which is, as it were, a centre of distribution for emigrants, stands up to her knees in the water of the thaw. The year has turned in earnest, and somebody is talking about the 'first iceshove' at Montreal, thirteen hundred or fourteen hundred miles east.

They will not run trains on Sunday at Montreal, and this is Wednesday. Therefore, the Canadian Pacific makes up a train for Vancouver at Winnipeg. This is worth remembering, because few people travel in that train, and you escape any rush of tourists running westward to catch the Yokohama boat. The car is your own, and with it the service of the porter. Our porter, seeing things were slack, beguiled himself with a guitar, which gave a triumphal and festive touch to the journey, ridiculously out of keeping with the view. For eight-and-twenty long hours did the bored locomotive trail us through a flat and hairy land, powdered, ribbed, and speckled with snow, small snow that drives like dust-shot in the wind—the land of Assiniboia. Now and again, for no obvious reason to the outside mind, there was a town. Then the towns gave place to "section so and so"; then there were trails of the buffalo, where he once walked in his pride; then there was a mound of white bones, supposed to belong to the said buffalo, and then the wilderness took up the tale. Some of it was good ground, but most of it seemed to have fallen by the wayside, and the tedium of it was eternal.

At twilight—an unearthly sort of twilight—there came another curious picture. Thus—a wooden town shut in among low, treeless, rolling ground, a calling river that ran unseen between scarped banks; barracks of a detachment of mounted police, a little cemetery where ex-troopers rested, a painfully formal public garden with pebble paths and foot-high fir trees, a few lines of railway buildings, white women walking up and down in the bitter cold with their bonnets off, some Indians in red blanketing with buffalo horns for sale trailing along the platform, and, not ten yards from the track, a cinnamon bear and a young grizzly standing up with extended arms in their pens and begging for food. It was strange beyond anything that this bald telling can suggest—opening a door into a new world. The only commonplace thing about the spot was its name—Medicine Hat, which struck me instantly as the only possible name such a town could carry. This is that place which later became a town; but I had seen it three years before when it was even smaller....

The Alberta town would remain singular in Kipling's affections for the rest of his life. In 1910, for instance, when some city fathers in Medicine Hat wanted to change the name of the town to something duller, a local citizen wrote to Kipling for help. Kipling replied in a letter (which would later be published around the world as a booklet) with a vigorous defense of the name's talismanic power:

Dear Sir …

You tell me that a public vote is to be taken on the question of changing the city's name. So far as I can make out from what I heard … and from the clippings you enclose the chief arguments for the change are (a) that some US journalists have some sort of joke that Medicine Hat supplies all the bad weather of the United States, and, (b) that another name would look better at the head of a prospectus.

Incidentally I note both arguments are developed at length by the Calgary *Herald*. I always knew that Calgary called Medicine Hat names, but I did not realize that Medicine Hat wanted to be Calgary's little god-child.…

Let us examine the name—Medicine Hat—I haven't my maps by me but I seem to remember a few names of places across the border such as Schenectady, Podunk, Schoharie, Poughkeepsie … etc. all of which are rather curious to the outsider, but times and the lives of men (it is people and not prospectuses that make cities) have sanctified the queer syllables with memories and associations for millions of our fellow creatures. Once upon a time these places were young and new and in process of making themselves. That is to say they were ancestors, with a duty to posterity, which duty they fulfilled in handing on their names intact; and Medicine Hat is today an ancestor—not a derivative, nor a collateral, but the founder of a line.

To my mind the name Medicine Hat has an advantage over all the names I have quoted. It echoes, as you so quaintly put it, of the old Cree and Blackfoot traditions of red mystery and romance that once filled the prairies. Also, it hints, I venture to think, at the magic that underlies the city, and as years go on, it will become more and more of an asset. It has no duplicate in the world; it makes men ask questions; and as I knew more than twenty years ago, draws the feet of the young men towards it; it has the qualities of uniqueness, individuality, assertion, and power. Above all, it is the lawful, original, sweat-and-dust-won name of the city and to change it would be to risk the luck of the city, to disgust and dishearten Old-Timers, not in the city alone, but the world over, and to advertise abroad the city's lack of faith in itself....

Forgive me if I write strongly, but this is a matter of which I feel strongly. As you know, I have not a dollar or a foot of land in Medicine Hat, but I have a large stake of interest and very true affection in and for the city and its folk. It is for this reason that in writing to you I have taken a liberty which to men who have known the city for several months or perhaps three years must seem inexcusable....

In conclusion it strikes me that the two arguments put forward for the change of name are almost equally bad. The second is perhaps a shade worse than the first. In the first case the town would change its name for fear of being laughed at. In the second it sells its name in the hope of making more money under an alias or as the Calgary *Herald* writes, for the sake of a name that "has a sound like the name of a man's best girl and looks like business at the head of a financial report."

But a man's city is a mere trifle more than a man's best girl. She is the living background of his life and love and toil and hope and sorrow and joy. Her success is his success; her shame is his shame; her honour is his honour; and her good name is his good name.

What then should a city be re-christened that has sold its name?—Judasville.

> Very sincerely yours
> Rudyard Kipling

The honeymooning couple continued their train journey westward until they reached the mountains, and here, for the first time in Canada, Kipling seems awed by the splendour of the scenery and the vastness of the wilderness:

That next morning brought us the Canadian Pacific Railway as one reads about it. No pen of man could do justice to the scenery there. The guide-books struggle desperately with descriptions, adapted for summer reading, of rushing cascades, lichened rocks, waving pines, and snow-capped mountains; but in April these things are not there. The place is locked up—dead as a frozen corpse. The mountain torrent is a boss of palest emerald ice against the dazzle of the snow; the pine-stumps are capped and hooded with gigantic mushrooms of snow; the rocks are overlaid five feet deep; the rocks, the fallen trees, and the lichens together, and the dumb white lips curl up to the track cut in the side of the mountain, and grin there fanged with gigantic icicles. You may listen in vain when the train stops for the least sign of breath or power among the hills. The snow has smothered the rivers ... One of the hillsides moved a little in dreaming of the spring and caught a passing freight train.

Our cars grind cautiously by, for the wrecking engine has only just come through. The deceased engine is standing on its head in soft earth thirty or forty feet down the slide, and two long-cars loaded with shingles are dropped carelessly atop of it. It looks so marvellously like a toy train flung aside by a child, that one cannot realise what it means till a voice cries, 'Any one killed?' The answer comes back, 'No; all jumped'; and you perceive with a sense of personal insult that this slovenliness of the mountain is an affair which may touch your own sacred self. In which case.... But the train is out on a trestle, into a tunnel, and out on a trestle again....

Once in Vancouver, the Kiplings set sail on April 4, 1892 for Japan and what was supposed to be the start of an extended tour of the East. But within a few weeks, Kipling learned that the bank, in which most of his funds were held, had failed, taking his money with it. With little option but to cancel the rest of the trip, Rudyard and Carrie headed home for Vermont, first sailing to Vancouver, then taking the trancontinental train to Montreal. The Canadian Pacific Railway offered them free tickets, happily accepted. In a decidedly less happy frame of mind because of his financial woes,

Kipling's account of this return journey across Canada, while still positive, even amusing, is perfunctory. He saved his best (albeit patronizing) comments for Winnipeg:

> Now from the province of Alberta to Brooklyn, USA, may be three thousand miles. A great stretch of that distance is as new as the day before yesterday, and strewn with townships in every stage of growth from the city of one round house, two log huts and a Chinese camp somewhere in the foothills of the Selkirks, to Winnipeg, with her league-long main street and her warring newspapers. Just at present there is an epidemic of politics in Manitoba, and brass bands and notices of committee meetings are splashed about the towns. By reason of their closeness to the States they have caught the contagion of foul-mouthedness, and accusations of bribery, corruption, and evil-living are many. It is sweet to find a little baby-city, with only three men in it who can handle type, cursing and swearing across the illimitable levels for all the world as though it were a grown-up Christian centre.

Once back in Vermont, Kipling began to set his house in order, literally: as income from his writings came flooding in, he and his wife decided to have a new residence built just north of Brattleboro. The construction was done by Jean Pigeon, a Quebecois, but despite the very Canadian appearance of the house, Kipling gave it a name from India: Naulakha. His residence there would prove to be relatively short, and in 1899, the Kiplings would leave the United States, Rudyard never to return.

Were it not for a single surviving letter to a cousin and a passing reference in Kipling's autobiography *Something of Myself,* we would not know that Kipling made a sightseeing trip with his father to Montreal, Quebec City, and the Saguenay Region in late July and early August 1893. The letter gives few details. Perhaps because of its personal nature, Kipling chose not to write about the vacation, either in letters or for publication, although one would have thought a honeymoon was just as personal, and the intimacy of that occasion certainly did not stop him from writing. Which leads to the tantalizing possibility that accounts of the Saguenay voyage linger unknown in letters still to be discovered.

A similar barreness of information envelopes Kipling's fourth trip to Canada, a fortnight-long fishing holiday to the Gaspé in the second half of June 1896. Mention of this trip appears, too, in just one extant letter, and a brief newspaper account.

In between these vacations in Quebec, diplomatic relations between England and America grew extremely tense, and in the summer of 1895, Kipling made serious plans for his family to emigrate promptly to Canada should war erupt. Cool heads prevailed, though, and the Kiplings' need to flee, like United Empire Loyalists one step ahead of the mob, was removed. In the same year, he made a fetching literary contribution to a magazine for children:

> There was a small boy of Quebec
> Who was buried in snow to the neck.
>   When they asked:—"Are you friz?"
>   He replied:—"Yes I is,
> "But we don't call this cold in Quebec."

A year after he wrote this limerick, the Bard of Empire published *The Seven Seas*, a collection which included a poem known as "Song of the Cities". Among the sixteen municipalities celebrated with quatrains were Victoria, Quebec, Montreal, and Halifax. The latter's peaen reads:

> Into the mist my guardian prows put forth,
>   Behind the mist my virgin ramparts lie,
> The Warden of the Honour of the North,
>   Sleepless and veiled am I!

Kipling, partly because he was living close to the border, but more because of his genuine interest, was always keenly aware of Canadian politics, especially Canadian foreign policy. So in 1897, when Joseph Chamberlain was struggling in England to see his Tariff Reform policy brought to fruition, the Canadian Prime Minister, Wilfrid Laurier, went far out on a political limb to give Chamberlain help; the Canadian Government passed a law which gave preferential tariffs to British goods. The significance of this important gesture was not lost on Kipling. He saw, with gratification, that Laurier had made a huge gamble to aid the mother country. But he could also see, from the tenor of the debate in Canada, and from the ultimate self-interest of the decision, that Canada was beginning to assert her political independence within the Empire. Primed by this Canadian loyalty, and not put off by the subject (surely the passage of a tax bill ranks among the most unpromising poetic subjects ever), Kipling wrote a glowing tribute to Canada, "Our Lady of the Snows", one of his most famous poems. Imagine his bewilderment when he learned that the poem, composed in admiration, was greeted by many of its its recipients with derision.

The title of the poem may have been inspired by Thomas D'Arcy McGee's poem "Our Ladye of the Snowe". Without doubt, Kipling had seen on earlier visits the renowned Montreal church Notre Dame des Neiges. Regardless, given that England and not France was the beneficiary of the preferential tariff, Kipling was probably trying to show sensitivity to Quebecois feelings by using the Catholic nomenclature. And as the passages quoted above attest, he certainly found Canadian snow awesome. But he did not foresee that many Canadians, overly sensitive to foreigners' ignorance of the clemency of our weather (and under-sensitive to literary nuance) would see the poem as just another dumb assertion that all of Canada was like the Arctic tundra. Only later did Kipling realize with a cringe that his frozen, snowy image also reinforced the terror (of the Canadian climate) felt by so many potential British emigrants—thus hardening their reluctance to move to Canada.

Prior to his next Canadian voyage, Kipling wrote one of his most famous science fiction tales. "With The Night Mail" is set in the year 2000 A.D. The plot centres on a trans-Atlantic voyage made by a super dirigible contracted to fly mail between the continents. Most

of the action takes place over the eastern Canadian seabord as the airship is bound for Quebec City. Kipling envisaged the airship and its
postal employees as little more than a railway car with hot air; nonetheless, reciting the destinations of the letters gave him a chance once
more to sing the prairie names that he found so magical: "I peer from
the fore end of the engine room over the hatchings into the coach. The
mail-clerks are sorting the Winnipeg, Calgary, and Medicine Hat
bags." The good ship *Postal Packet 162* soars over "Hudson Bay furri-
ers," "Keewatin liners," "Ungava petrol-tanks" when the narrator
offers this sage advice from the future: "It does not pay to 'fly' minerals
and oil a mile farther than is necessary; but the risks of transhipping to
submersibles in the ice-pack off Nain or Hebron are so great that these
heavy freighters fly down to Halifax direct." The story is also distinguished by one of Kipling's most poetic lines: "The clips parted with
a gesture of indignant dismissal, as though Quebec, glittering under
her snows, were casting out these light and unworthy lovers."

Kipling's sixth documented trip to Canada was undoubtedly his
most important. It was supposed to have taken place in 1899 when
McGill University offered him his first honorary doctorate, but illness and other matters prevented him from attending the convoca-
tion. In fact, his next trip to Canada did not transpire until 1907.
Several trips to England, concentration on solidifying his literary
career in London, and a lengthy trip to Africa intervened—as did
the sudden death of his young daughter.

The 1907 visit appeared to have the imprimatur of the fedcral Government—indeed, it was the only official or semi-official trip Kipling
ever made to a nation-member of the Commonwealth. Despite his
sometimes lordly claims for the Empire, Kipling actually had little
experience of that Empire: a few weeks in South Africa, less than a
fortnight in New Zealand, and less even than that in Australia were
typical lengths of stay in what were then termed the daughter countries of the Empire. Such brief encounters never stopped him from
pontificating on the merits or demerits of these countries, however.

Landing at Quebec City on September 27, 1907, the Kiplings
were given a deluxe private rail car by the head of the CPR, William

Van Horne. "Hitch on to any train you choose and stop off where you choose," Kipling quotes his host as generously offering. Apart from receiving his honorary doctorate at McGill (on October 17th), Kipling's few formal duties were limited mostly to speeches given to Canadian Clubs in Winnipeg (October 3rd), Vancouver (October 6th), Victoria (October 8th), Toronto (October 18th), Ottawa (October 21st) and Montreal (October 23rd). Kipling also made a breakneck stop in Calgary on October 4th, touring the city by car, while the train's scheduled departure was delayed for about two hours just for his convenience.

Ever the travel writer, Kipling used this 1907 trip not only to report on his immediate impressions (as he had done on his honeymoon trip of 1892) but to ruminate about Canada's singular, proud place in the world, about its future role, and about its responsibilities as the eldest daughter of the imperial association. His writings on this trip were collected and published as *Letters to the Family*—the "family" being the British Empire.

In a letter to his real children (as opposed to the metaphorical), written at the Place Viger Hotel in Montreal on September 29th, Kipling wrote:

> We have been in Canada since Friday morning and our adventures would fill a book.... We left the ship and found this stately splendour of a private car—its name was Dumfries—tacked on to the end of the passenger train. A stately negro received us with the airs of an archbishop: called us "Sir" and "Madam" in a deep resounding voice.... It was a fine day and the sight of the beautiful country—the maple leaves are just turning red—cheered us. We laughed with joy at the queer narrow French farms, which are only a hundred yards wide and run back from the river for two and a half miles. Each has a little wooden house and a pilliwinky windmill.

At the other end of the country, at Mount Stephen House in Field, British Columbia, Rudyard Kipling wrote to his young son

Illustration by Rudyard Kipling from a letter written in Montreal on September 29, 1907 to his children in England. "We laughed with joy at the sight of the queer narrow French farms, which are only a hundred yards wide and run back from the river for two and half miles."

how a scene, which many Canadians take for granted as part of their nation's vista, impressed him mightily: "We spent this morning in a buggy going out to see a lake called Emerald Lake. It is a wonderful, splendid deep emerald green. Enormous mountains capped with snow and covered with pine stand all round it and their reflections in the water are all tinted green.... I thought to myself and Mummy thought so too that after a few years, if all goes well, you and [your sister] will have a month's camping with us in this wonderful land."

At the adult level, Kipling made more provocative comments. Silly people who have not read him, but who have heard his phrase "the lesser breeds" (out of context) often believe him to have been a white supremacist. In fact, his thinking on deracination and immigration, while perhaps not in harmony with the majority opinion of Canadians today, was more complex than name-calling suggests. Having been raised as a preschooler in India, for example, and having lived there as a young adult, he was more than comfortable with the best of Indian culture, and in some ways, given the era, was close to colour blind. This ease with certain Asian cultures, and his avowed efforts to strengthen Empire meant that he was at a total loss to comprehend the desire of Canadians, especially those on the West

HAPPY THOUGHT!

(Rudyard to the Rescue.)

"I HAVE IT! LISTEN, NOW. CRAM THE COUNTRY FULL OF YOUR OWN KINSPEOPLE, AND THERE SIMPLY WON'T BE ROOM FOR THE ASIATICS!"

Front page editorial cartoon from *The Globe* (Toronto), October 19, 1907. Kipling's exhortation to Canadians to ignore skin colour when setting immigration policy but attend instead to the immigrants' loyalty to Empire aroused strong, often confused reactions. This cartoon, while far from savoury, is typical of the day.

Coast, to keep Asians out while welcoming white immigrants from northern European nations. These latter were people who shared a skin colour with the majority of Canadians, yes, but to Kipling they were a cancerous influence, for their loyalty to Empire was unproven, and they did not share the affection for the language and the mother country that his beloved Indians did. Against this backdrop, his remarks in Victoria, B.C. about potential immigrants from outside the Empire are as relevant today as they were a century ago: "The time is coming when you will have to choose between the

desired reinforcements of your own stock and blood, and the unde-
sired of races to whom you are strangers, whose speech you do not
understand, and from whose instincts and traditions you are separated by thousands of years." And addressing the Ottawa Canadian
Club on the immigration question and its impact upon international trade, with Laurier sitting right next to him at the head table,
Kipling boldly asked, "I do not understand how the Dominion pro-
poses to control the enormous Oriental trade and at the same time
hold herself aloof from the Asiatic influx which is the natural concomitant of that trade."

As he crossed Canada, Kipling met with some grumblings from
those who still felt betrayed by "Our Lady of the Snows". More serious murmurings were heard over his refusal to speak in theatres and
auditoriums where thousands could hear him. Those who pronounced such criticism seemed unaware that Kipling loathed public
speaking, indeed any public appearance. He agreed to speak to the
members of the Canadian Clubs solely because he believed, probably rightly at the time, that its membership comprised the nation's
most powerful opinion-makers. More typical of the response he
encountered in 1907 was this in Toronto: "When Mr. Kipling arose
he was greeted with hearty cheers, and the audience rose to its feet
and waved their napkins. "He's a jolly good fellow" was sung, and
then all gave another round of cheers that was prolonged several
minutes."

Despite his abhorence of public speaking, Kipling was very good
at it. He certainly knew how to play to the home crowd with lines
such as "I do not think you realize how largely Canada bulks, has
always bulked in the imagination of the other members of the imperial family." Or "I have realised here the existence of an assured
nationhood. The spirit of a people contented not to be another people or the imitators of any other people—contented to be themselves." And given Canadian fears in our own time of being
culturally assimilated by the Americans, Kipling's summary comment on the difference between the two nations is especially pointed:
"Always the marvel—to which Canadians seem insensible—was that

on one side of an imaginary line should be Safety, Law, Honour, and Obedience, and on the other, frank, brutal decivilization; and that despite this, Canada should be impressed by any aspect whatever of the United States."

Following his visit to Canada, Kipling was awarded the Nobel Prize for 1907. No proof exists that this is an example of cause and effect.

Perhaps because of the calibre of powermongers and politicians with whom he was able to meet, Kipling's interest in Canada deepened as a result of the 1907 cross-country tour. Also deepened after this excursion was his friendship with two Canadians residing in London who were to become crucially important to British (and thus, Empire) politics: Max Aitken and Andrew B. Law. Aitken is now better known by his titled moniker: Lord Beaverbrook; Bonar Law is recalled as a dedicated leader and the only Canadian ever to become Prime Minister of Britain.

Kipling's final visit to Canada came in 1930. In February of that year, he and his wife, their health atrocious, on doctor's orders had sailed for the West Indies. Carrie's poor health worsened drastically when she had an appendicitis attack, after which she was confined to a hospital in Bermuda for months. As the weeks without the physical presence of his wife dragged on, Kipling became more and more anxious to get her back to England for what he hoped would be superior care. It would have been easier for the couple to travel home to London via New York, but as Kipling told his American publisher (with words of disturbing and enduring relevance) America was "not a civilized country for the sick." Instead, Mr. and Mrs. Kipling sailed from Bermuda to Montreal. After a stay of a few days in June at the Ritz Carlton Hotel, where they met some members of Carrie's family who had travelled from the USA to meet them, the Kiplings sailed for Britain on the Canadian Pacific SS *Duchess of Bedford*.

Although his trips to Canada were now at an end, Kipling maintained interest in, and contact with, Canadians. He corresponded with dozens of leading authors and intellectuals in English Canada. In fact, on July 12, 1933, disregarding two of his rarely-broken cardinal

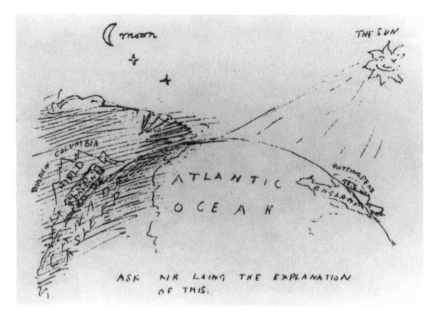

Illustration by Rudyard Kipling from a letter written in Field, B.C. on October 22, 1907 to his children. The drawing is an attempt to explain the effects of time zones, showing the Kiplings' private rail car in darkness ("Canada Asleep") while England basks in the sun.

rules (remain in seclusion, and never make public speeches), Kipling spoke at Claridge's at a banquet held in honour of a travelling group of writers from the Canadian Authors' Association.

His Canadian contacts, however, were not only with the high and mighty. On August 13, 1935 at Eastbourne, he made a touching gesture when he addressed eighty-four Canadian secondary school children on a summer visit to England. After telling them about his visits to Canada, he quizzed them about their own country, and then remarked sententiously: "England is as much a possession of Canada as Canada is a possession of England."

Kipling's only son had been killed in action in 1915, and in some soulful ways the father never recovered from the blow. Despite frail health, and as a silent homage to the memory of his son, Kipling became, in 1917 (and until he himself died in 1936), a Commissioner of War Graves. The part-time job charged him with overseeing the maintenance of military cemeteries wherever Empire soldiers had fought in World War One. Among his duties was the writing of epitaphs which would be carved into stone memorials around the world. Two were written for Canadian cenotaphs. The first is simply titled "Canadians":

> We, giving all, gained all.
>   Neither lament us nor praise;
> Only, in all things recall,
>   It is fear, not death, that slays.

The other inscription was composed for a Memorial in Sault Ste. Marie, Ontario:

> From little towns in a far land, we came,
> To save our honour, and a world aflame;
> By little towns in a far land, we sleep
> And trust those things we won, to you to keep.

Letters to the Family is unique among Kipling's works for it is the only non-fiction work dealing with a single Commonwealth nation. Regardless of this singular attention from a hugely popular author, Canadian response to the book was mixed. Predictable were the responses which basked in Kipling's praise. But thoughtful, darker responses were to be found in periodicals such as *Saturday Night*. This magazine, for example, saliently pointed out one rather large hypocritical aspect to Kipling's high regard for Canada:

> We turned out in crowds to see the author and poet, and listened to a set speech from an amateur politician of Empire.... Yet when, his tour completed, he sat down and wrote his "Letters to the Family," he sold them to a New York weekly paper. No doubt he secured a large price for the letters on condition that no Canadian paper was to secure the right to publish them until after they had all appeared in the New York paper, enabling that

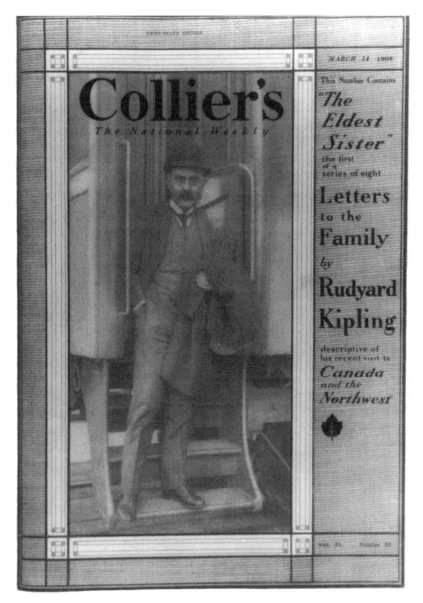

Rudyard Kipling about to board train that would take him across Canada in 1907. The photo shows the cover of *Collier's* magazine in which Kipling's lengthy examination of Canada ("the eldest sister" of the Commonwealth) first appeared. Kipling did not let Empire bolstering interfere with commerce: his contract with *Collier's* prohibited any major Canadian periodical from printing the essays. Photo courtesy of Princeton University Library.

journal to push its circulation in Canada and boast [of] its enterprise. Mr. Kipling, while making special appeals in favour of Imperialism, did not allow sentiment to interfere with his own business.

The "Letters to the Family" had been sold to *Collier's*, a New York weekly, on condition that newspapers and periodicals in central and eastern Canada could not print the same articles. *Collier's* exploited its monopoly of the Kipling series for weeks, running his photo on the cover of the March 14, 1908 issue in which the "Letters" first appeared, and publishing the "Letters" prominently every week thereafter until May 2, 1908.

The failure to sell serial rights to Americans rather than Canadians was not all that bothered some readers. The phenomenon of the instant "authority" also clearly rankled. Even today our media are clogged with reports by journalists who drop into world hot spots and within a week become "experts" on regional troubles, blithely ignorant of the millions of nuances and complexities behind those troubles. Some among the politically weathered in 1908 regarded Kipling in the same light:

> It is curious that a man who professes to interpret us to ourselves failed to learn that we would not care to have letters to this branch of the family addressed to us as if New York were our nearest post office.... Rapidly covering a country thousands of miles in extent a man gets his information piece-meal, hears one side of a story at a time and at his journey's end finds in his mind a tangle of observations and impressions of places, men and questions. In these letters, Kipling hampered himself with a mission. He wrote not as R.K. but as the disciple of Chamberlain. He was in the cramped pose of a schoolmaster, and at times the reader has the uncomfortable feeling that the lesson is to the infant class—that the letter is to the small child of the family.

> It has been reported that Kipling will come to Prince Edward Island to spend the summer. It is to be hoped that he will. A

book from his pen after a few leisurely months in Canada instead of a few hasty days would be worth while.

Kipling never made it to P.E.I. But stung, perhaps, by the negative response to the sale of first serial rights to an American periodical, he arranged for the first edition of the book version of the "Letters" to be published in Canada by Macmillan in the Fall of 1908 (the first American edition did not appear until 1913).

When Shostakovitch was alive, many refused to listen to his music because of his politics. Today, we are largely unaffected by the passions evoked by the politics of that time, and so are free to form an opinion about his music without reference to his possibly bizarre beliefs on the role of government. Kipling's account of Canada can be examined—even enjoyed—with equal disinterest.

from LETTERS TO THE FAMILY

I went across to Canada the other day, for a few weeks, mainly to ... see what our Eldest Sister was doing. Have you ever noticed that Canada has to deal in the lump with most of the problems that afflict us others severally? For example, she has the Double-Language, Double-Law, Double-Politics drawback in a worse form than South Africa, because, unlike our Dutch, her French can not well marry outside their religion, and they take their orders from Italy—less central, sometimes, than Pretoria or Stellenbosch. She has, too, something of Australia's labour fuss, minus Australia's isolation, but plus the open and secret influence of "Labour" entrenched, with arms and high explosives on neighbouring soil. To complete the parallel, she keeps, tucked away behind mountains, a trifle of land called British Columbia, which resembles New Zealand; and New Zealanders who do not find much scope for young enterprise in their own country are drifting up to British Columbia already.

Canada has in her time known calamity more serious than floods, frost, drought, and fire—and has macadamized some stretches of her road toward nationhood with the broken hearts of two generations. That is why one can discuss with Canadians of the old stock matters which an Australian or New Zealander could no more understand than a healthy child understands death. Truly we are an odd Family! Australia and New Zealand (the Maori War not counted) got everything for nothing. South Africa gave everything, and got less than nothing. Canada has given and taken all along the line for nigh on three hundred years, and in some respects is the wisest, as she should be the happiest, of us all. She seems to be curiously unconscious of her position in the Empire, perhaps because she has till lately been talked at, or down to, by her neighbours. You know how at any gathering of our men from all quarters it is tacitly conceded that Canada takes the lead in the Imperial game. To put it roughly, she saw the goal more than ten years ago, and has been working the ball toward it ever since. That is why her inaction at the last Imperial Conference made people who were interested in the play wonder why she, of all of us, chose to brigade herself with General Botha and to block the forward rush. I, too, asked that question of many. The answer was something like this: "We saw that England wasn't taking anything just then. Why should we have laid ourselves open to be snubbed worse than we were? We sat still." Quite reasonable—almost too convincing. There was really no need that Canada should have done other than she did—except that she was the Eldest Sister, and more was expected of her. She is a little too modest....

The St. Lawrence on the last day of the voyage played up nobly. The maples along its banks had turned—blood red and splendid as the banners of lost youth. Even the oak is not more of a national tree than the maple, and the sight of its welcome made the folks aboard still more happy. A dry wind brought along all the clean smell of their Continent—mixed odors of sawn lumber, virgin earth, and wood-smoke; and they snuffed it, and their eyes softened as they identified point after point along their own beloved river—places where they played and fished and amused themselves in holiday time. It must be pleasant to have a country of one's very own to show off. Understand, they did not in any way boast, shout, squeak, or exclaim—these even-voiced returned men and women. They were simply and unfeignedly glad to see home again, and they said: "Isn't it lovely? Don't you think it's beautiful? We love it."

At Quebec there is a sort of place, much infested by locomotives, like a coal-chute, whence rise the heights that Wolfe's men scaled on their way to the Plains of Abraham. Perhaps of all the tide-marks in all our lands the affair of Quebec touches the heart and the eye more nearly than any other. Everything meets there; France, the jealous partner of England's glory by land and sea for eight hundred years; England, bewildered as usual, but for a wonder not openly opposing Pitt, who knew; those other people, destined to break from England as soon as the French peril was removed; Montcalm himself, doomed and resolute, Wolfe, the inevitable trained workman appointed for the finish; and somewhere in the background one James Cook, master of HMS *Mercury*, making beautiful and delicate charts of the St. Lawrence River.

For these reasons the Plains of Abraham are crowned with all sorts of beautiful things—including a jail and a factory. Montcalm's left wing is marked by the jail, and Wolfe's right by the factory. There is, happily, now a movement on foot to abolish these adornments and turn the battlefield and its surroundings into a park, which by nature and association would be one of the most beautiful in our world.

Yet, in spite of jails on the one side and convents on the other and the thin black wreck of the Quebec Railway Bridge, lying like a dumped carload of tin cans in the river, the Eastern Gate to Canada is noble with a dignity beyond words. We saw it very early, when the under sides of the clouds turned chilly pink over a high-piled, brooding, dusky-purple city. Just at the point of dawn, what looked like the Sultan Harun-al-Raschid's own private shallop, all spangled

with coloured lights, stole across the iron-gray water, and disappeared into the darkness of a slip. She came out again in three minutes, but the full day had come too; so she snapped off her masthead
steering and cabin electrics, and turned into a dingy white ferry-
boat, full of cold passengers. I spoke to a Canadian about her. "Why,
she's the old So-and-So, to Port Levis," he answered, wondering as
the Cockney wonders when a stranger stares at an Inner Circle train.
This was his Inner Circle—the Zion where he was all at ease. He
drew my attention to stately city and stately river with the same
tranquil pride that we each feel when the visitor steps across our
threshold, whether that be Southampton Water on a gray, wavy
morning; Sydney Harbour with a regatta in full swing; or Table
Mountain, radiant and new-washed after the Christmas rains. He
had, quite rightly, felt personally responsible for the weather, and
every flaming stretch of maple since we had entered the river. (The
Northwester in these parts is equivalent to the Southeaster elsewhere, and may impress a guest unfavourably.)

Then the autumn sun rose, and the man smiled. Personally and
politically he said he loathed the city—but it was his.

"Well," he asked at last, "what do you think? Not so bad?"

"Oh, no. Not at all so bad," I answered; and it wasn't till much
later that I realized that we had exchanged the countersign which
runs clear round the Empire....

An up-country proverb says: "She was bidden to the wedding and
set down to grind corn." The same fate, reversed, overtook me on
my little excursion. There is a crafty network of organizations of
business men called Canadian Clubs. They catch people who look
interesting, assemble their members during the mid-day lunch-
hour, and, tying the victim to a steak, bid him discourse on anything
that he thinks he knows. The idea might be copied elsewhere, since
it takes men out of themselves to listen to matters not otherwise
coming under their notice and, at the same time, does not hamper
their work. It is safely short, too. The whole affair can not exceed an
hour, of which the lunch fills half. The Clubs print their speeches

annually, and one gets cross-sections of many interesting questions—from practical forestry to State mints—all set out by experts.

Not being an expert, the experience, to me, was very like hard work. Till then I had thought speech-making was a sort of conversational whist, that any one could cut in it. I perceive now that it is an Art of conventions remote from anything that comes out of an inkpot, and of colours hard to control. The Canadians seem to like listening to speeches, and, though this is by no means a national vice, they make good oratory on occasion....

When their winter comes, over the greater part of this country outside the cities, they must sit still, and eat and drink as the Aesir did. In summer they cram twelve months' work into six, because between such and such dates certain far rivers will shut, and, later, certain others, till, at last, even the Great Eastern Gate at Quebec locks, and men must go in and out by the side-doors at Halifax and St. John. These are conditions that make for extreme boldness, but not for extravagant boastings.

The maples tell when it is time to finish, and all work in hand is regulated by their warning signal....

Does any one remember that joyful strong confidence after the war, when it seemed that, at last, South Africa was to be developed—when men laid out railways, and gave orders for engines, and fresh rolling-stock, and labour, and believed gloriously in the future? It is true the hope was murdered afterward, but—multiply that good hour by a thousand, and you will have some idea of how it feels to be in Canada—a place which even an "Imperial" Government can not kill. I had the luck to be shown some things from the inside—to listen to the details of works projected; the record of works done. Above all, I saw what had actually been achieved in the fifteen years since I had last come that way. One advantage of a new land is that it makes you feel older than Time. I met cities where there had been nothing—literally, absolutely nothing, except, as the fairy tales say, "the birds crying, and the grass waving in the wind." Villages and hamlets had grown to great towns, and the great towns themselves had trebled and quadrupled. And the railways rubbed their hands and cried, like the Afrites of old: "Shall we make a city where no city is; or render flourishing a city that is desolate?" They do it too, while, across the water, gentlemen, never forced to suffer one day's physical discomfort in all their lives, pipe up and say: "How grossly materialistic!" ...

[A] man, to whom I did not talk, sticks in my memory. He had for years and years inspected trains at the head of a heavyish grade in the mountains—though not half so steep as the Hex—where all brakes are jammed home, and the cars slither warily for ten miles. Tire-troubles there would be inconvenient, so he, as the best man, is given the heaviest job—monotony and responsibility combined. He did me the honour of wanting to speak to me, but first he inspected his train—on all fours with a hammer. By the time he was satisfied of the integrity of the underpinnings it was time for us to go; and all that I got was a friendly wave of the hand—a master craftsman's sign, you might call it.

Canada seems full of this class of materialist.

Which reminds me that the other day I saw the Lady herself in the shape of a tall woman of twenty-five or six, waiting for her tram on a street corner. She wore her almost flaxen-gold hair waved, and parted low on the forehead, beneath a black astrachan toque, with a red enamel maple-leaf hatpin in one side of it. This was the one touch of colour except the flicker of a buckle on the shoe. The dark, tailor-made dress had no trinkets or attachments, but fitted perfectly. She stood for perhaps a minute without any movement, both hands—right bare, left gloved—hanging naturally at her sides, the very fingers still, the weight of the superb body carried evenly on both feet, and the profile, which was that of Gudrun or Aslauga, thrown out against a dark stone column. What struck me most, next to the grave, tranquil eyes, was her slow, unhurried breathing in the hurry about her. She was evidently a regular fare, for when her tram stopped she smiled at the lucky conductor; and the last I saw of her was a flash of the sun on the red maple-leaf, the full face still lighted by that smile, and her hair very pale gold against the dead black fur.

But the power of the mouth, the wisdom of the brow, the human comprehension of the eyes, and the outstriking vitality of the creature remained. That is how *I* would have my country drawn, were I a Canadian—and hung in Ottawa Parliament House, for the discouragement of prevaricators....

I had the good fortune to see the cities through the eyes of an Englishman out for the first time. "Have you been to the Bank?" he cried. "I've never seen anything like it!" "What's the matter with the Bank?" I asked: for the financial situation across the Border was at that moment more than usual picturesque. "It's wonderful!" said he—"marble pillars—acres of mosaic—steel grilles—might be a cathedral. No one ever told me." "I shouldn't worry over a Bank that pays its depositors," I replied soothingly. "There are several like it in Ottawa and Toronto." Next he ran across some pictures in some palaces, and was downright angry because no one had told him that there were five priceless private galleries in one city. "Look here!" he explained. "I've been seeing Corots, and Greuzes, and Gainsboroughs, and a Holbein, and—and hundreds of really splendid pictures!" "Why shouldn't you?" I said. "They've given up painting their lodges with vermilion hereabouts." "Yes, but what I mean is, have you seen the equipment of their schools and colleges—desks, libraries, and lavatories? It's miles ahead of anything we have and—no one ever told me." "What was the good of telling? You wouldn't have believed. There's a building in one of the cities, on the lines of the Sheldonian, but better, and if you go as far as Winnipeg, you'll see the finest hotel in all the world."

"Nonsense!" he said. "You're pulling my leg! Winnipeg's a prairie town."

I left him still lamenting—about a Club and a Gymnasium this time—that no one had ever told him; and still doubting all that he had heard of Wonders to come.

If we could only manacle four hundred Members of Parliament, like the Chinese in the election cartoons, and walk them round the Empire, what an all-comprehending little Empire we should be when the survivors got home!

Certainly the cities have good right to be proud, and I waited for them to boast; but they were so busy explaining they were only at the beginning of things that, for the honor of the Family, I had to do the boasting. In this praiseworthy game I credited Melbourne (rightly, I hope, but the pace was too good to inquire) with acres of municipal buildings and leagues of art galleries; enlarged the borders of Sydney harbor to meet a statement about Toronto's wharfage; and recommended folk to see Cape Town Cathedral when it should be finished. But Truth will out even on a visit. Our Eldest Sister has more of beauty and strength inside her three cities alone than the rest of Us put together. Yet it would do her no harm to send a commission through the ten great cities of the Empire to see what is being done there in the way of street cleaning, water-supply, and traffic-regulation....

One cannot leave a thing alone if it is thrust under the nose at every turn. I had not quitted the Quebec steamer three minutes when I was asked pointblank: "What do you think of the question of Asiatic Exclusion which is Agitating our Community?"

The Second Sign-post on the Great Main Road says: "If a Community is agitated by a Question—inquire politely after the health of the Agitator." This I did, without success; and had to temporize all across the Continent till I could find some one to help me to acceptable answers. The Question appears to be confined to British Columbia. There, after a while, the men who had their own reasons for not wishing to talk referred me to others who explained, and on the acutest understanding that no names were to be published (it is sweet to see engineers afraid of being hoist by their own petards) one got more or less at something like facts.

The Chinaman has always been in the habit of coming to British Columbia, where he makes, as he does elsewhere, the finest servant in the world. No one, I was assured on all hands, objects to the biddable Chinaman. He takes work which no white man in a new country will handle, and when kicked by the mean white will not grossly retaliate. He has always paid for the privilege of making his fortune on this wonderful coast, but with singular forethought and statesmanship, the popular Will, some few years ago, decided to double the head tax on his entry. Strange as it may appear, the Chinaman now charges double for his services, and is scarce at that. This is said to be one of the reasons why overworked white women die or go off their heads; and why in new cities you can see blocks of flats being built to minimize the inconveniences of housekeeping without help. The birth-rate will fall later in exact proportion to those flats.

Since the Russo-Japanese War the Japanese have taken to coming over to British Columbia. They also do work which no white man will; such as hauling wet logs for lumber mills out of cold water at from eight to ten shillings a day. They supply the service in hotels and dining-rooms and keep small shops. The trouble with them is that they are just a little too good, and when attacked defend themselves with asperity.

A fair sprinkling of Punjabis—ex-soldiers, Sikhs, Muzbis, and Jats—are coming in on the boats. The plague at home seems to have made them restless, but I could not gather why so many of them come from Shahpur, Phillour, and Jullundur way. These men do not, of course, offer for house-service, but work in the lumber mills, and with the least little care and attention could be made most valuable. Some one ought to tell them not to bring their old men with them, and better arrangements should be made for their remitting money home to their villages. They are not understood, of course; but they are not hated.

The objection is all against the Japanese. So far—except that they are said to have captured the local fishing trade at Vancouver, precisely as the Malays control the Cape Town fish business—they have not yet competed with the whites; but I was earnestly assured by many men that there was danger of their lowering the standard of life and wages. The demand, therefore, in certain quarters is that they go—absolutely and unconditionally. You many have noticed that Democracies are strong on the imperative mood. An attempt was made to shift them shortly before I came to Vancouver, but it was not very successful, because the Japanese barricaded their quarters and flocked out, a broken bottle held by the neck in either hand, which they jabbed in the faces of the demonstrators. It is, perhaps, easier to haze and hammer bewildered Hindus and Tamils, as is being done across the Border, than to stampede the men of the Yalu and Liaoyang.

But when one began to ask questions one got lost in a maze of hints, reservations, and orations, mostly delivered with constraint, as though the talkers were saying a piece learned by heart. Here are some samples:—

A man penned me in a corner with a single heavily capitalized sentence. "There is a General Sentiment among Our People that the Japanese Must Go," said he.

"Very good," said I. "How d'you propose to set about it?"

"That is nothing to us. There is a General Sentiment," etc.

"Quite so. Sentiment is a beautiful thing, but what are you going to do?" He did not condescend to particulars, but kept repeating the sentiment, which, as I promised, I record.

Another man was a little more explicit. "We desire," he said. "to keep the Chinaman. But the Japanese must go."

"Then who takes their place? Isn't this rather a new country to pitch people out of?"

"We must develop our Resources slowly, sir—with an Eye to the Interests of our Children. We must preserve the Continent for Races which will assimilate with Ours. We must not be swamped by Aliens."

"Then bring in your own races and bring 'em in quick," I ventured.

This is the one remark one must not make in certain quarters of the West; and I lost caste heavily while he explained (exactly as the Dutch did at the Cape years ago) how British Columbia was by no means so rich as she appeared; that she was throttled by capitalists and monopolists of all kinds; that white labour had to be laid off and fed and warmed during the winter; that living expenses were enormously high; that they were at the end of a period of prosperity, and were now entering on lean years; and that whatever steps were necessary for bringing in more white people should be taken with extreme caution. Then he added that the railway rates to British Columbia were so high that emigrants were debarred from coming on there.

"But haven't the rates been reduced?" I asked.

"Yes—yes, I believe they have, but immigrants are so much in demand that they are snapped up before they have got so far West. You must remember, too, that skilled labour is not like agricultural labour. It is dependent on so many considerations. And the Japanese must go."

"So people have told me. But I heard stories of dairies and fruit farms in British Columbia being thrown up because there was no labour to milk or pick the fruit. Is that true, d'you think?"

"Well, you can't expect a man with all the chances that our country offers him to milk cows in a pasture. A Chinaman can do that. We want races that will assimilate with ours," etc., etc.

"But didn't the Salvation Army offer to bring in three or four thousand English some short time ago ? What came of that idea?"

"It—er—fell through."

"Why?"

"For political reasons, I believe. We do not want People who will lower the Standard of Living. That is why the Japanese must go."

"Then why keep the Chinese?"

"We can get on with the Chinese. We can't get on without the Chinese. But we must have Emigration of a Type that will assimilate with Our People. I hope I have made myself clear?"

I hoped that he had, too....

After Politics, let us return to the Prairie which is the High Veldt, plus Hope, Activity, and Reward. Winnipeg is the door to it—a great city in a great plain, comparing herself, innocently enough, to other cities of her acquaintance, but quite unlike any other city.... All the country hereabouts is riddled with railways for business and pleasure undreamed of fifteen years ago, and it was a long time before we reached the clear prairie of air and space and open land. The air is different from any air that ever blew; the space is ampler than most spaces, because it runs back to the unhampered Pole, and the open land keeps the secret of its magic as closely as the sea or the desert.

People here do not stumble against each other around corners, but see largely and tranquilly from a long way off what they desire, or wish to avoid, and they shape their path accordingly across the waves, and troughs, and tongues, and dips and fans of the land.

When mere space and the stoop of the high sky begin to over-whelm, earth provides little ponds and lakes, lying in soft-flanked hollows, where people can step down out of the floods of air, and delight themselves with small and known distances. Most of the women I saw about the houses were down in the hollows, and most of the men were on the crests and the flats. Once, while we halted a woman drove straight down at us from the sky-line, along a golden path between black ploughed lands. When the horse, who managed affairs, stopped at the cars, she nodded mysteriously, and showed us a very small baby in the hollow of her arm. Doubtless she was some exiled Queen flying North to found a dynasty and establish a coun-try. The Prairie makes everything wonderful.

They were threshing the wheat on both sides of the track as far as the eye could see. The smoke of the machines went up in orderly perspective, alongside the mounds of chaff—thus: a machine, a house, a mound of chaff, a stretch of wheat in stooks—and then repeat the pattern over the next few degrees of longitude. We ran through strings of nearly touching little towns, where I remembered an occasional shack; and through big towns once represented by a name-board, a siding, and two troopers of the North-West Police. In those days men proved that Wheat would not grow north of some fool's line, or other, or, if it did, that no one would grow it. And now the Wheat was marching with us as far as the eye could reach; the railways were out, two, three hundred miles north, peopling a new wheat country; and north of that again the Grand Trunk was laying down a suburban extension of a few thousand miles across the Continent, with branches perhaps to Dawson City, certainly to Hudson Bay....

There are many local gods on the road through the Rockies: old bold mountains that have parted with every shred of verdure and stand wrapped in sheets of wrinkled silver rock, over which the sight travels slowly as in delirium; mad, horned mountains, wreathed with dancing mists; low-browed and bent-shouldered faquirs of the wayside, sitting in meditation beneath a burden of glacier-ice that thickens every year; and mountains of fair aspect on one side, but on the other seamed with hollow sunless clefts, where last year's snow is blackened with this year's dirt and smoke of forest-fires. The drip from it seeps away through slopes of unstable gravel and dirt, till, at the appointed season, the whole half-mile of undermined talus slips and roars into the horrified valley.

The railway winds in and out among them with little inexplicable deviations and side-twists, much as a buck walks through a forest-glade, sidling and crossing uneasily in what appears to be a plain path. Only when the track has rounded another shoulder or two, a backward and upward glance at some menacing slope, shows why the train did not take the easier-looking road on the other side of the gorge.

From time to time the mountains lean apart, and nurse between them some golden valley of slow streams, fat pastures, and park-like uplands, with a little town and cow bells tinkling among berry bushes; and children who have never seen the sun rise or set, shouting at the trains; and real gardens round the houses....

Time had changed Vancouver literally out of all knowledge. From the station to the suburbs, and back to the wharves, every step was strange, and where I remembered open spaces and still untouched timber, the tramcars were fleeting people out to a lacrosse game. Vancouver is an aged city, for only a few days previous to my arrival the Vancouver Baby—i.e., the first child born in Vancouver—had been married.

A steamer—once familiar in Table Bay—had landed a few hundred Sikhs and Punjabi jats—to each man his bundle—and the little groups walked uneasy alone, keeping, for many of them had been soldiers, to the military step. Yes, they said they had come to this country to get work. News had reached their villages that work at great wages was to be had in this country. Their brethren who had gone before had sent them the news. Yes, and sometimes the money for the passage out. The money would be paid back from the so-great wages to come. With interest? Assuredly with interest. Did men lend money for nothing in *any* country ? They were waiting for their brethren to come and show them where to eat, and later, how to work. Meanwhile this was a new country. How could they say anything about it ? No, it was not like Gurgaon or Shahpur or Jullundur. The Sickness (plague) had come to all these places. It had come into the Punjab by every road, and many—many—many had died. The crops, too, had failed in some districts. Hearing the news about these so-great wages they had taken ship for the belly's sake—for the money's sake—for the children's sake.

"Would they go back again?"

They grinned as they nudged each other. The Sahib had not quite understood. They had come over for the sake of the money—the rupees, no, the dollars. The Punjab was their home where their villages lay, where their people were waiting. Without doubt—without doubt—they would go back. Then came the brethren already working in the mills—cosmopolitans dressed in ready-made clothes, and smoking cigarettes.

"This way, O you people," they cried. The bundles were reshouldered and the turbaned knots melted away. The last words I caught were true Sikh talk: "But what about the money, O my brother?"

Some Punjabis have found out that money can be too dearly bought.

There was a Sikh in a sawmill, had been driver in a mountain battery at home. Himself he was from Amritsar. (Oh, pleasant as cold water in a thirsty land is the sound of a familiar name in a fair country!)

"But you had your pension. Why did you come here?"

"Heaven-born, because my sense was little. And there was also the Sickness at Amritsar."

(The historian a hundred years hence will be able to write a book on economic changes brought about by pestilence. There is a very interesting study somewhere of the social and commercial effects of the Black Death in England.)

In a wharf, waiting for a steamer, some thirty Sikhs, many of them wearing their old uniforms (which should not be allowed) were talking at the tops of their voices, so that the shed rang like an Indian railway station. A suggestion that if they spoke lower life would be easier was instantly adopted. Then a senior officer with a British India medal asked hopefully: "Has the Sahib any orders where we are to go?"

Alas he had none—nothing but goodwill and greetings for the sons of the Khalsa, and they tramped off in fours.

It is said that when the little riot broke out in Vancouver these "heathen" were invited by other Asiatics to join in defending themselves against the white man. They refused on the ground that they were subjects of the King. I wonder what tales they sent back to their villages, and where, and how fully, every detail of the affair was talked over. White men forget that no part of the Empire can live or die to itself.

Here is a rather comic illustration of this on the material side. The wonderful waters between Vancouver and Victoria are full of whales, leaping and rejoicing in the strong blue all about the steamer. There is, therefore, a whalery on an island near by, and I had the luck to travel with one of the shareholders.

"Whales are beautiful beasts," he said affectionately. "We've a contract with a Scotch firm for every barrel of oil we can deliver for years ahead. It's reckoned the best for harness-dressing."

He went on to tell me how a swift ship goes hunting whales with a bomb-gun and explodes shells into their insides so that they perish at once.

"All the old harpoon and boat business would take till the cows come home. We kill 'em right off."

"And how d'you strip 'em?"

It seemed that the expeditious ship carried also a large air-pump, and pumped up the carcass to float roundly till she could attend to it. At the end of her day's kill she would return, towing sometimes as many as four inflated whales to the whalery, which is a factory full of modern appliances. The whales are hauled up inclined planes like logs to a sawmill, and as much of them as will not make oil for the Scotch leather-dresser, or cannot be dried for the Japanese market, is converted into potent manure.

"No manure can touch ours," said the shareholder. "It's so rich in bone, d'you see. The only thing that has beat us up to date is their hides; but we've fixed up a patent process now for turning 'em into floorcloth. Yes, they're beautiful beasts. That fellow," he pointed to a black hump in a wreath of spray, "would cut up a miracle."

"If you go on like this you won't have any whales left," I said.

"That is so. But the concern pays thirty per cent, and—a few years back, no one believed in it."

I forgave him everything for the last sentence....

Canada possesses two pillars of Strength and Beauty in Quebec and Victoria. The former ranks by herself among those Mother-cities of whom none can say "This reminds me." To realize Victoria you must take all that the eye admires most in Bournemouth, Torquay, the Isle of Wight, the Happy Valley at Hong Kong, the Doon, Sorrento, and Camps Bay; add reminiscences of the Thousand Islands, and arrange the whole round the Bay of Naples, with some Himalayas for the background.

Real estate agents recommend it as a little piece of England—the island on which it stands is about the size of Great Britain—but no England is set in any such seas or so fully charged with the mystery of the larger ocean beyond. The high, still twilights along the beaches are out of the old East just under the curve of the world, and even in October the sun rises warm from the first. Earth, sky, and water wait outside every man's door to drag him out to play if he looks up from his work; and, though some other cities in the Dominion do not quite understand this immoral mood of Nature, men who have made their money in them go off to Victoria, and with the zeal of converts preach and preserve its beauties.

We went to look at a marine junk store which had once been

Esquimalt, a station of the British Navy. It was reached through winding roads, lovelier than English lanes, along watersides and parkways any one of which would have made the fortune of a town.

"Most cities," a man said, suddenly, "lay out their road at right angles. We do in the business quarters. What d'you think?"

"I fancy some of those big cities will have to spend millions on curved roads some day for the sake of a change," I said. "You've got what no money can buy."

"That's what the men tell us who come to live in Victoria. And they've had experience."

It is pleasant to think of the Western millionaire, hot from some gridiron of rectangular civilization, confirming good Victorians in the policy of changing vistas and restful curves.

There is a view, when the morning mists peel off the harbor where the steamers tie up, of the Houses of Parliament on one hand, and a huge hotel on the other, which as an example of cunningly fitted-in water-fronts and facades is worth a very long journey. The hotel was just being finished. The ladies' drawing-room, perhaps a hundred feet by forty, carried an arched and superbly enriched plaster ceiling of knops and arabesques and interlacings, which somehow seemed familiar.

"We saw a photo of it in *Country Life*," the contractor explained. "It seemed just what the room needed, so one of our plasterers, a Frenchman—that's him—took and copied it. It comes in all right, doesn't it?"

About the time the noble original was put up in England, Drake might have been sailing somewhere off this very coast. So, you see, Victoria lawfully holds the copyright.

I tried honestly to render something of the color, the gaiety, and the graciousness of the town and the island, but only found myself piling up unbelievable adjectives, and so let it go with a hundred other wonders....

RAYMOND
CHANDLER

O NE of the greatest mystery writers of the twentieth century
was also one of the most sought-after writers of screenplays.
Following the successful publication of his novels *The Big Sleep*
(1939) and *Farewell My Lovely* (1940) Raymond Chandler (1888-
1959) was lured to Hollywood by the usual bait: offers of money far
beyond any he could make from books. Despite his later claims that
he was not an adroit screenwriter, the big studios disagreed, and
Chandler certainly adapted to the form with ease.

His first film, co-written with Billy Wilder, was *Double Indem-
nity* (1943), and won for Chandler an Academy Award nomination.
He received another Oscar nomination for his second major screen
scenario, *The Blue Dahlia*, and these successes, combined with the
lucrative film adaptations of his novels, led to Chandler being
offered, in 1947, a contract such as no screenwriter had ever seen.

Until 1947, the film studios, while proclaiming great respect for
novelists not in their employ, loathed the individualism of the writers in their employ. A famed fiction writer's screenplay, no matter
how brilliant (or perhaps because it was brilliant), had to be edited,
changed, deformed and transmogrified first by other writers working for the studio, then by producers, actors and directors.

Raymond Chandler's stature was such, however, that in the spring
of 1947 Universal Pictures, to tempt Chandler from Paramount,

offered him a breathtaking salary of $4,000 per week to write an original screenplay on any subject of his choosing. As if this were insufficient reward, he was also offered a percentage of the box office receipts, and minimal questions from the studio about the progress of his screenplay. Under these immensely liberal circumstances, essentially free at last to write for the screen what he alone desired, Raymond Chandler chose to write *Playback*, a film set, not in the Los Angeles for which he was renowned (and where the studios assumed he would set the new picture), but in Canada—with a Canadian hero fighting American villains.

Although born in Chicago in 1888, the creator of Philip Marlowe moved with his mother to England when quite young and became a naturalized British subject in 1907 (thereby automatically losing his American citizenship). He received a classical education at Dulwich College, later earning a living in London as a freelance journalist, during the day writing for the *Westminster Gazette* or the *Spectator*, while at night writing unsellable poetry and pretentious arty fiction at home.

He returned to the USA in 1912, and was living in Los Angeles with his mother in 1917 when America finally entered World War One. Despite his renewed residency in the United States, Chandler had not bothered to reclaim his American citizenship, so he was ineligible for service in the American forces. But as a British subject he could serve, at that time, with the Canadians, and late in the summer he travelled from California to Victoria, British Columbia to enlist.

Private Raymond Thornton Chandler formally entered the Canadian Armed Forces on August 14, 1917 and was allocated service number 2025271. He was assigned to the celebrated (and kilted) Gordon Highlanders (later known as the Canadian Scottish Regiment) and began basic training near Victoria. Leave was rare for the new recruits, but on the few occasions when the men had a day off base, they really had only one destination open to them: the B.C. capital, and in Chandler's estimation, it was a dreary option.

In just three months, Chandler and the Highlanders, their basic training completed, were sent by train across Canada to Halifax, Nova Scotia. From there, their troop ship embarked on November 26, 1917.

Private Raymond Chandler in the dress uniform of the Canadian Army's Gordon Highlanders in 1917. The photo was probably taken near Victoria, British Columbia where Chandler trained with this venerable regiment before fighting in Europe. Chandler saw much slaughter: "My battalion (Canadian) had a normal strength of twelve hundred men and it had over fourteen thousand casualties." Photo courtesy of Bruccoli Clark Layman, Inc.

Upon arrival in Liverpool, England on December 7th, Chandler was assigned to the British Columbia Regiment and was stationed in Seaford, Sussex until March 18, 1918. Only then was his regiment finally shipped to France and the fighting. By this time, Chandler was with the Seventh Battalion of the First Canadian Division of what was then known as the Canadian Expeditionary Force. Being with this Battalion must have caused mixed emotions in Chandler: just prior to his arrival in France, the Battalion had fought in the famed battle at Vimy Ridge. It had also been part of the slaughter at Passchendaele where writer Ivor Gurney was gassed. So Chandler had a chance to be part of what was then thought to be a glorious and honourable affair; but he also faced a higher than usual probability of death.

As with many other men who saw heavy action at the front, Chandler rarely talked about what he witnessed in the trenches as a Canadian soldier, such was its horror. As the weeks of fighting continued, he was promoted in rank and within three months he made sergeant.

That he saw intense combat is certain. Decades later, in one of his few comments on The Great War, Chandler wrote to a friend,

> Courage is a strange thing: one can never be sure of it. As a platoon commander very many years ago I never seemed to be afraid, and yet I have been afraid of the most insignificant risks. If you had to go over the top somehow all you seemed to think of was trying to keep the men spaced, in order to reduce casualties. It was always very difficult, especially if you had replacements or men who had been wounded. It's only human to want to bunch for companionship in face of heavy fire. Nowadays war is very different. In some ways it's much worse, but the casualties don't compare with those in trench warfare. My battalion (Canadian) had a normal strength of twelve hundred men and it had over fourteen thousand casualties.

A few months later, in another letter to the same friend, he made this comment about his experience as a Canadian infantryman:

It seems that I have a serious anaemic condition. Not fatal, but quite serious. These diagnoses never make much impression on me, since I have lived my whole life on the edge of nothing. Once you have had to lead a platoon into direct machine-gun fire, nothing is ever the same again.

Chandler's war in the trenches ended in June 1918 when the blast of a German shell left him unconscious although unexplainably alive—because the same terrible explosion killed everyone else in his platoon. He was quickly shipped back to Great Britain to recuperate. Whether because he felt guilty at being the only one to survive the explosion, or because he had seen more than sufficient carnage in the trenches, or because some of his friends were now training to be pilots, Chandler asked for permission to transfer from the Army to the Air Force. He received permission to do so and was accepted as an officer cadet in July 1918, immediately beginning his training as a pilot. By coincidence, at the same time in Canada, and with the same rank, another eminent American writer was training with the hope of becoming a Canadian ace: Air Officer Cadet William Faulkner.

As with Faulkner, the Armistice prematurely ended Chandler's aviator training and neither author received his wings nor his officer's commission. Chandler returned to Canada by ship in January 1919 and by the beginning of February, still a soldier, he was in Vancouver. On February 20, 1919, with the British War Medal and the Victory Medal proudly on his chest, Sergeant Raymond Chandler was given an Honourable Discharge from the Canadian Expeditionary Force.

Within days, Chandler returned to the United States, and he appears to never have set foot in Canada again. Yet his year and a half as a Canadian soldier (of which less than four months was actually spent on Canadian soil) had a disproportionate impact on his psyche. His failure to return to Canada was due solely to his being reclusive, not to any animosity to the country or the people. Indeed, in a letter to the Canadian journalist Alex Barris, thirty years after he was last in Canada, Chandler could still write with vigour "[I have] strong pro-British feelings and also pro-Canadian, since I served in the CEF and spent months at Victoria in Gordon Highlands of Canada long ago." Despite his feeling that Victoria was "dull", Chandler also remarked, "If I called Victoria dull, it was in my time dullish as an English town would be on a Sunday, everything shut up, churchy atmosphere and so on. I did not mean to call the people dull. Knew some very nice ones."

In writing his screenplay, *Playback*, Chandler obviously relied on his recollections of the southwest corner of British Columbia. Most of the action is set in Vancouver, and a boat chase in the Strait of Juan de Fuca is dependent on a keen knowledge of the local weather conditions. Killian, the protagonist, is a Vancouver police detective, and the bad guys, many American, amusingly betray their citizenship through their ignorance of Canadian laws and customs.

Because he was free from the dictates of the studio, Chandler treated the writing of this screenplay as he had done no other, as if it were a novel, lingering over detail, honing dialogue. In spite of the generous terms under which he was commissioned to write the screenplay, he had the *chutzpah* to ask for not one, but two extensions to the deadline, delivering the final draft on March 24, 1948.

The formal response of the studio executives when they read the screenplay has not been preserved. One can imagine, though, that they uttered several thousand expletives—very loudly—followed by questions of genuine bewilderment: a movie set in Canada? With a Canadian as the hero? And Americans as the evildoers? For this we paid a quarter of a million dollars?

The film was never made. The studio, in a post-war recession, claimed that the expense of shooting on location in Canada prohibited development of the project. The executives wrote off the experiment as an expensive loss and the script was set aside, to be forgotten, indeed lost, for almost forty years.

The following excerpt is a conflation of two fairly adjacent scenes near the middle of the proposed movie. In the first, the Canadian homicide detective expresses his deepening affection for the American damsel in distress, Betty Mayfield. The second scene, one of the most emotional scenes in the script, is played against a background that is supposed to be anything but emotional: the changing of the guard. A wry smile must have crossed Chandler's face when he wrote this latter scene, for the soldier in the kilt, snapping to attention, could only have been modeled on his own warm memories: a young private, fresh from California, proud member of a legendary Canadian regiment.

This final draft of the screenplay was long thought to have been lost in the archives of Universal Studios. But it was discovered in the early 1980s by the American novelist and screenwriter John Sacret Young, and was published in 1985 in the United States with a forward by Robert B. Parker. Now that more than a decade has elapsed since the appearance of this impressive Canadian writing by Chandler, one hopes that a producer in this country will bring it to light as a film. In Chandler's own words, *Playback* was "one of the best films I wrote."

---

from PLAYBACK

Scene 62: A Wall at the Foot of the Hotel Gardens

Betty and Killaine are leaning on it, looking out over Puget Sound.

KILLAINE Down below's Stanley Park. On the other side of the trees, there's a beach. You can't see it.
(points over to left) Steveston's over there. Coast Guard station.
(points to right) There's the Yacht Club, and beyond it, the docks. Then over on the other side of the inlet, there's Grouse Mountain.

It's about four thousand feet high. There's a restaurant on top of it. Very nice restaurant.

(he turns to Betty) I'm sorry we couldn't have met in pleasanter circumstances, Miss Mayfield.

BETTY We wouldn't have met at all.

KILLAINE True. I was a bit irritable last night. I apologize.

BETTY You were a Galahad, compared to some cops I've known.

KILLAINE *(pouncing—but very quietly)* You've had dealings with the police before?

BETTY Who hasn't—one way or another?

KILLAINE But not in the investigation of a major crime, I hope.

BETTY Is it a crime?

KILLAINE We're ninety-eight per cent certain Mitchell was murdered. There are a lot of reasons.

(pause) Was he very drunk when you last saw him?

BETTY You were there when I last saw him.

KILLAINE I'd like to believe that. It's not too easy.

(Betty says nothing. Killaine looks away again) I've been talking to the Immigration Inspector who passed you across the border. He was a little suspicious of you. Mayfield isn't really your name, is it? *(Betty looks straight ahead, doesn't answer)* I'll find out, you know. Perhaps not today—perhaps not tomorrow. But in the end, I'll find out.

BETTY The police always do, don't they?

KILLAINE You've had an experience that you don't want to talk about. An unhappy marriage, for example.

(Betty turns away quickly) I wouldn't make you talk about it. My job is the death of Larry Mitchell. Why can't you give me your confidence?

BETTY You—or the Vancouver Police Department?

KILLAINE We try to be decent.

BETTY You're a police officer. A very nice one—but you have a job to do. I'm a girl who's in a jam, and it's your job to keep me there. Don't go considerate on me. I might start to bawl.

(Their eyes meet in a long look)

KILLAINE You won't tell me who you are. You won't even give me a chance to help you.

BETTY Nobody can help me. You, least of all.

KILLAINE *(suddenly)* If I understand what you mean by that.

BETTY You understand perfectly.

KILLAINE Then there isn't much I can do, is there?

BETTY There isn't anything you can do.
(He moves towards her, then turns abruptly and goes) ...

Scene 67: Interior of Corridor

Killaine comes out of his office, walks along briskly to a door, stops.

Scene 68: Close Shot of Door

It is lettered SUPERINTENDENT J. McKECHNIE. Killaine knocks, then starts in without waiting for an answer.

Scene 69: Interior of McKechnie's Office

McKechnie is at his desk. He is a military-looking Scotch-Canadian, with a white mustache. Beside the desk sits an elderly, prim-looking man in a dark suit with a black tie. Killaine comes up to desk.

MCKECHNIE Killaine, this is Mr. Mitchell, Senior. Young Mitchell's father. He just flew in from Toronto.

KILLAINE *(to Mitchell Sr.)* How do you do, sir.
(Mitchell Sr. nods)

MCKECHNIE I've explained the situation to Mr. Mitchell up to a point. Now about this Mayfield girl?

KILLAINE She's a suspect, naturally. But not the only one.

MCKECHNIE *(harshly)* She's the only one who had a dead man in her room. The only one who won't give an account of herself. The only one who tried to run away. And the only one, so far as I've been told, who went to such lengths to disguise her identity that she even removed the labels from her clothes. What more do you want?

MITCHELL, SR. She should have been arrested last night.

MCKECHNIE That's as may be.

(to Killaine) We've ample grounds to detain her for questioning. You can't deny that, surely.

KILLAINE No.

MCKECHNIE I hear she's a very pretty girl.

KILLAINE Which forces me to arrest her against my better judgment.

MCKECHNIE Aye. You have a point there.

MITCHELL, SR. If so, I must say that it escapes my attention, Superintendent. It is my son who has been murdered. He was not in all ways a good son—but he was my son. I want his murderer punished. The girl's obviously a criminal of some sort. Otherwise she'd give an account of herself. Arrest her, and you'll find out soon enough.

MCKECHNIE *(eyeing Killaine)* I think he's right.

KILLAINE *(standing up)* Am I to interpret that as an order to arrest Miss Mayfield?

MCKECHNIE When I give you an order, you'll not need it interpreted. *(glances up at clock on wall)*
You have an hour to make your mind up.
(he turns to Mitchell, Sr.) Well, are ye satisfied, Mr. Mitchell?

MITCHELL, SR. I'll be satisfied when my son's murderer is convicted and hanged.
(pause—his expression softens a little) You've given this young man a very difficult choice.

MCKECHNIE Aye. That was the point you said you didn't get.
(he turns back to Killaine) That's all. *(he makes a gesture of dismissal)*

KILLAINE Very good, sir.
(He turns. We PAN HIM TO THE DOOR, he starts out)

Scene 70:
Interior Corridor as Killaine Comes From McKechnie's Office

Starts back towards his own office.
Another plain clothes cop, DRISCOLL, is walking towards Killaine.
They meet just outside Killaine's office. Driscoll is a tall, solemn-looking Irishman.

DRISCOLL May I have a moment, Inspector?
(Killaine stops)
DRISCOLL The Harbor police have just picked a dead man out of the water.
KILLAINE Floater?
DRISCOLL Not a floater. Only just dead.
KILLAINE *(starting to turn away)* You're the waterfront specialist. Find out about it. I've got a murder to investigate.
DRISCOLL You have two murders to investigate. This man's head was beaten in. And there's nothing in his pockets.
(Killaine turns back, glances at his wrist watch)
KILLAINE Drunk-rolling job. They hit him too hard.
DRISCOLL *(annoyed with his manner)* I've been on the waterfront detail for twelve years. This man hadn't been dead an hour. He wasn't killed last night. He was killed today. In broad daylight. That's no drunk-rolling job.
KILLAINE *(starting to turn away again)* Let me know when you've identified him.
(Driscoll gives him a somber look and starts to leave)
KILLAINE *(calling after him)* And don't get too logical, Driscoll. In police business it doesn't work. I wish it did. But it doesn't.
DRISCOLL *(looking back)* I'm an Irishman, sir. An Irishman is *always* logical.
(Killaine frowns, then starts into his own little office)

Scene 71:
Close Shot—A Portion of a Tall, Spear-Topped Iron Railing along a Sidewalk

A man in a business suit is leaning against it. He is a plainclothes dick by the name of HANDLEY. Other people are standing near him, looking through the railing, as if waiting for something to happen. Handley is looking in the other direction, along the sidewalk. In the background, SOME TRAFFIC NOISE, and far off, BLAST OF A TUG WHISTLE. Handley gets a cigarette out and lights it, with his eyes still looking off to the side. CAMERA PANS SLOWLY ALONG THE RAILING, showing people standing in groups looking through. CAMERA PICKS UP BETTY AMONG THEM. Near at hand, there is a SHARP WHISTLE BLAST, and immediately snare drums are HEARD, first in spaced tap, then going into a tatoo.

Scene 72:
Long Shot—Gravelled or Paved Space in Front of an Official-Looking Building, built of stone, with broad steps. The Union Jack flies from a flagpole. On the space in front of the building, two small groups of soldiers are drawn up, and two bands. One group of soldiers is in battle dress, and the band which matches it is a bugle and drum band, also in battle dress. The other group is in the dress uniform of the Seaforth Highlanders, with kilts, Glengarrys, etc., and their band is a pipers' band, in kilts. What is taking place is a guard mount. (Subject to correct, as follows.) The old guard is stood at attention and inspected by the outgoing officer of the day, and during this inspection the drums and bugle band will march up and down in front of them, playing. The inspection over, the old guard will be formed into a marching column, the drum and bugle band will take position ahead of them, and the whole outfit will march across the parade ground and back again while the new guard stands at attention, its band silent. The old guard will then be halted, and faced towards the new guard, and will present arms. Then it will march off behind its band, while the kiltie guard is

*called to attention and presents arms. The outgoing and incoming offi-
cers of the day will salute each other. As the old guard marches off, their
band will stop playing, and the pipers will march and start playing the
bagpipes. This will continue while the new guard is inspected. Then
the new guard will be marched off behind the pipes, and the ceremony
is over. This is the background of the following scenes, and is going on
all the time. Whatever portion of it is to be shown is immaterial, but
the sound of it will be heard always, louder, not so loud, not loud at
all, according to what is going on and how far.off the bands are. Betty
is staring through the railing as the drum and bugle band goes into its
tattoo and starts marching. A moment later, the bugles join in.*

CUT BACK TO

Scene 73: Close-up of Handley

He is looking off in the other direction, makes a signal.

Scene 74: What He Sees

*A motorcycle officer standing beside the curb, near his motorcycle
which has a side car.*

Scene 75:

*Close Shot—Radio Dispatcher in Communications Division
of Police Headquarters.*

DISPATCHER (*into mike*) Go ahead, three-eight-six.
VOICE FROM LOUDSPEAKER Party I am detailed to observe is watching guard mount in front of Parliament buildings. Sergeant Handley is standing by.

(NOTE: There are no Parliament Buildings in Vancouver. They are in Victoria so some substitute must be found)

DISPATCHER *(into mike)* Message received. Stand by. One-two-five. *(He scribbles something on a pad, tears sheet off, and holds it out behind him without looking. A uniformed police officer takes it)*

Scene 76: Close Shot of Betty—Watching Through Railing

Scene 77: What She Sees

A Portion of Guard Mount Ceremonial

Scene 78: Close Shot of Handley—Standing By Railing, watching Betty

DRUM AND BUGLE MUSIC OVER SCENE.

Scene 79: Exterior of Street—Long Shot

A crowd against railing, motorcycle officer in foreground. A car ENTERS SHOT, stops behind motorcycle.

Scene 80: Close Shot—Car

Killaine gets out, crosses to motorcycle officer, who salutes him, then points out of scene.
KILLAINE I'll take over now. Wait for Handley.
He starts walking CAMERA WITH HIM, comes up with Handley, leans against the railing beside him.

KILLAINE I'm relieving you, Handley. Carry on with Gore at the hotel.
(Handley gives Killaine a curious look)

HANDLEY Very good, sir.

He goes out of shot. Killaine watches him, then moves along the railings (the guard mount ceremony is continuing all this time), comes up beside Betty.

KILLAINE This isn't a very good place to talk.

BETTY I don't want to talk.

KILLAINE I've come here to arrest you for murder.

DRUM AND BUGLE MUSIC IN BACKGROUND STOPS.

VOICE OF COMMAND *(over scene—very sharp and military)* Guard HALT!

A SOUND OF STAMPING FEET, THEN SILENCE.

VOICE OF COMMAND Right TURN!

A SOUND OF FEET, A STAMP, A SLAPPING OF HANDS AGAINST RIFLE SLINGS as guard brings its arms to order. *(Betty turns her head to look at Killaine)*

BETTY I expected nothing else.

KILLAINE I might be able to save you, if I knew enough.

BETTY You wouldn't even try. *(Killaine reacts, hurt)* There must be some copper in you, or you wouldn't be an inspector.

KILLAINE There must be—but when I'm with you, I can't find it.

VOICE OF COMMAND *(over scene)* Guard, Present ARMS!

APPROPRIATE SOUNDS ARE HEARD, THEN A ROLL STARTS ON THE TRAP DRUMS.

KILLAINE *(turning and looking through railing)* Everybody loves a guard mount—except the guard.

(he looks at his watch) My boss gave me an hour to make up my mind. The time's almost up.

(For the first time in the scene, Betty turns and faces him) I'm about to be very silly. A man passes a girl on the street—a very lovely girl—his eyes meet her eyes, and something reaches out and takes hold of his heart—and then she goes on and is lost in the crowd—and he says to himself, "There goes my lost love"—and it's true—if he never sees her again, it's still true. Of course, after a while, he forgets—or almost forgets—because after a while we forget almost everything.

(Betty is silent, staring in alarm) But this man is a copper. He gets orders—routine orders—to go to a place and investigate a murder—and everything points to a certain girl.

BETTY Points very straight to her.

KILLAINE He looks at the girl, looks into her eyes.

BETTY What does he see?

KILLAINE Palm trees against a sunset—waves breaking on a coral reef—the Taj Mahal by moonlight—roses in an English garden, just after a shower—

(he grins wryly) Clichés, one and all—but good ones, with a lot of mileage left in them—there's one thing he does not see—murder—and murder was what he was sent to find. Pretty ridiculous, isn't it?

BETTY Very ridiculous.

KILLAINE That's my hard luck—I'm man enough to tell you about it—and not be sorry.

BETTY What do your friends call you?—the ones that know you very well?—and like you very much?

KILLAINE They call me Jeff.

BETTY Jeff. Shall we go now, Jeff, and get it over with?

KILLAINE Not quite yet.

JOHN
GALSWORTHY

J OHN GALSWORTHY (1867-1933) began writing fiction for love. Not because he especially loved literature, but because he loved a woman who loved fine writing.

> If one has been brought up in an English public school and university, is addicted to sport and travel, has a small independent income, and is a briefless barrister, one will not take literature seriously, but one might like to please her of whom one was fond. I began. In two years I wrote nine tales. They had every fault.

Among the nine tales was one set in Canada, quoted below. They constitute the earliest published writing of a man who would eventually obtain global renown for his novels known collectively as *The Forsyte Saga*. In 1932, at the culmination of his career, he won the Nobel Prize for Literature.

Following graduation from Oxford, Galsworthy was called to the Bar but never practised law; rather, he took to travelling the four corners of the planet from 1891-1893, and on a sea voyage met, by chance, his near contemporary, Joseph Conrad, who also was just starting at the writer's trade. The two became fast friends for life.

One of Galsworthy's youthful trips was occasioned by his father's desire to prevent the development of a love affair between his son and "someone who wouldn't have done at all" as John Galsworthy later described the woman. Under the guise of probing a coal-mining operation, John Galsworthy was sent to British Columbia by his father in early 1891 to connect with his brother Hubert who was already in the country. Following a stay of indeterminate length in Quebec, he moved west to Victoria, eventually linking with his brother on August 9, 1891 at Nanaimo, B.C.

Pretence at inspecting the nearby mining operations soon gave way to preparations for a hiking foray into the interior of Vancouver Island. Apparently only a single letter survives from this period of Galsworthy's life, a letter to his sister Mabel, but it tells in unintentionally amusing detail (and sometimes outrageously arrogant detail), how the wilderness of Canada impressed itself upon him:

> We returned yesterday from our first camping out expedition, of which I will seek to give you some account. We made a start upon August 17th on a pouring wet morning, riding and accompanied by two other equestrians to bring back the horses. Our two pack horses, with loads of about two hundred lbs. each on board, had started about six or an hour earlier with Allen, our ex-mining, ex-teamster, ex-everything guide and our Indian Chief, Louis Goode (for very little). We rode mainly on Shank's mare for about fifteen miles over a regular mountain trail, five miles up Mt. Benson (two thousand feet up) then five miles on the level up there, and then another and down to the level of the lakes. It poured the whole way, and we were rather damp when we got there. We went straight to an unoccupied log cabin, where we fed, parted from our escort, who took the horses back, and made things snug for the night. Louis and I went out hunting, and before very long succeeded in losing ourselves, a gruesome sensation in those immense woods; the fool of an Indian, not knowing the country, had come without taking bearings or anything. While we were trying to determine our route we struck a "blaze" trail and followed it in diametrically the wrong

direction until, luckily for us, it became too dark to find it; and then, in making a desperate cast for the right direction, Louis caught sight of water, which we thought at first must be the second lake, miles from where we started, but which turned out to be the first. He wanted to follow it to the right and I to the left. Eventually I prevailed, and on we went, firing our rifles and shouting like blue blazes. At last we heard an answering shot, and then we made a plunge in that direction thro' some willow growth, as we didn't dare leave the lake again. That was the heaviest bit of going I have ever struck—up to your knees in water and over your head in thick growth. When we were about done we reached the other side, by which time it was pitch dark; but we could hear the answering shouts from the camp by this time, and so we guided ourselves by that. How many times I fell on my head I will not pause to relate! Suffice it to say that by the time (nine-thirty) that we struggled into camp we were about baked. You may talk about Wagner, but the sweetest music I ever heard was that first shout when we succeeded in locating the camp direction. It would have been awkward stopping out all night, as we were wet through, and, what was excessively foolish, had no matches or grub with us, only one brandy. This, as you may imagine, has made us a bit more cautious, but I must say that it was entirely the fool of an Indian's fault.

The next day, which was gloriously fine, we devoted to making a raft (hard work), composed of three logs of cedar split, twenty feet long and very heavy, joined together by pegs and cross beams, and which, launched at four-thirty, provided us with a capital boat. We went up the lake fishing from her and caught about fifteen trout, and I shot a couple of ducks but one got off. I tumbled in and had to spend the greater portion of the evening fishing in a shirt alone. We came back to the log cabin that night, but the next day we "packed" all our things down from the cabin to the raft (toughish work) and migrated to the head of the lake. There we pitched our tent and had an awfully jolly camp—lovely weather and scenery, and capital grub, as

Allen is an excellent cook. But alas, the hunting was a dead failure (very bad country for it) and the fishing not first-rate; we only got seventy trout while we were there—the weather was too hot and the water too deep for them to take. One day I started off to the head of the second lake about five miles (fearful walking) and took a couple of blankets, a rifle gun and fishing-rod, and camped under a cedar tree, where I had seen lots of deer marks the day before when out hunting that way. I waited up most of the night as it was very moonlight and they sometimes come down to the water to feed then; alas, no result, and I had a very uncomfortable night, being slightly mosquito- and other animile-bitten. However I caught a few fish, two of them weighing quite two lb. each, I should think, and giving me rare good sport. I had three meals off the very driest of bread and corned beef. The next morning, as the Indian ass did not turn up according to arrangement with a raft to bring me back, I was moved in an evil hour to take up my bed and all my belongings, weighing altogether some forty lbs., and walk. Oh! that walk was a sort of nightmare. The country there is too fearful to be described—it makes one's legs weak to think of it. However, I got back in four hours (one mile an hour is rather fast than otherwise there).

Finding the hunting no good there, we sent in a message by some people travelling down the lake and asked for the horses to be sent out to pack our things down on to Mt. Benson, where we expected to do better. We moved on Monday last, and camped at Wolf Creek ten miles from Nanaimo. Here, tho' we went out with great regularity, we couldn't get near the deer, tho' I should think there were plenty of them, as it looked very likely country; but it was so awfully dry that they could hear us half a mile off. The whole time I had three shots at deer (none of them easy) and Hue none at all. We got a few grouse but they were very scarce and altogether a stupid bird, of very indifferent flavour. Yesterday we returned here, having enjoyed our ten days very much in spite of the bad luck we had had shooting and fishing. I am going with a fellow to-morrow for a couple of days' deer-hunting in the neighbourhood here, and he says we shall have good sport, but I am no longer sanguine; and after that we shall probably go up to one of the islands along this coast, where they say sport is plentiful and easily got, and where there is no chance of getting lost (as they are so small). They are up Comox way, and we are trying to arrange to go up by the Comox boat next Wednesday and stay till the return boat on the Friday nine days later; after which Hue will probably go into the office and I shall commence my return journey.... I shall go down the Northfield mine shortly, and then shall have seen nearly everything as Robins has driven me about a great deal. I read a book on coal-mining while out camping. We go up to Robins' nearly every evening, and he remains as nice as ever. This evening we propose complying with an invitation from the parson here and giving him a look in, but I believe he is terrifying....

The two brothers did indeed advance to Comox for a couple of days, then to Denman Island for a week of hiking and hunting. By September 15, 1891 they had returned to Vancouver, from which city John Galsworthy returned to Britain.

Galsworthy made only one further trip to Canada that can be confirmed, and that was to Quebec City in late October 1920. During his many American trips, he may have made quick visits to Toronto to visit Pelham Edgar, the internationally renowned professor of English at the University of Toronto whom he had met in Italy while both were on vacation there, and with whom he established a regular correspondence and friendship. His voyages to the USA were for reasons of health—he enjoyed the dry hot climates of the southwestern states—and to lecture and attend openings of his plays. At the start of a lengthy tour in 1920, he entered the continent via Canada:

We left on October 20th by the Empress of France from Liverpool to Quebec, to winter in America.

Voyage uneventful; pleasant enough and very calm. Quebec very much changed since I saw it in 1891; then one drove in a calèche, now in taxi, up to the heights of Abraham. On Oct. 28 we reached Montreal. Made acquaintance with some of the McGill University folk, who were producing *The Pigeon* as their first amateur dramatic performance. One night in Montreal, and then on to New York....

Four years were to elapse between Galsworthy's 1891 trip to British Columbia and his first published fiction. But he put this western Canadian experience to some use in a story that appeared in his first collection, *From the Four Winds*, published under the pseudonym John Sinjohn in 1898.

While *From the Four Winds* does not have "every fault" as Galsworthy said above, it is clearly the work of a young and raw professional. The tales are set in India, Marseilles, the South Seas, the equatorial marine latitudes—everywhere in fact, that Galsworthy travelled as a young man in the early 1890s.

The sole narration with a Canadian setting appears to be partly autobiographical in that it is recounted by a young Briton travelling across Canada by train. In this story, "A Prairie Oyster", a Canadian travelling salesman regales his British listener with a tall tale of derring-do, a far-fetched drama of capture and escape at the hands of rebel Moors in Morocco. Although intrigued by the descriptions of fantastical minarets and sand dunes, Galsworthy's narrator appears content with the much more real pleasures offered by the beauty of the Canadian prairie.

A PRAIRIE OYSTER

I drink my love at the fall of night
    As the glow dies out of the Western sky
I drink to the whirr of the widgeon's flight,
    And the coyote's yowl, as we trundle by.

I drink my love in the prairie morn,
    With a "Hey! farewell!" to the falling moon,
To the stars a-point at the flush of dawn,
    And the waking cry of the watchful loon.

I drink my love in the heat and glare,
    With the sun a-flame on the silent lake;
I drink to the hum of the quivering air,
    To the beat and throb of the world awake.

Here's a toast to them all! And it's sung refrain
Is the clink and jar of a westward train.

We droned along in one of those fits of despondency peculiar to trains that have an immensity of flat ground in which to pick up their lost time.

The night was a lovely one, hot, with a bright moon silvering the prairie, and trying vainly to throw shadows in a shadowless space. In a meditative mood, I lounged on the platform against the open door of the smoking car, and it seemed to me that I was taking a lesson in the comprehension of infinity. A rolling plain as far as the eye could reach—not a tree—not a house—as limitless and as empty as the sky itself.

A peculiar feeling of rest and freedom at first possessed me; I was, or thought I was, beginning to understand many things hitherto unrevealed, to have a sympathy with Simon Stylites, and an appreciation of Mahatmaism; but soon a wild desire to project myself indefinitely into space seized upon me. The moonlight and the vastness were getting into my brain—a little more, and I might have leapt from the train, and run until nature or prairie-dog holes should assert their influence upon me;—and then with a saving grace, a couple of coyotes appeared from behind a hillock, and played with their tails in the moonlight—and the spell was broken.

I became conscious that my cigar was out, that the mosquitoes were annoyingly attentive. Better to be a limited being in a smoking car and not itch, than to be an unlimited being outside it and itch most "demnibly." I went back into the smoking-room.

Empty, thank heaven—no professionals from the Golden City to talk faro and rowdyism; no commercials to bombard one with down Eastern brag, the decline of Winnipeg, or the future of Vancouver and the C. P. R.; no globe-trotting sportsman to bewail his luck in the Rockies, or abuse the British Columbian for a liar.

"Empty, thank God."

"Take a light, sir?" said a soft, rather high-pitched, drawling voice under my left elbow. I jumped, and, to disguise it, smote my cheek, where a mosquito might have been, but was not.

A man of about forty, a long figure in a sleeping suit, with a lean, brown, clean-shaven face, courteously bending forward, held towards me the lighted end of a cigar.

"Thanks very much, sir; delighted to find I'm not alone."

"*Not* empty, thank God;" said Mr. Dick Denver, in an unmoved voice.

"My dear sir," said I, sitting down next to him, "I shouldn't have dreamed of that remark, if I'd seen you; but you were so completely tucked away in that corner, that I'd no idea you were here, and I must confess I was uncommonly glad not to see our 'Frisco friends, or the bummers" (*Anglice* commercial travellers).

"Guess you're right; they are kind of tiring."

"What beats me," I went on, "is the way people like that, who really have nothing to say, insist upon saying it, and, by Gad, enjoy saying it, and are certain you enjoy hearing them say it, and set you down as a condemned fool if you don't say it yourselves!"

"Right," said Mr. Denver: "for a man that spreads himself around to be dull, give me a woman first, and then a bummer. And yet," he went on meditatively, "there are some profoundly interesting beetles amongst that last tribe; and—amongst the other too." He sighed, and relapsed into the silent puffing of his cigar. I had not travelled from Montreal nearly to Calgary with Mr. Denver without discovering that he was a silent man on all subjects, and on the subject of women a dumb, and apparently a deaf image. Try him upon the subject of "bummers" the oyster might open for once, I thought, but without much hope....

"Did you ever have anything to do with any curious specimen?" I said carelessly.

"Some," he said; "one mainly—Irishman—he travelled in wine; I guess he was the smartest coon I ever struck, but no head—or rather too much head, like a glass of stout."

"All Irishmen are like that," I said, sententiously and untruthfully; then, with a cautious insertion of the opener, "what was his name?"

"Kinahan; we called him Kinjan," and—more to himself than to me—"Jupiter! I was in the tightest kind of a hole with that cuss and one other.'

"Really tight?" said I.

"Never tighter, except about three times, and those I don't take much stock in talking of."

"Women?" I said hardily. He nodded.

"And others," he added, as if he had thereby over-committed himself.

"It seems to me," said I, feeling the opener deepening in the shell, "you don't 'take much stock' in talking of anything, considering that you really have got something to say; tell me this yarn of Kinjan, and be a benefactor to a poor sleep-forsaken devil."

Mr. Denver chewed the end of his cigar.

"Bore you world without end," he said.

"Try me," I besought.

"We must have drinks, then." He heaved himself up, and called melodiously over the car platforms.

When the materials had been brought, Mr. Denver constructed himself his favourite pick-me-up, in which raw egg and cayenne pepper formed the chief ingredients.

"Let me mix you one," he said; "guess you won't weaken on it; it's short, but it's breezy."

We drank together, and our hearts were opened within us, and we became as brothers. Through the open door and window the wonderful silver prairie night came in, and the lamp of the smoking-room flickered and went out before its breath. We swallowed another prairie oyster each, and the strings of Mr. Denver's tongue were unloosed, and he spake plain, if a little through his nose.

And as he spake, the snoring from the sleeping-saloon and the snorting of the engine became to me as the roaring of the surf upon the sea-shore, and the rolling prairie as the sands of the desert, and afar off a lone clump of trees, shining white under the moon as the minarets of a distant Moorish city....

He lounged back in his seat with a far-away look in his sunken eyes, and I had to jog him with questions once or twice before he took up the word again ... he stopped, turning his head to gaze out of the window.

"Look," he said, "there's the dawn." And sure enough, far away behind us on the eastern horizon, a pale salmon streak slowly lengthened and spread; between us and it on the dim prairie lay a still, murky sheet of water. In front of the train, in its western way-faring, the young slopes of the Rockies rose shadowy and faint in the growing light. As we stepped out on to the car platform the shrill tragic cry of the loon came floating to us, through the wreathing mist, from across the reedy pools. We watched the sun rise—and those who are watching the sun rise on the prairie and the flushing of the early mountain slopes in the reflected light, are not greatly given to talk. But when it was over, I turned to Dick Denver. His brown, lean face looked drawn and haggard, and he shaded his eyes with his hand. Presently he raised his hand to his hat, and taking it off, stood looking long and steadily at the now risen sun, and his lips moved. If I hadn't known him for a hardened and notorious sinner, I should have said he was muttering a prayer. The impression was so strong upon me that I waited to speak until he had replaced his hat.... He turned and went back into the smoking car. The oyster was closing fast.

"Just one question," I hazarded; "what became of the other two men afterwards?" He drew out a pack of cards, and began shuffling them, and I had to repeat the question.

"Oh! I guess Kinjan would be alive,—why certainly he would be; unless he might have been caught up in a flame of fire, there wouldn't be any other kind of a death for him," he said with the ghost of a smile.

"And Torin?"

"Gone out, I reckon," he said impassively.

The curt grimness of this remark jarred upon me, though why it should have, I don't know; why expect sentiment from Dick Denver, who lived from day's end to day's end with his life in his hands?

"In heaven's name, why indeed?" I said aloud to myself, as I turned once again before going through the door to my berth— Dick Denver was dealing a set of poker hands, and humming softly to himself. It was broad daylight, and the train still droned along. I was dead tired; and as I shut the door softly, and turned into my bunk, instead of an intelligent moral deduction from the story and its teller, all I could think of was the children's grace, "Thank God for a good dinner."

JAMES OLIVER CURWOOD

N o other American author loved Canada as rapturously, as corporeally, as enduringly, and with such an aw-shucks pride, as James Oliver Curwood (1878-1927).

He grew up in his native Michigan. After graduating from university, he pursued journalism, eventually becoming editor of the *Detroit News*, one of the nation's largest newspapers. But in 1907, he resigned the post to be a full-time writer of fiction, rapidly becoming one of the bestselling authors of his day. Total copies sold of his titles number, staggeringly, in the many millions, and the French literary critics of the day sincerely, if not perversely, hailed him as the equal of Jack London and Upton Sinclair. Many of his novels were translated in his own day into motion pictures, further augmenting his astonishing popularity. Today, in his hometown of Owosso, Michigan, he is immortalized by the Curwood Museum, an institution preserving his home, his writing and the record of his extensive efforts at animal conservation.

Curwood had been, by his own admission, just another greedy, bloodthirsty North American big-game hunter. But an encounter (described below) with a grizzly in the Canadian bush converted him to the environmentalist cause. He later mined his encounter for a novel titled *The Grizzly King* (1916). Decades after its publication, *The Grizzly King* would inspire the French filmmaker Jean-Jacques

James Oliver Curwood posing for a publicity photo as a freelance ranger and propagandist for the Canadian North. "The Canadian Government offered me eighteen hundred dollars a year, plus all expenses, to explore the picturesque provinces of the West and then go into the North to gather material for articles and stories intended to induce settlers into the country."
Photo courtesy of Ivan A. Conger.

Annaud to make *The Bear* (1988), one of the largest-grossing films in the history of cinema. (Since its first appearance in 1952, the French translation of *The Grizzly King* has never been out of print in France.) Thereafter, Curwood spent, when he could, every summer in the Canadian Far North—he called Canada "God's Country"—and most of his thirty-one novels were set in the wilder territories. Such was his infectious devotion to Canada that the Canadian federal government, in a move of such breathtaking intelligence it makes one question how the government could have been involved, hired him on contract as a freelance ranger, and as an official propagandist to lure tourists and settlers.

> During the year 1902, in which I returned to the *News*, I became acquainted with M.V. MacInness, "Mac" to all his friends, then representing the Canadian Immigration Department in Detroit.... To him I went when in need of counsel, entertainment, or merely relaxation.
>
> He was rather portly and always in jovial humor. He never tired of painting vivid word pictures for me of his beloved Canada, more particularly the vast panorama of unexplored wilderness toward the north and west. His mind was filled with information concerning that magnificent expanse of territory, and he never lost an opportunity to introduce me to Canadians who came to his office. I met many Dominion immigration officers, members of Parliament, Hudson's Bay Company officials, officers of the Grand Trunk and Canadian Pacific, members of the Royal Northwest Mounted Police and scores of others.... The Canadian government offered me eighteen hundred dollars a year, plus all expenses, to explore the picturesque provinces of the West and then go into the North to gather material for articles and stories intended to induce settlers into the country. The opportunity to become a part of the great and glorious land whose far frontiers had been a part of my dreams for years thrilled me as no other event in my life....

Not all of Curwood's books were set in the western half of our nation. One of his last novels, *The Black Hunter*, is subtitled *A Novel of Old Quebec*. Three of the principal characters are Anne St. Denis, ("daughter of a fighting seigneur"), David Rock ("a son of the forests and their dangers, who carves on his powder horn an angel in the form of Anne"), and the Black Hunter ("a weird and mysterious wanderer of the wilderness, a weaver of romance and tragedy, not quite forgotten even to this day").

While many Canadian readers might be amused at his characterizations, or his sense of what our forebears were really like, it is worth recalling, before we chuckle too patronizingly, that like so many American novelists, and unlike too many Canadians, he regarded our history as more than a worthy subject for fiction:

> Probably no period in the history of the North American continent offers to the writer of romance a field richer in incident or one more filled with the picturesque and thrilling life of the pioneer than that with which this novel opens…. Yet it is a curious and interesting fact that these years, beginning with the English and French struggle for supremacy in 1755 and ending a few years before the War of Independence, have seldom been called upon, and almost never with any degree of historical accuracy, to furnish material for the writer of fiction.

Given the immensity of his book sales, it is daunting to contemplate the impact of Curwood on the world's perception of ourselves. In *The Flaming Forest*, for example, subtitled *A Novel of the Canadian Northwest*, the hero is a solitary, rugged Mountie, surviving by his own wits, tougher than any bad guy, but, at the core, ever sensitive to the beautiful: this is how we were perceived internationally, thanks to Curwood, by millions. With the failure of our own culture to promulgate worthy alternatives, Curwood's were the images whose verisimilitude would be rarely questioned by outsiders:

An hour ago, under the marvelous canopy of the blue northern sky, David Carrigan, Sergeant in His Most Excellent Majesty's Royal Northwest Mounted Police, had hummed softly to himself, and had thanked God that he was alive. He had blessed McVane, superintendent of the "N" Division at Athabasca Landing, for detailing him to the mission on which he was bent. He was glad that he was traveling alone, and in the deep forest, and that for many weeks his adventure would carry him deeper and deeper into his beloved north. Making his noonday tea over a fire at the edge of the river, with the green forest crowding like an inundation on three sides of him, he had come to the conclusion—for the hundredth time, perhaps—that it was a nice thing to be alone in the world, for he was on what his comrades in the Landing called a "bad assignment."

The places to which Curwood usually chose to travel in Canada were rough-hewn at best, and dangerously wild, which probably accounts for the paucity of writing accomplished while he was actually in the bush. So we have the odd fact that almost all of his hundreds of thousands of words about Canada were penned while he was not in Canada, but snug at home in Michigan. The sample of his writing below (from one of his autobiographies, *God's Country: The Trail to Happiness*, 1921) is sincerely representative because it typifies his deliberately elementary approach to prose and because it conveys his romanticized—but yes, heartfelt—passion for northern Canada.

from GOD'S COUNTRY:
THE TRAIL TO HAPPINESS

As I sit here now, clicking my typewriter in the still heart of the forest, it is a wonder to me that some colossal spirit of vengeance does not rise up out of it and destroy me. And yet, when I consider, I know why that vengeance does not come—and in the face of this "great reason," I see my littleness as I have never seen it before. It is because, very slowly, my egoism is crumbling away. And as it crumbles, my big brother—all nature—grips my hand ever more closely, and whispers to me to tell others something of what I have found. And that big brother is not only the spirit of the heart-beating things about me, but also the spirit and voice of the trees, of the living earth that throbs under my feet, of the flowers, the sun, the sky. It is all reaching out to me with a great show of friendliness, and I seem to feel that fear and misunderstanding have slipped away from between us. It is inviting me to accept of it all that I may require, yet to cherish that which I cannot use. It is telling me, as it has whispered to me a thousand times before, the secret of life; that the life in my own breast and all this that is about me are one and the same—and that, in our partnership for happiness, we each belong to the other. And there must be no desire for vengeance between us.

Yet, to me, it does not seem like justice, looking at it from the warped and narrow point of view of my human mind. It is the human instinct to demand an eye for an eye and a tooth for a tooth. And I cannot see why my God of nature should give me such reward of peace and friendship after what I have done. It has always been my logic that life is the cheapest thing in existence. There is just so much earth, so much water, so much air about us; but of life there is no end. So we go on destroying. If nature would keep this destroyed life unto herself for a few generations, instead of giving it back to us

James Oliver Curwood with his dogs and bear skins in "God's Country", better known as Canada. Curwood, one of the most popular authors of his time, was first attracted to the Canadian wilderness for its wealth of big game. But an encounter with a grizzly transformed him into a leading environmentalist. Photo courtesy of Ivan A. Conger.

in her unvengeful way, the earth would soon become a desert. Then we would learn our lesson.

I am thinking, as I write this, of a beautiful little forest in a wonderful valley in the heart of the British Columbia mountains. It was a glorious thing to look down upon that day when I destroyed it. I call it a forest, though there was not more than an acre of it, or two at the most. And the valley was really a "pocket" among the mighty peaks of the Firepan Range. It was of balsams and cedars, rich green, and densely thick—a marvelous patch of living tapestry, vibrant with the glow and pulse of life in the sunset of that day. Into its shelter we had driven a wounded grizzly which had refused to turn and fight. And so thick and protecting was the heart of it that we could not get the grizzly out. Night was not far away, and in its darkness we knew our game would escape us. And the thought came to us to burn that little paradise of green. There was no danger of a spreading fire. The mountain walls of the "pocket" would prevent that. And it was I who struck the match!

In twenty minutes, the little forest was a sea of writhing, leaping flame. It cried out and moaned in the agony of conflagration. The bear fled from its torture and its ruin, and we killed him. That night, the moon shone down on a black and smoldering mass of ruin where a little while before had been the paradise.

In our camp, we laughed and exulted. The egoism of man made us feel our false triumph. What it had taken a thousand years to place in that cup of the mountains we had destroyed in half an hour—yet we felt no regret. We had destroyed a thousand times more life than filled our own pitiable bodies, yet did the false ethics of our breed assure us that we had done no wrong—simply because the life we had destroyed had not possessed a form and tongue like our own.

"This man must be losing his reason," I hear some of my readers say. Is it that, or is a bit of reason just returning to me, after a million years of sleep? If it is madness, it is of a kind that would comfort the world could all be mad as I am mad. Life is Life. It is a spark of the same Supreme Power, whether in a tree, a flower, or a thing of flesh and blood. To me, as I view it now, the wanton destruction of that little paradise was as tragic as the destruction of life carried about on two legs or four. I feel that the crime of its destruction was as great as that of another day which I recall most vividly in these moments.

I was in another wonderland of the northern mountains, and my companion was a grizzled old hunter who had learned the art of killing through a lifetime of experience. With our pack-outfit of seven horses, we were hitting for the Yukon over a trail never traveled by white man before. So glorious was the valley we were in on this day of which I write that at noon we struck our camp. So awesome was the vastness and beauty of it that my soul was held spellbound with the magic of it. On all sides of us rose the mighty mountains, with snowcrowned peaks rising here and there out of the towering ranges. The murmur of rippling water filled the soft air with soothing song; green meadows, sweet with the perfume of wild hyacinths, violets, and a hundred other flowers, carpeted the rich earth about us; on the sunwarmed rocks, whistlers lay in fat contentment, calling to one another like small boys whistling between their teeth; the slopes were dotted with ptarmigan; a pair of eagles soared high above us, and from the patches and fingers of timber came the cry and song of birds. With my back propped against a pile of saddles and panniers I carefully scanned the slides and slopes through my hunting-glasses. High up on the crag of a mountain-shoulder, I picked up a nanny-goat feeding with her kid. Still farther away, on a green "slide" at least two miles from camp, I discovered five mountain-sheep lying down. And after that, swinging my glasses slowly, I came to something which sent a thrill through my blood. It was a mile away, a great, slow-moving hulk that I might have mistaken for a rock had my eyes not been trained to the ways and movement of game. It was a grizzly.

Alone I went after him, armed with man's deadliest weapon of extinction, a .405 Winchester. Inside of half an hour I was well in the teeth of the breeze coming up the valley, and almost within gunshot of my victim. I came to a coulee and crept up that, and when I reached the table-land meadow where it began, a thousand feet above the valley, I found myself within a hundred yards of the grizzly.

He was digging like a dog for a gopher. And, then, suddenly, my heart gave a thump that almost choked me. In a twist of the mountain-bench, not more than seventy or eighty yards above me, were two more grizzlies. I hesitated, and looked back down the coulee, for a moment doubtful whether to retreat or declare war. Then I decided. In my hands was a killer of the deadliest and surest kind. I was an expert shot and my nerves were steady. I began. I think I fired five shots in perhaps thirty seconds, and the three big grizzlies died almost in their tracks. A conqueror returning in his triumph to old Rome could not have been more elated than I. I remember that I leaped and danced and shrieked out at the top of my voice in the direction of camp. I was mad with joy. Three thousand pounds of flesh and blood lay hot and lifeless under my eyes, and I, the human near-god, with my own two insignificant hands and a mechanical thing, had taken the life from it!

I sat down on one of the huge carcasses that still breathed under me. I wiped my face, and my blood was running a race that heated me as if with fire. And the thought came to me: "Oh, if the world could only see me now—here in my glorious triumph—with these great beasts about me!" For it was a mighty triumph for man, the egoist. In thirty seconds I had destroyed a possible one hundred years of throbbing, heart-beating life, a hundred years of winter, a hundred years of summer, a hundred mating-seasons, and the thousand other lives that now would never be born! I stood up, and shrieked again toward the camp, and far above me out of the blue of the sky I heard an answering cry from one of the eagles....

When I sat down at my typewriter an hour ago, I had planned to begin immediately the telling of what I have wandered somewhat away from—the story of a few incidents which helped to bring about my own regeneration, and which at last impressed upon me this great Golden Rule of all nature—live and let live. The big dramatic climax in that part of my life happened over in the British Columbia mountains, where my love of adventure has taken me on many long journeys.

But the change had begun to work in me before then. My conscience was already stabbing me. I was regretting, in a mild sort of way, that I had killed so much. But I was still the supreme egoist, believing myself the God-chosen animal of all creation, and when at any time I withheld my destroying hand, I flattered myself with a thought of my condescension and human kindness.

At the particular time I am going to write about, I was on a big grizzly-hunt in a wild and unhunted part of the British Columbia mountains. I had with me one man, seven horses, and a pack of Airedales trained to hunt bear. We had struck a grizzly-and-caribou paradise, and there had been considerable killing, when, one day, we came upon the trail of Thor, the great beast that showed me how small in soul and inclination a man can be. In a patch of mud his feet had left tracks that were fifteen inches from tip to tip, and so wide and deep were the imprints that I knew I had come upon the king of all his kind. I was alone that morning, for I had left camp an hour ahead of my man, who was two or three miles behind me with four of the horses and the Airedale pack. I went on watching for a new campsite, for the thrill of a great desire possessed me—the desire to take the life of this monster king of the mountains. It was in these moments that the unexpected happened. I came over a little rise, not expecting that my bear was within two or three miles of me, when something that was very much like a low and sullen rumble of far-away thunder stopped the blood in my veins.

Ahead of me, on the edge of a little wallow of mud, stood Thor. He had smelled me, and, I believe, it was the first time he had ever smelled the scent of man. Waiting for this new mystery in the air, he had reared himself up until the whole nine feet of him rested on his haunches, and he sat like a trained dog, with his great forefeet heavy with mud, drooping in front of his chest. He was a monster in size, and his new June coat shone a golden brown in the sun. His forearms were almost as large as a man's body, and the three largest of his five knife-like claws were five and a half inches long. He was fat and sleek and powerful. His upper fangs, sharp as stiletto-points, were as long as a man's thumb, and between his great jaws he could have crushed the neck of a caribou. I did not take in all these details in the first startling moments; one by one they came to me later. But I had never looked upon anything in life quite so magnificent. Yet did I have no thought of sparing that splendid life. Since that day, I have rested in camp with my head pillowed on the arm of a living grizzly that weighed a thousand pounds. Friendship and love and understanding have sprung up between us. But in that moment my desire was to destroy this life that was so much greater than my own. My rifle was at my saddle-horn in its buckskin jacket. I fumbled it in getting into action, and in those precious moments Thor lowered himself slowly and ambled away. I fired twice, and would have staked my life that I had missed both times. Not until later did I discover that one of my bullets had opened a furrow two inches deep and a foot long in the flesh of Thor's shoulder. Yet I did not see him flinch. He did not turn back, but went his way.

Shame burns within me as I write of the days that followed; and yet, with that shame, there is a deep and abiding joy, for they were also the days of my regeneration. Day and night, my one thought was to destroy the big grizzly. We never left his trail. The dogs followed him like demons. Five times in the first week we came within long shooting-range, and twice we hit him. But still he did not wait for us or attack us. He wanted to be left alone. In that week, he killed four of the dogs, and the others we tied up to save them. We trailed him with horses and afoot, and never did the spoor of other game lure me aside. The desire to kill him became a passion in me. He outgeneraled us. He beat all our games of trickery. But I knew that we were bound to win—that he was slowly weakening because of exhaustion, and the sickness of his wounds. We loosed the dogs again, and another was killed.

Then, at last, came the splendid day when Thor, master of the mountains, showed me how contemptible was I—with my human shape and soul.

It was Sunday. I had climbed three or four thousand feet up the side of a mountain and below me lay the wonder of the valley, dotted with patches of trees and carpeted with the beauty of rich, green grass, mountain violets and forget-me-nots, wild asters and hyacinths. On three sides of me spread out the wonderful panorama of the Canadian Rockies, softened in the golden sunshine of late June. From up and down the valley, from the breaks between the peaks, and from the little gullies cleft in shale and rock that crept up to the snow-lines came a soft and droning murmur. It was the music of running water—music ever in the air of summer, for the rivers and creeks and tiny streamlets gushing down from the melting snow up near the clouds are never still. Sweet perfumes as well as music came to me; June and July—the last of spring and the first of summer in the northern mountains—were commingling. All the earth was bursting with green; flowers were turning the sunny slopes and meadows into colored splashes of red and white and purple, and everything that had life was giving voice to exultation—the fat whistlers on their rocks, the pompous little gophers on their mounds, the squirrel-like rock-rabbits, the big bumblebees that buzzed from flower to flower, the hawks in the valley, and the eagles over the peaks.

Earth, it seemed, was at peace.

And I, looking over all that vastness of life, felt my own greatness thrust upon me.

For had not the Creator of all things made this wonderland for *me*?

There could be no denial. I was master—master because I could think, because I could reason, because I held the reins to an unutterable power of destruction. And then the vastness of time seized upon me like a living thing. Yesterday, a thing had happened which came strongly into my thoughts of to-day. Under a great overhanging cliff I had found a part of monster bone, as heavy as iron—a section of a gigantic vertebra. Two years before I had found part of the skeleton of a prehistoric creature, identical with this, and, from photographs which I took of it the scientific departments of the University of Michigan and the government at Ottawa agreed that the bones were part of the skeleton of a mammoth whale that once had swum where the valleys and peaks of the Rocky Mountains now disrupt the continent.

And on this Sunday, looking down, I thought of the monster bone I had found yesterday in the dry shale and sand under the cliff. When the Three Wise Men saw the star in the east, that bone was as I had found it. It was there when Christ was born. It was there, unmoved and untouched, before Rome was founded, before Troy died in the mists of the past, before history, as we know history, began. It was there a million years ago, ten million, fifty, a hundred. And, thinking of this, I felt myself growing smaller and smaller; my egoism died away, and I saw these mountains obliterated and under the blue of a vast ocean, and rising out of that ocean I saw other continents, peopled with other people, moved by other religions, beating to the pulse of other civilizations long dead....

I climbed higher up the mountain. I felt my greatness gone. Kindly, something had told me how pitiful I was. I was not mighty. I was no more in the ultimate of things than a blade of grass. My egoism, on that glorious Sunday, began to crumble in my soul. And then, by chance if you will have it so, came the climax of that day.

I came to a sheer wall of rock that rose hundreds of feet above me. Along this ran a narrow ledge, and I followed it. The passage became craggy and difficult, and in climbing over a broken mass of rock, I slipped and fell. I had brought a light mountain-gun with me, and in trying to recover myself I swung it about with such force that the stock struck a sharp edge of rock and broke clean off. But I had saved myself from possible death, and was in a frame of mind to congratulate myself rather than curse my luck; fifty feet farther on I came to a "pocket" in the cliff, where the ledge widened until, at this particular place, it was like a flat table twenty feet square. Here I sat down, with my back to the precipitous wall, and began to examine my broken rifle.

I laid it beside me, useless. Straight up at my back rose the sheer face of the mountain; in front of me, had I leaped from the ledge, my body would have hurtled through empty air for a thousand feet. In the valley I could see the creek, like a ribbon of shimmering silver; two or three miles away was a little lake; on another mountain I saw a bursting cascade of water leaping down the heights and losing itself in the velvety green of the lower timber. For many minutes, new and strange thoughts possessed me. I did not look through my hunting-glasses, for I was no longer seeking game. My blood was stirred, but not with the desire to kill.

And then, suddenly, there came a sound to my ears that seemed to stop the beating of my heart. I had not heard it, until it was very near—approaching along the narrow ledge.

It was the click,—click,—click of claws rattling on rock!

I did not move. I hardly breathed. And out from the ledge I had followed came a monster bear!

With the swiftness of lightning, I recognized him. It was Thor! And, in that same instant, the great beast saw me.

In thirty seconds I lived a lifetime, and in those thirty seconds what passed through my mind was a thousand times swifter than spoken word. A great fear rooted me, and yet in that fear I saw every-thing to the minutest detail. Thor's massive head and shoulders were fronting me. I saw the long naked scar where my bullet had plowed through his shoulder; I saw another wound in his fore leg, still ragged and painful, where another of my soft-nosed bullets had torn like an explosion of dynamite. The giant grizzly was no longer fat and sleek as I had first seen him ten days ago. All that time he had been fighting for his life; he was thinner; his eyes were red; his coat was dull and unkempt from lack of food and strength. But at that distance, less than ten feet from me, he seemed still a mighty brother of the mountains themselves. As I sat stupidly, stunned to the immobility of a rock in my hour of doom, I felt the overwhelming conviction of what had happened. Thor had followed me along the ledge, and, in this hour of vengeance and triumph, it was I, and not the great beast, who was about to die.

It seemed to me that all eternity passed in these moments. And Thor, mighty in his strength, looked at me and did not move. And this thing that he was looking at,—shrinking against the rock,—was the creature that had hunted him; this was the creature that had hurt him, and it was so near that he could reach out with his paw and crush it! And how weak and white and helpless it looked now! What a pitiful, insignificant thing it was! Where was its strange thunder? Where was its burning lightning? Why did it make no sound?

Slowly Thor's giant head began swinging from side to side; then he advanced—just one step—and in a slow, graceful movement reared himself to his full, magnificent height. For me, it was the beginning of the end. And in that moment, doomed as I was, I found no pity for myself. Here, at last, was justice! I was about to die. I, who had destroyed so much of life, found how helpless I was when I faced life with my naked hands. *And it was justice!* I had robbed the earth of more life than would fill the bodies of a thou-sand men, and now my own life was to follow that which I had destroyed. Suddenly fear left me. I wanted to cry out to that splen-did creature that I was sorry, and could my dry lips have framed the words, it would not have been cowardice—but truth.

I have read many stories of truth and hope and faith and charity. From a little boy, my father tried to teach me what it meant to be a gentleman, and he lived what he tried to teach. And from the days of my small boyhood, mother told me stories of great and good men and women, and in the days of my manhood, she faithfully lived the great truth that of all precious things charity and love are the most priceless. Yet I had accepted it all in the narrowest and littlest way. Not until this hour on the edge of the cliff did I realize how small can be the soul of a man buried in his egoism—or how splendid can be the soul of a beast.

For Thor knew me. That I know. He knew me as the deadliest of all his enemies on the face of the earth. Yet until I die will I believe that, in my helplessness, he no longer hated me or wanted my life. For slowly he came down upon all fours again, and, limping as he went, he continued along the ledge—*and left me to live!*

I am not, in these days, sacrilegious enough to think that the Supreme Power picked my poor insignificant self from among a billion and a half other humans especially to preach a sermon to that glorious Sunday on the mountainside. Possibly it was all mere chance. It may be that another day Thor would have killed me in my helplessness. It may all have been a lucky accident for me. Personally, I do not believe it, for I have found that the soul of the average beast is cleaner of hate and of malice than that of the average man. But whether one believes with me or not, does not matter, so far as the point I want to make is concerned—that from this hour began the great change in me, which has finally admitted me into the peace and joy of universal brotherhood with Life. It matters little how a sermon or a great truth comes to one; it is the result that counts.

I returned down the mountain, carrying my broken gun with me. And everywhere I saw that things were different. The fat whistlers, big as woodchucks, were no longer so many targets, watching me cautiously from the rocktops; the gophers, sunning themselves on their mounds, meant more to me now than a few hours ago. I looked off to a distant slide on another mountain and made out the half-dozen sheep I had studied through my glasses earlier in the day. But my desire to kill was gone. I did not realize the fullness of the change that was upon me then. In a dull sort of way I accepted it as an effect of shock, perhaps as a passing moment of repentance and gratitude because of my escape. I did not tell myself that I would never kill sheep again except when mutton was necessary to my camp fire. I did not promise the whistlers long lives. And yet the change was on me, and growing stronger in my blood with every breath I drew. The valley was different. Its air was sweeter. Its low song of life and running waters and velvety winds whispering between the mountains was new inspiration to me. The grass was softer under my feet; the flowers were more beautiful; the earth itself held a new thrill for me.

STEPHEN GRAHAM

THE DIFFERENCES between a tramp and a hobo are nearly if not completely blurred in contemporary English usage. But close to one hundred years ago, the nuances were easily delineated. So when writers Jack London or W.H. Davies tramped in Canada, they did so, yes, of course, in part because it seemed romantic and they could convince themselves that by tramping they were closer to nature and the ur-matters of the spirit. But these poor writers hoboed primarily because they lacked the funds to travel by any other means. For Stephen Graham (1884-1975) and Vachel Lindsay, however, tramping in Canada was undertaken not because of a want of cash, but because it seemed to provide a genuine means, a sincere conduit, by which to have meaningful contact with the land and its people.

Although a novelist, Stephen Graham was better known in his day (and in our own day is best remembered) as a writer of what we now term literary travel writing. He was also a globally recognized expert on Russian affairs.

Graham admitted that he was won to the genius of Russia by the spell of its novelists, and as a young man he left his native London to live what he hoped would be a Tolstoyan, idyllic existence. He lived for a while in Moscow, and then chose to live in the country with peasants. He walked and walked and talked and listened. Not content with tramping the Caucasus and Ural Mountains, he traversed

Crimea on foot. From there, still walking, he visited the Russian north.

Some sense of his drive can be had simply by citing the places he explored:

[He] accompanied Russian peasants to Jerusalem. He also "followed up the tide of emigration from Europe to America", going steerage with a party across the Atlantic and tramping to the farms of the West. In 1914, he was in Central Asia; the next year in Egypt, Bulgaria and Roumania; and in 1916 he traveled to northern Norway and Murmansk.... He toured Mexico in 1922-23.... In 1925 he was in Dalmatia and the Balkans; in the Carpathians in 1926; in New York in 1928; Bosnia in 1929-30; Macedonia in 1935; and Swaziland and the Transvaal in 1936.

All of these trips were described, often movingly, in his many books and in articles for the *Times* of London.

In 1922, Stephen Graham published an account of his previous year's tramp in the United States and Canada with the eminent American poet Vachel Lindsay. Approximately one-quarter of the book is given to a description of their time in this country.

Graham had befriended Vachel Lindsay in 1920 in London when Lindsay, at the height of his literary acclaim, had made a triumphal tour of Cambridge, Oxford, and London, giving poetry readings, and being feted by such lions of English literature as Ezra Pound, Robert Bridges, Robert Graves and John Masefield.

Two more unlikely travelling companions than Graham and Lindsay are hard to imagine. Lindsay was swollen with pride at what he regarded as the unparalleled genius of America; Graham was "the accepted interpreter of the greatness of the Russian soul to English readers through his translations, introductions and editions." Where Lindsay had next to no first-hand knowledge of nations beyond his own, Graham had, it seemed, walked the entire planet. But more challengingly, Lindsay was a political, even annoying *naif*, blind to the hypocrisies of his own country; Graham, already aware of the betrayals of the Russian Revolution, had a longer, more sophisticated view of the weather-vane ethics of most politicians.

In the first half of his *Tramping With A Poet In The Rockies* Graham pays appropriate homage to the splendours of their starting point, Glacier National Park in Montana. Between these passages of natural description, Graham patiently, heuristically tries to rehabilitate Lindsay's political astigmatism, to miniscule avail. In the interests of concord, he gives up the attempt—until five weeks later when they approach the Canadian border.

By his comments to Vachel Lindsay, Graham implies that he has been to Canada before, but when such a visit might have occurred is unrecorded. This tramp with Stephen Graham also marks Vachel Lindsay's first time in Canada, and Lindsay is the only major foreign author to have made his initial visit to this country, not through the usual ports of entry, but rather via Alberta. The Canadian territory described in the following excerpt is approximately two hundred kilometres due south of Calgary.

———————

from TRAMPING WITH
A POET IN THE ROCKIES

"As we approach the British Empire," says Vachel facetiously, "the huckleberries grow more plentiful, the raspberry-bushes larger, the trees loftier, the air purer." In the poet's mind politics and hymns gave way to desire of huckleberries. I luxuriated in raspberries. He was Huckleberry Finn. I was a character in Russian folk-lore—the hare with the raspberry-coloured whiskers. "When we get to a Canadian hotel let us register as H. Finn and R.C.W. Hare," said the poet.

We had slept on the hoar-frosted grass of mountain meadows near the sky; we had slept among the beavers on the banks of the Kootenai; we tramped in the radiant upper air; we tramped in the gloom of ancient forests. Mount Cleveland lifted its dome of snow high o'er the lesser mountains. Trapper Mountain receded. We listened one night to the coyotes caterwauling in their loneliness. Their superfluous lugubrious laments reminded me of modern West of Ireland poetry. Vachel laughed at the comparison. We came to a deserted cabin, once the habitation of a ranger, now littered with Alberta whisky bottles, and here we read a pencilled remark written years ago: "Slept here last night. Visited by a bare who came into cabin and et two sides of bacon." Another pencilled notice, apparently by the same hand, said: "Don't leave garbig lying about but put it in the Garbig Holl." An Indian came and offered to lead us to a boat on Lake Waterton and give us a ferry to Canada. We preferred to walk, but it occurred to me afterwards that he was not so much interested in boating as in bottles. I don't doubt he could have got us a drink. Then a grand mounted party came past us with guides and pack-horses, coming from over Brown Pass, going over Indian Pass. This was a rich American family on holiday: here were father and mother, grown children, young children, cousins, and in the midst of them Aunt Jemima, looking very proud and stiff, with an expression on her face which signified *"Never again!"* They had been twenty-eight days in the mountains, camping out all the time.

Vachel's ankle was rather weak, and he much preferred sitting to walking. He called himself "the slow train through Arkansas." We stopped at stations, half-stations, and halts. "All I lack, Stephen, is steam," said he. But every now and then he would take courage and say, "Lots of walk in me to-day—Canada to-night!"

The excitement of finding the "Canadian Line" cheered my companion. The face which in the morning had looked contrite and penitent as that of one just released from jail, lighted up with new mirth and facetious intent. He began to get steam....

"Except for the King," said Vachel, "we are much the same people." He loathed kings. "There's not much difference between Canada and the United States," he went on.

"We'll see," I answered. "Canadians are subjects of a monarch; Americans are citizens of a Republic. Canadians look to the King. More than a mere line divides the two halves of North America. You'll see."

So we tramped on. We had a last lunch and finished the ham, the apricots, and the coffee. As one remarkable fact, we met no Canadians on the American side; we met no Americans going to Canada either. Yet there were no restrictions whatever. Out in the Rockies the unguarded line is literally unguarded; no patrols, no excise or passport officers. You can come and go as you please. The United States would encourage Canada to a communion of perfect freedom. Whilst America puts nothing in Canada's way, Canada for her part could not afford to police a four-thousand-mile line. All is therefore free.

Still, it is clearly the wild animals that take advantage of freedom, and they abound and are happy in the region about the line. It is a very strange line, straight and absolute on the map, the essence of political division, an absurdity in geography. There is no river, no main mountain-range, no change of the colour of the soil, but only the invisible hypothesis called 54.40—the "Fifty-four Forty or fight" of the boundary dispute. It would have been difficult to find the line but for the fact that a sixteen-foot swathe has been cut in the forest. We had been told to look out for that. We found it at last, and it was afternoon, and we stood in No-man's land together.

It was a curious cut, a rough glade, an alley through the tall pines. We walked along it a short way; we discerned where it stretched far over a mountain-side, a mere marking in the uniform green of the forest-roof. We came down to where the lake water was lapping on the shore, and the great mountains in their fastnesses stood about us. We found frontier post No. 276, and then I stood on the Canada side and Vachel Lindsay stood on the America side, and we put our wrists on the top of the post. As we two had become friends and learned to live together without quarreling, so might our nations. It was a happy moment in our tramping.

Then, as it was four in the afternoon, I proposed having tea, much to the mirth of the poet. For had we not finished the last of our coffee at our last American resting-place? Fittingly we began on tea when we entered the Empire.

There was a change of scenery; fresher air, aspen groves, red hips on many-briars. A beautiful mountain lifted its citadelled peak into a grey unearthly radiance. We climbed Mount Bertha, and the hill-sides were massed with young slender pines that never grow hoary or old, but die whilst they are young, and are supplanted by the ever-new—forests of everlasting youth. The grandeur of the mountains increased upon us till all was in the sublimity of the Book of Job and of the Chaldean stars. There was nothing petty anywhere—but an eternal witness and an eternal silence....

So we entered the Dominion National Park of Waterton Lakes. We climbed the next mountain after Mount Bertha and saw on every hand the pinnacled and pillared tops of the Canadian mountains, crags surmounted by mighty teeth of stone blackly silhouetted against a radiant sky. Some Dominion officials came into these parts last year, cancelled the old names of the mountains, and gave them a new set—Mount Joffre, Mount Foch, and the rest, as if they were No. 1 and No. 2 of Great War villas. I see by old maps that Mount Cleveland used to be called Kaiser Peak. How war changes the names of places! It changed St. Petersburg to Petrograd, Pressburg to Bratislava; it has even changed the names of the Rocky Mountains....

At last we came to a Canadian camping ground and a group of people clustered around a Ford touring car. A Ford car used for touring. Here there happened to be on holiday a professor of English, and he recognized Lindsay at first sight—such is the fame of the poet in American universities and schools.

This camping-group told us we were in a land predominantly inhabited by Mennonites, Mormons, and Dukhobors, and they whetted our curiosity considerably regarding our new neighbors.

We had arrived in a part of Canada which was rather obscure and certainly little visited by either Americans or Englishmen.

We came to a ramshackle inn and a village and a dance-hall, and it was the last dance of the season. The Mormon, German, and Russian belles checked in their corsets at the cloakroom, and prepared for fun. It was a log-cabin hall, but the floor was waxed, and from the beams hung coloured-paper lanterns. There were a score or so of black bear-skins hung on the walls all the way round. On the bear-skins were white sashes with these words printed on them: *I Do Love To Cuddle;* and on the main beam of the ceiling was written: *Patrons are respectfully requested to park their gum outside.* The whole front of the piano was taken out so that there should be more noise. Splotches on the floor showed how in the past, patrons had surreptitiously brought in their gum and had accidents. Many couples assembled, and we saw the human species, though not at its best.

We issued from the mountains on to the southern Alberta plain, and then looking back, saw every great mountain we had ever crossed. "We've found the real sky-scrapers," said Vachel. "Instead of the Times Building, Heaven's Peak; instead of the Flatiron, Flat Top Mountain; instead of the World Building, Going-to-the-Sun; and instead of the building raised by dimes, the temple not made by hands. The way to these wonders is not by Broadway, but by primitive trails." The poet conducted the orchestra of the universe with the long blossoming stem of a basket flower—"instead of the Stock Exchange, the Star Granary over Waterton Lake," he murmured. We named the beautiful grouping of mountains about the lake as the Star Granary. For at night with stars above and star-reflections below, it was as if the barns were full of Heaven's harvest.

We tramped away northward toward the Crow's Nest, where a great forest fire was raging, and we came to the "cow-town" of Pincer Creek. The Canadian Wild West seemed much wilder than the Wild West south of the line—or rather, the population seemed wilder. One missed the gentleness and playfulness of the United

States. The men were harder than down south, and they looked at us with a contempt only modified by the thought that we might be potential harvest hands. The Canadian-English looked more askance at Vachel than they did at me. He looked poetical. They couldn't have put a name to it, but that is what it was. But whatever it was, I could feel their aversion. They disapproved of tramps, but preferred them to poets. I could see also they didn't care for Vachel's accent, but they rejoiced in mine and spoke to me just to get me to reply so that they could hear once more the voice of the Old Country. We were clearly in the Empire and not in the Republic. The Union Jacks in the little log-cabins were wreathed with flowers.

The Stars and Stripes had disappeared. We were so struck with the change of feeling in the air that we bought ourselves a school-history of Canada and read it assiduously. The very way of man looking to man was different. Then the first popular song which sounded in our ears was:

We never get up until the sergeant
Brings our breakfast up to bed.
O it's a lovely war!

which is a purely British army song. The Englishman in Alberta is an overman in the midst of a miscellaneous foreign under-population. The Englishman's word is law. He is stronger, rougher in his language and his ways—not educated. But this sort of fibre is best suited for the outposts of Empire.

"We Americans are just a bunch of playful kittens," said Vachel.

There was nothing very playful about the Alberta pioneers.

"Did you light that fire on the side of the road a mile back? Well, you dam well go back and put it out."

"We did put it out."

"I tell ye, ye didn't. I won't waste my breath talking to you. If you set the prairie afire, I'll have you both in jail by sundown."

"All right, we'll go back."

We had not anticipated coming into the neighborhood of the Dukhobors. It was an interesting surprise. I had promised myself I would make a special pilgrimage some day to Western Canada just to find out what the Dukhobors thought about life, and how they were getting on now. And then to come on them accidentally.

The Dukhobors, or "Spirit wrestlers," are a Russian religious community brought to Canada in 1898. They claim to have been in existence in Russia for over three hundred years. They are primitive Christians akin to Quakers, but more uncompromising. They are Communists, pacifists, anti-state, anti-church, anti-law. Theologically they consider Christ as a good man and teacher, but not divine. Tolstoy's teachings show him very close to the Dukhobors in theory. He greatly sympathized with them in the persecution which they suffered at the hands of the Russian Government, and it was in part due to him, and more largely to the Society of Friends in England, that the expatriation of the Dukhobors was accomplished. Tolstoy is said to have put aside the profits of his novel *Resurrection* to defray in part the expenses of transporting the Russians. There are several thousand of them, and first they were taken to Cyprus where at least the British Navy got acquainted with them, as they were naturally a curiosity. Cyprus was not suitable, and so Canada was chosen for a habitat. The community was taken to Saskatchewan, and later migrated in large part to British Columbia. They did not find their path strewn with roses in Canada, and have had a hard time. But despite persecution they have prospered. They are notorious for a naked procession they once made "in quest of the Messiah" some forty miles in bitter winter weather, displaying "the naked truth" to the Canadians—the pilgrimage to Yorktown which has been described with much gusto in the American and Canadian Press. They have refused to take steps to relinquish their Russian nationality, refused to fight, refused to pay taxes. So naturally they have been a thorn in the side of the Canadian.

The Rocky Mountains stretching away in their majesty must remind some Russians of the grand array of the Caucasus as seen from the north—and the prairie is the steppe. Far away you discern the white and brown buildings of a settlement, and then, ten times as large as anything else, pale-blue grain-elevators. The circumambient moor is many coloured, and a dove-coloured sky is flecked with softest cloud. There are snow fences at many points of the road to protect from drifts in winter. A never-ceasing wind which brings no rain is driving over the corn-fields. As you approach the village you begin to see Russian peasant men and women working on the fields hoisting the wheat-sheaves to the harvesting carts, hoisting the sheaves to the top of the stacks. A stalwart peasant-wife in cottons stands on top of the stack, pitchfork in her hand, and she catches the sheaves as they come up to her. The grain-elevators rise mightily into vision, and then the words printed on them in large black letters—THE CHRISTIAN COMMUNITY OF UNIVERSAL BROTHERHOOD....

I thought I detected a curious homesickness among many of them. The violent rumours and persistent bad news of Russia comes to a primitive community that cannot read in a more disturbing and dramatic way than through newspapers. They complained sadly of conditions in Canada; of droughts, of plagues of grasshoppers, of bygone hardships and persecutions in Saskatchewan.

"Here there will be a Bolshevik revolution too," said one. "We shall not take part in it. But we know it is preparing. There is much discontent in the neighboring settlements and in the mines. Oh yes, there is trouble brewing here too."

This Dukhobor had been talking to brother Poles and Ruthenians, but he was quite out of perspective. I asked how the Dukhobors had fared under the Conscription Act. Apparently they did not suffer much; Canada did not trouble the Dukhobors. They had an easier time than their brothers the Mennonites in the United States. They told me there had been a considerable influx of Mennonites by way of the unguarded line: they also are pacifists and utterly opposed to personal service in war. So struck are they by what happened to them in America through the war that there is much talk of their deserting both Canada and the States and seeking a refuge in Mexico.

The Dukhobors, however, have a strong hold in Canada, and as long as Peter Verigin, their unofficial patriarch and leader, lives, they will most probably hold on to their settlements in British Columbia and Saskatchewan. Perhaps in a new era, a new Russia may again take the Dukhobors to herself. Canada does not assimilate them. And they are, and they feel, as Dostoevsky said, like "a slice out of a loaf."

We tramped from ranch to ranch by the rutty roads that skirt the sections, walked away from the mountain-walls, and ever as we went the terrain extended. The sky had become wider; no rocky walls closed us in. The backs of our necks became swollen from the unusual heat of the sun on them. We kicked up dust as we walked, dust again! Our eyes traversed the scene to light, not on cascades or possible camping-grounds, but on far-away farmhouses. We met the oats and wheat and barley fields striving over the moors, and walked till all moor disappeared, till there was nothing in front of us but gold. Made dream-like by the forest fires, the long range of the Rockies seemed unreal—the mountains which we had climbed became remote and shadowy—and not part of our destiny. Our only reality was golden Alberta, which seemed to extend to infinitude, the plateau only gradually losing its altitude, unfolding and undulating downward—one vast resplendent area of golden harvest fields.

The sun gleamed on numberless shocks on the right, on the left, and ahead, and the whole horizon was massed with newly mobilized golden armies. We walked the rutty roads and were exhilarated, and counted the wheat fields which we passed, knowing that each, being a whole section, was a whole mile long....

We boiled our pot by the side of the road; we sought milk and bread at farmhouses; we slept at night in the wheat with shocks piled on three sides of us to keep out the wind, and a broken shock underneath us to keep us soft—and the night sky above us was of swans' plumage, and all the golden stalks and stubble about us and above us were exaggerated among the stars.

Night was very different on the plains from night in the mountains. No sound of waters, no castellated peaks rising in the moonlight, no sense of vast unevenness and dissected rocks; but instead, a feeling of being in a great encampment where the swarming stocks of wheat were tents, the tents of such a host that the numbers took away one's breath. The poet rejoiced. He loved it. The odor of the yellow stalks was a new breath of life to him—for he was a prairie boy.

The dawn-twilight was long and quiet, and the mornings were serene. No workers were in sight. The disparity in numbers between men and wheat was remarkable to my eyes. In Russia, the whole plain would have been alive with the gay cottons of peasant lads and lasses. But here, harvesting machinery displaces whole populations of men and women.

Indians began to be numerous on the road as we approached the Blood Reservation: Indian farm-wagons with women and children sprawling on the hay at the bottom, and then Indians on horseback, all one piece with their horses. We left the golden grain behind and crossed the Reserve. Vachel explained what a squaw man is—a white who marries an Indian girl in order to get hold of her portion of land, the Indians of to-day being almost all of them endowed with land by the Government. We found again the Kootenai, now brawling through the plains, and bathed again, and reverted in spirit to those mountains. Then we tramped from tent to tent across the green wilderness where the Indians lived. Indian boys in many-coloured garments pranced on their horses, chased lines of cattle and horses, and kept the lines straight by galloping incessantly between them from left to right to one end of the line, and then right to left to the other end.

We met Indians in voluminous seedy clothes, walking with a stoop; men with gloomy ruminating faces who tried to avoid contact with a white man. We talked to them; they raised their red romantic faces and glared at us like owls startled by light. They could not speak English, so they answered nothing, but just turned out of our way and slouched on. Or the livelier ones made signs to us. The stout squaws stared at us. The slender girls on their horses were almost indistinguishable from boys.

What a beaten-down and untidy place a Reservation is, strewn with jetsam from the wigwam, hoofed till not a flower remains. The Indians spend more time on horseback than on foot—they can't farm, or won't farm, and possess only the roughest of comforts. We came to a Government Practice Farm where Indians were being taught, and saw squaws working there—but very little sign of decent cultivation on the reservations. The Indian asks enough on which to live. He wants no more, will work for no more. He makes plentiful use of canned foods, and lives from hand to mouth. Hence you never hear of Indian cooks. It is curious to contrast the genius of the Negro for cooking and the absence of a taste for cooking in the Indians.

After the Indians we came to the Mormons. They were as much surprised as the Dukhobors. How should Mormons be here? Perhaps we are the first to make the discovery that the Mormons have invaded Canada. These are the first Mormons to invite the shelter of the Empire. As usual, they have made their settlement in a very obscure part, far from the centre of authority. And if trouble should arise they have only to trek through the Rockies, and then Uncle Sam and Senator Snoot will protect them.

We were regaled at farmhouses by sweet Mormon brides, who gave us bannocks, who gave us of their simmering greengages out of the great cauldron on the stove. Elders on horseback very politely, and with many details, showed us the way to Cardston and the Mormon Temple. We were happily and sympathetically disposed towards the Mormons, and Vachel, who has taught the Salt-Lake-City girls to dance whilst he chanted to them "The Queen of Sheba," has a soft spot in his heart for the sect....

Cardston, which at length we reached, is largely a Mormon city. The Temple, a remarkable structure, exteriorly chaste and beautiful, dominates the scene, and the clouds rest upon it, obscuring its upper storeys in cloudy weather. It is not used for general worship; for that purpose there is a sufficiently ugly tabernacle. It is almost exclusively for the Mormon sacraments, the sealing of wives and children, and for the meditational recreation of the elders. Once the building has been completed and consecrated it will remain inaccessible to outsiders, but in order to avert suspicion, visitors are shown over it until that time. We were lucky, as the Temple is very nearly finished, and it is a rare experience for an outsider to gain access. There are only eight Mormon Temples in the world, and the rites performed therein are entirely secret.

The town is mostly inhabited by Mormons, and the great business "pull" of the sect is evidenced in the technical and structural growth of the place. The land between the city and the reservations is theirs, and also much that lies beyond. A strong propaganda for the sect is carried on all over America, and also in England and in Europe. Women converts seem especially desired. On the other hand, men of proved sincerity or simplicity are not rejected. The Mormons have land at their disposal, and they exert considerable influence on settlers and pioneers of the West. The elders help to organize business and to mormonise the community as much as possible. They can be of great help to any young Mormon starting life. On the other hand strange dooms are said to await any Mormons who give away their secrets, and apostasy is infrequent....

With that our tramping ended. We left our pine-staffs leaning against a Cardston wall. We slept in beds again and bought our coffee at a shop. Gathering prose invaded the clear blue of our poetry. Some sadness, like a shadow, settled on us. And it was goodbye to the mountains.

VACHEL LINDSAY

W HEN Vachel Lindsay (1879-1931) arrived in Toronto in December 1925 to read from his work, both the *Globe* and the *Toronto Star* considered his appearance so important they accorded it front-page treatment. This was far from the first time that the visit of a poet had received such an honour. William Butler Yeats, for example, was regularly profiled on the front pages when he visited Toronto. Today, that the arrival of any creative writer would merit front-page coverage seems a laughable possibility, given our media's page-one obsession with the shenanigans of politicians and our culture's alleged uninterest in the utterances of literary authors. Before World War Two, however, such estimable placement was regularly accorded eminent visiting British authors (of any genre) and for illustrious visiting American novelists—but rarely for American poets, no matter how distinguished. But Vachel Lindsay, internationally renowned as much for his long feats of tramping throughout the States as for his poetic work, was so famous the newspaper editors could presume that the majority of their readers would be familiar with his name.

It is difficult now to value, to obtain even a sense of how revitalizing Vachel Lindsay was for the writing world of North America at the beginning of the twentieth century:

Lindsay is to be credited with influencing American life along two more or less related fronts. He began to publish and recite his ballads and "rhymes" at a time when contemporary poetry was dying the death of standardization, gentility and dullness. The revolt that followed is generally traced to the "imagists" and free verse writers stemming from the anthology "Des Imagistes" (1914), edited by Ezra Pound, but Lindsay had a rich share in the awakening. Likewise, he was an instrument in carrying the idea of beauty out of eclecticism into the consciousness of rural America.

An adroit draughtsman, Lindsay originally studied art in New York City (with Rockwell Kent and George Bellows as classmates) before turning to poetry. He had little luck in selling either, but an experiment he conducted on the streets of Manhattan in 1905 did much to colour his thinking about the place of the fine arts in American life. He illustrated one of his own poems and had the combination printed as a broadside. Standing on the cold sidewalk, he attempted to give away the broadsides to passers-by. No one would take his poem. Then, he offered the broadsides for two cents each; there were several buyers. He felt the priorities of his compatriots had been established.

Unemployed but hardly despondent, he set off on a long walking tour of Florida, literally singing, chanting or reciting his poems for his supper. Along the way, he sold booklets of his own verses, and developed (concocted might be more accurate) a politically unsophisticated but strongly held belief in the inherent majesty of the common people of America. Vachel Lindsay quickly came to see himself as a missionary of aesthetics to these people, a hortatory tendency abetted by his superb rhetorical skills. These skills were inate, but were honed by his ability to learn from, even mimic, southern preachers. He was especially eloquent when he spoke in favour of the banning of booze.

In his several tramps across America, he could convince himself that he was coursing through, actually savouring democracy, that the mantle of Whitman was his. The naivety of his self-perception should not blind us to the augustness of what he was attempting, nor to the respectful fame he garnered: in our own time, when poetry in North America seems irrelevant to most people, seems the seduced hostage of professors, much of what Vachel Lindsay aspired to—craved—could be devoutly wished for today.

The high spirits could not be sustained. In 1931, deeply depressed and fatigued, Lindsay swallowed an entire bottle of lye, an appallingly excruciating suicide. He was only fifty-two years old.

In the summer of 1921, Vachel Lindsay strolled through Glacier National Park in Montana (abutting the international frontier with Alberta) with the English writer Stephen Graham. From the beginning, perhaps in deference to Graham's nationality, the duo planned to cross into Canada (i.e., into what Vachel Lindsay regarded as the British Empire) and explore the Waterton Lakes area of Alberta. Lindsay had walked throughout the American side of the Park before but he had never crossed into Canada. When he did so with Graham, he was shocked. The border's liberality, its freedom from the restrictions ordinarily conveyed by the term "frontier", all this meshed seductively with his own thinking, and he was to remark later on several occasions upon how ideal was that frontier between the two countries. Indeed, for Vachel Lindsay, what was interesting about Canada was not Canada (for his few descriptions of the nation betray a belief that it was nothing more than an extension of Britain), but rather the border between Canada and the USA. No other foreign author was so intrigued by that international line, as invisible, as intangible, yet as real as sleep.

Stephen Graham published in 1922 an account of their vagabond expedition titled *Tramping With A Poet In The Rockies*. The year following, Vachel Lindsay published two books: his *Collected Poems*, and *Going-To-The-Stars*, a response in verse to Graham's perceptions of the trip. In both volumes, he refers to the seductive attraction that the world's longest undefended border has upon him.

In a foreword to the *Collected Poems* he also speaks of the absence of boundaries as only an American citizen would, in that the absence of borders represents for him an idyllic freedom from the idiocies and rivalries of men. That the absence of a Canadian-American border might be a nightmare for Canadians, that the abolition of the border for Edenic reasons might just be Manifest Destiny in disguise, seems not to have occurred to him—ever.

> And it seems to me Mason and Dixon's line runs around every country in the world, around France, Japan, Canada, or Mexico or any other sovereignty. It is the terrible line, that should be the line of love and goodwill, and witty conversation, but may be the bloody line of misunderstanding. When Graham and I climbed into Alberta, Canada, from Glacier Park, Montana, we crossed a Canadian-American line almost obliterated. Every line should be that way.

In an essay in *Going-To-The-Stars* Vachel Lindsay and his wife refer to a walk they made together in the same region where Graham and Lindsay had walked earlier. Once again, he crossed into Canada but this later venture has the air of a Sunday outing about it. Far more important is Vachel Lindsay's description of the feelings he ascribes to Stephen Graham, but one suspects there is more Lindsay than Graham in these reflections:

> With even more emphasis, we thought of him as a guide, philosopher, and friend when we crossed the Canadian line on Waterton Lake. One needs a British shepherd in the British Empire. Some boundaries are guarded by soldiers or by Chinese walls. Stephen is now tramping in bristling, difficult eastern Europe, still meditating on his philosophy of boundary lines.... He is sometimes in Saskatoon, Saskatchewan, sometimes holding the hand of Lady London. There is no boundary in the world that is more the property of Stephen Graham than the Canadian, a wide swath cut in the lonely unguarded forest where any man may walk east or west. North or south, east or west in this forest, a man will find nothing but friends.

At the conclusion to his Preface to *Going-To-The-Stars*, Lindsay again refers to the path he and Graham discovered which held such theoretical weight for them both:

> On the southern side of the Canadian-United States boundary, just as we reached it, our coffee gave out. Most symbolical happening! There in the deep woods, as we passed to the northern side, Graham said with a sigh of insatiable anticipation: "Now we will have some tea." We had had tea all along, alternated with coffee. But now Stephen, on his own heath, was emphatic about it. So he made tea, a whole potful, with a kick like a battering ram, and I drank my half.
>
> Certainly, the most worth-while thing in Stephen's book, and mine, is a matter known to all men long before the books were written. That is, that a Britisher and a United Stateser can cross the Canadian-American line together and discover that it is hardly there; can discover that an international boundary can be genuine and eternal and yet friendly. If there is one thing on which Stephen and I will agree till the Judgement Day, it is that all the boundaries in the world should be as open, and as happy as the Canadian-United States line. To many diplomats such a boundary is incredible, and yet it exists, one of the longest in the world.

No evidence appears to exist that either Lindsay or Graham ever visited Saskatoon, Saskatchewan. Further recondite research in the Saskatoon City Archives might reveal a December visit. The mellifluous name of the city may have tickled Linday's poetic ear sufficiently that he felt no need to actually visit the city itself. Whatever. The following, written in November 1922, remains the only poem Vachel Lindsay ever published with Canada as its subject.

SASKATOON, SASKATCHEWAN

The Shakespearean Christmas Tree

In Saskatoon, Saskatchewan,
Shakespeare's voice seemed in the air,
And something in the prairie line,
Something in the wheat field fair,
Something in the British hearts
That gave me welcome in my need
Made my soul a splendid flower,
Out of a dry and frozen weed.

And something in the stubbly fields
And their young snow to end the year,
Brought a sob and a great wind,
Each snowflake was a frozen tear.
The sky rained thoughts, and a great song
In the Elizabethan tongue
Swept from the Canadian fields!
New broken sod, too sad, too young,
Yet brother fields to Kansas fields,
Where once I worked in sweat and fire
To give the farmer his ripe wheat,
And slake my patriarch desire,
For wheat sheaves for my eyes and arms
A satisfaction vast and strange.
And now I reaped dim fields of snow
And heard the song from the wide range.

All prairies in the world are mine,
For I was born upon the plain.
And I can plant the wheat I choose,
In alien lands, in snow or rain.
I heard a song from Arden's wood,
A song from the edge of Arcady.
Rosalind was in the snow.
Singing her arch melody,
Although the only tree there found,
In alien, cold Saskatoon,
Was heaven's Christmas Tree of stars,
Swaying with a Shakespearean croon.
The skies were Juliet that night,
And I was Romeo below.
The skies Cordelia and Lear
And I the fool that loved them so.
I shook my silly bells and sang
And told young Saskatoon good-by.
And still I own those level fields
And hear that great wind's noble cry.

SINCLAIR LEWIS

T HE FIRST AMERICAN to win the Nobel Prize for Literature, Sinclair Lewis (1885-1951) succumbed to the curse of the Nobel: he did his finest writing up to the moment he won the Prize; following the ceremony, he wrote some of his least consequential fiction. Indeed, in the opinion of most literary critics, his best prose was written within a mere ten-year period: 1920 to 1930. In the midst of this decade-long peaking of his career, a period that saw the publication of his masterpieces *Main Street*, *Babbitt*, *Arrowsmith*, and *Elmer Gantry*, Sinclair Lewis wrote yet another novel, *Mantrap*, a work that has been unjustly neglected, even forgotten, by critics, especially American critics. This oblivion ensued, perhaps, in part, because the novel is set, not in the American cities where the critics are most comfortable, but in Canada.

Sinclair Lewis made at least six trips to this country. The first (for which we have evidence) came near the end of a long camping trip Lewis made in 1916 with his first wife, Grace. Having crossed much of the northern USA, the couple, while in Seattle, decided to steam to Vancouver. Gracie Hegger Lewis, whose pet name for Sinclair was "Hal", wrote later in describing the trip:

We were excited by our sail to Vancouver and stepping on British soil. And we thought Vancouver itself—the red pillar boxes with the royal crown and the bobbies with straps under their chins, Hindoos with turbans driving vegetable carts, and Chinamen balancing long poles with baskets swaying at either end—equally thrilling. "Furrin!" said Hal.

His second stop in Canada came as part of a North American lecture tour in 1921, a tour spawned by the fame which had greeted *Main Street*, published the previous year.

On that tour Toronto was the first stop of two in Canada (the other location was Hamilton) where he spoke to the American Women's Club. His remarks at the time are revealing because they imply that he had already journeyed through the western provinces and because, in his remarks, Lewis displayed a grasp of Canadian literature not usually shared by other visiting authors at that time—a knowledge no doubt abetted by the fact that his mother was a Canadian citizen, born in London, Ontario. Indeed, Lewis was quoted by the Toronto newspapers as beginning his speech with a claim that he was "half Yankee, half Canadian" and that he regarded serious rifts between the two countries as unthinkable: "If we can't work together then, by Heaven, let us give up the game—there is no hope for civilization." This passionate exclamation was met with long applause, but Lewis, now having fed the audience some sugar fed it some bitter medicine: "I was thinking of what Canada will, but has never done in literature … I've never read anything about Canada that gave me the slightest idea of what I've seen since I came." He then trashed the bestselling novelist Ralph Connor for either distorting or even missing most of the interesting aspects of the Canadian west, claiming "the most interesting things are the tremendous changes in agriculture and industry, in the turning of the farm from pioneering to a big business." He continued,

> There are most astounding opportunities for splendid fiction in Canada, and what is required to produce it is ability and sweat, ability to see, then work, ability to see how actually interesting are the things in Toronto, in hotel and street … I cannot understand why none of your writers has yet given you stories of your

silos. What, after all, are mountains compared to them. They stand for so much. Mountains just loaf around, but silos feed the people. A silo against a violet sunset is just as beautiful as a mountain.

He concluded the specifically Canadian section of his speech by recommending Harvey O'Higgins to the audience, a Canadian author he much admired.

A return visit to Canada seems to have been in his mind almost from the time he finished his Ontario lectures in 1921. By 1923 he is writing to his literary agent describing indistinct plans for an expedition to the "Canadian wilds". In that same year, Lewis wrote to his brother, Claude:

> Do you remember speaking to me, a year and a half ago, about some expedition which goes all through Northern Canada every summer, getting entirely away from civilization, and taking two or three months to make the trip? Does it occur every year? Would there be any way in which I could go with them—they might be glad to be "written up," and of course I'd stand my share of the expenses. I live far too sedentary a life, and I'd like to do something of that kind.

A more concerted effort to prepare for the trip can be dated to January 1924. Lewis, vacationing in England, wrote to a friend, George Brown, the European representative of the CPR, about a trip Lewis and his brother, Claude, wanted to make in the Canadian north. He asked Brown for information about "an annual party sent out in Canada, either by the Hudson's Bay Company or the Department of Indian Affairs; it is, I believe, called the Indian Treaty Party Trip."

Brown, knowing that his railroad could not help (where Sinclair Lewis wanted to go, steel rails did not exist), arranged for Lewis's query to be forwarded to Ottawa. The gods must have been smiling on Lewis because his letter eventually came into the hands of the Secretary of the Department of Indian Affairs, a fellow professional writer, the legendary Canadian poet Duncan Campbell Scott. Scott handled Lewis's request personally. Had it been otherwise, Lewis would never have written *Mantrap*.

At that time the federal government, no doubt partly because of the formal nature of the encounters, and allegedly from a desire to shield the natives from what it regarded as contaminating contact with the southern world, refused virtually all non-essential requests from outsiders to accompany Indian Agents on their annual forays into Indian country. It was on these visits, for example, that the Agents dealt with legal matters that had arisen among the natives in the previous year. It was also on these trips that the Agents conferred on the Indians the pitiful sums obligated by the treaties. That an outsider, unfamiliar with the territory, would be a liability for an Agent on such a trip was a given, but that an outsider with absolutely no experience of the North—or natives—would be allowed on such a trip was too silly, too dangerous even for serious contemplation. Yet Duncan Campbell Scott used his authority to authorize just such a trip, perhaps with the hope that Lewis would write a flattering account of northern Canada for one of the large-circulation American magazines, or would write a romantic northern tale *à la* James Oliver Curwood.

Sinclair Lewis was to prove no Curwood, being neither an adept outdoorsman nor a chronicler of the joys of the wilderness.

From the first of their correspondence, Duncan Campbell Scott took an avuncular interest in the Lewis brothers' trip, his concern ranging from philosophical advice on how they could best savour the land and experience the real North, to the picayune choice of fly repellant. In between were recommendations on how to select the right canoe, tent, motor, and, not least, counsel on the hiring of several Indians who would paddle for the Lewises and carry most of their gear during portages.

The brothers boarded the train from their hometown of Sauk Center, Minnesota on June 5, 1924, headed for Winnipeg. Eventually they were supposed to meet the Indian Agent, William Taylor, travel to the end of steel at Big River, Saskatchewan, and then begin their formal journey by canoe. But before then, Sinclair Lewis had arranged to give public lectures or talks in a number of prairie towns.

On June 6th, arriving in Winnipeg from Minnesota, he was greeted "by a Mr. Parker, Secretary of the local Kiwanis Club and a photographer from the *Free Press.*" Alas, the photos taken by the newspaper seem not to have survived. The *Winnipeg Free Press* interview with Lewis does survive, however, in the form of an excellent article, followed by an account of Lewis's speech on "British and American Relationships" given to the Kiwanis at the Fort Garry Hotel. After the speech, the author toured the city in the company of a local bookseller before returning to his room at the Royal Alexandra Hotel for a night of serious boozing with more reporters and apparently numberless hangers-on.

On June 9th the pair headed for Regina where Sinclair would happily wallow in the trio of hard drinking, public speeches, and newspaper interviews. After lunch at the Assiniboine Club ("Of course, the elite were all there—two Generals, two Colonels, three judges, a Major, a Captain, etc. You'd have thought it was a council of war.") they explored the town of Regina before Sinclair spoke at the Trading Company's banquet hall. One trusts the hall was large enough to accommodate the clubby throng, for the lecture was held under the joint auspices of the Women's Canadian Club and the Regina branch of the Canadian Authors' Association with guests from the Rotary Club, Kiwanis Club, and Men's Canadian Club also present. The speech out of the way, Claude reports in his journal,

> At 11:30 p.m. we dropped in at a Mr.—'s house on the way home for a drop of Scotch. Harry [Sinclair Lewis] sure has a good nose for it. This province is dry and all these judges and generals who raise cain with the common people about liquor seem to have a large supply on hand.... Everyone was rather languid the next day.... But we had to be up and about for we were invited to the barracks of the Northwest Mounted Police for 10 a.m.... Major Duffis, the commander in charge, showed us all the wonderful

horses and had some of his men do stunts for us. You'd have thought the Prince of Wales was on an inspection tour.

Regina proved deliciously distracting for Sinclair Lewis. He was wined and dined so seductively that he extended his stay, even though this meant the Indian Agent, already cooling his heels waiting for the duo, had to postpone the departure of his entourage for the North.

From Regina, the brothers took an overnight train to Saskatoon, arriving on the morning of June 13, 1924. They were billeted for the day in the home of Dr. A.L. Lynch. Lewis was scheduled to speak at the King George Hotel, but an announcement of the speech in the local newspaper suggests that these Prairie speaking engagements were rather hastily organized, and may have been the author's subconscious way of delaying the actuality of his trip to the North (where alcohol would be scarce):

> As the luncheon is being arranged on short notice, members are requested to be sure to get their tickets tomorrow if possible and so help the executive. They will be on sale at Pinder's Drug Store and at the cigar stand in the entrance of the Canada Building.

From Saskatoon, Sinclair and Claude Lewis travelled by train to Prince Albert, Saskatchewan, arriving in the evening. Claude Lewis reported:

> We landed here at 10:10 and had thought that no one knew we were coming. Sad mistake. The town representatives were all there and conducted us in great state to the hotel. Then they all piled into the room and a booze party began. This lasted until about 12:30 when I went up to bed and the crowd finally had sense enough to go home.

For the next few days, the Prince Albert hotel room became Party Central: visitors and well-wishers without end, and drinking fiestas well into the small hours of the morning. Interspersed among the bouts of liquid camaraderie were a noon-hour talk to the Rotary Club, a gala dinner and speech to the Kiwanis Club, and a round of golf with His Worship, the Mayor of Prince Albert.

Finally, their wilderness escapade could be delayed no further, and the expedition departed on June 18, 1924. The group took a slow freight from Prince Albert bound for the railhead at Big River, from which point they would canoe for the remainder of the voyage. Bill Taylor (the Indian Agent) and Claude Lewis each had a canoe with a motor and two Indians, while Sinclair Lewis, in a canoe with two natives but no motor, was towed by his brother. The Indians in Sinclair's canoe spoke no English, and he spoke no Cree; as the trip progressed, the inability to converse must have become more tiresome by the minute.

Sinclair Lewis's impression of the aboriginal helpers is in stark contrast to that of his brother. Claude, in his account of the excursion, consistently speaks of them in the highest terms ("I should have thought those Indians who rowed or paddled all day would have been dead, but they were as bright and cheerful as ever."). His brother, however, conveyed, in his fiction, at least, a different reaction:

> [He] had been brought up on the Fenimore Cooper tradition of Indians. He expected all of them to look like the chieftain on the buffalo nickel, like the statue which in all proper parks stands between Goethe in marble and General Sherman in bronze—a sachem eagle-nosed, tall, magnificently grave. His heart was pinched as he saw shambling toward them four swart and runty loafers…. They did not look in the least like lords of the wilderness engaged in watching, under lean shadowing hands, the flight of a distant eagle. They looked like undersized Sicilians who had been digging a sewer, and their only human expression was their supercilious, self-conscious grins. Feathers and blankets they wore not, but rusty black suits from the cheaper kind of white man's back-street shops. The one sign of

Indian art was their moccasins and one hectic bead belt displaying the Union Jack.

For Sinclair Lewis, the trip seems to have started well, although with pathetic fallacy, the expedition, on its first day of paddling, had to stop early because of contrary winds. As the Agent wanted to take advantage of the long daylight hours in the north, the group, when the weather permitted, would arise at four or five in the morning, breakfast quickly, then canoe until nine at night, a formidably long day.

Their route took them to Lac la Plonge and then to Lac Ile-à-la-Crosse, where they paused for a week's rest. Lewis used the occasion to write to his publisher on June 30th:

> The trip is going beautifully. I've already quite lost my jumpiness, my daily morning feeling-like-hell; I haven't had a drink for eleven days and haven't missed it in the least. I don't *have* to do any work at all—the Indians do that—but I paddle enough to get a lot of exercise. The ground no longer feels hard to sleep on, and I wake at four, ready for bacon and coffee, with great cheerfulness. I shoot *at* ducks; catch pike; and listen to the agent's stories—he is a delightful fellow, knows the wilds, and has a sense of humor. All goes beautifully....

Their next stop was Wapachewunak, followed by portaging and paddling on several lakes that were part of the Churchill River system.

Somewhere between Ile-à-la-Crosse and a Hudson Bay Post known as Stanley (which they reached on July 11th), Sinclair Lewis decided he had had enough, and he told his brother and the Agent that at the next main stop, Pelican Narrows, rather than travel farther north with the group to Reindeer Lake, he would abandon the expedition and head south for the Saskatchewan River. On the Saskatchewan he could catch a steamboat to The Pas, and then train to Winnipeg and home. His brother, Claude, whose journal indicates that he, at least, found the entire trip marvellous, tried to persuade Sinclair to remain with the trek, but Lewis was unrelenting in wanting to escape south. By July 26th he was back in the Manitoba capital, and shortly thereafter, in Minnesota.

Although he telegraphed a positive report to his family and friends ("Weather fine and party is ahead of schedule and I have cut off last loop of trip so am back at railhead feeling superb real rejuvenation.") the month in the wilds of Canada left Sinclair Lewis shocked and confused. Shocked, because like the Babbitt he had mocked in an earlier novel, Lewis himself had been proven naive about the cleansing power of Nature; confused because the demons he had thought were a product of "civilization" were as prevalent in the wilderness as they had been in New York and Europe.

There is no solid indication that Lewis, prior to his departure, intended to write a novel based on his Saskatchewan and Manitoba adventure. And the complexities of his responses to the trip meant that months would have to elapse before he could sort out those responses and shape them into a novel. But within two years, his perceptions digested, he published *Mantrap*, a novel which had modest sales, the sales aided, no doubt, by the release of a successful film version within a month of the book's publication. The film was directed by Victor Fleming (better known for having directed *Gone With the Wind* and *The Wizard of Oz*) and starred Clara Bow in what many consider her finest performance.

From the point of view of Canadian literary history, Lewis's 1924 trip to Saskatchewan was the most consequential. However, Sinclair Lewis did make one other significant trip to Canada.

In October 1929, the month of the stockmarket Crash, Lewis came to Toronto for about ten days to cover the annual convention of the American Federation of Labor. For almost a decade, Lewis had wanted to write, as his magnum opus, a great novel about the working class. Despite this professed desire, his research for the novel had been lackadaisical, marked mostly by occasional and very brief trips to mill towns where he would gather bits of dialogue or record his first impressions. But a chance to witness at close hand the machinations of American labour was too tantalizing an opportunity for an author determined to write the real story of the labour movement. So Sinclair Lewis happily accepted an invitation from the United Press wire service to report on the convention.

The convention was held at the Royal York Hotel in Toronto. At the table reserved for the media, Lewis met Carl Haessler, a journalist covering the convention for a labour wire service known as Federated Press. The two men took an instant liking to each other, and over a drink in his hotel room, Lewis described his labour-novel-to-be to Haessler. Indeed, recognizing in Haessler someone who could give him continual inside access to the world of the working class and to the labour movement, Lewis impetuously offered Haessler a contract as his advisor. Given that Lewis was hiring Haessler to do labour, the terms, of course, had to be generous: their contract, penned by Lewis on the spot on Royal York letterhead, offered Haessler one hundred and fifty dollars a week, plus expenses, for a trial month and, if both parties were happy, then the same terms each month until the research was completed plus five per cent of the royalties from the novel.

Haessler and Lewis toured the northeastern quarter of the United States for about five weeks, but by Christmas 1929 Lewis's enthusiasm for exploring mill towns, much like his previous enthusiasm for exploring the Canadian wilderness, had altogether evaporated. His Great American Labour Novel would never be written.

Nineteen twenty-nine was also the year in which Sinclair Lewis wrote to his nephew about the Canadian novelist Morley Callaghan:

> Are you and your fellow geniuses watching the work of Morley Callaghan ... along with that of Ernest Hemingway? I should think that these may be the children who will kick me off my chair of honour in a few more years. Callaghan seems to me particularly to have a really authentic power to making his impressions of life—mad life or lugubriously sane life—completely vivid.

Lewis made two other brief visits to Canada, both to Toronto. In late February 1939, he appeared at the Royal Alexandra Theatre as an on-stage commentator in the play *Angela Is Twenty-Two*, a play which was, he claimed (with a poor grasp of arithmetic) "three-quarters Canadian" because he co-wrote it with the Canadian-born actress Fay Wray. The play, including Sinclair Lewis's performance, received lukewarm reviews during its week-long, pre-Broadway run. While in Toronto, Lewis also took time to endorse, by his very public presence at its rehearsals, a left-wing theatrical group, and to give warm praise to a Canadian playwright since forgotten, Brian Doharty.

His final visit to Canada came in December 1943. He appeared for a one-night stand with the Jewish scholar and novelist Lewis Browne in a staged debate on the topic "Is Machinery Wrecking Civilization?" The pair were touring the continent with the debate, which, by the time it reached Toronto, might have been stale. The reviewer for the *Globe and Mail* stated otherwise:

> For two months the writers have publicly debated this topic across the United States, and their style rejects the prepared argument in favour of the quick parry and thrust of witty ad libbing.... For almost two hours the writers who in private life are fast friends slugged verbally at each other with no quarter asked and none given, while the audience chuckled at their sallies.... Who won? Nobody seemed to know or care, least of all the debaters.

The excerpt below is from *Mantrap*, the novel that more than any other by Lewis has been misunderstood by critics. Because *Mantrap* had been written by Lewis, one of the foremost writers in America, the reviewers, American reviewers especially, were discreet in veiling their disappointment in what they thought was an ordinary love story with a western setting. Academic critics who wrote later were not so discreet; most have dismissed the novel as the worst, or next to worst book which Sinclair Lewis ever published.

Today it is hard to fathom how their readings could have been so wrong. *Mantrap* was published immediately after the appearance of three Lewis books which the critics agreed were masterpieces. And *Mantrap* was immediately followed by *Elmer Gantry*—which they also agreed was a masterpiece. Yet their critical responses to *Mantrap* give no hint that they questioned their first, negative impressions of the book. They seem to have believed that an author of ferocious talent, having produced brilliant satires one after the other, merely stumbled badly (but temporarily) by writing a western romance (which they thought was not a satire)—only to regain his equilibrium immediately thereafter with one of the most influential satires of the twentieth century. The opinion makers were American, but the novel's setting was Canadian, and it was this difference which blinded them to the now obvious reality that Lewis intended *Mantrap* to be as much a satire as *Babbitt* or *Elmer Gantry*, that Lewis intended to eviscerate the myths propogated by his furiously despised rival on the bestseller lists, Zane Grey.

When the book was published in 1926, Zane Grey had been the king of the bestseller lists for some time. Lewis, miffed that a writer he regarded as his inferior should outsell him, constantly quizzed his agent and publisher about where he stood on the bestseller lists *vis-à-vis* Zane Grey.

If Zane Grey in his books, like Fenimore Cooper before him, wished to portray natives as Rousseau's Noble Savage, then Sinclair Lewis in *Mantrap* ensured that the Indian's all too human frailties would be brought to the fore. In a formulaic Grey novel, the dude from the eastern states would inevitably be ennobled by his brief exposure to the splendours of the West. In Lewis's novel, the easterner's experience of Nature in the west is not ennobling at all but disheartening: the weather is cold and rainy, the ground becomes harder the more the fatigued paddler wants to sleep, and the mosquitoes never relent. In a Grey western, the effete easterner goes west to be transformed into a Real Man by following the example of the Real Men bred by the West. In *Mantrap*, the American protagonist, fearing he may be a sissy, enters the wilds of Saskatchewan craving transformation, only to find that the supposedly tough Canadians sleep in silk. As one of the backwoodsmen says:

> When I come here first, a real eastern swell with an extra shirt, I started teaming, then trapping, before I got into the wicked wiles of trading. Well, at first, I certainly did want to be a real, hard-boiled, dyed-in-the-wool roughneck. So I used to sleep in my pants, even on hot nights. But—well—tell you—here's how it is ... my friend, summer nights, I wear pajamas, especial' when I'm out on the hike. And they're silk pajamas, friend, and I'd rather give up my bow-man ... than give up the nice pillow I've lugged around for five years! ... I travel just as soft as I can.

Sinclair Lewis also had reconfirmed in Canada the knowledge that the West did not transform women into the noble beings who peopled Zane Grey's novels. So, in *Mantrap*, the lead female character is even more morally dissolute in the wilderness than she ever was in the city. Indeed, Lewis has wicked fun with Zane Grey's pedestaled view of women: where the formula western would culminate with a shoot-out between two men for the love of one splendid woman, *Mantrap*, at its conclusion, has the two male leads come together, not to kill each other, but to have a polite conversation where each agrees to save the other from a woman whom, they realize belatedly, is a shameless flirt.

Had Lewis set his satire in the American West, these lampoons of myths central to the American imagination would have been clear to American critics. But the Canadian setting—so different in texture and colour and climate and population from American models—seems to have completely disoriented the reviewers, and rendered the academic critics blind. Nearly sixty years have had to elapse before the purpose—and the burlesque power—of the novel have come to be seen.

In the following excerpt, Ralph Prescott, an American businessman, is trying to flee from northern Saskatchewan with the help of

an Indian guide. Ralph is fleeing because he has eloped with
Alverna, the wife of Joe Easter, a Canadian backwoods trader.

---

from MANTRAP

It had taken them all one day to make the three-mile portage behind
Mantrap Landing, behind Moose Mountain, to the Ghost Squaw
River.

Lawrence Jackfish had at first refused to go with them. He had
been won by a promise of two dollars extra a day, and for two dollars
a day, which meant ever so many red shirts and red silk handkerchiefs and cigarettes and mouth-organs, Lawrence would have committed murder—several murders.

But if he continued as their guide, he was not their servant; and
his yellowish eyes peeped at them, his crooked teeth leered at them,
till Ralph thought with relish of using an axe when Lawrence's back
was turned.

All afternoon they panted on the hot secret trail.

It was a foot-wide path through pine thickets. The air was lifeless
as in a shuttered and abandoned house on an August afternoon.

Following Lawrence, who carried the upturned canoe on his
shoulders, Ralph toiled with such a load of flour and bacon and
blankets as he would never have believed himself able to lift. He was
not walking—he was merely putting one foot before the other, endlessly, forever, with a separate effort of his will at each step. He was
not alive. All of him was dead save scorching shoulders, wrenched
small of his back, and plodding feet. He was a quarter aware that
behind him, carrying almost as large a load as his own, Alverna was
panting. But it was only when he had laboriously revolved the

thought in his cloudy brain for ten minutes that he came to life sufficiently to suggest: "You've got too much to carry, child. Put down part of it, and we'll pick it up later."

"No," she said, breathlessly but stoutly. "I'm going to do my share."

He pitied her, the white and golden moth fluttering in a cobweb, but he was too paralyzed with fatigue to do anything about it. The most spirited part of his cerebration was the fear that some one, crossing over the mountain from Mantrap Landing, should see them and bring a raging Joe down upon them.

As to whether he was virtuous in rescuing Alverna, or vile in treachery to Joe, or maddeningly both at once—such frail philosophies could not make themselves heard in the torment of his toil.

If they could but get this portage done, if they could be joyfully away, in the freedom of the racing rivers, the wide and desolate lakes—

He learned to trot the back trail burdenless, like Lawrence, when he returned for another load, and behind him he heard Alverna forlornly pattering through the dry pine needles. He did not look at her, but he felt her comradeship.

They labored till the late dusk. Then only they boiled the kettle and, with fingers stiffened into hooks, devoured their bacon and bannock. Lawrence withdrew a little, and Ralph was happy in sitting with her by a low fire, coals glowing in a hollow of glittering quartz sand. He had never supposed that she could display such brilliant and lucid and endearing silence. And treacherously that silence drifted into sleep.

Ralph woke bewildered. The spell of slumber was like an eiderdown quilt over his head, and fumblingly he thrust it aside. In the light of ash-filmed coals, under the thin mistiness of northern midnight, Alverna was curled in stillness and Lawrence was snoring in his blankets, under a mosquito-bar. Mosquitoes. Ralph realized dully that it had been nothing more romantic than a mosquito which had roused him.... Then he perceived that Alverna was looking at him. Though her cuddling childish body had not moved, it seemed to him that her eyes were open. She was very near him, they two alone.

She peered at him drowsily and rolled into his arms.

His hands gripped her sides, then remained cramped and unmoving, not daring to move. A thousand times he had wondered, a thousand times pictured himself gallant in love. Now he worried, over and over, "What does she expect me to do?"

Terror, sheer terror and incapacity for life, began to shadow his embarrassment. He wanted to escape from her.

The fire was low. He had more imagined than seen her. But her shoulders were close to his eyes now; her sailor blouse was gaping, and torn with toil on the portage. Terror and anxiety vanished from him as he irresolutely kissed the hollow beside her collar-bone. He awaited a second for her indignation but she sighed and moved closer. She said nothing save a slow sighing "Oh, my dear!" and he forgot all the world of Ralph Prescott.

They were on the portage again at dawn; and by noon, with relief so profound that their panting was like the sob of wailing women, they teetered into the canoe and slowly paddled up the Ghost Squaw River.

There were two more portages, immediately, but they were short; they were almost luxurious. And then for the first time Ralph took his share in shooting rapids.

Though their general direction was up-river, they had cut across the curves of an S in the current, and for two miles they went down-stream. Thus it was that the Ralph who a few days ago had shivered before rapids found himself shooting them and depending not on guides but on his own muscle, his own nerve.

They came to Ghost Rapids, silently, ignoring their peril.

Lawrence took the bow. He stood there, pointing with his paddle at the one inevitable way through the welter of rapids. Where Ralph would have steered to the right through an apparently even current, Lawrence read the cryptic manuscript of the water and directed him to a crazy zigzag left, then right, left again, and straight ahead, almost grazing a fanged rock.

It was Ralph's hour of test. Without for a moment ceasing to be afraid, he was steady at the steering paddle, abrupt at wrenching the canoe from side to side, all the while cursing hideously under his breath.

Suddenly they were in the last gush of the water, the bow of the canoe leaping five feet in the air, while Ralph chewed his lip. As suddenly they shot into the calm water beyond the rapids, and in relief Ralph sighed above his lifted paddle, so that Alverna looked back in wonder, and Lawrence loosed his hissing snicker.

For a week there was a nightmare of portages and snaky creeks up which they had to pole, of mosquitoes and the inferno of endless paddling; and Ralph's only solace was the unbroken gallantry, the smiling kindness of Alverna, as she took her turn at the paddle, as she plodded on the portage, as she sat by the camp-fire, her lacerated little hands twined about her knees, in a mud-smeared garment which had once been a white linen skirt.

He had courage because she believed that he had courage. When she slipped a trusting hand into his and murmured, "You've been so wonderfully good to me!" he was rewarded for his labor.

As he watched her sleeping, under wretched and insufficient blankets, in the cold nights which swooped down after the panting sun-drenched days, his dry heart blossomed in tenderness.... To think that he had once esteemed people because they understood Goossen's music or James Joyce's fiction, because they wore sleek clothes and were clever at the use of forks, because they could set up wooden words as a barricade against roaring life!

Tenderly he covered her with his own blanket, and lay shivering under a tarpaulin. And in the morning when side by side they washed their streaky faces in the chill water of a northern lake and their cheeks stung with sudden life, they smiled at each other and intelligently said nothing at all, and Ralph Prescott was no longer a cautious forty-odd, but twenty and aware of all romance.

Now this was their route, set down for any lunatic who shall of his own will leave wife and lawn and sheltered porch and stagger from Whitewater by the back way to Mantrap Landing, or from Mantrap dolorously to Whitewater.

By the Ghost Squaw River and Ghost Rapids and Bucking Rapids, up which they poled, with that chastening feeling of leaning out over the side of the canoe and wondering how soon the pole will slip and you will flop into the river, then by portage to Lost River, a portage half of sun-broiling rocks that were torturing to moccasined feet and half of swamp reeking with vast mosquitoes poisonous to sweaty neck and straining wrist, they came on Pike Lake. For five miles they sailed there more luxuriously than Cleopatra and Antony in scarlet-pinioned caravels.

Ralph marveled that he could ever have felt uneasy in a sailing canoe. By contrast with portages and the ache of paddling, to loll in the shadow of the bending sail, to feel the breeze on his scorching cheeks, to hear Alverna softly singing, yet all the time to be on their way, each moment safer from the menace of Joe Easter's fury—this was a heaven he had never known.

Another portage, a reeling madness of five miles through thickets, and they came again to the openness of Thunder Bird Lake. But there was no breeze; they had to paddle all the shoreless and blistering plain of that dead expanse. And then, slowly, they perceived and acknowledged a danger.

Ralph had wondered at the persistent fogginess of the air in full sunshine. The shore was indistinct; the sun was a red ball at which he could stare undazzled; and the sun's reflection was a necklace of rubies on the pallid ripples of the pearl-gray water.

He looked back from the bow. "Getting foggy," he suggested.

"Yeh. Forest fire some place—smoke," said Lawrence.

"Forest fire? Near us?"

"Don't know. Maybe."

"I noticed it quite a while ago. But I guess it's pretty far off," Alverna made pretense. "Smoke will carry hundreds of miles."

Ralph had forgotten his fear of Joe's pursuit. But new danger stirs the imagination, and now to the travail of sixteen toiling hours a day was added a desperate wonder as to where the forest fire might be, and when they would burst out in a horror of arching flame.

And there was nothing he could do about it. He must go on. He was as helpless as though he were on a steamer in mid-ocean.

Where once he would have thought only of saving his own hide, he thought now of Alverna. Lawrence Jackfish might burn like a pitch-pine torch, and welcome; but if they should be caught by the fire (he pictured it, slowly, painfully, his mind dulled by paddling) he would protect her; he would cover her with his jacket, souse her in the lake…

Their chart showed that they were to pass from Thunder Bird Lake to Lake Midnight—the largest body of water on their route— by way of Weeping River. Here the streams turned southward. They would go downstream, and Ralph hoped for swift and easy passage to Lake Midnight.

They camped at the beginning of the Weeping River, in a sunset of crimson clouds murky with the impalpable smoke. The sun was red-eyed and irate as it set; the dusk was thick; and over the whole world was a sense of brooding fate.

They were wearily silent when they rose next dawn. There was no freshness in the air, and somberly they started down Weeping River.

It started out promisingly enough, with a gush of brown water between sandy banks monotonously lined with low willows. But the river became so shallow that the canoe scraped the sandy bottom. Presently they had but three inches of water, littered everywhere with rocks over which the canoe had to be lifted, in terror lest it be slashed beyond repair and leave them abandoned, starving, in the wilderness.

Instead of darting down a pleasant stream, they made less than a mile an hour, wading in slippery pools, tugging at the canoe. Alverna was still plucky, but her face was drawn, and Ralph bore all her suffering with his.

Mosquitoes joyously clouded round them, more portentous in their venomous insignificance than the black-winged fates.

"We'll have to give it up and hit cross-country for Lake Midnight. Looks here on the map as if we could get across to Mudhen

Creek, which flows into Midnight ... Course the map may not be right. So much of this country is unexplored," said Ralph.

"All right. Let's," said Alverna, listlessly.

But Lawrence Jackfish said nothing at all, and Lawrence scowled, and Ralph wondered: "What's he thinking? What's he planning to do? How long can I make him take orders?"

They did, in fact, reach Mudhen Creek, and so came at last on the open waters of huge Lake Midnight. But the history of that passage would be a confused and unchroniclable nightmare. Ralph could never put it together; never determine whether they took three and a half days or four and a half from Weeping River to Lake Midnight. The portage to Mudhen Creek was a delirium of quaking muskeg which let them down to drenched knees, of swamps crawling with scum, of brush which slashed their unprotected faces as they staggered with their loads, of airy mosquitoes singing their contempt, of persistent bulldog flies circling round and round their eyes, lighting and circling again, with a *zizz* which made the lords of creation shriek like lunatics, broken as they were with weariness.

And the cloud of smoke from the forest fires was over them always, but that menace had become as distant as Joe's possible pursuit.

They began to admit their shortage of food. It was Alverna who had the courage to speak of it.

Not always had Ralph plodded beside her in ecstasy. Before breakfast coffee and in the strain of the portage he had often been irritated by her humming, her trick of pushing back her hair, the cruelty with which she split infinitives, and her bland supposition that everything which was not fierce or awful was either cute or nice. But these annoyances scarce rose to perception in his mind. For her strength and patient courage he had such affectionate admiration as he had once given to Joe.

"We got to start starving ourselves," she blurted. "Hardly enough grub to last us down Lake Midnight. The map says there's a trading-station near the south end of the lake. Once we hit it, I guess we'll be on a real good trail, and we can get some grub there. But our stuff has to last— Maybe we better cut it down to two meals a day now, and one a day pretty soon."

"I suppose so," sighed Ralph.

Bacon thrice daily had come to be all of his concept of heaven that was not comprised in Alverna.

"Hey, you, Lawrence, don't hog so much bannock! We got to go slow," Alverna observed, as sweetly as possible, but the Indian scowled.

To piece out the larder, they stopped at every swamp which promised a pickerel. But there were few fish, and the long delays made the fear of approaching forest fire more lively.

So hour by day-long hour they lumbered through swamp and muskeg and thicket, blind and mute, and when at last they came through a cool birch grove and found Mudhen Creek, Alverna stood weeping with relief, her face smeary as a muddy child's, and Ralph was too frayed to feel relief, too tired even to comfort her.

But after an hour of swift paddling down the Mudhen, helped by the current, on their way to Lake Midnight now, on their way to sailing and sacred food, his spirits rose and they two smiled again.

But they were so hungry!

At a pool below shallow rapids in the Mudhen, Ralph flung in his trolling-hook and drew in, hand over hand, a ten-pound muskalonge more beautiful than the silver doe of heaven. They lit a fire, but scarce waited for the fish to broil; they tore at it half cooked, black-handed savages, and when Ralph gave Alverna his bit of better-cooked fish, it was his one heroism in life.

He was sure now that their toil was over—but he was not quite sure that he was sure. When the Mudhen flowed into the magnificent stretches of Lake Midnight, apprehension once more gathered round him.

There was a sinister look to those cruel waters. He understood the name of Lake Midnight when he saw that vasty stretch, the color of a bottomless spring. The lake was smooth enough; it reached out in a floor of black marble. But to venture on that frowning immensity in a canoe was like risking open ocean.

"Looks tricky, somehow. And no islands for shelter. Wonder if there's many squalls on it?" Ralph meditated. He kept his worry from Alverna.

There were squalls.

A breeze lifted before they had paddled half a mile. But it was a fair wind and they had to use it. Ralph was relieved that Lawrence kept as close to the east shore as possible, but that was not particularly close, for the shore-line was broken by many indentations. They were never more than a mile from land, Ralph calculated, yet they might as well have been a hundred. Neither he nor Alverna could swim half a mile, if they capsized, and the chicken-faced Lawrence would not try to save them.

Was it really only a mile to those distant trees, that secure beach? Ralph gazed to south, to west—a hundred and twenty miles it was to the south end of the lake, and to the west shore, forty. From the low plane of their canoe, the swart vastness of Lake Midnight was more engulfing than the round of desert.

He played with these thoughts and put them from him. He could not afford now the luxury of being timid; and when Lawrence suggested that they land and boil the kettle, though being ashore would provide half an hour of surcease from the feeling of danger he snapped: "No, go on. Wind may change."

They were, their map asserted, more than halfway to Whitewater and the high civilization of Bert Bunger's hotel when they camped that evening on the shore of Lake Midnight.

They had for supper only bacon and milkless tea.

When Ralph rose, a little after four, and came out rubbing his sandy eyes, the world was a mystery of fog. Only a patch of gray lake was visible, motionless except for faint etchings of ripples. He felt the vigor of the damp fog. The earth seemed new, recreated in a doubtful youth, and but for the specter of Joe, he would have rejoiced and felt ready for any venture.

He grew conscious that something was wrong with the scene, something very wrong, something missing. There was no canoe turned properly upside-down on the beach. There was no canoe anywhere. Nor was Lawrence Jackfish in sight, under his mosquito-bar.

"Lawrence! Lawrence!" Distress gave awe to his voice.

Alverna appeared at the flap of their tent, tousled and sleepy.

"What is it, Ralph?"

"Apparently Lawrence and the canoe are gone. Oh, probably he's out on the lake, to catchum fish for breakfast. You can't see far in this fog."

She stared; she hastened to the tarpaulin which covered their stores.

"No. He's skipped out for keeps," she said resolutely. "He's taken all our grub except a little flour and a quarter of a pail of lard and a teeny bit of tea. He's taken everything. He expects us to die here."

WALLACE STEGNER

"I ESTIMATE that I missed becoming Canadian by no more than an inch or two of rain," Wallace Stegner sagely remarked in an essay recollecting his youth in Eastend, Saskatchewan, a village near the border with the United States. "My family homesteaded on the Montana-Saskatchewan border in 1915, and burned out by 1920, after laying the foundation for a little dust bowl by plowing up a lot of buffalo grass. If the rains had been kind, my father would have proved up on that land and become a naturalized citizen."

Wallace Stegner (1909-1993) is one of America's greatest novelists. He was also—more than any other American author—consistently the most perceptive about Canada. That such intelligence evolved from a mere six-year residence in Saskatchewan (when he grew from a five-year-old child to one aged eleven) is testimony not only to his remarkable powers of observation as a novelist, but also to the powerful hold that the Prairie had in forming his sense of self. Saskatchewan, he would later write, "is the richest page in my memory."

Born in 1909 in Iowa to a father forever chasing rainbows and the quick buck without having to work for it, Stegner, in adulthood, could recollect little of his childhood until he arrived in Canada. His father, far from downhearted by the failure of his previous get-rich-quick schemes in America, was convinced that homesteading in Canada provided just the ticket for instant wealth. Despite understandable misgivings, Mrs. Stegner, with her two young sons in tow, in late spring 1914, joined her husband in Eastend, in the new province of Saskatchewan, to become, they hoped, wheat farmers extraordinaire. Events conspired against them. But their half-decade residence in Eastend marked their longest residence as a family in any one place; hitherto, twelve months in one spot had seemed an eternity. "I used to think that I was shaped by motion," Stegner wrote in a memoir recollecting Eastend, "but I find on thinking it over that what most conditioned me was … where we stayed long enough to put down roots and develop associations and memories and friends and a degree of self-confidence." Later, he was to reconfirm Eastend's importance to his life and to his writing career: "The years during which I participated in the birth of that town were the shaping years of my life. I have never forgotten a detail of them." Stegner was perceptive enough about his own writing to grasp that the primitive surroundings of Eastend determined, in some ways, not only what he wrote about, but also the manner, the style in which he wrote. When the American historian Richard Etulain asked Stegner why he described himself as an old-fashioned novelist, Stegner replied,

I felt like a nineteeth century anachronism, and I still feel a little that way. I really don't belong in the twentieth century; I grew up in the nineteenth century, even though it was technically on the calendar as the twentieth. What I was growing up in was 1914 Saskatchewan, but in its development, it was about like 1860 Kansas. I never literally—you won't believe this, Dick— but I never saw a water closet or a bathtub till I was twelve years old. I never saw a lawn until I was twelve years old. It never occured to me that people lived with such grace.

Among his many fond descriptions of this formative place is this, in which Wallace Stegner recounts his arrival:

Eastend when we arrived was the Z-X ranch house and a board-inghouse for the crews building the grade for a Canadian Pacific branch line down from Swift Current … Within a few weeks, when the rails were laid, the town grew by several derailed box cars, old Pullmans, and a superannuated dining car. We lived the first winter in that dining car, considered pretty classy. Later we lived in a rented shack. After two years, my father built a house and a small barn down in the west end, on the [Frenchman] river.

In this pioneer setting, Stegner learned to swim, fight, shoot, fish, trap, and lead what seems, in retrospect, to have been an enviable Tom Sawyerish existence. But for the new kid on the block, his five-year-old American past was catching up to him:

Around Christmas we all watched the first soldiers go off to war, and then and afterward we had trouble with Canadian kids who said the United States was too yellow to get in the fight. They had a song for us:

> Here's to the American eagle
> He flies over mountain and ditch
> But we don't want the turd
> of your goddamed bird
> You American son of a bitch

My brother, who was big for his age, and tough, fought every kid his size, and some bigger, in defense of America's honor. But we were ashamed, and we got an instructive taste of how it felt to be disliked for tribal affiliations that we hadn't really known we had.

Despite these occasional schoolboy reminders of his roots, by the end of his stay in Eastend, so pervasive was the influence of Canadian schooling, a Canadian home, and Canadian neighbours, Stegner concluded, "I wasn't sure whether I was American or Canadian."

The family had two residences in Eastend: rooms in town where

Wallace Stegner, second from right, seated at a swimming hole in Eastend, Saskatchewan. From the age of five until he was eleven, Stegner lived in or near this prairie town. "The years during which I participated in the birth of that town were the shaping years of my life. I have never forgotten a detail of them." Photo courtesy of Mary Stegner.

they wintered for nine months of the year, and a shack, as of 1915, where they summered on the acres the elder Stegner had purchased as part of his homesteading dream. The immigration (or, depending upon one's politics, the invasion) by those of European ancestry was so new, so recent, Stegner's plough, and the ploughs of his neigh-bours, as late as 1915, were the first to break the sod in those sections.

In interviews, in essays, and in his fiction, Stegner reveals again and again that the years in Canada were among the happiest of his life. So influential were those years, they inspired three books set wholly or in large part in Saskatchewan: *On A Darkling Plain* (1940), *The Big Rock Candy Mountain* (1943), and *Wolf Willow* (1962). The latter two are masterpieces.

Taking its title from Matthew Arnold's poem "Dover Beach", *On A Darkling Plain* is not among Stegner's finest works, although the novel is laden with several redeeming aspects. The author would later say to an astute critic that it was "psychologically naive". But Canadian readers, especially, will be struck by its brilliant descriptions of the prairies: the climate, animal life, and sky that make that countryside so unique, so dauntingly addictive, are here described with unashamed respect, even love.

Edwin Vickers, the hero of the tale, is a veteran of the Princess Pats and battles at several renowned sites, including Vimy Ridge. Having been gassed in the trenches in the penultimate year of World War One, he eschews returning to his home in Vancouver (and the sophisticated literary life he had formerly led there), in order to find himself—and to find the meaning of life—by living alone on a homestead in previously unfarmed southern Saskatchewan. Within a day of his arrival, Vickers finds that he cannot survive on the prairie without the aid of a neighbour, and in describing the need for this neighbourly succour Stegner inherently declares for the first time in his oeuvre his revisionist belief that the West, far from being a place of rugged individualism, is too brutal, too big to allow for anything but mutual reliance. This bold contradiction of a reigning myth would become a hallmark of Stegner's ruminations about the West, typical of the contrary thinking that would make him such a seminal theorist.

The Big Rock Candy Mountain is Stegner's largest work of fiction. Despite its size and its mastery of storytelling, the novel is disgracefully under-celebrated and undervalued in eastern North America and abroad. As an aesthetic construct, it is addressed mainly to Stegner's reconciliation with the ghost of his foolhardy, shiftless, overbearing and sovereign father. But the book's allegiances to Stegner's own life mean that the Saskatchewan chapters are among the novel's most engaging, and, when the family's hopes fail, are among the most heartbreaking.

In none of his other novels does the weather play such a crucial role as it does in *The Big Rock Candy Mountain*. The reader, conscious of the fate of the crops if rain doesn't come, holds his breath with Bo Mason and his family as they search the sky, and pray, and, initially, at least, are rewarded:

> Things greened beautifully that June. Rains came up out of the southeast, piling up solidly, moving toward them as slowly and surely as the sun moved, and it was fun to watch them come, the three of them standing in the doorway. When they saw the land east of them darken under the rain Bo would say, "Well, doesn't look as if it's going to miss us," and they would jump to shut windows and bring things in from yard or clothesline. Then they could stand quietly in the door and watch the good rain come, the front of it like a wall and the wind ahead of it stirring up dust, until it reached them and drenched the bare packed earth of the yard, and the ground smoked under its feet, and darkened, and ran with little streams, and they heard the swish of the rain on roof and ground and in the air.

Deeply affecting as this novel is, its sense of place can sometimes confound the Canadian reader. There are, for example, occasional references that indicate the family is in a country other than the USA. And the narrative point of view shifts dramatically: until the family reaches Canada, the narrator is principally the mother. But as soon as the family reaches Canada, the narrator becomes Stegner's alter-ego, the child Bruce Mason. But the differences between the histories of the two nations, and differences between the character of the citizenry are rarely remarked upon by Stegner. When they are cited, Stegner describes them in the novel as akin to the dissimilarities that merely differentiate states within the Union rather than mark national attributes. Stegner later confessed that at the time he wrote *Big Rock Candy Mountain*, "It hadn't occured to me that there was a difference between the American West and the Canadian, and I knew very little." However, within two decades he was to know a great deal, and distilled that knowledge of history about the Canadian West—and knowledge of how to write—into the breathtakingly superb *Wolf Willow*.

Stegner was later to recall that he could not pinpoint when it was that he began to be interested in the history of the Canadian West as something specifically different from that of the American West. His best estimate placed the first rumblings of curiosity in the 1950s. Commencing his research, he soon discovered that there was little hard information available with which to satisfy his inquisitiveness:

> The more I got interested the harder I had to hunt for sources. I went back to the town and went through the whole file of town papers carefully, photographing a lot of them, bringing them home for further study. There was a paper that ran consecutively from 1914 to … I don't know, whenever I was up there in the fifties.

His curiosity about the history of Eastend and the surrounding territory was spawned by a desire to learn something about his own past. But the history of the area was so exciting, so affecting, he started to research aspects of that history for its own sake, regardless of its immediate relevance to his own life. His researches became formidable, and it wasn't long before Stegner realized that just as his father had been among the first to break the ground on their prairie homestead, he was breaking new ground in the formal study of Western Canada. In 1980, Stegner reviewed the effect of his contributions, including a 1978 conference at Banff that is now regarded as having been seminal for academic study of the West:

> I wouldn't be at all surprised if one of the reasons why historians are commenting on the differences between the Canadian and American Wests now is that I told them to. I don't ordinarily say

things about myself that way. But going up to that conference in Banff shocked me almost ... how much *Wolf Willow* was the beginning of a tradition. I hadn't really thought I was the Herodotus of those hills, but I obviously was.

In addition to bringing a novelist's breadth of vision to his perceptions and descriptions of southern Saskatchewan and Alberta, Stegner also brought a wealth of pithy insight. For example, in contrasting emigration patterns to the Wests of the States and Canada, he adds almost by way of aside, "It's interesting to note that most of the Canadian prairie provinces were settled not by covered wagon but by train."

Wolf Willow takes its name from the plant prevalent throughout southern Saskatchewan. When Stegner returned to Eastend in the fifties for the first time since he had left it at the age of eleven, he was struck immediately, like Proust by madeleines, by a smell which catapulted him into the past. "I couldn't figure out what the smell was. It took me two days to find out. I ate leaves of every shrub in the valley, I think, before I found the right one."

Despite this introductory essay's emphasis on Stegner's connections to the West, the attentive reader of his work will quickly discover that he is not a regional writer. Quite the contrary. "Quality is a whole lot more lasting than regional piety," is just one of his exhortations to fellow Westerners. At a time when too many reviewers and publishers across Canada wallow in, even relish, their blinkered parochialism, boasting endlessly that their neck of the woods is unique, such is its awesome wealth of literary geniuses, Stegner's intelligence about the role of place in a definition of aesthetics is more salient than ever:

I'm a Westerner to the extent that I think I'm entitled to write about the life I know and that that life is as legitimate a life as the life of anybody. I resent the condescension [from the East] that often happens. On the other hand, I don't think you can just go around resenting condescension. For one thing, you're very likely to get into a kind of mode and overvalue yourself and overvalue anything from your region. Somebody, because he or she is local, is likely to look good to you, and that's not at all safe … I don't want to become a guru for any regional movement. I really don't believe in it.

Apart from his few months at Eastend doing research in the fifties, Wallace Stegner lived in Canada on only one other occasion: for the 1973-74 academic year he was the Claude T. Bissell Professor of Canadian-American Studies at the University of Toronto. Arriving in the city when nationalist feeling was still soaring, Stegner was surprised to discover that the feelings of Canadians about the USA were almost identical to the feelings held by western Americans about the power centres of their eastern seaboard. The adjective "almost" is crucial however, for it is typical of Stegner's widsom that he could detect, even after just a few weeks in Canada, subtle, essential variations:

> Part of the charm of regionalism is that it permits us to disavow the industrial civilization, the zoo cities, the eastern arrogances, the anomie and malaise of our country. So do Canadians with respect to the United States, conceived as a monolith. Just as they do not always recognize how large a component of regionalism there is in their nationalism, so they don't always realize that in their local patriotism and their feelings towards the sources of power and domination, they sound almost exactly like an American province. But it would not do to tell them too bluntly, for what they do not want to be is anything American…. It is actually extremely instructive to see some of one's own dilemma acted out in another place by another combination of people…. I have rebelled against the influence of aspects of America that were antipathetic to me and the region I felt I belonged to. I have resented the cultural and economic colonialism forced upon the West by the East: no Canadian could have resented American domination more. I have felt that if America was the last best hope of earth, as it started out to be, then the West was the place

where the worst mistakes might be avoided and the best of the promises paid off. The average Canadian feels the same way. He feels more moral than Americans, and he has a lot more faith in his country than most Americans can generate.

On a couple of occasions, Stegner would make remarks that are heart-stopping to a Canadian nationalist. To Canadian journalist Douglas Fetherling, Stegner said during his stay in Toronto, "The western US and western Canada share so much and, as with the rest of the two countries, the similarities, I think, are more interesting than the differences." Twenty years later, he said to journalist Paula Simon, "The international boundary is a kind of artificial line." Are such comments damning evidence of a will to Manifest Destiny, evidence contradicting what he said earlier about the differences between the Canadian and American Wests? Stegner claimed not. Indeed, in a splendidly intelligent essay written while he was living in Toronto in 1973, Stegner took pains to explain the context of his criticisms of Canada:

> I don't want to infuriate anyone; and although I will defend the United States on most counts, even in the deplorable year 1973, I don't come as a Yankee freebooter bent upon annexing Canada. If there was ever a Manifest Destinarian in me, he exhausted himself on the way West, and doesn't operate north-south. Moreover, my loyalties are mixed, for I spent a half dozen of my most impressionable years on a Saskatchewan homestead.... So if I say something detestable, please remember that I am trying to speak simultaneously from within and without the family. I am an American visitor but also I am a kind of knot-headed country cousin, more to be pitied than censured, and more to be loved than reviled.

The essay addresses cunningly and with sophisticated discrimination the differences between the literary evolutions of the United States and Canada. Since Canadian nationalism was fervid, even white hot when Stegner wrote his essay, his perspicacity was nearly matched by his courage. While some of his comments were cast directly at issues of the day, his more general conclusions in the essay resonate today with the same loudness and clarity that train whistles do at night-time country crossings.

Except for one paragraph, which he himself recognized as paradoxical, certainly provocative:

> I feel completely at home in the Canadian literary climate, even when its winds get shrill. I could be enlisted as a b.b. calibre Lafayette. Nothing in New York or Detroit, or for that matter in Mississippi, tells me anything about my identity or my roots. As I said in *Wolf Willow*, I came back to Saskatchewan looking for those roots; and what Saskatchewan did not put into me, Montana and Utah and California did. I am content to have my world citizenship rooted in the West, though I don't want to be just a regionalist—and I will now risk outraging some of you by saying that it doesn't much matter whether the West means Canadian or American. I don't see much difference.

In his lifetime, Wallace Stegner won practically every literary award his country could bestow. In his descriptions of Western life, he was one of the first writers to portray the lives of adults other than cowboys, Mounties, gunslingers and sheriffs. As a creative writing teacher based in the West he counted among his students, and had large effect on the early writing of, such currently renowned writers as Larry McMurtry, Ken Kesey, Tom McGuane, Edward Abbey, Robert Stone, Raymond Carver, Tillie Olsen, and Philip Levine. Without doubt, Stegner was the leading role model for several generations of authors coming to maturity in the West. The distinguished Canadian writer Sharon Butala is passionate and forthright in delineating Stegner's importance to her and other authors of the Prairie:

> Was he a great man? For the children of the West, Wallace Stegner was the father of a new dream, a new vision. He took a

clear-eyed look around him and said, "This is the West, and this and this and this." And he was right, and he articulated it for the first time as it really is, he created it, and gave us the right to settle in with a sigh of relief, that all those things about our country we had known in our bones and that coursed through our blood were real and true and a part of us.

We are not a failed Europe, a failed East; we are a new society mired in the muck and struggle and relentless wonder of nature, and we are the first generation to see ourselves as such, to push away the understanding of this place that came from Europe and the East and, as a society, in what looks like ruin and despair, to begin to recreate ourselves as we ought to have been in the first place, as Wallace Stegner saw that we might be and hoped against hope we would be. That is greatness.

Wallace Stegner looked at Canada with an erudition fostered by decades of study, formal and informal, noting with irony the similarities of the two nations, but wisely, as well, noting their differences. He saw them, like the hemispheres of the brain, parietal, superficially identical, divided into regions, but underneath, saw, too, that each thought discretely.

------

from WOLF WILLOW

The Cypress Hills discovered that they had a history when the Old Timers' Association of Maple Creek planted some historical markers in 1942. In coming first to Fort Walsh they acknowledged that this was the true capital of the first stage of that frontier. In the old post cemetery, where the police graves were identifiable but the civilian ones a scramble of unmarked mounds, they erected crosses, and where they knew, they placed the appropriate names: Clark, Dumont, LaBarge, Quesnelle, McKay, Chief Little Bird—white, *métis,* Scotch halfbreed, Indian. From the graveyard they moved on to plant a cement monument where Abe Farwell's post had stood, and another where the wolfers and the Assiniboin had fought across Battle Creek. The foundations of Farwell's post were still faintly discernible after nearly seventy years, but the battlefield they could locate only through the memory of an old *métis* who as a boy of eighteen, in 1880, had kicked up human bones while herding the police beef herd on that ground.

Once discovered, history is not likely to be lost. But the first generation of children to grow up in a newly settled country do not ordinarily discover their history, and so they are the prime sufferers from discontinuity. If I, for instance, wanted a past to which I could be tribally and emotionally committed, I had to fall back on the American Civil War (my grandfather, whom I had never seen, had fought in it), or upon Norway (my maternal grandfather and grandmother had emigrated from it). Being a mama's boy, I chose Norway, which made a real hash of my affiliations. All through my childhood I signed my most personal and private books and documents with the Norwegian name that my grandfather had given up on coming to America. It seems to me now an absurdity that I should have felt it necessary to go as far as the Hardanger Fjord for a sense of belonging. I might have had—and any child who grows up in the Cypress Hills now can have—Fort Walsh, and all that story of buffalo hunter, Indian and halfbreed, Mounted Policeman and wolfer, which came to its climax just here.

The very richness of that past as I discover it now makes me irritable to have been cheated of it then. I wish I could have known it early, that it could have come to me with the smell of life about it instead of the smell of books, for there was the stuff of an epic there, and still is for anyone who knows it right—perhaps for some *métis* or Cree, a descendant of Gabriel Dumont or Big Bear or Wandering

Spirit, who can see the last years of the Plains frontier with the distance of history and with the passion of personal loss and defeat. Often as it has been summarized, no one has properly told the story of the defeat of the Plains people, a people of many tribes but one culture. Fort Walsh saw its last years. This was where some of the last hopes flickered out and the irreconcilables gathered in hope of a last stand: Canadian Indians and American Indians, Cree and Assiniboin and Blackfoot who belonged, and Sioux and Nez Percé and Gros Ventre who fled here because of the Medicine Line and because here were the last of the buffalo. A way of life extremely rich in human satisfactions both physical and spiritual came to an end here. From their headquarters at Fort Walsh, a little over a hundred redcoated men patrolled its final agonies. A few years after it was essentially over for the Indians, the *métis* who lived by the same skills and were shaped to a similar habit of life broke out in their own final desperation, drawing with them some of their Indian relatives, and that could be another epic.

All of it was legitimately mine, I walked that earth, but none of it was known to me. I wish our homes or schools had given us stereopticon slides of Fort Walsh's old log stockade with its inward-facing buildings, its officers' and non-coms' quarters, its powder magazine, its blacksmith and carpenter shop, its thirty-horse stable, its kitchen, bakery, guardroom, quartermaster's store—all of it whitewashed clean and shining in the valley under the jackpine hills. I wish I had seen the Union Jack obeying the prairie wind from its tall pole, and heard the commands of drill and parade in that compound, and seen how competition among the troops brought out the spit and polish. They made full-dress parades in red coats, white helmets, pipe-clayed buckskin breeches, glittering boots. Sometimes, when a man was immaculately prepared for competition, his comrades carried him across the parade ground for fear he would get a wrinkle or a fleck of dust on him.

We were not informed in school that the graces of imported civilization first appeared here at Fort Walsh: amateur theatricals, pets, music, sports. Saskatchewan's first play, *Dick Turpin*, was acted by constables who had been out on patrol to pick up an offender called Four Jack Bob, and who barely had time to throw Bob in the guardhouse and get into their costumes before the curtain. The pets were young antelope, baby buffalo, a Canada goose who sat on a rock and alerted the guard when men sneaked in late from a pass, and who finally made the mistake of chasing an Indian dog, which killed him. The music was provided by men from F Troop, transferred from Calgary after Fort Walsh was made the headquarters of the force in 1878. The band died a riotous death, and one oddly incongruous with the traditional discipline of the Mounties, when its members, celebrating a British victory in Afghanistan, were betrayed by Commissioner Macleod's special issue of grog, and began beaning one another with the instruments.

The games, like the parades, often had the ceremonial full-dress quality that is reputed to keep men British in a far land. It must have been a rather remarkable sight to see cricketers and tennis players in white flannels walking across the compound, or bare-kneed constables and sub-constables lining up for a scrum at rugger. Sometimes they enlisted *métis* and Indians in their games, and educated them in how to take a rough body block or a kick in the shins without going for a knife. Sometimes they went out to meet the inhabitants, and raced horses against them outside the stockade. They kept an eye on sun dances where youths who had made a vow tore themselves from boyhood into manhood by hurling themselves against rawhide thongs threaded under their breast muscles. At Christmas or New Year there might be a banquet, even a dance. Outside the walls a village of three hundred families, mainly *métis,* had assembled by the late 1870's. It boasted a hotel, a restaurant, a log pool hall, a barber shop, and even a photographer's shop, for whose presence any historian has reason to give thanks. In the valley ringed by its timbered hills there might be at any time several hundred Indians. As the buffalo grew scarcer and hunger came as an unwelcome guest in the lodges, the hundreds grew into thousands, for whatever the Indians had coming to them by treaty was distributed here, and if new treaties were contemplated, this was where they would be discussed, and if non-treaty Indians wanted to beg a share of the dole, this was the place one begged in.

They were of many tribes, and their simultaneous presence might mean trouble either because of hereditary hostilities, or because of competition for the remaining game, or even because of the never quite quiet threat that they might ally in hostility against the whites. From Fort Walsh the Mounties patrolled south as far as Kennedy's Crossing on the Milk River, near the present hamlet of Wild Horse; and east through a chain of detachment posts to Wood Mountain. Disregarding Isaac Cowie's burned Hudson's Bay Company post, my home town dates from 1879, when Sitting Bull and his Teton Sioux made their winter camp on its site among the bends of the White-mud. They were the first recorded inhabitants. That same winter, Walsh established a detachment post on the site of Cowie's cabins. Later we saw the chimneys of the police cabins sticking up through the grass and chokecherry bushes near the other line of chimneys from the old *métis* village when we went berrying in Chimney Coulee. It would have offended our Fenimore-Cooper-trained sensibilities to know that they were the relics not of savagery but of law.

Still, I wish we had known it. I wish we had heard of the coming of the Sioux, when they rode northward after annihilating Custer's five troops on the Little Big Horn, a whole nation moving north, driving the buffalo before them, and with the soldiers from every army post between Canada and Texas on their track. In December, 1876, there were three thousand Ogalalas, Minneconjous, Hunkpapas, Sans Arcs, and Two Kettles camped near White Eagle's hundred and fifty lodges of Canadian Sissetons on Wood Mountain, and these were not all. Sitting Bull was reported to be on the Red Water, south of the Line, with a large band of Tetons, and there was a big band of agency Sioux, Yanktons under Medicine Bear and Black Horn, at a place called Burnt Timber, below where the Frenchman crossed the forty-ninth parallel. These agency Indians too, though technically responsible to the authorities at Fort Peck, on the Missouri, had made sounds of wanting to cross the Line.

I wish somebody had told us how the tough Irishman Walsh,

friendly to Indians but a realist, a good policeman and absolutely
without nerves, rode in upon the camp of the first three thousand
hostiles on Wood Mountain. With twelve men he rode through a
fringe of warriors some of whom carried carbines wrenched from the
hands of Custer's dying cavalrymen, past a horse herd many of
whose horses and mules wore the United States Army brand, among
lodges where American scalps still hung drying in the smoke, and in
a meeting with White Eagle, Black Moon, Spotted Eagle, Little
Knife, Long Dog, and their surly warriors, he told them how they
would behave if they wanted to stay in the Great Mother's country.
They said they were tired of war and wanted peace. Fine. They
would do no injury to man, woman, or child; they would steal nothing, not so much as a horse; they would not fight, either among
themselves or with the Canadian Indians; they would not hide
behind the Medicine Line for the winter and then go raiding down
south as soon as the prairies dried, they would not ever hunt beyond
the Medicine Line, and they would smuggle no ammunition over it
to their friends.

How bold a speech, how sublime a faith in the rightness of the
Canadian occupation and the strength of Canadian law, considering
that these Indians had hardly cooled from a bloodletting of white
soldiers unmatched since Braddock's defeat, and that the police,
outnumbered thirty or forty to one, had no chance of help nearer
than several hundred miles. He told them the rules and they said they
would obey: White Eagle, the Sisseton, had told them that the White
Forehead Chief was a man of his word. They asked, almost humbly,
for ammunition to hunt the buffalo, which they were forced now to
lasso or to kill with lances made of knives bound to poles. Almost as
if he possessed the power he assumed, Walsh granted to Jean Louis
Legaré, the Wood Mountain trader destined to escort Sitting Bull
back to captivity five years later, the right to sell the Sioux ammunition they could have taken by force any time they chose.

Later in the spring of 1877 Walsh repeated his lecture to fifty-
seven lodges of Tetons under Four Horns, whom he intercepted just
as they moved into Canada along the Frenchman. The Tetons were

not as amenable as the first camp. One of their number persuaded them that Walsh could not be trusted, and they held him and his scouts in camp until messengers could be sent to confer with the Yanktons down at Burnt Timber. Next morning Medicine Bear and Black Horn and two hundred warriors painted for war poured across the Line and up to the Mud House Ford ready to revenge upon their own people any harm that might have come to Walsh. The nameless Teton who had called Walsh a Long Knife spy slid away in the excitement of the speech-making, and so saved his scalp.

Not too many days after that, Walsh repeated his lecture for the third time, this time to Sitting Bull himself, who had encamped with his band of Tetons near Pinto Horse Butte, between Wood Mountain and the Cypress Hills. He got from Sitting Bull the same answer he had had from Spotted Eagle and Four Horns and Long Dog. They were tired of war, they wanted to make their homes in the Great Mother's country, they would keep the peace.

Having clamped the lid on the kettle before it had a chance to boil, Walsh and later his replacement, Inspector L.N.F. Crozier, had to keep it on. The Sioux were not the only American Indians wandering north of the Line in 1877. Two months after Sitting Bull crossed over, there came a big encampment of South Assiniboin under Crow's Dance. They announced their arrival by roughing up a small camp of Canadian Saulteaux and demanding that the Saulteaux join them and submit to their hunting rules. Instead, the Saulteaux chief Little Child went to Walsh, and Walsh with seventeen men went directly to the camp of Crow's Dance.

Arriving early in the morning, he left the surgeon and three men to build a barricade on which the others could fall back if a fight started. Then he and the other thirteen went into camp, entered the lodges, came out with twenty-two chiefs as prisoners, and bluffed their way out to the barricade, from which they stood off the Assiniboin frenzy without firing a shot. Crow's Dance and Crooked Arm, the head men, spent some months in a Mounted Police jail. The rest learned what the Sioux had had the wit to accept early: the law applied to everybody.

It kept the Mounties busy applying it. Time after time a handful of constables and scouts had to pluck horse thieves or stolen horses out of the midst of threatening clots of warriors. The daughter of the trader at Wood Mountain had the experience of being held with a knife at her throat while her Sioux captors demanded flour from her father, and her father stood with a pistol at the head of a powder keg threatening to blow them all up if the Sioux moved. Who made the move, finally, was a group of Mounties and ex-Mounties who burst in and threw the Sioux out—a procedure for which Walsh himself had set a precedent when he once threw Sitting Bull out the door, seizing the great man of the Sioux nation by the scruff and the seat and pitching him out in the dirt and then defying the furious stir of rage and threats until it subsided.

Through the almost five years of the Sioux visitation, from the end of 1876 to the summer of 1881, the Mounted Police kept the lid on, throttled the whiskey traffic, rode thousands of miles on patrol, noted in their patrol books the passage of every stray Indian or white or *métis*, every stray horse, every unfamiliar brand. When, in August, 1877, word came that the Nez Percé were headed for the Line pursued by General Howard and General Gibbon, Walsh had warning speeches to make to the aroused councils of the Sioux with all the war chiefs present. They were hot to start south to help the Nez Percé and have another go at the American cavalry. Walsh reminded them that if they went they would not be back; under those circumstances they would find the red coats hunting them as the blue coats hunted them now. The Sioux stayed. But when the refugees from Chief Joseph's long-running battle limped in, wounded, exhausted, stripped of everything but horse and gun, there was more need for Walsh's iron hand. He again calmed the angry Sioux, and he gave the Nez Percé sanctuary and his lecture on Canadian law. They were White Bird and ninety-eight men, fifty women, and about fifty children, the battered remnant of a tribe that their conqueror General Miles called "the boldest men and the best marksmen" he had ever known. They had been friends of the whites since Lewis and Clark first met them under their other name of Chopunnish. Half Americanized, some of them Christians, house-dwellers, farmers, they had been cheated and abused until they made one of the last, the most desperate, and certainly one of the most heroic of the Indian revolts against the system that was destroying their life.

The heartbreaking Nez Percé refugees were not likely in themselves to add to the police burden. They were simply, like the Sioux and Gros Ventre and Assiniboin that kept drifting in, part of the ethnic junk heap that was piling up between Wood Mountain and the Cypress Hills as the Plains frontier worked toward the end of its first phase. But their condition so infuriated the Sioux, who were still powerful and capable of war, that there was constant fighting talk, and when Walsh brought word that General Alfred Terry and an American commission wanted to confer with the Sioux at Fort Walsh, it took all the prestige Walsh had, and all his argumentative persistence, to persuade Sitting Bull to attend. He would come only on the assurance that he had the protection of the Mounted Police, and he would promise nothing.

With twenty chiefs, Walsh left the camp near Pinto Horse Butte, and midway between there and Fort Walsh, probably near the bends where the Frenchman eased out of the Hills and where my town would later stand, they met Commissioner Macleod coming from the west, and they camped and feasted together. I know how that October river bottom would have looked and smelled with the skin lodges and the willow fires and the roasting meat—the smells of autumn and the muddy banks, the Indian Summer pungency of drying leaves and rose hips, the special and secret smell of wolf willow, the glint of yellow and red leaves shaking down over the camp in a chilly night wind. It is an actual pleasure to think that their boots and moccasins printed the gray silt of those bottoms where my bare feet would kick up dust years later. I like the thought of them camping there, great men of their time and kind, bent upon an errand that would bring other great men from below the forty-ninth parallel, including correspondents from the New York *Herald* and the Chicago *Times*. Except for Henri Julien, who had accompanied the Mounties on their march west in 1874 as artist and correspondent for the *Canadian Illustrated News,* those were almost the only newspapermen who were ever lured to our Hills by anything.

The conference for which Sioux, red coats, and American officers assembled at Fort Walsh on October 17, 1877, was one of the briefest and least productive in history. There was one meeting. General Terry offered the Sioux amnesty, reservations, cattle, and allotments, and suggested that they had better come on home. The Sioux rose one by one and said that the Americans were liars, that they had never kept a promise, and that the Sioux would be fools to believe them now after having been cheated and deceived so often. They ironically introduced the squaw of Bear That Scatters, a move that in itself was an insult, since women did not sit on Indian councils. The wife of Bear That Scatters had been coached in a short speech. The Long Knives, she complained, were not giving her time to breed. She would like to stay here and have some children. The chiefs, for their part, said many times that they would not go back, that they wanted to be Canadian Indians. They shook hands many times with Macleod and Walsh, and wrapped their robes around them when it might have been time to shake hands with General Terry or his commissioners. So the commissioners gave it up and went home, and the Sioux stayed around Fort Walsh and made themselves sick on plum pudding and other items that Macleod had brought over for the occasion.

But the Sioux were not, whatever their desire, Canadian Indians, and Walsh and Macleod had to tell them so. They were not entitled to payments under any of the seven treaties which Canada had made with the tribes, and when others came in for treaty money the Sioux were left out. In 1877 there were still plenty of buffalo along the Frenchman, but by 1879 they were almost gone, and when starvation began to look in the lodge flaps of all the Indians on that border, it looked longest and most hungrily in on Sioux and Nez Percé. By persistent tactics of never dealing with Sitting Bull as head chief, but undercutting his power by consulting others, Walsh and Crozier whittled the great magician of the Tetons down to smaller and smaller size, and by 1880 had whittled away more than twelve hundred of his followers and persuaded them to return to agencies south of the Line. On July 11, 1881, Sitting Bull and his last supporters, quarreling over a few bags of flour and bitter at what they had been brought to, started out from Willow Bunch with Louis Legaré, and made their scarecrow march southward through the whitened buffalo bones. A week later they met Captain Clifford at the place now called Plentywood, Montana. The day after that, the gates of Fort Buford closed behind them and their guns were stacked in the yard and the Plains Indians were done.

Fort Walsh was almost done, too. It had never been a healthful site. Unexplained fevers swept it and its satellite village; the water from Battle Creek, polluted by buffalo and horse carcasses in the swamps above, brought typhoid into their tin cups and canteens. And two great movements of history, one just closing and one about to begin, united in persuading the police that another headquarters would serve them better, and that even as a post Fort Walsh should not be maintained. After the starving winters it became clear that reservations farther north, in the fertile belt along the North Saskatchewan, would provide more chance for farming and Indian self-sufficiency. More than that, the Hills were too close to the border. However successfully the police might deal with Sitting Bull's exiles, they were never able to control the horse-stealing that went on in both directions across the Line, and it seemed sound policy to move the Canadian Indians far enough north so that they would neither be tempted to raid, nor be tempting objects of raids from the American side. Finally, the Canadian Pacific was building very rapidly west, and one of the major police jobs of the new era would be protecting the men who were doing the building. By the winter of 1882, headquarters had been moved to Wascana or Pile o' Bones Creek, on the CPR main line, and the city that was being built there and called Regina after the queen. In May, 1883, Fort Walsh was dismantled and as much of its building material as could be salvaged was hauled to Maple Creek, on the railroad, to be used in building detachment posts there and in Medicine Hat, farther west on the

South Saskatchewan. From the Maple Creek post, patrols could still ride the trail south to Kennedy's Crossing, or east to Eastend, Pinto Horse Butte, and Wood Mountain.

The wild and dangerous frontier had gone out like a blown match. Instead of taming wild men in wild places, the Mounted Police would increasingly find themselves protecting civilized men in places rapidly becoming tame. As for the Cypress Hills, only a little more than a decade after Cowie moved cautiously into them they lay all but empty from Medicine Lodge Coulee to Eastend, cleared of their grizzlies and elk, their flanks swept clean of buffalo, their ravines and valleys emptied of Indians. Only a few transitional figures remained. Abe Farwell, now ranching on a tributary of the Frenchman near where it flows out of Cypress Lake, was one; several Mounted Policemen who had served their terms and taken their allotments of land, certain *métis* who had squatted along the creeks, certain hide hunters who had seen the handwriting on the wall, made a thin and scattered population. Little by little, in the next twenty-five years, cattle would replace the buffalo, some of them whiteface and "shorthorn"—meaning anything not a longhorn— and some of them ringy old longhorns driven all the way up from the Rio Grande to stock the northern ranges. There would be room in the history of the Hills for one cowboy generation, and like its earlier counterpart it would be made up of many kinds: drifters from the American Plains all the way from Texas to Montana, Irish immigrant boys, venturesome English youths with too little self-control or too many elder brothers, made-over Mounties, French aristocrats, *métis* squatters, reformed whiskey traders. They would have this kingly range to themselves until 1906, long after nesters, barbed wire, and weather had pinched off the open-range running of cattle in the States.

I wish I had known some of this. Then, sunk solitary as a bear in a spider-webby, sweaty, fruit-smelling saskatoon patch in Chimney Coulee on a hot afternoon, I might have felt as companionship and reassurance the presence of the traders, *métis*, Indians, and Mounties whose old cabins were rectangles of foundation stones under the long grass, and whose chimneys crumbled a little lower every year. Kicking up an arrowhead at the Lazy-S ford, I might have peopled my imagination with a camp among the bends of the Whitemud and had the company of Sitting Bull, Long Dog, Spotted Eagle, Walsh, Macleod, Léveillé—some Indian Summer evening when smoke lay in fragrant scarves along the willows and the swallows were twittering to their holes in the clay cutbanks and a muskrat came pushing a dark-silver wedge of water upstream. I knew the swallows and the muskrats, and was at ease with them; we were all members of the timeless natural world. But Time, which man invented, I did not know. I was an unpeopled and unhistoried wilderness, I possessed hardly any of the associations with which human tradition defines and enriches itself.

I have sat many times all alone just inside the edge of one of the aspen coulees that tongued down from the North Bench, and heard the soft puffs of summer wind rattle the leaves, and felt how sun and shadow scattered and returned like disturbed sage-hen chicks; and in some way of ignorance and innocence and pure perception I have bent my entire consciousness upon white anemones among the white aspen boles. They were rare and beautiful to me, and they grew only there in the dapple of the woods—flowers whose name I did not know and could not possibly have found out and would not have asked, because I thought that only I knew about them and I wanted no one else to know.

Those are most peaceful images in my mind. I don't know why, remembering them, I think of Marmaduke Graburn. Perhaps because his grave lies under the same sky, with the same big light and the same quiet over it; perhaps because he died in such a coulee as this, and died young.

In 1879 he was nineteen years old, a rookie sub-constable recently recruited in Ottawa, a boy with an itch for adventure and a name that might have come out of a Victorian novel. Graburn Coulee, back of Fort Walsh a few miles, is the name the maps now give to the draw where he rode alone after an axe he had left behind, and was followed and shot in the back of the head by Star Child, a Blood

Indian with a grudge. He died alone and uselessly, the victim of brainless spite. *Métis* trackers led by Jerry Potts and Louis Léveillé found first the tracks of his shod horse where they were joined by two barefoot Indian ponies, then his pillbox forage cap beside the trail; then his body, dumped into a ravine. He was not the first Mountie to die on the job. Others had died of fever, or gone under in the quicksand of rivers, but he was the first to die by violence. In their first five years, from the beginning of the march from Fort Dufferin to the time when Star Child raised his sawed-off fusee behind the unsuspecting boy in an aspen-whispering coulee in 1879, the Mounted Police had neither killed nor been killed. Merely by the unusualness of his death young Graburn demonstrated the quality of the force to which he belonged. They had come to the Cypress Hills in 1875 to smother a hornet's nest. In 1883 they left the Hills pacified and safe, almost as peaceful as when I wandered through the coulees with a .22 and found nothing more dangerous than cottontails and anemones, or a lynx that might have been the product of my yearning imagination.

NOTES

  2 "heroic adventurers": My thanks to Robert McGhee of the Archeological Survey of Canada for his thoughts on the importance—then and now—of the Fifth Thule Expedition.

  4 "but was thinking in Inuit": Edmund Carpenter, telephone conversation with Greg Gatenby, March, 1993.

  29 "the same short stretch of track": See my introduction to Jack London in Greg Gatenby, *The Wild Is Always There,* 148 ff. For a discussion of contemporary newspaper accounts of Davies' accident, see Richard Stonesifer, *W.H. Davies: A Critical Biography,* 236, n. 28.

  45 "*The Frozen Deep*": See my introductions to Wilkie Collins and Charles Dickens in Gatenby, *The Wild Is Always There,* 297 ff. and 295 ff.

  49 "than anything imaginable": Belloc to Mrs. Reginald Balfour, 9 March 1923, *Letters from Hilaire Belloc,* ed. Robert Speaight, 135.

  50 "two sides of the border": Belloc, 135.

  54 "critique of British manners": J. Balteau et. al., eds., *Dictionnaire de Biographie Francaise,* vol. 6, 723.

  63 "I don't know yet": Lloyd C. Douglas, "Impatient Idealists," in *The Empire Club of Canada: Addresses Delivered to the Members During the Year 1942-43,* 258.

  63 "sermons were a success": Virginia Douglas Dawson and Betty Douglas Wilson, *The Shape of Sunday,* 220.

  64 "business when they feel like it": Dawson, 10.

  64 "to say nothing of the whiffle": Dawson, 290. Douglas visited Toronto in November 1932 to give a sermon at Deer Park United Church. While in the city his Canadian publisher Thomas Allen took Douglas to meet R.E.

Knowles, the *Toronto Star* reporter assigned (for years, alas) to interview liter- ary celebrities. In a typically insufferable article, Knowles tells us almost nothing about Lloyd C. Douglas except that Douglas had "once preached in Mr. Bennett's church in Calgary." (R.E. Knowles, "No Author is Indifferent to Money, Douglas Claims," *Toronto Star*, 25 November 1932, 1-2). Exactly when Douglas was in Calgary and whether he preached in or visited other Canadian cities remains unknown.

72 "a man thirteen years her senior": Raymond E. Fitch, *Breaking With Burr: Harman Blennerhassett's Journal, 1807*, xi.

73 "of moral obliquity": *The National Cyclopaedia of American Biography*, 3:5.

74 "before any monies were paid": I say "probably penniless" because the only reference to her death (apart from its announcement) occurs in the Aaron Burr entry in *The National Cyclopedia of American Biography*, 3:6, where she is said to have been buried by the Sisters of Charity in New York City. The paucity of information about Margaret Blennerhassett is unfortunate. Apart from a two-page essay by Mary Lu MacDonald "Margaret Blenner- hassett," in *Canadian Writers Before 1890*, ed. W.H. New, vol. 99 of *The Dictionary of Literary Biography*, 28-29), I know of no separate study of her life or work. I looked at the Harmann Blennerhassett file at the Library of Congress, and although the *Handbook of Manuscripts* of the Library main- tains that the file contains "a number of poems by his wife, Adeline Agnew Blennerhassett" these have disappeared, and despite an extensive search in 1992 by several librarians at the Library of Congress, the missing poems were not found.

76 "vehicles available for education": Magnus Magnusson and Herman Palsson, *The Vinland Sagas*, 35.

85 "alienated all his paying clients": Quoted in George Perkins et. al., eds., *Benet's Reader's Encyclopedia of American Literature*, 239.

86 "a complete bath of it": Richard Henry Dana, Jr., *The Journal of Richard Henry Dana, Jr.*, ed. Robert F. Lucid, 1:312.

86 "Quebec City with approval": James Doyle, *Yankees in Canada*, 87-8.

86 "Canadian territorial waters": Quotation from his actual address to the Commission is arduous because it is a legal document, numbingly long and often technical. But the serious student of American perceptions of Canada will find it pays re-reading, despite its taxing length, because it betrays a learned knowledge of, and undisguised respect for Canadian maritime his- tory and the Maritimes' economy. In his remarks on free trade between Canada and the USA, and how much fish it was right for foreign fleets to take, Dana was disturbingly clairvoyant. A Canadian fisheries dispute, coin- cidentally, would involve another American writer just four years later. The distinguished poet James Russell Lowell, in his capacity as Minister to the Court of Saint James, handled American negotiations during an extended

battle of words over the rough treatment of American fishermen by their counterparts in Fortune Bay, Newfoundland. Unlike Dana, Lowell seems not to have made passage to Canada.

88 "in a semi-somnolent state": Richard Henry Dana, Jr., *Speeches in Stirring Times and Letters to a Son,* 348-9.

88 "his tobacco-chewing": Ibid., 349-50.

106 "either story might have awakened": Frederick S. Cozzens, *Acadia; or, A Month with the Blue Noses,* 300.

107 "under whatever disguise": Cozzens, 306. Cozzens is also a compelling retailer of historical legends. While I cannot vouch for the accuracy of his facts, I am eager to applaud his wonderful recountings of episodes in Nova Scotian history. Would that more Canadian teachers of history were as excited by the personages of our past, and told their students the tales as vivaciously.

107 "Henry W. Longfellow": Henry Wadsworth Longfellow, *The Letters of Henry Wadsworth Longfellow,* ed. Andrew Hilen, 4:137.

109 "is holy and sublime": Cozzens, 200-203.

109 "have shone to advantage": Ibid., 292.

110 "this is a wonderful country": Ibid., 205-6.

111 "it is somewhere in Newfoundland": Ibid., 131-4.

112 "memorial of heroic womanity": Ibid., 238-9.

112 "my own stand-point is defective": Ibid., 258-9.

124 "a heart-stopping 130 million copies": Ann Ronald, "Zane Grey," in *American Novelists, 1910-1945,* ed. James J. Martine, vol. 9, part 2 of *The Dictionary of Literary Biography,* 87.

124 "the Mountie's boss was named 'McKenzie'": For the fullest description of the Sergeant King comics, see Maurice Horn, *Comics of the American West,* 31-4.

126 "a daily strip was added in March 1936": See the entry for "King of the Royal Mounted" in Maurice Horn, ed., *The World Encyclopedia of Comics,* 428-9.

126 "good and bad were clearly defined": The episodes in the comics inspired a series of books (in reality they were half comic book, half novel) in the late 1930s, with Zane Grey cited as the author. The series was part of a larger series known collectively as The Big Little Books. For the record the relevant titles are: *King of the Royal Mounted* (Racine: Whitman Publishing, 1936); *King of the Royal Mounted and the Northern Treasure* (Racine: Whitman Publishing, 1937); *King of the Royal Mounted in the Far North* (Racine: Whitman Publishing, 1938); *King of the Royal Mounted Gets His Man* (Racine: Whitman Publishing, 1938); *King of the Royal Mounted Policing the Far North* (Racine: Whitman Publishing, 1938); *King of the Royal Mounted and the Great Jewel Mystery* (Racine: Whitman Publishing, 1938). Diehard collectors

or researchers may wish to investigate the possibility that there is yet another book: *King of the Mounted and the Ghost Guns of Roaring River* (1946?) I was unable to locate a copy of this book anywhere, so cannot verify that it is similar to the first seven *King of the Royal Mounted* titles.

126 "in the history of comics": The comic books of *King of the Royal Mounted* made their first appearance in 1936. Dell Comics eventually took over the series and greatly expanded the audience for the comic books. Zane Grey's name was exploited on the cover until the issue of June-August 1956. For exhaustive detail on this and other Greyiana see G. M. Farley, *Zane Grey, A Documented Portrait,* 68-9. The first artist to work on King of the Mounted was Alan Dean. Maurice Horn writes: *"King of the Royal Mounted* is chiefly remembered for Allen Dean's solid, and at times brilliant, artwork." Horn, *Comics,* 34.

128 "cracking the saplings": Zane Grey, "The Great Slave," in *Tappan's Burro and Other Stories,* 87-8.

128 "along the Canadian coast": Frank Gruber, *Zane Grey: A Biography, 127.*

128 "the urgent needs of life": Zane Grey, "Bonefish," *Field and Stream Magazine,* August 1918, 297-302.

128 "Campbell River, Vancouver Island": Zane Grey, *Tales of Fresh-Water Fishing,* 56.

128 "a quaint little old English town": Ibid., 57.

129 "hideous to me": Ibid., 57.

129 "beauty of the surroundings": Ibid., 58.

129 "for any angler": Ibid., 64.

130 "in the track of commercialism": Ibid., 66.

130 "of his piscatorial writing": Carlton Jackson, *Zane Grey,* 157, n.23.

130 *"Isiophorus greyi"*: Ibid., 114.

131 "this one was the greatest": Zane Grey, *Tales of Swordfish and Tuna,* 68. The International Game Fish Association is the body which recognizes world records. At the time that Grey fished in Nova Scotia, the International Angling Rules of the IGFA were not established; indeed, record-keeping was a far from sophisticated business. However, as with the claims of birders, the honour system ruled, and fraudulent claims—and claimants—would be shunned and ignored. As far as I can determine, no one ever challenged any of Grey's claims for world record catches.

159 "by Hovenden Walker": Marion L. Kesselring, *Hawthorne's Reading 1828-1850: A Transcription and Identification of Titles Recorded in the Charge-Books of the Salem Athenaeum,* 24, 25, 54, and 63.

159 "till I have visited Canada": Letter to Franklin Pierce. See Nathaniel Hawthorne, *The Letters, 1813-1843,* ed. Thomas Woodson et al., 224.

160 "September 28, 1832": Hawthorne, *The Letters, 1813-1843,* 227, n. 2

160 "while it awes the mind": Nathaniel Hawthorne, "My Visit to Niagara," *New-England Magazine* 8 (February 1835): 94.

164 "French in the forecastle": Nathaniel Hawthorne, "An Ontario Steam-boat," *American Magazine of Useful and Entertaining Knowledge* 2 (March 1836): 270-72.

164 "*Evangeline*": For a discussion of *Evangeline,* and of Longfellow's relationship to Canada, see my introduction to Longfellow in Gatenby, *The Wild Is Always There,* 244 ff.

165 "by starlight and torchlight": Julian Hawthorne, *Nathaniel Hawthorne and His Wife: A Biography,* 2:16-17.

166 "these speculations secret": Nathaniel Hawthorne, *The Letters, 1857-1864,* ed. Thomas Woodson et al., 354-5.

174 "do I still make there": Quoted in S.D. Scott, "William Cobbett," *Acadiensis* 5 (1905): 215.

175 "without stockings or shoes": William Cobbett, *Life and Adventures of Peter Porcupine,* 35.

175 "other than the sky": William Cobbett, *The Emigrant's Guide; In Ten Letters Addressed to the Taxpayers of England; Containing Information of Every Kind, Necessary to Persons Who Are About to Emigrate...,* 6.

176 "I am for the latter": Ibid., 40-2.

177 "compelled to obey": Cobbett, *Political Register,* 17.6.1809, quoted in Daniel Green, *Great Cobbett,* 60-1.

179 "roaring drunk": Cobbett, *Political Register,* 19.6.1809, quoted in Green, 63.

179 "as a curiosity": Cobbett, *Political Register,* 17.6.1809, quoted in Green, 65.

180 "four hundred men": Scott, 209-10.

180 "in the course of a year": Scott, 214-15.

181 "got safe to England": Quoted in George Spater, *William Cobbett, The Poor Man's Friend,* 1:28.

182 "at his frequent worst": Douglas Fetherling, "Obit for Cobbett: in praise of the polemicist's art," *Quill & Quire* 48 (May 1982), 22.

195 "as well as possible": Thomas Hughes, *Vacation Rambles,* 116.

195 "their country and her prospects": Ibid., 116-7.

196 "a self-sufficing and unambitious life": Ibid., 118-9.

197 "the act of living in this country": Ibid., 121.

200 "were I beginning life again": Ibid., 125-6.

202 "with Northern lights": Ibid., 127-8.

212 "my favourite country": Khushwant Singh, "Khushwant Singh," in *Contemporary Authors: Autobiography Series,* ed. Mark Zadrozny, 9:230.

212 *"first book of stories"*: Ibid.

214 "a soppy sentimentalist": Khushwant Singh, "Orient Pearl in the World Oyster," in *Man and His World: The Noranda Lectures,* 49-50.

219 "Canada or Canadians": Besides the Rossini, Donizetti, and Mozart, I know of only one other opera featuring a Canadian: *Le Huron* by André Ernest Modeste Grétry based on the novel *L'Ingenu* by Voltaire. For discussion of *L'Ingenu,* see my entry on Voltaire in Gatenby, *The Wild Is Always There,* 177-196. Grétry (1741-1813), an enormously prolific composer, and the dominant force of his day in *opéra-comique,* actively collaborated with Voltaire on the opera, which premiered in 1768. For a full discussion of Grétry and this opera, see David Charlton, *Grétry and the Growth of Opera-comique* (Cambridge: Cambridge University Press, 1986).

In operetta, the most distinguished—is that the word?—example is *Rose Marie* (1924) composed by Friml, with lyrics by Oscar Hammerstein II. This is the operetta which features "The Indian Love Call" among other laughable "quotations" from Canadian lore.

220 "Canada again and again": Act One, Aria No. 15 *"Rivolgete a lui lo sguardo"* sung by Guglielmo:

*... Se si parla poi di merto
Certo io sono, ed egli e certo
Che gli uguali non si trovano
Da Vienna al Canada.*

["... If we're going to discuss merits
I'm certain, as is he,
that our equals cannot be
found from Vienna to Canada."]

Mozart wrote this aria with a specific tenor in mind: one of his favourite singers, Francesco Benucci. Benucci was also Mozart's first Figaro, and the first Leporello. The libretto was by Lorenzo da Ponte, an old colleague, and the opera had its premiere on January 26, 1790.

220 "designed for—the Opera-Comique": William Ashbrook, *Donizetti and His Operas,* 160.

220 "a substantial revival": The opera is available on digital CD, each using a slightly variant text. The earliest recording I've been able to find is an Italian LP, probably dating from the 1950s, on the "Cetra" label (no number given) featuring Giuseppina Arnaldi, Carlo Franzini and Paolo Montarsolo and the Orchestra Sinfonica di Torino. A recent disc records a live performance made in Palermo in 1991, featuring Adelina Scarabelli, Pietro Ballo and Alessandro Corbelli and the Orchestra da Camera Siciliana. It is on the "Nuova Era" label, No. 7045. Another recent digital pressing dates from September 1990

featuring Susanna Rigacci, Ugo Benelli and Romano Franceschetto with the Orchestra da Camera dell'Associazione on the Bongiovanni label, No. GB 2109/102.

220 "The following translation": As a literary person rather than a musical specialist I was amazed to discover that *Rita* had never been published in English translation, just as *La Cambiale di Matrimonio* by Rossini had never been published in translation in book form (see my entry on Rossini in Gatenby, *The Wild Is Always There*). With Dr. Francesca Valente of the Italian Cultural Institute, Toronto, I intend to publish books about these operas, including complete libretti in Italian and English, along with histories and illustrations of the productions.

226 "Sylvia Bradshaw in Dreiser biographies": My efforts to locate "Sylvia Bradshaw" were in vain, despite the help provided anonymously by Dreiser specialists.

227 "and do nothing. Nothing": *Toronto Evening Telegram,* 21 September 1942, 3.

230 "East River to drown himself": John J. McAleer, *Theodore Dreiser: An Introduction and Interpretation,* 40.

244 "of the intellect": P.J. Kavanagh, ed., *Selected Poems of Ivor Gurney,* xi.

254 "the Great American Cataract": Letter from Bryant to Charles Folson, New York, 8 December 1826, quoted in Stanley Thomas Williams, *The Spanish Background of American Literature,* 146.

254 "the rest of his life": Charles H. Brown, *William Cullen Bryant,* 139.

261 "by Hudson Bay, Labrador, and Canada": François René, vicomte de Chateaubriand, *Travels in America,* trans. Richard Switzer, 6.

262 "to acknowledge its power": André Maurois, *Chateaubriand,* trans. Vera Fraser, 60-1.

262 "out of the abyss": François René, vicomte de Chateaubriand, *Atala,* trans. Irving Putter, 78-9.

264 "the Man with the Long Beard": George Painter, *Chateaubriand: A Biography,* 1:233.

269 "of her own absolutism": Quoted in "Harriet Martineau" by Ira Nadel in *Victorian Novelists Before 1885,* ed. Ira B. Nadel and William E. Fredeman, vol. 21 of *The Dictionary of Literary Biography,* 230-2.

269 "are alike taken seriously": Virginia Blain et al., eds., *The Feminist Companion to Literature in English,* 724.

270 "in the Victorian period": Nadel, 232.

270 "in guilt towards them": Harriet Martineau, *Harriet Martineau's Letters to Fanny Wedgwood,* ed. Elisabeth Sanders Arbuckle, 6.

270 "between capitalists and labourers": Letter to her cousin Henry Reeve, 26 June 1871, from Harriet Martineau, *Selected Letters,* ed. Valerie Sanders, 227-8.

271 "as well as I could": Harriet Martineau, *Autobiography*, 129.

271 "[back to] Detroit": Harriet Martineau, *Society in America*, 1:xiv.

272 "time again for the excursion": Ibid., 1:314.

272 "wild and singular beauty": Ibid., 2:19-21.

281 "shrewd critics of their society and responsibilities": Blain, 277. Her second visit to Canada was occasioned by a talk she gave at Eaton Auditorium to the Women's Canadian Club, February 11, 1937.

290 "had known in the United States": Joyce Carol Oates, *Wonderland*, 488.

290 "from competing record stores": Ibid., 489-90.

290 "an American city after all": Ibid., 490.

291 "its trim of gold and blue": Ibid., 509.

306 "with a unique affection": Sir Angus Wilson, the late novelist, and the author of one of the best biographies on Kipling, remarked on this singular regard when writing about one of Kipling's later trips to Canada:

> Now they went on their way. Up from New York through the near mid-West, that Kipling already knew, in order to cross into Canada. In the articles he then wrote of America, love was certainly predominant in the love-hate mixture. Yet already, before they crossed over into Canada, a little British note creeps into his comments.... It is the first time that Canada registers as a centre of value.... Indeed, Canada, despite set-backs Kipling attributed usually to French-Canadian interest, was of all the Imperial or Anglo-Saxon hopes of Kipling's life the most lasting. It was not only her response to England's call in the Boer War and in the Great War; other white colonies and his beloved Indians could show that. It was, I think, her constant resistance to the siren voice of the States that, despite all the disappointments over British immigration discouraged, or Imperial preferences unfulfilled, kept Canada a constant source of hope to Kipling's political dreams. (See Angus Wilson, *The Strange Ride of Rudyard Kipling*, 179.)

One of the largest repositories of Kipling material in the world is found at Dalhousie University in Halifax, Nova Scotia, and I am grateful to the Kipling Librarian, Karen Smith, for her generous help with Kipling-in-Canada matters.

307 "under the shadow of the old flag": Rudyard Kipling, *From Sea to Sea: Letters of Travel*, vol. 2, 18.

307 "I thanked God for it": Ibid., 51-2. The distinguished Canadian poet Earle Birney has taken lines from this description of Vancouver and transformed them into a found poem. See Birney, *The Collected Poems of Earl Birney*, vol. 2, 169.

308 "a man buys a piece of tobacco": Kipling, *From Sea to Sea*, 52-3.

308 "investment in Vancouver was lost": Kipling would later appear to confuse

the years in which he bought this property. In his autobiography *(Something of Myself,* 64) he indicates that he bought the land when he reached Vancouver as part of his honeymoon in 1892. But since *From Sea to Sea* was published three years before his honeymoon, and since it is in *From Sea to Sea* that he describes the land purchase, the 1889 date must be the more accurate. The autobiography is amusing, however, for giving Kipling's discovery of the dupe:

> But there was a catch in the thing, as we found many years later when, after paying taxes on it for ever so long, we discovered it belonged to someone else. All the consolation we got then from the smiling people of Vancouver was: "You bought that from Steve, did you? Ah-ah, *Steve! You* hand't ought to ha' bought from Steve. No! Not from *Steve!"* And thus did the good Steve cure us of speculating in real estate.

Quite when Kipling made the discovery of the fraud is unclear. Thomas Pinney, the renowned Editor of the exhaustive edition of Kipling's letters, indicates that Kipling "held" his Vancouver property until 1928 (See Kipling, *The Letters of Rudyard Kipling,* ed. Thomas Pinney, vol.1, 326, n.9). The entire question of where, and when, and how Kipling bought property in Vancouver remains a vexing one, and if it can be resolved will require extensive research in the tax and registry archives of British Columbia.

308 "the retired go to Victoria": Kipling, *From Sea to Sea,* 54.

308 "as I ought to have been": Kipling, *Letters of Rudyard Kipling,* vol.1, 335.

310 "when it was even smaller": Rudyard Kipling, *Letters of Travel,* 24-26. The prairie would be toasted in a poem written by Kipling not long after his first visit. In "The Native-Born" (1894) there is the following stanza:

> To the far-flung, fenceless prairie
> Where the quick cloud-shadows trail,
> To our neighbour's barn in the offing
> And the line of the new-cut rail;
> To the plough in her league-long furrow
> With the grey Lake gulls behind—
> To the weight of a half-year's winter
> And the warm, wet western wind!

(Rudyard Kipling, *Rudyard Kipling's Verse: Inclusive Edition,* 191.)

312 "Judasville": Kipling to Francis Fatt, 9 December 1910, *Kipling's Advice To "The Hat": in response to an appeal from an old-timer of Medicine Hat, Alberta.*

313 "out on a trestle again": Kipling, *Letters of Travel,* 26-32.

314 "a grown-up Christian centre": Ibid., 81-2. Winnipegers should not feel they are the only butts of this sarcastic tone. A similar slur was penned about his English compatriots: "North of London stretches a country called 'The Midlands', filled with brick cities, all absolutely alike, but populated by natives who, through heredity, have learned not only to distinguish between

them but even between the different houses." Quoted in Wilson, 321.

314   "a single surviving letter": Kipling, *Letters of Rudyard Kipling,* vol. 2, 106.

314   *"Something of Myself"*: Kipling, *Something of Myself,* 75.

315   "a brief newspaper account": Kipling, *Letters of Rudyard Kipling,* vol. 2, 245. The letter was addressed to W.A. Fraser, a Toronto journalist and fiction writer. The article appeared in the Saint John (New Brunswick) *Daily Telegraph,* 18 June 1896 in an article headlined simply "Kipling". Thomas Pinney was most generous in drawing this newspaper account to my attention and in sending me a copy of the article.

315   "we don't call this cold in Quebec": Kipling, *Letters of Rudyard Kipling, vol. 2,* 177-8.

315   "Victoria, Quebec, Montreal, and Halifax": Rudyard Kipling, *The Seven Seas,* 13. John Bell in his *Halifax: A Literary Portrait,* 107, claims that Kipling "visited Halifax in the 1890s" but he gives no evidence for such a claim, and I have found none.

317   "the Winnipeg, Calgary, and Medicine Hat bags": Rudyard Kipling, "With the Night Mail," in *Actions and Reactions,* 133.

317   "fly down to Halifax direct": Ibid., 154.

317   "light and unworthy lovers": Ibid., 155.

318   "just for his convenience": Kipling's speeches in Winnipeg, Toronto and Montreal were published in his *A Book of Words* (1928). The Ottawa speech was published in *Addresses Delivered Before the Canadian Club of Ottawa 1903-1909,* ed. Gerald Brown. The Vancouver and Victoria speeches appear not to have been published in their entirety, but excerpts were published in *The Times* of 11 October 1907. For a description of the pit stop in Calgary, see the *Calgary Herald,* 4 October 1907 where Kipling says, "This is the wonder city of Canada ... Of all the cities I have seen in the West, this beats them all."

318   "pilliwinky windmill": Rudyard Kipling, "O *Beloved Kids": Rudyard Kipling's Letters to his Children,* ed. Elliot Gilbert, 42-3.

319   "in this wonderful land": Ibid., 50.

320   "immigrants from northern European nations": The most intelligent discussion of Kipling's views on race, immigration and Canada is found in Chapter 5 of Angus Wilson's *The Strange Ride of Rudyard Kipling.*

321   "separated by thousands of years": Quoted in The Front Page, *Saturday Night,* 26 October 1907, 1.

321   "concomitant of that trade": Ibid.

321   "prolonged several minutes": "Canada's Great Outlook One of "Big Four" Nations," *The Mail and Empire,* 19 October 1907, 9. Other measures of affection were more public and more lasting. In Saskatchewan, for example, a town was named in his honour. Kipling, the town, lies just west of the

metropolis of Moosomin. Torontonians, not to be outdone by this prairie hospitality in 1907, named a new dirt road after the British author. Kipling Avenue is now one the city's major thoroughfares.

321 "of the imperial family": Kipling, "Canada's Path to Nationhood," in *Addresses Delivered Before the Canadian Club of Ottawa 1903-1909,* ed. Gerald H. Brown, 118.

321 "contented to be themselves": Kipling, *Book of Words,* 33.

322 "whatever of the United States": Kipling, *Something of Myself,* 116.

322 "SS *Duchess of Bedford*": See Lord Birkenhead, *Rudyard Kipling,* 338-40 for an interesting account of the Montreal stay.

323 "the Canadian Authors' Association": G.K. Chesterton also spoke at the banquet. A 16mm film with sound was made of this event; it was screened later in the year at the annual convention in Toronto of the C.A.A. but my efforts to locate either a print or the negative of the film have been in vain. Kipling's remarks to the group were comprised of sententious phrases about the role of the writer in the world, but a few lines dealt directly with Canada: "For it was given me once to see Canada *en bloc.* I had known portions of it, of course, many years before, but this was one prodigious sweep from Quebec to Victoria and back again. Through three amazing weeks it was my turn to be shown things—to listen to prophecies which within the next 10 years fell short of the facts; and to feel the moral pulse of a land and a people free as their own airs and yet set in most ancient and sane practices of justice, honour and self-control...." See "Canadian Authors," *The Times,* 13 July 1933, 8. The banquet was announced in "Broadcasting," *The Times,* 12 July 1933, 12.

323 "Canada is a possession of England": News and Notes, *The Kipling Journal* 35 (Sept. 1935): 7071.

324 "to you to keep": Rudyard Kipling, *Rudyard Kipling: Selected Poems,* ed. Peter Keating, 170.

326 "interfere with his own business": The Front Page, *Saturday Night,* 16 May 1908, 1.

327 "a few hasty days would be worthwhile": Ibid.

327 "the first American edition did not appear until 1913": James Stewart, *Rudyard Kipling: A Bibliographic Catalogue,* 255.

345 "service number 2025271": National Archives of Canada, Government Records Branch, *Statement of Service in the Canadian Armed Forces: Raymond Thornton Chandler,* compiled by Bill Wood, 6 August 1991.

347 "fourteen thousand casualties": Chandler to Deirdre Gartrell, 2 March 1957, *Selected Letters of Raymond Chandler,* ed. Frank MacShane, 423-4.

348 "nothing is ever the same again": Chandler to Deirdre Gartrell, 25 July 1957, *Selected Letters of Raymond Chandler,* ed. Frank MacShane, 455

348 "Air Officer Cadet William Faulkner": For details of Faulkner's connections

to Canada, both in his life and his writing, see the William Faulkner entry in Gatenby, *The Wild Is Always There*, 1-20.

348   "Canadian Expeditionary Force": Many of the details concerning Chandler's military career are taken from Frank MacShane's excellent biography. See especially pages 27-31 of his *The Life of Raymond Chandler.*

348   "set foot in Canada again": Because of, or in order to maintain his Canadian ties, Chandler, upon returning to the USA, seems to have worked briefly for an American branch of the Bank of Montreal. See MacShane, 31.

349   "Knew some very nice ones": Chandler to Alex Barris, 16 April 1949, *Selected Letters of Raymond Chandler,* 165.

349   "for almost forty years": Ibid. See *Raymond Chandler's Unknown Thriller: The Screenplay of Playback,* for the complete version of the final draft and for a summary of the evolution of the scenario.

350   "one of the best films I wrote": Quoted by James Pepper in his Preface to Chandler, *Playback.*

360   "They had every fault": Stanley Kunitz [Dilly Tante, pseud.], *Living Authors: A Book of Biographies,* 140.

364   "I believe he is terrifying": Quoted in Harold Vincent Marrot, *The Life and Letters of John Galsworthy,* 70-3.

364   "Galsworthy returned to Britain": Harold Vincent Marrot, *The Life and Letters of John Galsworthy,* 73.

365   "then on to New York": Marrot, 500.

371   "Jack London and Upton Sinclair": Allen Johnson and Dumas Malone, eds., *Dictionary of American Biography,* vol.2, 622-3.

373   "the history of cinema": From the Introduction by Jean-Jacques Annaud to James Oliver Curwood, *The Bear: A Novel,* a re-issue of *The Grizzly King,* xiii. Curwood himself was heavily involved in the early years of the film industry, and wrote willingly for the screen. Later, he became active as a producer. In addition to original screenplays, he adapted some of his own prose for films, while other screenwriters made yet more cinematic adapatations of his fictions. According to one source, at least one hundred and twenty-two films were based on Curwood's prose (Bernard A. Drew, *Lawmen in Scarlet,* 152). For a discussion of Curwood's extensive involvement with the film industry, including some of the earliest movies ever made in Canada, see Judith A. Eldridge, *James Oliver Curwood: God's Country and the Man,* 139 ff. This latter is a poorly written text, but would seem to be the only book which treats Curwood's Canadian film ventures.

373   "no other event in my life": James Oliver Curwood, *Son of the Forests,* 198-201.

374   "for the writer of fiction": James Oliver Curwood, *The Black Hunter,* page v.

375   "a bad assignment": James Oliver Curwood, *The Flaming Forest,* 1.

389 "and Swaziland and the Transvaal in 1936": Stanley J. Kunitz and Howard Haycraft eds., *Twentieth Century Authors,* 560-1.

389 "his translations, introductions and editions": Ibid., 561.

390 "they approach the Canadian border": With an affection engendered by longer hindsight, Stephen Graham recalled this trip quite fondly in his 1964 autobiography. See Stephen Graham, *Part of the Wonderful Scene,* 238-48.

402 "front-page treatment": The *Toronto Star,* in fact, put a captioned photo of Lindsay on the front page on both Saturday, December 5, 1925 and Monday, December 7th. The *Globe* ran a captioned photo on December 5th on the front page of the City Section. Both newspapers gave extensive coverage to his visit, as did the *Evening Telegram* and the *Mail & Empire.* The reading, attended by the literary luminaries in the city (including Bliss Carman who happened to be in town for a brief visit) took place on December 8, 1925. Two days later, Lindsay gave an address to the Empire Club in which he made no reference to Canada, but rather spoke extensively about the similarities and minor differences between citizens of America and the British Empire. One infers from his address that the term "Canadian" was but a subdivision of the the larger and far more important and complimentary appellation "British". Perhaps, given the era in which he spoke, his perception of his (Establishment) audience's leanings—and their sense of themselves—was correct.

403 "consciousness of rural America": *The National Cyclopaedia of American Biography,* vol. 23, 230.

405 "Every line should be that way": Vachel Lindsay, *Collected Poems,* 24. The Foreword is dated October 15, 1922.

405 "a man will find nothing but friends": Quoted in Vachel Lindsay, *The Poetry of Vachel Lindsay,* ed. Dennis Camp, vol. 3, 978-9.

406 "one of the longest in the world": Vachel Lindsay, *Going-To-The-Stars,* 6-7.

410 "'Furrin!' said Hal": Grace Hegger Lewis, *With Love From Gracie,* 104.

410 "through the western provinces": Born and raised in Minnesota, Lewis could have easily driven through the Canadian prairies. Whether he actually did so is undetermined.

411 "as beautiful as a mountain": For coverage of, and quotations from, Sinclair Lewis's Toronto speech, see "Bright Future for Literature," *The Globe,* 13 April 1921; "Don't Write Fairy Tale, Write About Real Life," *The Toronto Daily Star,* 13 April 1921; "Give Real Canada to World: It Teems with Bigness," *The Evening Telegram,* 13 April 1921; and "Not To Be Bound By Conventions," *The Mail and Empire,* 13 April 1921. It was during this speech that Lewis betrayed the presence in Toronto of Willa Cather. See Gatenby, *The Wild Is Always There,* 215.

411 "a Canadian writer he much admired": Lewis's affection for the writing of O'Higgins may have been influenced by the fact that O'Higgins was

adapting *Main Street* for the National Theatre in New York City in the same year that Lewis spoke in Toronto. O'Higgins (1876-1929) was born, like Lewis's mother (nee Kermott), in London, Ont. He was educated at the University of Toronto but soon after emigrated to the United States where he became one of the more famous magazine short story writers of his time. His plays were forgettable melodramas, but the novels he wrote at the end of his life remain important for their pioneering use of Freudian thinking. The last prose he wrote, for example, was one of the first articles to deal openly with Walt Whitman's alleged homosexuality.

411   "Canadian wilds": Sinclair Lewis, *From Main Street to Stockholm: Letters of Sinclair Lewis, 1919-1930,* edited by Harrison Smith, 149.

411   "something of that kind": Mark Schorer, *Sinclair Lewis: An American Life,* 390. The best account of Lewis's 1924 trip to Canada is found in the excellent *Treaty Trip: An Abridgement of Dr. Claude Lewis's journal of an expedition made by himself and his brother, Sinclair Lewis, to northern Saskatchewan and Manitoba in 1924,* edited by Donald Greene and George Knox. Quotations from some otherwise unpublished letters, and further facts about the trip are found in Schorer.

411   "Indian Treaty Party Trip": Claude Lewis, *Treaty Trip,* 6.

412   "their gear during portages": Ibid., 7.

413   "from the *Free Press*": Ibid.

413   "in the form of an excellent article": See "Sinclair Lewis in Unusual Interview," *Manitoba Free Press,* 7 June 1924, 4. Lewis is quoted as saying that he had never been to Winnipeg before, but that he had been to both coasts of Canada. When he made the Canadian east coast visit is unknown.

413   "a council of war": Lewis, *Treaty Trip,* 9.

413   "Trading Company's banquet hall": "Women's Canadian Club To Hear Sinclair Lewis," Regina *Leader,* 9 June 1924, 7. See also *The* [Regina] *Leader's* editorial on Sinclair Lewis, 11 June 1924, 4, and its coverage of his speech on page 5. See also *The Leader's* "Lewis and Party Leave For North", 13 June 1924. Grace Hegger Lewis discusses the Regina stopover, among others on this trip, in *With Love From Gracie,* 274-81.

414   "on an inspection tour": Lewis, *Treaty Trip,* 9-10.

414   "the entrance of the Canada Building": "Sinclair Lewis To Speak Here," *Saskatoon Phoenix,* 12 June 1924. On June 14th *The Phoenix* wrote another article ("'Dirty Truth' Is Great Yarn") reporting on the speech, in which Lewis is quoted as saying "I am not a professional lecturer, and being only a poor amateur, will only say I like this country a lot and I like you...."

414   "sense enough to go home": Lewis, *Treaty Trip,* 11.

415   "as bright and cheerful as ever": Ibid., 15. Other remarks by Claude Lewis in his journal reinforce this assessment. A few examples: "The speed with which

those Indians can stick up a camp and cook supper is amazing … They don't argue among themselves as to who shall do the work, but all hustle to do the work as quickly as possible." [p.14]; "To me it was really wonderful how those Indians would go into a strip of foaming water with rocks sticking out everywhere and know exactly the right place so as not to smash the canoe all to pieces." [p.16]; "I am always amazed at the rapidity with which these Indians can unload vast amounts of stuff in these canoes and be ready for the night." [p.22].

416 "displaying the Union Jack": Sinclair Lewis, *Mantrap,* 36-7.

416 "All goes beautifully": Lewis, *From Main Street to Stockholm,* 161.

417 "feeling superb real rejuvenation": Ibid., 162.

417 "about the working class": One of Lewis's biographers regards the year 1929 as seminal: "But by far the most crucial factor bearing upon Lewis's career after 1929, perhaps the turning point in it, was his failure to complete a novel dealing with the American labor movement." See Sheldon Norman Grebstein, *Sinclair Lewis,* 123.

418 "royalties from the novel": These details are taken from Schorer, 523. See also Lewis's letters to various persons in the Fall of 1929 in Lewis, *From Main Street to Stockholm,* 280-84.

418 "completely vivid": Quoted by Tony Kilgallin, "Toronto Life in Literature, Part IV: Ernest Hemingway: Toronto Took Five Years Off My Life,'" *Toronto Life 1,* no. 6 (April 1967): 25.

419 "Canadian-born actress Fay Wray": "Sinclair Lewis Wants Play Open At End For Change," *Toronto Telegram,* 27 February 1939.

419 "a left-wing theatrical group": *Toronto Telegram,* 28 February 1939, two photos and caption "Author-Playwright Sees Toronto Rehearsal [of Theatre of Action]". For a fuller description of the impact of Lewis's visit on the troupe, see Toby Ryan, *Stage Left,* 176-8.

419 "Brian Doharty": *Toronto Telegram,* 27 February 1939, 12, "Sinclair Lewis Wants Play Open At End For Change."

419 "Is Machinery Wrecking Civilization?": See "Author Declares Titles Hurt Anglo-US Unity," Toronto *Globe and Mail,* 5, 9 December 1943; "Literary Heavies Clash; Who Won—Who Knows?" Toronto *Globe and Mail,* 10 December 1943, 4; "Two Authors Debate Merit of Machinery," Toronto *Telegram,* 10 December 1943, 2. The debate took place in the Eaton Auditorium.

419 "least of all the debaters": "Literary Heavies Clash; Who Won—Who Knows?" Toronto *Globe and Mail,* 10 December 1943, 4.

419 "next to worst book which Sinclair Lewis ever published": A brief sampling of some of the negative comments: "Little can be said in defense of the way *Mantrap* was written." (James Lundquist, *Sinclair Lewis,* 76); "To put it

bluntly, *Mantrap is* a bad book ... it is worse than anything he had done except *The Innocents.* " (Grebstein, 98); "So he wrote instead, on his return, *Mantrap*—which is perhaps a thin cut above *The Innocents,* the most deplorable of all his books." (Schorer, 422); *"Mantrap,* a very poor novel that can be disposed of quickly ..." (Martin Light, *The Quixotic Vision of Sinclair Lewis,* 98).

420   "Zane Grey": Robert E. Fleming was the first to elucidate the connection between Lewis and Grey. The essay in which he fully explores the satirical connection is a model of what academic literary criticism should do, and is a model of how it should be written. See Robert E. Fleming, "Sinclair Lewis vs. Zane Grey: *Mantrap* as Satirical Western," *MidAmerica IX, the yearbook of the Society for the Study of Midwestern Literature.* A helpful essay that is complementary to Fleming's is Sanford E. Marovitz, "Ambivalences and Anxieties: Character Reversals in Sinclair Lewis' *Mantrap,"* *Studies in American Fiction* 16:2 (Autumn 1988): 229-36.

421   "I travel just as soft as I can": Lewis, *Mantrap,* 90-91.

421   "a shameless flirt": The parallels with Donizetti's *Rita* are obvious, although coincidental.

432   "an inch or two of rain": Wallace Stegner, *Where the Bluebird Sings to the Lemonade Springs,* 59.

432   "a naturalized citizen": Ibid.

432   "the richest page in my memory": Ibid., 30.

433   "a degree of self-confidence": Ibid., 3-4.

433   "never forgotten a detail of them": Ibid., 5.

433   "lived with such grace": Wallace Stegner and Richard W. Etulain, *Conversations with Wallace Stegner on Western History and Literature,* 197.

434   "on the Frenchman river": *Bluebird,* 5-6.

434   "really known we had": Ibid.

434   "American or Canadian": Stegner and Etulain, 148.

434   "the happiest of his life": See, for example, Stegner and Etulain, 50

436   "psychologically naive": Ibid., 36.

437   "among the most heartbreaking": Ibid., 41 ff. Note especially page 47: "The Saskatchewan episodes are much the closest to autobiography. Those are memories of my childhood, most of them."

437   "roof and ground and in the air": Wallace Stegner, *The Big Rock Candy Mountain,* 191.

438   "I knew very little": Stegner and Etulain, 61. In the transcription of portions from another interview (in 1992 with journalist Paula Simons), Wallace Stegner demonstrates that the issue was still a confounded one for him. At one point in the interview he declares the "international boundary is a kind of

artificial line." Yet, a minute later, the man who could see next to no difference between the prairie of Canada and the northern plains of the USA could cite an intangible nuance explaining why Missourians are not true Westerners: "There's always been literature about the West. But the kind of literature I keep looking for is literature which is written from inside the West and not by tourists or by recent visitors, some of whom were brilliant—like Mark Twain and so on, but he wasn't a Westerner, he was a Missourian. And there is a difference, which I can recognize but not detail!" See "The West of Wallace Stegner," interview by Paula Simons, July, 1992, *Brick* 46 (Summer 1993): 26-31.

438 "the breathtakingly superb *Wolf Willow*": Among the many who admired this work was Vladimir Nabokov who described it in a letter to Stegner as "enchanting, heartrending, and eminently *enviable.*" Nabokov was familiar with Stegner's Saskatchewan territory:

> "Many passages I read with nostalgic excitement: I have had some unforgettable butterfly collecting in the Glacier Park region ... and at many points between Browning and the Dakotas—which is not far from *your* collecting localities, and I think I smelled your *Shepherdia* (henceforth to be known as *Stegneria....*" See Nabokov to Wallace Stegner, 18 February 1967, *Selected Letters 1940-1977,* ed. Dmitri Nabokov and Matthew J. Bruccoli, 401.

438 "different from that of the American West": Stegner and Etulain, 61.

438 "whenever I was up there in the fifties": Ibid., 62

439 "but I obviously was": Ibid.

439 "not by covered wagon but by train": Ibid., 157

439 "before I found the right one": Ibid., 162

439 "exhortations to fellow Westerners": Ibid., 129

440 "really don't believe in it": Stegner, "The West of Wallace Stegner," 30.

441 "than most Americans can generate": Wallace Stegner, "Letter From Canada," *The American West* 11, no.1 (January 1974): 28-30.

441 "more interesting than the differences": Doug Fetherling, "Canadians always crossing novelist Stegner's path," *Toronto Star,* 26 November 1973, D6.

441 "a kind of artificial line": Stegner, "The West of Wallace Stegner," 29.

441 "more to be loved than reviled": Wallace Stegner, "The Provincial Consciousness," *The University of Toronto Quarterly* 43, no. 4 (Summer 1974): 299.

442 "I don't see much difference": Ibid., 307.

443 "That is greatness": Sharon Butala, "The Night Wallace Stegner Died," *Brick* 46 (Summer 1993): 24.

EXCERPT SOURCES

Belloc, Hilaire. *Letters from Hilaire Belloc.* Edited by Robert Speaight. London: Hollis & Carter, 1958. Reprinted by permision of Peters Fraser & Dunlop Group Ltd.

Blennerhassett, Margaret. "To a Humming-Bird." In *The Widow of the Rock and Other Poems, by A Lady.* Montreal: E. V. Sparhawk, 1824.

Blouet, Paul [Max O'Rell, pseud.] *A Frenchman in America.* New York: Cassell Publishing Company, 1891.

Bryant, William Cullen. *Letters of a Traveler: or, Notes of Things Seen in Europe and America.* London: Richard Bentley, 1850.

Chandler, Raymond. *Raymond Chandler's Unknown Thriller: The Screenplay of "Playback."* Preface by James Pepper. New York: The Mysterious Press, 1985.

Chateaubriand, François René, vicomte de. *Travels in America.* Translated by Richard Switzer. Lexington: University of Kentucky Press, 1969. Copyright © 1969 by The University of Kentucky Press.

Cobbett, William. *Advice to Young Men.* London: George Routledge and Sons, 1887.

Cozzens, Frederick S. *Acadia: or, A Month with the Blue Noses.* New York: Hurd and Houghton, 1877.

Crowley, Aleister. *The Confessions of Aleister Crowley.* Edited by Julian Symonds and Kenneth Grant. London: Jonathan Cape, 1969.

Curwood, James Oliver. *God's Country: The Trail to Happiness.* New York: Cosmopolitan Book Corporation, 1921.

Dana, Richard Henry, Jr. *The Journal of Richard Henry Dana, Jr.* Volume 1. Edited by Robert F. Lucid. Cambridge, Massachusetts: The Belknap Press of Harvard University Press, 1968.

Davies, W.H. *The Autobiography of a Super-Tramp.* London: Jonathan Cape, 1908.

Delafield, E.M. *The Provincial Lady in America.* New York: Harper, 1934.

[Donizetti, Gaetano.] Vaez, Gustavo. *Rita.* Music by Gaetano Donizetti. Original translation by Francesca Valente and Greg Gatenby.

Douglas, Lloyd C. *The Shape of Sunday: An Intimate Biography of Lloyd C. Douglas by his Daughters,* by Virginia Douglas Dawson and Betty Douglas Wilson. Cambridge, Mass.: The Riverside Press, 1952.

Dreiser, Theodore. *Sister Carrie.* Edited by John C. Berkey, Alice M. Winters, James L.W. West III, and Neda M. Westlake. Philadelphia: University of Pennsylvania Press, 1981. Reprinted by permission of the University of Pennsylvania Press.

Eirik's Saga. In *The Vinland Sagas.* Translated by Magnus Magnusson and Herman Pálsson. London: Penguin Books, 1965. Reproduced by permission of Penguin Books Ltd.

Freuchen, Peter. *Vagrant Viking.* Translated by Johan Hambro. New York: Julian Messner, Inc., 1953. Copyright © 1953 by Silver, Burdett and Ginn, Simon & Schuster, Elementary. Used by permission.

Galsworthy, John [John Sinjohn, pseud.]. "A Prairie Oyster." In *From the Four Winds.* London: T. Fisher Unwin, 1897.

Graham, Stephen. *Tramping With A Poet In The Rockies.* New York: D. Appleton & Company, 1922. Copyright © 1922, renewed 1950 by Stephen Graham. Used by permission of Dutton Signet, a division of Penguin Books, USA Inc.

Grey, Zane. "Giant Nova Scotia Tuna." In *Tales of Swordfish and Tuna.* New York: Grosset & Dunlap, 1927.

Gurney, Ivor. "Canadians." In *Collected Poems of Ivor Gurney.* Edited by P.J. Kavanagh. New York: Oxford University Press, 1982.

Hawthorne, Nathaniel. *Famous Old People: Being the Second Epoch of Grandfather's Chair.* Boston: Tappan & Dennet, 1842.

Heredia, José María. "Niagara." Translated by William Cullen Bryant and an unknown collaborator. In *The Literary History of Spanish America.* New York: MacMillan, 1916.

Hughes, Thomas. "Preface." In *Guide Book to the Canadian Dominion, Containing Full Information for the Emigrant, the Tourist, the Sportsman, and the Small Capitalist,* by Harvey J. Philpot. London: Edward Stanford, 1871.

Kipling, Rudyard. *Letters to the Family.* Toronto: Macmillan Company of Canada, Ltd., 1908.

Lewis, Sinclair. *Mantrap.* New York: Grosset & Dunlap, 1926.

Lindsay, Vachel. "Saskatoon, Saskatchewan." In *The Poetry of Vachel Lindsay.* Vols. 2-3. Edited by Dennis Camp. Peoria, Illinois: Spoon River Poetry Press, 1985, 1986.

Martineau, Harriet. *Retrospect of Western Travel.* New York: Harper & Brothers, 1838.

Oates, Joyce Carol. "Natural Boundaries." In *Crossing the Border.* New York: The Vanguard Press, Inc., 1976.

Parkes, Bessie Rayner. "The Fate of Sir John Franklin." In *Poems of Places,* edited by Henry Wadsworth Longfellow. Vol. 23, *America.* Boston: Houghton, Osgood and Company, 1879.

Singh, Khushwant. "When Sikh Meets Sikh." In *The Mark of Vishnu and Other Stories.* London: The Saturn Press, 1950.

Stegner, Wallace. *Wolf Willow.* Lincoln, Nebraska: University of Nebraska Press, 1962. Copyright © 1955, 1957, 1958, 1959, 1962 by Wallace Stegner. Reprinted by permission of Brandt & Brandt Literary Agents, Inc.

Vaez, Gustavo. *Rita.* Music by Gaetano Donizetti. Original translation by Francesca Valante and Greg Gatenby.

BIBLIOGRAPHY

Ashbrook, William. *Donizetti and His Operas*. Cambridge: Cambridge University Press, 1982.

Balteau, J., Barroux, M., Prevost, M. et al., eds. *Dictionnaire de Biographie Francaise*. *19* vols. Paris: Librarie LeTouzey et Ane 1937-94.

Bell, John. *Halifax: A Literary Portrait*. Lawrencetown Beach, Nova Scotia: Pottersfield Press, 1990.

Belloc, Hilaire. *Letters from Hilaire Belloc*. Edited by Robert Speaight. London: Hollis & Carter, 1958.

Birkenhead, Lord. *Rudyard Kipling*. London: Weidenfeld and Nicholson, 1978.

Birney, Earle. *The Collected Poems of Earl Birney*. Vol. 2. Toronto: McClelland and Stewart Limited, 1975.

Blain, Virginia; Grundy, Isobel; and Clements, Patricia, Editors. *The Feminist Companion to Literature in English*. New Haven: Yale University Press, 1990.

Brown, Charles H. *William Cullen Bryant*. New York: Charles Scribner's Sons, 1971.

Butala, Sharon. "The Night Wallace Stegner Died." *Brick* 46 (Summer 1993).

Carpenter, Edmund. Telephone conversation with Greg Gatenby, March 1993.

Chandler, Raymond. *Raymond Chandler's Unknown Thriller: The Screenplay of "Playback."* Preface by James Pepper. New York: The Mysterious Press, 1985.

———. *Selected Letters of Raymond Chandler*. Edited by Frank MacShane. New York: Columbia University Press, 1981.

Chateaubriand, François Rene, vicomte de. *Atala/Rene*. Translated by Irving Putter. Berkeley and Los Angeles: University Press, 1952.

———. *The Genius of Christianity*. Baltimore: John Murphy and Company, 1856.

———. *Travels in America*. Translated by Richard Switzer. Lexington: University of Kentucky Press, 1969.

Charlton, David. *Grétry and the Growth of Opera-comique.* Cambridge: Cambridge University Press, 1986.

Cobbett, William. *The Emigrant's Guide; In Ten Letters Addressed to the Taxpayers of England; Containing Information of Every Kind, Necessary to Persons Who Are About to Emigrate …* London: Mills, Jowett, and Mills, 1830.

——. [Peter Porcupine, pseud.] *Life and Adventures of Peter Porcupine.* Philadelphia: W. Cobbett, 1796.

Crowley, Aleister. *The Confessions of Aleister Crowley.* Edited by Julian Symonds and Kenneth Grant. London: Jonathan Cape, 1969.

Cozzens, Frederick S. *Acadia: or, A Month with the Blue Noses.* New York: Hurd and Houghton, 1877.

Curwood, James Oliver. *The Bear: a Novel* (Original title: *The Grizzly King).* Introduction by Jean-Jaques Annaud. New York: Newmarket Press, 1989.

——. *The Black Hunter.* The Copp Clark Co. Limited, 1926.

——. *The Flaming Forest.* The Copp Clark Co. Limited, 1921.

Curwood, James Oliver, and Bryant, Dorothea A. *Son of the Forest.* New York: Grosset & Dunlap, 1930.

Dana, Richard Henry, Jr. *The Journal of Richard Henry Dana, Jr.* 2 vols. Edited by Robert F. Lucid. Cambridge, Massachusetts: The Belknap Press of Harvard University Press, 1968.

——. *Speeches in Stirring Times and Letters to a Son.* New York: Houghton Mifflin Company, 1910.

Davies, W.H. *The Autobiography of a Super-Tramp.* London: Jonathan Cape, 1908.

Dawson, Virginia Douglas, and Betty Douglas Wilson. *The Shape of Sunday: An Intimate Biography of Lloyd C. Douglas by his Daughters.* Cambridge, Mass.: The Riverside Press, 1952.

[Donizetti, Gaetano.] Vaez, Gustavo. *Rita.* Music by Gaetano Donizetti. [Sound Recording, Digital CD] Featuring Adelina Scarabelli, Pietro Ballo and Alessandro Corbelli and the Orchestra da Camera Siciliana. "Nuova Era" label (No. 7045), 1991.

——. Vaez, Gustavo. *Rita.* Music by Gaetano Donizetti. [Sound Recording, Digital CD] Featuring Susanna Rigacci, Ugo Benelli and Romano Franceschetto with the Orchestra da Camera dell'Associazione. Bongiovanni label, No. GB 2109/10-2, September 1990.

——. Vaez, Gustavo. *Rita.* Music by Gaetano Donizetti. [Sound Recording, LP]. Featuring Giuseppina Arnaldi, Carlo Franzini, and Paolo Montarsolo and the Orchestra Sinfonica di Torino."Cetra" label (no number given), 1950s?

Douglas, Lloyd C. "Impatient Idealists." In *The Empire Club of Canada: Addresses Delivered to the Members During the Year* 1942-43. Toronto: T.H. Best Printing Co., Ltd., 1943.

Doyle, James. *Yankees in Canada.* Downsview, Ontario: ECW Press, 1980.

Drew, Bernard A. *Lawmen in Scarlet: An Annotated Guide to Royal Canadian Mounted Police in Print and Performance.* Metuchen, New Jersey: The Scarecrow Press, 1990.

Eldridge, Judith A. *James Oliver Curwood: God's Country and the Man.* Bowling Green, Ohio: Bowling Green State University Popular Press, 1993.

Farley, G.M. *Zane Grey: A Documented Portrait*, Tuscaloosa, Alabama: Portals Press, 1986.

Fetherling, Douglas. "Obit for Cobbett: in praise of the polemicist's art." *Quill & Quire* 48 (May 1982), 22.

Fitch, Raymond E. *Breaking With Burr: Harman Blennerhassett's Journal, 1807.* Athens, Ohio: Ohio University Press, 1988.

Fleming, Robert E. "Sinclair Lewis vs. Zane Grey: *Mantrap* as Satirical Western." In *MidAmerica IX: the yearbook of the Society for the Study of Midwestern Literature,* edited by David D. Anderson. East Lansing: Michigan State University Press, 1982.

Freuchen, Peter. *Vagrant Viking.* Translated by Johan Hambro. New York : Julian Messner, Inc ., 1953.

The Front Page. *Saturday Night,* October 26, 1907, 1.

The Front Page. *Saturday Night,* May 16, 1908, 1.

Gatenby, Greg. *The Wild Is Always There.* Toronto: Alfred A. Knopf Canada, 1993.

Graham, Stephen. *Part of the Wonderful Scene.* London: Collins, 1964.

Grebstein, Sheldon Norman. *Sinclair Lewis.* New York: Twayne Publishers, 1962.

Green, Daniel. *Great Cobbett: The Noblest Agitator.* Hodder and Stoughton, Toronto: 1983.

Grey, Zane. "Bonefish." *Field and Stream Magazine,* August 1918, 297-302.

——. "The Great Slave." In *Tappan's Burro and Other Stories.* New York: White Lion Publishers, 1974.

——. *Tales of Fresh-Water Fishing.* New York: Grosset & Dunlap, 1928.

——. *Tales of Swordfish and Tuna.* New York: Grosset & Dunlap, 1927.

Gruber, Frank. *Zane Grey: A Biography.* New York: World Publishing Company, 1970.

Gurney, Ivor. *Selected Poems of Ivor Gurney.* Edited by P. J. Kavanagh. Oxford: Oxford University Press, 1982.

Hawthorne, Julian. *Nathaniel Hawthorne and his Wife.* New York: Houghton, Mifflin and Company, 1889.

Hawthorne, Nathaniel. *The Letters, 1813-1843.* Edited by Thomas Woodson et al. Columbus, Ohio: Ohio State University Press, 1984.

——. *The Letters, 1857-64.* Edited by Thomas Woodson et al. Columbus, Ohio: Ohio State University Press, 1987.

——. "My Visit to Niagara." *New-England Magazine* 8 (February 1835): 91-96.

——. "An Ontario Steam-boat." *American Magazine of Useful and Entertaining Knowledge* 2 (March 1836): 270-72.

Horn, Maurice. *Comics of the American West.* New York: Winchester Press, 1977.

Horn, Maurice, ed. *The World Encyclopedia of Comics.* New York: Chelsea house Publishers, 1976.

Hughes, Thomas. *Vacation Rambles.* London: Macmillan, 1895.

Jackson, Carlton. *Zane Grey.* (Revised Edition.) Boston: Twayne Publishers, 1989.

Johnson, Allen, and Malone, Dumas, eds. *Dictionary of American Biography.* Vol. 2. New York: Charles Scribner's Sons, 1958.

Kesselring, Marion L. *Hawthorne's Reading 1828-1850: A Transcription and Identification of Titles Recorded in the Charge-Books of the Salem Athenaeum.* New York: The New York Public Library, 1949.

Kilgallin, Tony. "Toronto Life in Literature, Part IV: Ernest Hemingway: Toronto Took Five Years Off My Life.'" *Toronto Life* 1, no. 6 (April 1967): 24-25.

Kipling, Rudyard. *A Book of Words.* Garden City, New York: Doubleday, Doran, & Company, Inc., 1928.

——. "Canada's Path to Nationhood." In *Addresses Delivered Before the Canadian Club of Ottawa 1903-1909,* edited by Gerald H. Brown. Ottawa: The Mortimer Press, 1910.

——. *From Sea to Sea: Letters of Travel.* Vol. 2. New York: Doubleday & McClure Company, 1899.

——. *Kipling's Advice To "The Hat": in response to an appeal from an old-timer of Medicine Hat, Alberta.* Charles River, Mass.: Sign of the George, 1922.

——. *The Letters of Rudyard Kipling.* Vols. 1-2. Edited by Thomas Pinney. London: The Macmillan Press Ltd, 1990. *Letters of Travel (1892-1913).* London: Macmillan and Co., Limited, 1920.

——. *"O Beloved Kids": Rudyard Kipling's Letters to his Children.* Edited by Elliot Gilbert. London: Weidenfeld and Nicholson, 1983.

——. *Rudyard Kipling's Verse: Inclusive Edition.* London: Hodder and Stoughton Limited, 1933.

——. *Selected Poems.* Edited by Peter Keating. London: Penguin Books, 1993. *The Seven Seas.* London: Methuen and Co., 1909

——. *Something of Myself.* Edited by Thomas Pinney. New York: Cambridge University Press, 1990.

——. "With the Night Mail." In *Actions and Reactions.* New York: Charles Scribner's Sons, 1909.

Kunitz, Stanley J. [Dilly Tante, pseud.]. *Living Authors: A Book of Biographies.* New York: The H. W. Wilson Company, 1931.

Kunitz, Stanley J., and Haycraft, Howard, eds. *Twentieth Century Authors.* New

York: The H.W. Wilson Company, 1961. *British Authors of the Nineteenth Century.* New York: The H.W. Wilson Company, 1936.

Lewis, Claude. *Treaty Trip: An Abridgement of Dr. Claude Lewis's journal of an expedition made by himself and his brother, Sinclair Lewis, to northern Saskatchewan and Manitoba in 1924.* Edited by Donald Greene and George Knox. Minneapolis: University of Minnesota Press, 1959.

Lewis, Grace Hegger. *With Love From Gracie.* New York: Harcourt, Brace, and Company, 1955.

Lewis, Sinclair. *From Main Street to Stockholm: Letters of Sinclair Lewis, 1919-1930.* Edited by Harrison Smith. New York: Harcourt, Brace, and Company, 1952.

———. *Mantrap.* New York: Grosset & Dunlap, 1926.

Light, Martin. *The Quixotic Vision of Sinclair Lewis.* West Lafayette, Indiana: Purdue University Press, 1975.

Lindsay, Vachel. *Collected Poems.* New York: The Macmillan Company, 1925.

———. *Going-to-the-Sun.* New York: D. Appleton & Co. 1923.

———. "The Modern Troubadour". In *Empire Club of Canada: Addresses Delivered to the Members During the Year 1925.* Toronto: The Macoomb Press, 1926.

———. *The Poetry of Vachel Lindsay.* Volumes 2-3. Edited by Dennis Camp. Peoria, Illinois: Spoon River Poetry Press, 1985.

Longfellow, Henry Wadsworth. *The Letters of Henry Wadsworth Longfellow. Vol. 4, 1857-1865.* Edited by Andrew Hilen. Cambridge, Massachusetts: The Belknap Press of Harvard University Press, 1972, 1982.

Lundquist, James. *Sinclair Lewis.* New York: Frederick Ungar Publishing Co., 1973.

MacDonald, Mary Lu. "Margaret Blennerhassett." In *Canadian Writers Before 1890,* edited by W.H. New. Vol. 99 of *The Dictionary of Literary Biography.* Detroit: Gale Research Inc., 1990.

MacShane, Frank. *The Life of Raymond Chandler.* New York: E.P. Dutton & Co., Inc., 1976.

Marovitz, Sanford E. "Ambivalences and Anxieties: Character Reversals in Sinclair Lewis' *Mantrap.*" *Studies in American Fiction* 16:2 (Autumn 1988): 229-36.

Marrot, Harold Vincent. *The Life and Letters of John Galsworthy.* New York: Scribner's Sons, 1936.

Martineau, Harriet. *Selected Letters.* Edited by Valerie Sanders. Oxford: Clarendon press, 1990.

Harriet Martineau's Autobiography. London: Smith, Elder, & Co., 1877.

———. *Harriet Martineau's Letters to Fanny Wedgwood.* Edited by Elisabeth Sanders Arbuckle. Stanford, California: Stanford University Press, 1983.

———. *Society in America.* London: Saunders and Otley, 1966.

Maurois, André. *Chateaubriand: Poet, Statesman, Lover.* Translated by Vera Fraser. New York: Harper & Brothers, 1938.

McAleer, John J. *Theodore Dreiser: An Introduction and Interpretation*. New York: Holt, Rinehart, and Winston, Inc., 1968.

Nabokov, Vladimir. *Selected Letters 1940-1977*. Edited by Dmitri Nabokov and Matthew J. Bruccoli. New York: Harcourt, Brace, Jovanovich, 1989.

Nadel, Ira B. "Harriet Martineau." In *Victorian Novelists Before 1885*. Vol. 21 of *The Dictionary of Literary Biography*, edited by Ira B. Nadel and William E. Fredeman. Detroit: Gale Research Co., 1983.

National Archives of Canada, Government Records Branch, Personal Records Centre, Ottawa, Ontario. *Statement of Service in the Canadian Armed Forces: Raymond Thornton Chandler*. Compiled by Bill Wood, 6 August 1991.

The National Cyclopaedia of American Biography. New York: James T. White and Company, 1933.

News and Notes. *The Kipling Journal* 35 (Sept. 1935): 69-78.

Oates, Joyce Carol. *Wonderland*. New York: The Vanguard Press, 1971.

Painter, George. *Chateaubriand: A Biography. Volume One (1768-93): The Longed-for Tempests*. London: Chatto & Windus, 1977.

Perkins, George; Perkins, Barbara; and Leininger, Phillip, eds. *Benet's Reader's Encyclopedia of American Literature*. New York: HarperCollins Publishers, 1991.

Ronald, Ann. "Zane Grey." In *American Novelists, 1910-1945*, edited by James J. Martine. Vol. 9 Part 2 of *The Dictionary of Literary Biography*. Detroit: Gale Research Company, 1981.

Ryan, Toby. *Stage Left: Canadian Theatre in the Thirties: A Memoir*. Toronto: CTR Publications, 1981.

Safford, William H. *The Life of Harman Blennerhassett*. Cincinnati, 1853.

Schorer, Mark. *Sinclair Lewis: An American Life*. New York: McGraw-Hill Book Company Inc., 1961.

Scott, S.D. "William Cobbett." *Acadiensis* 5 (April-July 1905), 182-215.

Singh, Khushwant. "Khushwant Singh." In *Contemporary Authors: Autobiography Series*, edited by Mark Zadrozny, vol. 9. Detroit: Gale Research Inc., 1989.

Singh, Khushwant. "Orient Pearl in the World Oyster." In *Man and his World: The Noranda Lectures*. Toronto: University of Toronto Press, 1968.

Spater, George. *William Cobbett, the Poor Man's Friend*. New York: Cambridge University Press, 1982.

Stegner, Wallace. *The Big Rock Candy Mountain*. New York: Penguin Books, 1991.
"Letter From Canada." The American West 11, no. 1 (January 1974): 28-30.

——. "The Provincial Consciousness." *The University of Toronto Quarterly* 43, no. 4 (Summer 1974): 299-310.

——. "The West of Wallace Stegner." Interview by Paula Simons, July, 1992. *Brick* 46 (Summer 1993): 26-31.

——. *Where the Bluebird Sings to the Lemonade Springs.* New York: Random House, 1992.

Stegner, Wallace, and Etulain, Richard W. *Conversations with Wallace Stegner on Western History and Literature.* Salt Lake City: University of Utah Press, 1983.

Stewart, James. *Rudyard Kipling: A Bibliographic Catalogue.* Toronto: Dalhousie University Press and University of Toronto Press, 1959.

Stonesifer, Richard J. *W.H. Davies: A Critical Biography.* London: Jonathan Cape, 1963.

Vaez, Gustavo . *Rita* . Music by Gaetano Donizetti . [Sound Recording, Digital CD] Featuring Adelina Scarabelli, Pietry Ballo and Alessandro Corbelli and the Orchestra da Camera Siciliana. "Nuova Era" label (No. 7045), 1991

——. *Rita* . Music by Gaetano Donizetti. [Sound Recording, Digital CD] Featuring Susanna Rigacci, Ugo Benelli and Romano Franceschetto with the Orchestra da Camera dell'Associazione. Bongiovanni label, No. GB 2109/10-2, September 1990.

Rita. Music by Gaetano Donizetti. [Sound Recording, LP]. Featuring Giuseppina Arnaldi, Carlo Franzini and Paolo Montarsolo and the Orchestra Sinfonica di Torino."Cetra" label (no number given), 1950s?

Williams, Stanley Thomas. *The Spanish Background of American Literature.* New Haven: Yale University Press, 1955.

Wilson, Angus. *The Strange Ride of Rudyard Kipling.* London: Pimlico, 1994.

Zane Grey's King of the Royal Mounted and the Northern Treasure. Racine, Wisconsin: Whitman Publishing, 1937.

Newspapers

Calgary Herald
The Times [London UK]
The Leader [Regina]
Daily Telegraph [Saint John, New Brunswick]
Saskatoon Phoenix
Globe [Toronto]
Globe and Mail [Toronto]
Mail and Empire [Toronto]
Toronto Star
Toronto Telegram
Manitoba Free Press [Winnipeg]

ACKNOWLEDGEMENTS

Many people helped in the construction of this book. Accolades must go to Dr. Francesca Valente and Dr. Branko Gorjup for their scholarly help as well as practical counsel. Gibraltar is not more steady than their friendship. Wide-ranging help came from many antiquarian booksellers; David Mason, Debra Dearlove and Steven Temple in particular were, and are, generous in citing possible authors for inclusion and helping with bibliographies. Richard Landon, ever the model librarian, remains ever prompt in making his daunting knowledge (and the formidable resources of the Thomas Fisher Rare Book Library) available to me.

For substantial assistance with certain authors, or because of service above and beyond the call of duty, I am indebted to the following: Ivan Conger of Owosso, Michigan; June Flegg, Local History Room, Saskatoon Public Library; Dr. Loren Grey, son of Zane Grey; Nicholas Lindsay, son of Vachel Lindsay; Thomas Pinney, English Department, Pomona College; Karen Smith, Kipling Librarian, Dalhousie University Library, Halifax; Mary Stegner, wife of the late Wallace Stegner; the staff of the rare book room of the University Library, University of California, Irvine; Toronto Public Library System, Interlibrary Loan Service (particularly the North York and Yorkville Branches).

The following also deserve special thanks for the help they afforded: the staff of the Baldwin Room of the Metropolitan Toronto Public Library. George Brandak, Curator of Manuscripts, Special Collections, University of British Columbia. Cameron Campbell. Martha Clevenger, Associate Archivist, Missouri Historical Society. Michael Coren. Major Yvon Desjardins, Public Affairs Officer, Ministry of National Defense, Toronto. Daye Doobrajh, Interlibrary Loan Service, Princeton University. Perkins Library Staff, Duke University, Durham, North Carolina. Anne Ferdinands, Communications Coordinator, Ministry of the Environment, Lands, and Parks, British Columbia. Janet Fetherling. Northrop Frye. C. H. Gervais. Graham C. Greene. Ms. Lilace Hatayama, Special Collections, UCLA. P.J. Kavanagh. Dan Kislenko of the *Hamilton Spectator.* James Lahey. Robert

Lingeman. Alberto Manguel. David Mason. Robert McGhee, Archaeological Survey of Canada. Ken McGoogan of the *Calgary Herald*. Phillip Ower, University of Toronto Reprographics. Staff of Pratt Library, Victoria College, University of Toronto. Dr. Judith Priestman of the Bodleian Library, Oxford. James Quandt. Stewart Renfrew, Archivist, Queen's University Archives. Arthur Smith of Opera America. Ray Swick of the Blennerhassett Historical State Park, West Virginia. Bruce Whiteman, McGill University Library. Stephany Wilken, World Record Secretary, International Game Fish Association, Pompano Beach, Florida. Bill Wood, the National Archives of Canada.

My staff at the Harbourfront Reading Series, while not directly involved in the creation of this book, have performed their jobs so admirably that they freed my free time from extraordinary worries. So special thanks to Geoff Taylor, Christine Rassias, Laura Comello, Janet Harron and Barbara Edwards. For a remarkable punctiliousness that would have put Cobbett to shame, and for his scholarly rigour, doggedness in the trenches, and inventiveness when others would have given up, my deepest gratitude, too, to Peter LaRocca.

INDEX

police (see also Royal Canadian Mounted Police) 23, 36-38, 227-28, 231, 349-59, 409
Pond Inlet, N.W.T. 4
Porcupine, Peter, pseud. – see Cobbett, William
Port Mouton, N.S. 135
Potawatomi Indians 250
poverty and the poor (see also beggars and begging) 28, 32-39, 85, 94, 98, 160, 179-80, 254, 273, 275, 388
prairie 248, 272, 309, 311, 333, 337, 365-70, 392-401, 404-08, 410-17, 432-56
"A Prairie Oyster" (John Galsworthy) 365-70
Presbyterians 89-90, 121
press, Canadian 40, 52, 205, 212, 226-29, 396, 402, 469 American 228, 396, 418
priests and clerics 41, 52, 57, 63, 65-71, 94, 95, 100, 195, 364
Prince Albert, Sask. 414-5
Prince Edward Island 175, 180, 326-27
Prince Regent Strait, N.W.T. 21
Princess Patricia's Canadian Light Infantry 436
prisons 16, 36-37, 181, 329, 395, 449
privateers – see pirates
Prohibition 403
prospecting – see mining
prostitution 88, 93-101
Protestantism 51-52, 58, 70, 90
The Provincial Lady in America (E.M. Delafield) 281, 282-8
"A Psalm of Montreal" (Samuel Butler) 75
pseudonyms 55, 181, 280, 365,

Quakers – see Society of Friends
Quebec, province of (see also Lower Canada) 56, 57, 158, 159, 200, 315, 361, 374

Quebec City, Que. 31, 55, 56, 73, 86, 159, 163, 172, 195-7, 204, 287, 314, 315, 317, 329, 331, 342, 364
Queen's Hall, Montreal 61
Queenston, Ont. 274, 276-78

RCMP – see Royal Canadian Mounted Police
racism xiii, 214, 217, 319-21, 334-37, 466
radio 212, 356
railways 29, 36, 39, 52, 204, 312, 313, 317, 323, 329, 331, 332, 337-9, 411, 415, 417, 434, 453
Rasmussen, Knud 1-4, 11
Rebellion of 1837 270
Regina, Sask. 470
Regina Leader 470
Reindeer Lake, Sask. 416
Renfrew, Ont. 29, 38-43
Repulse Bay, N.W.T. 13-15
Retrospect of Western Travel (Harriet Martineau) 270, 272-9
Rideau Hall, Ottawa 61, 62
Rita (Donizetti) 219-22
Ritz Carlton Hotel, Montreal 322
The Road (Jack London) 29
Roman Catholicism 49, 53, 57, 58, 94, 230, 252, 263, 280, 316
Rose Marie (Hammerstein/Harbach and Friml/Stothart) 462
Round Island, Ont. 275
Royal Alexandra Hotel, Winnipeg 413
Royal Alexandra Theatre, Toronto 419
Royal Canadian Mounted Police 3, 16, 17, 124, 216, 228, 291, 309, 310, 338, 373, 375, 413, 444, 448-56
Royal York Hotel, Toronto 226, 228, 418
Russell Hotel, Ottawa 61, 62
Russia and Russians 31, 60, 222, 226, 388, 394, 396-9